HARCOURT

Math

INTERVENTION
Skills

Grade 4

Harcourt

Orlando   Austin   Chicago   New York   Toronto   London   San Diego

Visit *The Learning Site!*
www.harcourtschool.com

CONTENTS

▶ Using *Intervention • Skills* .... **IN**ix

▶ Chapter Correlations .... **IN**xi

▶ Skills

   ▶ **Number Sense, Concepts, and Operations:**
   Number Sense and Place Value

     1   Place Value: 4-Digit Numbers **IN3**

     2   Benchmark Numbers **IN7**

     3   Place Value Through Millions **IN11**

     4   Order Numbers on a Number Line **IN15**

     5   Order Numbers **IN19**

     6   Round to Nearest 10 and 100 .... **IN23**

     7   Round Numbers **IN27**

   ▶ **Number Sense, Concepts, and Operations:**
   Whole Number Addition

     8   2-Digit Addition **IN33**

     9   Algebra: Add 3 Numbers **IN37**

   ▶ **Number Sense, Concepts, and Operations:**
   Whole Number Subtraction

     10   2-Digit Subtraction **IN43**

     11   Fact Families **IN47**

   ▶ **Number Sense, Concepts, and Operations:**
   Whole Number Multiplication

     12   Arrays **IN53**

     13   Multiplication Table Through 12 .... **IN57**

     14   Explore Multiplying 2-Digit Numbers **IN61**

     15   Multiply 2-Digit Numbers **IN65**

     16   Multiplication Patterns **IN69**

     17   Estimate Products **IN73**

     18   Multiply 3- and 4-Digit Numbers **IN77**

     19   Mental Math: Multiplication Patterns **IN81**

     20   Multiplication Properties **IN85**

▶ **Number Sense, Concepts, and Operations:**
Whole Number Division

21   Meaning of Division **IN91**

22   Multiply and Divide Facts Through 5 . . . . **IN95**

23   Multiply and Divide Facts Through 10 . . . . **IN99**

24   Practice Division Facts. **IN103**

25   Divide with Remainders **IN107**

26   Division Procedures **IN111**

27   Estimate Quotients **IN115**

28   Place the First Digit **IN119**

29   Zeros in Division **IN123**

30   Mental Math: Division Patterns **IN127**

▶ **Number Sense, Concepts, and Operations: Fractions**

31   Parts of a Whole **IN133**

32   Parts of a Set **IN137**

33   Equivalent Fractions. **IN141**

34   Mixed Numbers. **IN145**

35   Read and Write Fractions **IN149**

▶ **Number Sense, Concepts, and Operations: Decimals**

36   Decimals and Money. **IN155**

37   Relate Fractions and Decimals **IN159**

38   Decimals to Thousandths. **IN163**

▶ **Measurement**

39   Tell Time **IN169**

40   Dates on a Calendar. **IN173**

41   Length: Customary Units **IN177**

42   Length: Metric Units **IN181**

43   Perimeter. **IN185**

44   Area **IN189**

▶ Geometry and Spatial Sense

45   Line Segments and Angles **IN195**

46   Classify and Measure Angles **IN199**

47   Plane Figures **IN203**

48   Quadrilaterals **IN207**

49   Polygons **IN211**

50   Symmetry **IN215**

51   Congruent Figures **IN219**

52   Slides, Flips, and Turns **IN223**

53   Solid Figures **IN227**

▶ Algebraic Thinking, Patterns, and Functions

54   Missing Addends **IN233**

55   Number Patterns **IN237**

56   Find a Rule **IN241**

57   Algebra: Missing Factors **IN245**

58   Ordered Pairs **IN249**

59   Expressions **IN253**

60   Expressions with Variables **IN257**

▶ Data Analysis and Probability

61   Use a Pictograph **IN263**

62   Use Data from a Survey **IN267**

63   Bar Graphs **IN271**

64   Make Bar Graphs **IN275**

65   Possible Outcomes **IN279**

66   Probability **IN283**

Answers **IN287**

Check What You Know Enrichment

▶ Chapter 1   How Many? • Benchmark Numbers **IN323**
             Crack the Code • Numbers to Thousands **IN324**

▶ Chapter 2   Off to School • Compare and Order Numbers/
             Compare, Order, and Round **IN325**

▶ Chapter 3   Play Ball! • Two-Digit and Column Addition **IN327**
             Giraffe Story • Add and Subtract Three Digits **IN328**

▶ Chapter 4   What's Missing? • Missing Addends/Fact Families **IN329**
             Party Time • Number Patterns **IN330**

▶ Chapter 5   Tick Tock • Time **IN331**
             A Month of Fun Days • Use a Calendar **IN332**

▶ Chapter 6   I'll Buy It! • Read Pictographs **IN333**
             My Favorite Color • Frequency Tables **IN334**

▶ Chapter 7   What's the Weight? • Bar Graphs **IN335**
             Pictographs in Class • Read a Pictograph **IN336**

▶ Chapter 8   Silly Symbols • Multiplication and Division **IN337**

▶ Chapter 9   Number Clues • Missing Factors **IN339**
             Little Rascal • Multiplication Patterns **IN340**

▶ Chapter 10 Model Matching • Model Multiplication **IN341**
             Facts Search • Multiplication Facts **IN342**

▶ Chapter 11 Shortcut • Multiply by 10s, 100s, 1,000s **IN343**
             Food Fuel • Find Products **IN344**

▶ Chapter 12 Paper Products • Multiply 1-Digit Numbers/Estimate Products **IN345**

▶ Chapter 13 Picture That • Division Facts IN347
            The Bear Facts • Find the Quotient IN348

▶ Chapter 14 Starry Quotients • Division/Compatible Numbers IN349

▶ Chapter 15 A Riddle of Zeros • Divide by 1-Digit Divisors IN351
            Number, Please! • Divide with Remainders IN352

▶ Chapter 16 Sporty Products • Multiplication Facts IN353
            A Sad Bird • Fact Families IN354

▶ Chapter 17 Find the Figures • Identify Geometric Figures IN355
            Straw Angles • Identify Angles IN356

▶ Chapter 18 What's the Angle? • Classify Angles IN357
            Plane Figure Puzzle • Identify Plane Figures IN358

▶ Chapter 19 Cut It Out! • Compare Figures/Slides, Flips,
            and Turns/Identify Symmetric Figures IN359

▶ Chapter 20 Place to Place • Read Number Lines IN361
            Being Happy • Points on a Grid IN362

▶ Chapter 21 They're All Equal • Parts of a Whole IN363
            How Many Parts? • Parts of a Group IN364

▶ Chapter 22 How Many? • Parts of a Whole/Compare Fractions IN365
            All Mixed Up! • Mixed Numbers IN366

▶ Chapter 23 What Are the Chances? • Outcomes IN367
            Legs and Laundry • Parts of a Set IN368

▶ Chapter 24 Map Maker • Measurement IN369
            Lost Digits • Multiplication/Division IN370

▶ Chapter 25   A Turtle Crawl • Measurement **IN371**
                Going Up, and Up, and Up. . . • Multiply by 10, 100, 1,000 .... **IN372**

▶ Chapter 26   Pieces and Parts • Model Decimals **IN373**
                Riddle Me This • Decimals **IN374**

▶ Chapter 27   Methuselah • Round Whole Numbers **IN375**
                A Place for a Pattern • Decimal Place Value **IN376**

▶ Chapter 28   Perimeter Puzzles • Find Perimeter **IN377**
                Overall Expressions • Expressions with Variables **IN378**

▶ Chapter 29   Mystery Multiplication • Expressions with Variables **IN379**
                Polyominos • Find Area **IN380**

▶ Chapter 30   It's Solid • Solid Figures **IN381**
                The Missing Half • Plane Figures/Multiply Three Factors **IN382**

Answers **IN383**

Using *Intervention • Skills*

The *Intervention • Skills* will help you accommodate the diverse skill levels of students in your class and prepare students to work successfully on grade-level content by targeting the prerequisite skills for *each chapter* in the program. The following questions and answers will help you make the best use of this rich resource.

How can I determine which skills a student or students should work on?

Before beginning each chapter, have students complete the "Check What You Know" page in the Student Edition. This page targets the prerequisite skills necessary for success in the chapter. A student's performance on this page will allow you to diagnose skill weaknesses and prescribe appropriate interventions. *Intervention • Skills* lessons are tied directly to each of the skills assessed. The *Check What You Know Enrichment* activities are also correlated to the skills targeted on the "Check What You Know" page. A chart at the beginning of each chapter correlates the skill assessed to the appropriate intervention materials. The chart appears in the HARCOURT MATH Teacher Edition.

In what format are the *Intervention • Skills* materials?

A. **Copying masters** provide the skill development and skill practice on reproducible pages. These pages in the *Intervention • Skills Teacher's Guide with Copying Masters* can be used by individual students or small groups. You can also allow students to record their answers on copies of the pages. This guide provides teaching suggestions for skill development, as well as an alternative teaching strategy for students who continue to have difficulty with a skill. Sixty pages of *Check What You Know Enrichment* activities provide additional practice of these skills.

B. **CD-ROM** provides the skill development and practice in an interactive format. *Check What You Know Enrichment* activities are provided as printable PDF files.

Are manipulative activities included in the intervention resources?

The teaching strategies included in the teacher's materials for the *Intervention • Skills* lessons do require manipulatives, easily gathered classroom objects or copying masters from the *Teacher's Resource Book*. Since these activities are designed for only those students who show deficits in their skill development, the quantity of manipulatives will be small. For many activities, you may substitute materials, such as squares of paper for counters, coins for two-color counters, and so on.

How can I organize my classroom so that I have time and space to help students who show a need for these intervention strategies and activities?

You may want to set up a Math Skill Center with a folder for each of your students. Based on a student's performance on the *Check What You Know* page, assign appropriate skills by marking the student's record folder. The student can then work through the intervention materials, record the date of completion, and place the completed work in a folder for your review. You may wish to assign students to a partner, assign a small group to work together, or have a specified time during the day to meet with one or more of the individuals or small groups to assess their progress and to provide direct instruction. You may wish to assign *Check What You Know Enrichment* activities to those who perform satisfactorily on the *Check What You Know* pages.

How are the lessons structured?

Each skill begins with a model or an explanation with a model. The first section of exercises, titled *Try These,* provides 2–4 exercises that allow students to move toward doing the work independently. A student who has difficulty with the *Try These* exercises might benefit from the Alternative Teaching Strategy activity for that skill described in this Teacher's Guide before they attempt the *Practice on Your Own* page. The *Practice on Your Own* page provides an additional model for the skill and scaffolded exercises, which gradually remove prompts. Scaffolding provides a framework within which the student can achieve success for the skill. At the end of the *Practice on Your Own*, there is a *Quiz*. The *Quiz* provides 2–4 problems that check the student's proficiency in the skill. Guidelines for success are provided in the teacher's materials.

Intervention • Skills
Chapter Correlations

Number Sense, Concepts, and Operations

Number Sense and Place Value

Skill Number	Skill Title	Chapter Correlation
1	Place Value: 4-Digit Numbers	1, 14
2	Benchmark Numbers	1
3	Place Value Through Millions	2
4	Order Numbers on a Number Line	20
5	Order Numbers	2
6	Round to Nearest 10 and 100	2, 27
7	Round Numbers	3

Whole Number Addition

Skill Number	Skill Title	Chapter Correlation
8	2-Digit Addition	3
9	Algebra: Add 3 Numbers	28

Whole Number Subtraction

Skill Number	Skill Title	Chapter Correlation
10	2-Digit Subtraction	3, 14
11	Fact Families	4

Whole Number Multiplication

Skill Number	Skill Title	Chapter Correlation
12	Arrays	8, 16
13	Multiplication Table Through 12	9, 16, 24, 29
14	Explore Multiplying 2-Digit Numbers	10
15	Multiply 2-Digit Numbers	11, 12, 24
16	Multiplication Patterns	11
17	Estimate Products	12
18	Multiply 3- and 4-Digit Numbers	24
19	Mental Math: Multiplication Patterns	25
20	Multiplication Properties	30

Whole Number Division

Skill Number	Skill Title	Chapter Correlation
21	Meaning of Division	8
22	Multiply and Divide Facts Through 5	9, 10, 16, 29
23	Multiply and Divide Facts Through 10	9, 10, 13, 16, 29
24	Practice Division Facts	13
25	Divide with Remainders	14
26	Division Procedures	15
27	Estimate Quotients	15
28	Place the First Digit	24
29	Zeros in Division	24
30	Mental Math: Division Patterns	25

Fractions

Skill Number	Skill Title	Chapter Correlation
31	Parts of a Whole	21
32	Parts of a Set	21, 23
33	Equivalent Fractions	22
34	Mixed Numbers	22
35	Read and Write Fractions	26

Decimals

Skill Number	Skill Title	Chapter Correlation
36	Decimals and Money	26
37	Relate Fractions and Decimals	27
38	Decimals to Thousandths	27

Measurement

Skill Number	Skill Title	Chapter Correlation
39	Tell Time	5
40	Dates on a Calendar	5
41	Length: Customary Units	24
42	Length: Metric Units	25
43	Perimeter	28
44	Area	29

Geometry and Spatial Sense

Skill Number	Skill Title	Chapter Correlation
45	Line Segments and Angles	17
46	Classify and Measure Angles	18
47	Plane Figures	18
48	Quadrilaterals	18
49	Polygons	30
50	Symmetry	19
51	Congruent Figures	19
52	Slides, Flips, and Turns	19
53	Solid Figures	30

Algebraic Thinking, Patterns, and Functions

Skill Number	Skill Title	Chapter Correlation
54	Missing Addends	4
55	Number Patterns	4
56	Find a Rule	9
57	Algebra: Missing Factors	16
58	Ordered Pairs	20
59	Expressions	28
60	Expressions with Variables	29

Data Analysis and Probability

Skill Number	Skill Title	Chapter Correlation
61	Use a Pictograph	6
62	Use Data from a Survey	6
63	Bar Graphs	7
64	Make Bar Graphs	7
65	Possible Outcomes	23
66	Probability	23

Number Sense, Concepts, and Operations

Number Sense and Place Value

15 Minutes

OBJECTIVE Write the value of the digits in numbers to thousands

MATERIALS base-ten blocks

You may wish to use base-ten blocks to model the example.

Begin by having the students look at the place-value chart, and recall that the place-value labels show the value of each digit in a number. Remind them also that they can use the place-value labels to help them write a number in different ways.

Have students look at Step 2. As they read the value of each digit, suggest that stu-dents display the appropriate base-ten blocks.

Ask: **What is the value of the digit 1? 1 thousand or 1,000 How do you know? The 1 is in the thousands place.**

Continue asking similar questions. Guide students as they see that the value of the digit 1 is greater than the value of the digit 2; the value of the digit 2 is greater than the value of the digit 7, and so on.

In Step 3, point out how the place-value words help with writing the number two ways. Have students read the number aloud. Have them note the position of the comma in 1,275.

Ask: **What does the comma separate? the hundreds from the thousands**

TRY THESE Exercises 1 and 2 provide practice in using place-value charts to write the value of digits.

- **Exercise 1** Value of the digits in 7,569.

- **Exercise 2** Value of the digits in 6,403.

PRACTICE ON YOUR OWN Review the example at the top of the page. Discuss why the value of 0 hundreds is 0, and why it is necessary to write a zero in that place.

QUIZ Determine if students know the names of the places in the place-value chart, and can tell the value of the given digits. Success is determined by 2 out of 2 correct responses.

Students who successfully complete the **Practice on Your Own** and **Quiz** are ready to move to the next skill.

COMMON ERRORS

- Students may be able to write the number of ones, tens, hundreds, and thousands, but be unable to relate that number to the value of the digit.

- Students may have trouble identifying the value of 0; for example, they may write a number such as two thousand, twenty-seven as 227 instead of 2,027.

Students who made more than 1 error in the **Practice on Your Own,** or who were not successful in the **Quiz** section, may benefit from the **Alternative Teaching Strategy** on the next page.

Alternative Teaching Strategy
Use Models to Show Place Value to Thousands

20 Minutes

OBJECTIVE Use base-ten blocks to model place value to thousands

MATERIALS base-ten blocks

Write the number 2,438 in a place-value chart. Then guide students as they use base-ten blocks to model the number.

Point to the thousands place. Explain that the 2 in the thousands place means $2 \times 1{,}000$ or 2,000.

Ask: **What is the value of the 2 in the chart? 2 thousands, or 2,000 How many thousands blocks will you use? 2**

The 4 in the hundreds place means 4×100, or 400. What is the value of the digit 4? 4 hundreds or 400 How many hundreds blocks will you use? 4

Continue to ask similar questions as the students model the remaining digits.

As students focus on the model, ask them which digit has the greatest value and which has the least value. Students can see that the thousands place has the greatest value, and the value of the places decrease from left to right.

Relate the model to the number, and write and say the number two ways.

2 thousands, 4 hundreds 3 tens 8 ones
2,438

Repeat the activity several times with other 4-digit numbers. Include examples with zeros in ones, tens, or hundreds places, such as 3,026, 1,407, and 4,580.

When students show an understanding of place value to thousands, have one partner choose a 4-digit number and write it in a place-value chart, while the second partner uses base-ten blocks to model the number. Have the partners record the number two ways. Then have them reverse roles to complete another example.

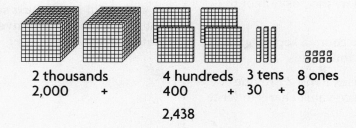

2 thousands   4 hundreds   3 tens   8 ones
2,000   +   400   +   30   +   8

2,438

Grade 4
Skill 1

Place Value: 4-Digit Numbers

Write the value of each digit in the number 1,275.

Step 1 Use a place value chart.

TH	H	T	O
1	2	7	5

Step 2 Write the value of each digit.

The value of the **1** is 1 thousand or 1,000.
The value of the **2** is 2 hundreds or 200.
The value of the **7** is 7 tens or 70.
The value of the **5** is 5 ones or 5.

Step 3 Use place value words to write the number.

1 thousand, 2 hundreds 7 tens
5 ones = 1,275

▲ Try These

Write the value of each digit.

1 **7,569**

TH	H	T	O
7	5	6	9

The value of the **7** is ☐ thousands or ☐.

The value of the **5** is ☐ hundreds or ☐.

The value of the **6** is ☐ tens or ☐.

The value of the **9** is ☐ ones or ☐.

☐ thousands ☐ hundreds ☐ tens ☐ ones
= **7,569**

2 **6,403**

TH	H	T	O
6	4	0	3

The value of the **6** is ☐ thousands or ☐.

The value of the **4** is ☐ hundreds or ☐.

The value of the **0** is ☐ tens or ☐.

The value of the **3** is ☐ ones or ☐.

☐ thousands ☐ hundreds ☐ tens ☐ ones
= **6,403**

Go to the next side.

Practice on Your Own

Skill (1)

Example:

Write the value of each digit of the number 2,063.

TH	H	T	O
2	0	6	3

The value of the **2** is 2 thousands or 2,000.
The value of the **0** is 0 hundreds or 0.
The value of the **6** is 6 tens or 60.
The value of the **3** is 3 ones or 3.
2 thousands 0 hundreds 6 tens 3 ones = **2,063**

Write the value of each digit.

1 3,079

TH	H	T	O
3	0	7	9

The value of **3** is ☐ thousands or ☐.

The value of **0** is ☐ hundreds or ☐.

The value of **7** is ☐ tens or ☐.

The value of **9** is ☐ ones or ☐.

2 7,503

TH	H	T	O
7	5	0	3

The value of **7** is ☐ thousands or ☐.

The value of **5** is ☐ hundreds or ☐.

The value of **0** is ☐ tens or ☐.

The value of **3** is ☐ ones or ☐.

3 8,290

TH	H	T	O
8	2	9	0

The value of **8** is ☐ thousands or ☐.

The value of **2** is ☐ hundreds or ☐.

The value of **9** is ☐ tens or ☐.

The value of **0** is ☐ ones or ☐.

4 6,100

TH	H	T	O
6	1	0	0

The value of **6** is ☐ thousands or ☐.

The value of **1** is ☐ hundred or ☐.

The value of **0** is ☐ tens or ☐.

The value of **0** is ☐ ones or ☐.

▶ Quiz

Write the value of the underlined digit.

5 <u>4</u>,066 ☐

6 2,0<u>7</u>8 ☐

OBJECTIVE Estimate how many squares will cover a figure using benchmark numbers

MATERIALS graph paper

You may wish to have the students verify how many squares are in each benchmark shape by counting. They may also write a multiplication problem to match the number of rows and columns and find the product to verify the number of squares in each.

Direct students' attention to Example A.

Ask: **Which benchmark numbers are about the same length or width as the figure? 10, 50, and 100 are all about the same length Which benchmark numbers are too wide? 25, 50, and 100 are all too wide How many groups of 10 will cover the figure? 3 groups Three groups of 10 are how many squares? 30 How does the area of the 30 squares compare to the area in the figure? It is about the same as the area in the figure.**

Continue to ask similar questions as you work through Example B.

TRY THESE Exercises 1-3 model the type of exercises students will find on the **Practice on Your Own** page.

- **Exercise 1**   Benchmark number 10.
- **Exercise 2**   Benchmark number 25.
- **Exercise 3**   Benchmark number 50.

PRACTICE ON YOUR OWN Review the example at the top of the page. Ask students why benchmark number 100 was used to estimate the number of squares it would take to cover the figure. **Possible response: The figure is large, so it makes sense to use the largest benchmark that will fit on the figure.**

QUIZ Make sure that the students select the appropriate benchmark number to estimate. Success is determined by 2 out of 3 correct responses.

Students who successfully complete the **Practice on Your Own** and **Quiz** are ready to move on to the next skill.

COMMON ERRORS

- Student may select a benchmark number that is too large.
- Students may not use enough of the benchmark number to cover the figure.

Students who made more than 2 errors in the **Practice on Your Own,** or who were not successful in the **Quiz** section, may benefit from the **Alternative Teaching Strategy** on the next page.

Alternative Teaching Strategy
Modeling Benchmark Numbers

OBJECTIVE Use benchmark numbers made from graph paper to estimate the number of squares it takes to cover a figure

MATERIALS benchmark numbers 10, 25, 50, and 100 on grid paper as shown in the lesson, blank figures labeled A through E, Figure A is a rectangle 5 units by 10.8 units, Figures B through E can be any size

Distribute a set of benchmark numbers and blank figures to each student.

Say: **Look at Figure A and the benchmark numbers. Which benchmarks fit in the figure without going over the edges?** Benchmark numbers 10, 25, and 50 **Which is the largest benchmark number you could use?** 50

How many times does the benchmark number 50 fit in the figure? 1 **Does the benchmark match the figure precisely?** No **What is an estimate for the number of squares it will take to cover the figure?** 50

Repeat this activity with similar examples. When the students show understanding of the estimating process, remove the benchmark numbers from students desks. Display one set of benchmark numbers on the chalkboard and have students try an exercise using only paper and pencil. Ask students to explain why they chose a particular benchmark number.

Figure A

Benchmark Numbers

10   25   50

Grade 4
Skill
2

Benchmark Numbers

Benchmark numbers are useful numbers such as 10, 25, 50, and 100. They help you estimate about how much or about how many without counting.

Example A

Choose a benchmark number. Tell about how many squares will cover the figure.
Look at the figure. Choose 10. Estimate.

Think: About 3 groups of 10 will cover the figure.

$10 + 10 + 10 = 30$
So, about 30 squares will cover the figure.

Example B

Choose a benchmark number. Tell about how many squares will cover the figure.
Look at the figure.

Think: About 3 groups of 25 will cover the figure.

Choose 25.

Estimate.

$25 + 25 + 25 = 75$
So, about 75 squares will cover the figure.

Try These

Use the benchmark number to estimate. Tell about how many squares will cover the figure.

1 About [ ] groups of 10 will cover the figure.

About [ ] squares will cover the figure.

2 About [ ] groups of 25 will cover the figure.

About [ ] squares will cover the figure.

3 About [ ] groups of 50 will cover the figure.

About [ ] squares will cover the figure.

Go to the next side.

Practice on Your Own

About 4 groups of 100 will cover the figure.

$100 + 100 + 100 + 100 = 400$

So, about 400 squares will cover the figure.

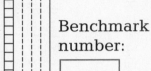

Think: Use benchmark numbers to estimate.

Skill 2

....

Use benchmark numbers to estimate. Tell about how many squares cover the figure.

1
Benchmark number:

Estimate: [   ] squares

2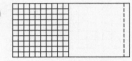
Benchmark number:

Estimate: [   ] squares

3
Benchmark number:

Estimate: [   ] squares

4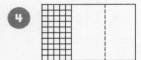

Benchmark number:

Estimate: [   ] squares

5
Benchmark number:

Estimate: [   ] squares

6
Benchmark number:

Estimate: [   ] squares

▶ **Quiz**

Use benchmark numbers to estimate. Tell about how many squares cover the figure.

7
Benchmark number:

Estimate: [   ] squares

8
Benchmark number:

Estimate: [   ] squares

9

Benchmark number:

Estimate: [   ] squares

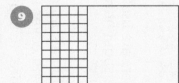

20 Minutes

OBJECTIVE Read and write numbers to millions

MATERIALS place-value chart

You can begin by using base-ten blocks to model how a number can be expressed in different ways. Explain that the number in a place value chart can be written in expanded form, in standard form, and in words. Review the names of each column of the place-value chart. Remind students that each *period* includes ones, tens, and hundreds.

Say: **Look at the place-value chart in Example 1. What is the value of each digit in the number 5,729,146? Possible answer: 5 millions, 7 hundred thousands, 2 ten thousands, 9 thousands, 1 hundred, 4 tens, and 6 ones**

On the board write the number in expanded form as students provide the value. Explain to students that when they know the value of the digits they can read the number by using the word form.

Ask: **How do you read the number 5,729,146 using words? five million, seven hundred twenty-nine thousand, one hundred forty-six**

Point out that knowing the value of the digits can also help students when they write the number in standard form.

Ask: **How do you write the number in standard form? 5,729,146**

Have students read the headings for the place-value chart in Example 2. Then, ask questions similar to those in the first example. Remind students that a comma is used to separate the periods.

TRY THESE Exercises 1–2 give students an opportunity to express numbers in different ways.

- **Exercise 1** Express an 8-digit number.

- **Exercise 2** Express a 7-digit number.

PRACTICE ON YOUR OWN Review the examples at the top of the page. Exercises 1–2 help students write numbers in word form. Exercise 3 allows students to write a number in expanded form. Exercise 4 lets students write a number in standard form. Remind students to look at the position of each digit in the number.

QUIZ Determine if students can find the value of a given digit, and can express the number in different ways. Success is indicated by 2 out of 3 correct responses.

Students who successfully complete the **Practice on Your Own** and **Quiz** are ready to move on to the next skill.

COMMON ERRORS

- Students may have difficulty using the expanded form to write the standard form.

- Some students may omit a zero in a number such as four hundred five.

Students who make more than one error in the **Practice on Your Own**, or who were not successful in the **Quiz** section, may benefit from the **Alternative Teaching Strategy** on the next page.

Alternative Teaching Strategy
Use Models to Read and Write Numbers

20 Minutes

OBJECTIVE Use models to read and write numbers to thousands

MATERIALS base-ten blocks

Give each student a set of base-ten blocks. Have students show 2 hundreds, 9 tens, and 3 ones to represent 293. Have students express in different ways the number that the model represents.

Ask: **What blocks did you use? 2 hundreds, 9 tens, 3 ones What is the number in expanded form? 200 + 90 + 3**

Explain that the expanded form can help students write the number in standard form and in words. To write the number in standard form, students can use mental math to add.

Ask: **What is the number in standard form? 293 How would you write the expanded form as words? two hundred ninety-three**

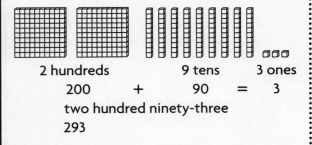

2 hundreds   9 tens   3 ones
200   +   90 = 3
two hundred ninety-three
293

Repeat the activity several times, having students read and write 3-digit numbers.

Then, on the board write 1,000.

Ask: **What would I need to show this number? 10 hundreds blocks** Have volunteers combine their blocks to show 1,000. Stack them in a tower.

Ask: **What do we need to add to these 10 hundred blocks to show 1,421? 4 hundreds, two tens, 1 one**

Have other volunteers contribute the missing base-ten blocks. Ask students to write the number in expanded and standard form.

Ask: **How would I write the expanded form of the number 3,421? 3,000 + 400 + 20 + 1 How would I write that number in standard form? 3,421**

Continue to have students write the expanded and standard form of 3-, 4-, 5-, 6-, 7-, 8-, and 9-digit numbers. When students show an understanding of place value, have them read and write numbers to 999 million without the expanded form.

Grade 4
Skill 3

Place Value Through Millions

Read and write the number.

Example 1

MILLIONS			THOUSANDS			ONES		
Hundreds	Tens	Ones	Hundreds	Tens	Ones	Hundreds	Tens	Ones
		5,	7	2	9,	1	4	6

Standard Form: 5,729,146

Word Form: five million, seven hundred twenty-nine thousand, one hundred forty-six

Expanded Form:
5,000,000 + 700,000 + 20,000 + 9,000 + 100 + 40 + 6

Example 2

MILLIONS			THOUSANDS			ONES		
Hundreds	Tens	Ones	Hundreds	Tens	Ones	Hundreds	Tens	Ones
	2	9,	3	5	2,	4	6	3

Standard Form: 29,352,463

Word Form: twenty-nine million, three hundred fifty-two thousand, four hundred sixty-three

Expanded Form:
20,000,000 + 9,000,000 + 300,000 + 50,000 + 2,000 + 400 + 60 + 3

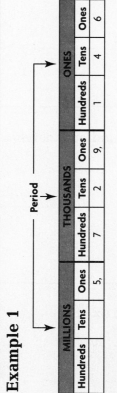

Try These

Complete.

1)

MILLIONS			THOUSANDS			ONES		
Hundreds	Tens	Ones	Hundreds	Tens	Ones	Hundreds	Tens	Ones
	1,	6,	7	8	3,	5	7	6

[1] ten millions [6] millions [7] hundred thousands
[8] ten thousands [3] thousands [5] hundreds [7] tens [6] ones

Standard Form: 16,783,576

Word Form: sixteen million, seven hundred eighty-three thousand, five hundred seventy-six

Expanded Form:
10,000,000 + 6,000,000 + 700,000 + 80,000 + 3,000 + 500 + 70 + 6

2)

MILLIONS			THOUSANDS			ONES		
Hundreds	Tens	Ones	Hundreds	Tens	Ones	Hundreds	Tens	Ones
		1,	4	6	2,	5	7	3

[ ] millions [ ] hundred thousands [ ] ten thousands
[ ] thousands [ ] hundreds [ ] tens [ ] ones

Standard Form: _____

Word Form: one million, four hundred sixty-two thousand, five hundred seventy-three

Expanded Form:
1,000,000 + 400,000 + 60,000 + 2,000 + 500 + 70 + 3

Go to the next side.

Practice on Your Own

Example:

Period

MILLIONS			THOUSANDS			ONES		
Hundreds	Tens	Ones	Hundreds	Tens	Ones	Hundreds	Tens	Ones
1	5	7,	2	7	4,	1	6	3

Standard Form: 157,274,163

Word Form: one hundred fifty-seven million, two hundred seventy-four thousand, one hundred sixty-three

Expanded Form:

100,000,000 + 50,000,000 + 7,000,000 + 200,000 + 70,000 + 4,000 + 100 + 60 + 3

Think: 1 hundred million 5 ten millions 7 millions 2 hundred thousands 7 ten thousands 4 thousands 1 hundred 6 tens 3 ones

Complete.

1

MILLIONS			THOUSANDS			ONES		
Hundreds	Tens	Ones	Hundreds	Tens	Ones	Hundreds	Tens	Ones
		1,	3	5	2,	4	2	2

Word Form: _____ , three hundred _____ thousand, _____

Expanded Form: 1,000,000 + 300,000 + 50,000 + 2,000 + 400 + 20 + 2

2 18,534,453

Word form: _____

3 4,951,308

Expanded Form: _____

4 three hundred million, six hundred four thousand, one hundred ninety-six

Standard form: _____

▶ Quiz

Complete.

5 4,651,741

Word form: _____

6 seventeen million, three hundred twenty-five thousand, six

Standard Form: _____

7 641,901,862

Expanded form: _____

OBJECTIVE Order numbers on a number line

Direct students' attention to Example 1 at the top of the page. Have them locate and point to the number line shown.

Ask: **How are the numbers on the number line arranged?** Possible response: The numbers are arranged from least to greatest going from left to right.

Locate each of the three numbers on the number line.

Say: **Find 411 and circle the point on the number line with your pencil.**

Follow the same procedure to help students find and mark 401 and 406 on the number line.

Ask: **Which of the three numbers is located furthest to the left on the number line?** 401 **So which number has the least value?** 401 **Which number is located next on the number line, going left to right?** 406 **Which number is located furthest to the right on the number line?** 411 **So which number has the greatest value?** 411

Direct students' attention to Example 2 at the top of the page. Have them locate and point to the number line shown.

Say: **Find 887 and circle the point on the number line with your pencil.**

Follow the same procedure to help students find and mark 878 and 880 on the number line.

Ask: **Which of the three numbers is located farthest to the left on the number line?** 878 **So which number has the least value?** 878 **Which number is located next on the number line, going left to right?** 880

Which number is located farthest to the right on the number line? 887 **So which number has the greatest value?** 887

TRY THESE In Exercises 1–3 students practice ordering numbers from least to greatest using a number line.

• **Exercise 1**   Students order 1 number.

• **Exercise 2**   Students order 2 numbers.

• **Exercise 3**   Students order 3 numbers.

PRACTICE ON YOUR OWN Review the example at the top of the page. Remind students that the numbers on the number line increase in value from left to right. Mention that they can order more than 3 numbers on a number line by using the technique they just learned. Remind students to find all the numbers on the number line before recording their order.

QUIZ Determine if students can use a number line to order a set of numbers.

Success is indicated by 2 out of 3 correct responses.

Students who successfully complete the **Practice on Your Own** and **Quiz** are ready to move to the next skill.

COMMON ERRORS

• Students may transpose numbers and fail to find the number on the number line or find the wrong number. Encourage students to check the final order of the numbers to see if it makes sense.

Students who make more than 2 errors in the **Practice on Your Own**, or who were not successful in the **Quiz** section may benefit from the **Alternative Teaching Strategy** on the next page.

Alternative Teaching Strategy
Order Numbers on a Meter Stick

20 Minutes

OBJECTIVE Order numbers on a meter stick

MATERIALS meter stick

Begin by assigning students into groups of 3. Lay a meter stick on the ground. One at a time, have the 3 students stand with their toes at one end of the stick and then have them take a normal stride. (If a measurement within a group of 3 repeats, have the student take another stride.)

Ask a volunteer to measure the point where the back of the forward foot lands for each stride. On the board, record the measurements to the nearest centimeter. Write the measurements in groups of 3 in the order they occurred.

Once all the students have taken a turn, note the greatest and least measurements and use them as parameters for drawing a segment of the meter stick on the board. Begin your meter-stick segment with a number that is 2 or 3 centimeters less than the least measurement, and extend the segment 2 or 3 centimeters beyond the greatest measurement. Mention to students that a meter stick is a number line.

Direct students' attention to the first set of numbers. Work with students to find and circle each measurement on the number line segment on the board.

30 31 32 33 34 35 36 37 38 39 40 41 42 43 44 45 46 47 48 49 50 51 52

After the measurements are marked, ask: **Which measurement is furthest to the left on the number line? Answers will vary; check answer. So, which number is the least? same as previous answer**

Remind students that as you move from left to right on a number line, the values increase.

Ask: **Which measurement comes next on the number line? Check answer. Which measurement comes furthest to the right on the number line? Check answer. So which measurement is the greatest? same as previous answer**

Point out that the shortest stride was the least measurement and the longest stride was the greatest measurement on the number line.

Repeat the activity, if necessary, or expand it to include 4, 5, or 6 measurements.

Grade 4
Skill 4

Order Numbers On a Number Line

Put the numbers in order from the least to greatest.
A number line can help you find the order.

Example 1

411   401   406

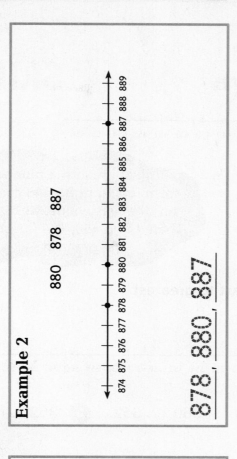

400 401 402 403 404 405 406 407 408 409 410 411 412 413 414 415

To order from least to greatest, go from left to right.

__401__, __406__, __411__

Example 2

880   878   887

874 875 876 877 878 879 880 881 882 883 884 885 886 887 888 889

__878__, __880__, __887__

▶ Try These

Write the numbers in order from least to greatest.
Use the number line to help you.

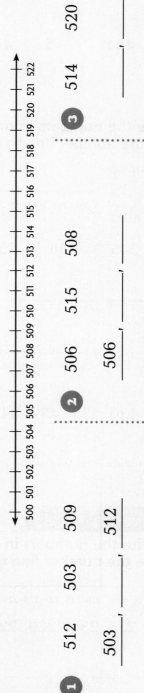

500 501 502 503 504 505 506 507 508 509 510 511 512 513 514 515 516 517 518 519 520 521 522

1 512   503   509

__503__, ____, ____

2 506   515   508

__506__, ____, ____

3 514   520   502

____, ____, ____

Go to the next side.

Practice on Your Own

Skill  4

444 445 446 447 448 449 450 451 452 453 454 455 456

454   445   449   450

> **Think:** I read the number line from left to right. 445 comes first. It has the least value. Next, I find 449. Then, I find 450. 454 is last. 454 has the greatest value.

**Write the numbers in order from least to greatest.
Use the number line to help you.**

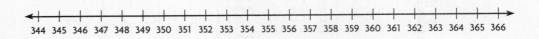

344 345 346 347 348 349 350 351 352 353 354 355 356 357 358 359 360 361 362 363 364 365 366

1 345   356   354   **2** 353   360   352   **3** 362   358   355

_____, _____, _____   _____, _____, _____   _____, _____, _____

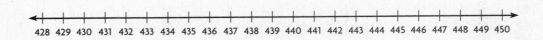

428 429 430 431 432 433 434 435 436 437 438 439 440 441 442 443 444 445 446 447 448 449 450

4 430 435 432 442   **5** 445 431 434 440   **6** 435 443 447 439

___, ___, ___, ___   ___, ___, ___, ___   ___, ___, ___, ___

▶ Quiz

**Write the numbers in order from least to greatest.
Use the number line to help you.**

225 226 227 228 229 230 231 232 233 234 235 236 237 238 239 240 241 242 243 244 245 246 247

7 235 238 229 227   **8** 230 240 234 228   **9** 234 229 232 231

___, ___, ___, ___   ___, ___, ___, ___   ___, ___, ___, ___

Skill 5

Order Numbers

OBJECTIVE Order numbers from least to greatest or from greatest to least

MATERIALS base-ten blocks and place-value charts

15 Minutes

You may wish to begin the lesson by reviewing place-value to ten thousands.

Direct students' attention to the three numbers in Step 1. Have them read the numbers aloud. Then say: **To order these numbers, start with the thousands place. Which place is the thousands?** the first place at the left **Are the numbers in thousands place all the same or different?** the same

Then direct students to Step 2.

Ask: **Are the numbers in hundreds place the same?** no Say: **9 is greater than 7, and 7 is greater than 1. The hundreds are not the same, so the hundreds place will determine the order of the three numbers.**

Proceed to Step 3 and point out that the numbers in hundreds place are compared. Say: **So, you will start with the number with a 9 in the hundreds place. Which number is greatest?** 3,927 **Which numbers are next?** 3,762 followed by 3,101 **Why?** because 9 > 7 > 1 and the greatest numbers come first

Ask: **What if all the numbers in the hundreds place were the same? Where would you look next to put the numbers in order?** Look at the tens then at the ones.

TRY THESE Exercises 1–9 provide practice in ordering numbers from greatest to least.

- **Exercises 1–3** Compare the thousands.
- **Exercises 4–6** Compare the hundreds.
- **Exercises 7–9** Compare the tens.

PRACTICE ON YOUR OWN Review the examples at the top of the page. Guide students to conclude that the numbers are ordered by first comparing the ten thousands. Help students notice that the numbers are being ordered from least to greatest. Then have students begin the exercises. In Exercises 1–6, they are to order numbers from least to greatest. In Exercises 7–12, they order numbers from greatest to least. Remind students to read the directions to be sure they know what they are being asked to do.

QUIZ Determine if students can order numbers to ten thousands from least to greatest and from greatest to least.

Success is indicated by 4 out of 6 correct responses.

Students who successfully complete the **Practice on Your Own** and **Quiz** are ready to move on to the next skill.

COMMON ERRORS

- Students may start by comparing the digits in the place-value positioned from right to left rather than from left to right.

- Students may compare digits in different place-value positions.

- Students may confuse the order in which they are asked to write the numbers.

Students who made more than 3 errors in the **Practice on Your Own**, or who were not successful in the **Quiz** section, may benefit from the **Alternative Teaching Strategy** on the next page.

Alternative Teaching Strategy
Ordering Numbers by Using Grids

20 Minutes

OBJECTIVE Use a grid to order numbers from greatest to least

MATERIALS wide-ruled notebook paper, index card

Write these numbers on the board: 32,685; 32,717; 32,459. Say: **We will order these three numbers from greatest to least.**

Have students take the notebook paper and turn it sideways, so that the lines run up and down. Say: **We will use the lines on the paper as guidelines to help us order the numbers.**

Direct students attention to the board.

Ask: **What is the greatest place-value position in these three numbers?** ten thousands Have them choose a column and label it *Ten Thousands*. **What is the next greatest place-value position?** thousands Have them label the next column *Thousands*. Have students continue labeling the columns with the names of the remaining place-values. *Hundreds, Tens, Ones*

Say: **Write at the top of your paper the order in which you will arrange the numbers.** greatest to least

Say: **Write the first number on your paper. In which column will you place the 3?** ten thousands column **In which columns will you place the next numbers: 2, 6, 8 and 5?** in the thousands, hundreds, tens, and ones columns

Direct students to look at the board and copy the remaining numbers onto their papers. Say: **Use the columns to line up the place-value positions. Check students' papers for accuracy.**

Say: **Place your index card next to the ones column. Slide it left until it covers the hundreds and the thousands columns.**

Demonstrate how to cover the columns, leaving only the thousands exposed.

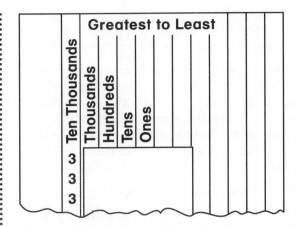

Say: **Are the numbers in the ten thousands column the same or different?** the same **Which column do we uncover next?** the thousands **Are the thousands all the same or different?** the same **Which column do we uncover next?** the hundreds **Are the hundreds all the same or different?** different **What does this mean?** We use the numbers in the hundreds column to order the 3 numbers.

Say: **Are we ordering the numbers from greatest to least or from least to greatest?** greatest to least **Which number in hundreds column is greatest?** 7 Write greatest next to 32,717.

Say: **Which of the numbers remaining in the hundreds column is the least? Write least next to 32,459.**

Now ask students to copy the numbers in order from greatest to least onto their papers separating them with the greater than symbol.

So, the numbers in order from greatest to least are 32,717 > 32,685 > 32,459.

Order Numbers

Grade 4
Skill 5

Write these numbers in order from greatest to least: 3,927; 3,101; and 3,762.

Step 1
Line up the numbers by place-value. Look at the digit in the place-value position on the left first. Compare the thousands.

3,927
3,101
3,762
↑

All the thousands are the same.

Step 2
Now look at the next place-value position. Compare the hundreds.

3,927
3,101
3,762
↑

The hundreds places are not the same.

Step 3
Write the numbers in order from greatest to least.

Think: The number with 9 in the hundreds place is the greatest. The number with 1 in the hundreds place is the least.

9 > 7 > 1

So, the order from greatest to least is 3,927 > 3,762 > 3,101.

Try These

Write these numbers in order from greatest to least.

1 2,957; 7,968; 4,960

2 1,987; 2,897; 3,789

3 7,898; 8,000; 1,999

4 4,999; 4,001; 4,500

5 9,500; 9,249; 9,350

6 5,877; 5,787; 5,699

7 3,700; 3,750; 3,735

8 8,877; 8,887; 8,899

9 6,728; 6,705; 6,753

Go to the next side.

Practice on Your Own

Write these numbers in order from least to greatest: 59,712; 52,085; 56,436.

First, line up the numbers by place-value. Compare the ten thousands. 59,712 52,085 56,436 The digits in ten thousands place are the same.	**Next,** look at the digits in the next place-value position to the right. Compare the thousands. 59,712 52,085 56,436 The thousands are different.	Order the numbers in thousands place from least to greatest. $2 < 6 < 9$ **So,** the order from least to greatest is $52,085 < 56,436 < 59,712$.

Write the numbers in order from least to greatest.

1 88,727; 99,545; 63,258

2 52,759; 55,865; 51,917

3 94,976; 94,388; 94,095

4 75,656; 75,156; 75,428

5 85,443; 87,489; 86,416

6 23,564; 51,215; 34,111

Write the numbers in order from greatest to least.

7 31,532; 51,594; 61,626

8 70,388; 78,036; 73,805

9 77,564; 77,878; 77,901

10 27,256; 35,512; 48,064

11 54,095; 54,121; 54,292

12 33,222; 35,420; 34,911

▶ Quiz

Write the numbers in order from least to greatest.

13 34,824; 44,873; 24,256

14 51,402; 58,321; 50,693

15 64,875; 64,737; 64,949

Write the numbers in order from greatest to least.

16 93,872; 13,012; 33,792

17 12,587; 15,576; 16,525

18 10,872; 10,974; 10,716

OBJECTIVE Round to tens and hundreds

MATERIALS number line

20 Minutes

You may wish to begin by reviewing how to round 2-digit numbers on a number line.

Remind students that they have learned to round numbers two ways. They can use a number line or they can use the rounding rules.

Say: **You are rounding 1,463 to the nearest ten on the number line. 1,463 is between which two tens? 1,460 and 1,470 What number is halfway between 1,460 and 1,470? 1,465 Is 1,463 closer to 1,460 or 1,470? 1,460** So, 1,463 rounded to the nearest ten is 1,460.

Ask similar questions for rounding 1,463 to the nearest hundred.

As you work through the example with the students using rounding rules, you may wish to suggest that students underline the digit to be rounded and circle the digit to the right. Marking in this way will help the students focus on the correct digits.

TRY THESE Exercises 1 and 2 give students the opportunity to round both ways.

- **Exercise 1** Round up to the nearest ten.
- **Exercise 2** Round down to the nearest hundred.

PRACTICE ON YOUR OWN Review the example with the students. Remind them to read the directions carefully, so they will know to which place they are rounding.

QUIZ Students may choose to use either a number line or the rounding method to complete the **Quiz.** Success is indicated by 3 out of 4 correct responses.

Students who successfully complete the **Practice on Your Own** and **Quiz** are ready to move on to the next skill.

COMMON ERRORS

- Some students may look at a digit in the wrong place; for example to round to the nearest 10 they may use the digit in the tens place instead of the ones place.

- Some students may round to the nearest ten instead of the nearest hundred and vice versa.

Students who made more than 2 errors in the **Practice on Your Own,** or who were not successful in the **Quiz** section, may benefit from the **Alternative Teaching Strategy** on the next page.

Alternative Teaching Strategy
Round to Tens and Hundreds

15 Minutes

OBJECTIVE Use a place value chart to round to tens and hundreds

MATERIALS place-value chart, number cards

Provide students with place-value charts or have them make the charts. Display a card showing 62. Then explain to the students that they are to round 62 to the nearest ten. Have them tell you the two tens that 62 is between. **60 and 70**

Display a card showing 60 and a card showing 70. Place 62 between 60 and 70 and ask the students to decide whether to round 62 up to 70, or round it down to 60. Have them write 62 in the place-value chart in preparation for rounding.

Have them underline and label the digit in the tens place to show that it's the rounding place. Then have them circle the digit in the ones place.

Hundreds	Tens	Ones	
	6 rounding place	**2**	← Think: digit to the right

Say: **This is the digit to the right of the rounding place. You use this digit to decide how to round.**

Have students use the rounding rules to determine that since 2 < 5, they need to round down. So, 62 rounded to the nearest ten is 60.

Repeat the activity several times, having students round two digit numbers to the nearest ten. Then move on to rounding numbers to the nearest hundred.

When students show an understanding of the rounding process, have them round numbers without the place-value chart.

Grade 4
Skill 6

Round to Nearest 10 and 100

Round 1,463 to the nearest ten using a number line.

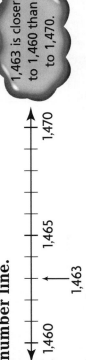

1,460   1,465   1,470

1,463

1,463 is closer to 1,460 than to 1,470.

1,463 rounded to the nearest ten is 1,460.

Round 1,463 to the nearest hundred.

1,400   1,450   1,500

1,463

1,463 is closer to 1,500 than to 1,400.

1,463 rounded to the nearest hundred is 1,500.

To round to the nearest **ten,** look at the digit in the ones place. If the digit is less than 5, the digit to be rounded stays the same.

3 < 5

digit to
be rounded ⌐   ⌐ ones place
    1 , 4 6 3

1,463 rounded to the nearest ten is 1,460.

To round to the nearest **hundred,** look at the digit in the tens place. If the digit is 5 or greater, the digit to be rounded increases by 1.

6 > 5

digit to
be rounded ⌐   ⌐ tens place
    1 , 4 6 3

1,463 rounded to the nearest hundred is 1,500.

▲ Try These

Complete.

1 Use a number line. Round 126 to the nearest ten.

120   125   130
          126

126 is closer to ☐ than to ☐.

126 rounded to the nearest ten is ☐.

2 Use rounding rules. Round 1,617 to the nearest hundred.

1, 6 1 7   The digit in the tens place is ☐.

The digit to be rounded is ☐.

1,617 rounded to the nearest hundred is ☐.

Go to the next side.

Name _____ Skill _____

Practice on Your Own
Skill 6

Round 259 to the nearest hundred.

Number Line

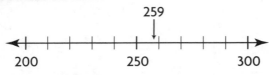

Look at the number line.

259 is closer to 300 than to 200.

Rounding Rules

To round to the nearest hundred, look at the tens digit.

⌐ tens digit
↓
2 **5** 9

If the digit is 5 or greater, the digit to be rounded increases by 1. If the digit is less than 5, the digit to be rounded stays the same.

So, 259 rounded to the nearest hundred is 300.

Round to the nearest ten.

1
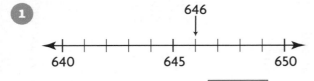

646 to the nearest ten is ☐.

2
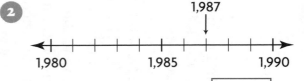

1,987 to the nearest ten is ☐.

Use rounding rules to round the numbers to the nearest hundred.

3 380   ↓

        <u>3</u> **8** 0

380 rounded to the nearest

hundred is ☐.

4 1,794   ↓

        1, <u>7</u> 9 4

1,794 rounded to the nearest

hundred is ☐.

Round to the place of the underlined digit.

5 4<u>6</u>2

6 6,9<u>2</u>7

7 <u>2</u>65

8 3,<u>8</u>78

_____ _____ _____ _____

▶ **Quiz**

Round to the place of the underlined digit.

9 5<u>8</u>6

10 9,0<u>3</u>8

11 <u>6</u>30

12 5,<u>6</u>83

_____ _____ _____ _____

OBJECTIVE Use rounding rules to round numbers from the nearest thousand to the nearest million

You may wish to review place value before beginning this lesson.

Direct students' attention to Step 1.

Ask: **Why is the arrow pointing to the 3? 3 is in thousands place. How do you know that 163,987 is between 163,000 and 164,000?** If I count by thousands, the next greater thousand is 164,000.

Direct students' attention to Step 2.

Ask: **What digit is in the hundreds place? 9** Remind students that when they are asked "Is 9 greater or less than 5?", they are comparing digits in hundreds place and that 900 is greater than 500.

Direct students' attention to Step 3.

Ask: **What digit is in the rounding place? 3 To what number is the three rounded? 4** Review the thought cloud so students understand that all the digits to the right of the rounded place should contain zeros.

Then ask: **What if the hundreds digit were a 5 instead of a 9? Would you increase the rounding digit by 1 or not? Increase it. Would you increase the rounding digit by 1 if the hundreds digit were a 4? no**

TRY THESE Exercises 1–16 allow students to apply the rules of rounding.

- **Exercises 1–4**   Round to the nearest thousand.

- **Exercises 5–16**   Round each number to the place value of the underlined digit.

PRACTICE ON YOUR OWN Review the example at the top of the page. It shows how to round down and apply rounding rules to numbers in the millions. In Exercises 1–4, students round to the nearest thousand; and in Exercises 5–16, to the place value of the underlined digit.

QUIZ Determine if students can round to the nearest thousand, ten thousand, hundred thousand, and million. Success is indicated by 6 out of 8 correct responses.

Students who successfully complete the **Practice on Your Own** and **Quiz** are ready to move on to the next skill.

COMMON ERRORS

- Students will round to the wrong place.

- Students will see a 5 next to the rounding place and not know to increase the digit in the rounding place by 1.

- Students will not change digits to the right of the rounded place to zeros.

- Students will forget to keep the digits to the left of the rounding place the same.

Students who make more than 4 errors in the **Practice on Your Own**, or who were not successful in the **Quiz** section, may benefit from the **Alternative Teaching Strategy** on the next page.

Alternative Teaching Strategy
Using Number Cards to Round Numbers

20 Minutes

OBJECTIVE Use rounding rules to round numbers

MATERIALS index cards, markers

Each student or pair of students should have two sets of index cards labeled with the digits 1–9 on one side and 0 on the opposite side. Also make three cards with a comma on each.

Have students use these index cards to create the number 837,265,149. Say: **We will round this number to the nearest thousand, ten thousand, hundred thousand, and million.**

Say: **Use your pencil to point to the digit in the thousands place. What is the digit to the right of this number? 1 Is it 5 or more, or less than 5? less than 5 What do you do then? Keep the 5 the same and make the digits to the right of the 5 zeros.**

Have students turn over the three index cards to the right of 5 to show zeros. The number in front of students should now be 837,265,000.

Say: **What is the digit in the ten thousands place? 6 Is the digit to the right of this number 5 or more, or less than 5? 5 or more What do you do then? It is 5 or more, so I add 1 to the number in the rounding place. I turn the digits to the right into zeros.**

Have students use their index cards to display the rounding. The number in front of students should now be 837,270,000.

Say: **What is the digit in the hundred thousands place? 2 Is the digit to the right of this number 5 or more or less than 5? 5 or more What do you do then? It is 5 or more, so I add 1 to the number in the rounding place. I make the digits to the right into zeros.**

Have students use their index cards to display the rounding. The number in front of students should now be 837,300,000.

Say: **What is the digit in the millions place? 7 Is the digit to the right of this number 5 or more or less than 5? less than 5 What do you do then? It is less than 5, so I keep the digit the same. I make the digits to the right into zeros.**

Have students use their index cards to display the rounding. The number in front of students should now be 837,000,000.

Continue rounding until the number in front of students becomes 800,000,000.

Repeat these steps using the number 743,612,859.

Round Numbers

Round 163,987 to the nearest thousand.

Step 1
Find the place to which you want to round.

↓ place to be rounded
163,987

163,987 is between 163,000 and 164,000.

Step 2
Look at the digit to its right.

↓ place to be rounded
163,**9**87

Look at the hundreds digit. Is 9 greater or less than 5?

Step 3
Since 9 is greater than 5, the digit in the rounding place increases by 1.

So, 163,987 rounded to the nearest thousand is 164,000.

Use these rules:
- If the digit is *less than 5*, the digit in the rounding place stays the same.
- If the digit is *5 or more*, the digit in the rounding place increases by 1.

> All of the digits to the right of the rounded place become zeros.

Try These

Round each number to the nearest thousand.

1 598,457

2 87,430,984

3 316,554

4 4,159

Round each number to the place value of the underlined digit.

5 24,<u>5</u>40,871

6 <u>1</u>6,726

7 6<u>1</u>,361

8 729,<u>4</u>97

9 7<u>5</u>8,475

10 5,4<u>6</u>8,795

11 48,<u>5</u>96

12 5<u>6</u>8,795

Go to the next side.

Practice on Your Own

Round 105,190,328 to the nearest million.

Think: Find the place to which you want to round. ↓ place to be rounded 105,190,328	**Next,** Look at the digit to its right. ↓ place to be rounded 105,190,328 Is 1 greater or less than 5?	Since 1 is less than 5, the digit in the rounding place stays the same. **So,** 105,190,328 rounded to the nearest million is 105,000,000.

Round to the nearest thousand.

1. 109,387
2. 473,098
3. 78,943,789
4. 9,821,501

Round to the nearest ten thousand.

5. 109,387
6. 473,098
7. 78,943,789
8. 9,821,501

Round to the nearest million.

9. 3,132,466
10. 67,613,429
11. 150,510,536
12. 819,453,021

Round each number to the place value of the underlined digit.

13. 8,6̲75,309
14. 49̲2,586
15. 2̲,105
16. 454,45̲2,505

▶ Quiz

Round each number to the place value of the underlined digit.

17. 251̲,622
18. 238̲,296
19. 48̲5,514
20. 224̲,016

21. 244̲,484
22. 368̲,812
23. 91̲,696,783
24. 141̲,786,442

Number Sense, Concepts, and Operations

Whole Number Addition

15 Minutes

OBJECTIVE Add 2-digit numbers, regrouping ones as tens

Explain to students that in this skill they will be finding the sum of 2-digit numbers. Point out the place-value labels and suggest that students use them to remember the value of each digit as they add.

Draw students' attention to Step 1. Have them add the ones.

Ask: **You have more than 9 ones. What can you do next? Regroup the ones.**

Work through the regrouping with students. Have them look at Step 2.

Ask: **How do you regroup the ones? There are 13 ones, I regroup 10 ones as 1 ten 3 ones.**

Emphasize that the regrouped digit is placed in the tens column.

Ask: **How do you show the regrouping? I write 3 in the ones place of the sum, and write the 1 ten in the tens column.**

As students complete the addition in Step 3, remind them to add the regrouped digit when they add the tens.

TRY THESE Exercises 1–4 prepare students for the regrouping exercises they will find on the **Practice on Your Own** page.

- **Exercise 1**   Regroup 14 ones.
- **Exercise 2**   Regroup 10 ones.
- **Exercise 3**   Regroup 11 ones.
- **Exercise 4**   Regroup 12 ones.

PRACTICE ON YOUR OWN Review the example at the top of the page. Ask students to explain how they use the place value labels to help them in the regrouping process. Encourage students to use terms such as *ones*, *tens*, *regroup*, *place*, and *sum*.

QUIZ Determine if students can regroup when they add 2-digit numbers. Success is indicated by 3 out of 4 correct responses.

Students who successfully complete the **Practice on Your Own** and **Quiz** are ready to move on to the next skill.

COMMON ERRORS

- Students may forget to add the regrouped digit.
- Students may place the regrouped digit in the wrong column.
- Students may not know their addition facts.

Students who made more than 4 errors in the **Practice on Your Own**, or who were not successful in the **Quiz** section, may benefit from the **Alternative Teaching Strategy** on the next page.

Alternative Teaching Strategy
Model 2-Digit Addition: Regrouping Ones as Tens

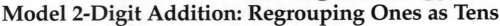

OBJECTIVE Use base-ten blocks to model addition of 2-digit numbers, regrouping ones as tens

MATERIALS base-ten blocks, paper

Explain to students that they will be reviewing the regrouping process for adding 2-digit numbers.

First, review regrouping ones. Have students take 18 ones. Explain that since there are more than 9 ones, they can regroup 10 ones as 1 ten. Note that now they have 1 ten 8 ones. Help students recognize that 18 ones and 1 ten 8 ones represent 18.

Next, have students work in pairs. One partner models with the blocks, the other records the addition on paper. Present this addition example.

tens	ones
2	4
+3	7
□	□

Explain that the place-value labels can help students remember the value of the digits as they add. The grid helps them to write the digits in the correct place. Have the students show the addends 24 and 37 with the blocks.

Say: **Begin by adding ones. Group the ones blocks together. How many ones do you have in all? 11 ones You have more than 9 ones. What do you do next? Regroup 11 ones as 1 ten 1 one. Where do you put the regrouped ten? with the other tens**

Remind students to write the regrouped digit above the 2 in tens column.

When you add the tens, what must you remember to do? Add the regrouped digit. What is the sum? 61

Repeat the activity with similar examples. When students show understanding of the regrouping process, encourage them to add using only paper and pencil.

24 →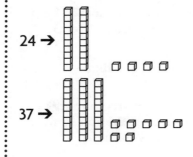

37 →

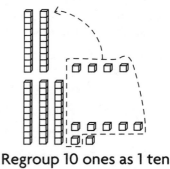

Regroup 10 ones as 1 ten

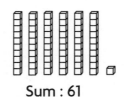

Sum : 61

Grade 4
Skill
8

2-Digit Addition

Find 36 + 27 = ■.

Step 1 Add the ones.

Tens	Ones
3	6
+ 2	7

$6 + 7 = 13$ ones

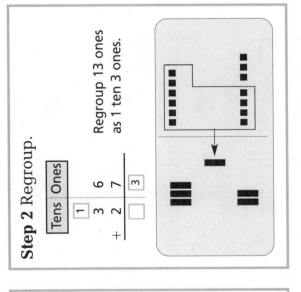

Step 2 Regroup.

Tens	Ones
1	
3	6
+ 2	7
	3

Regroup 13 ones
as 1 ten 3 ones.

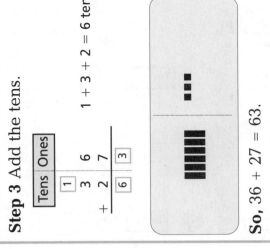

Step 3 Add the tens.

Tens	Ones
1	
3	6
+ 2	7
6	3

$1 + 3 + 2 = 6$ tens

So, 36 + 27 = 63.

Try These

Find the sum.

1

Tens	Ones
	8
+ 4	6

2

Tens	Ones
	9
5	1
+ 3	

3

Tens	Ones
	3
3	8
+ 4	

4

Tens	Ones
	6
1	6
+ 7	

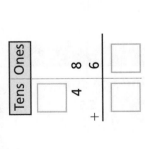
Go to the next side.

Practice on Your Own

 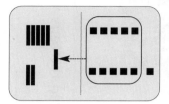

Think:
Regroup ones when the sum of
the digits is 10 or greater.

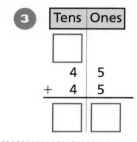
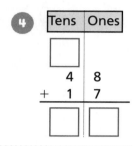

	Tens	Ones
	1	
	5	5
+	2	6
	8	1

Find the sum.

1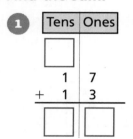

Tens	Ones
1	7
+ 1	3

2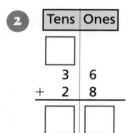

Tens	Ones
3	6
+ 2	8

3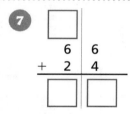

Tens	Ones
4	5
+ 4	5

4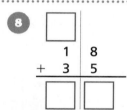

Tens	Ones
4	8
+ 1	7

5
```
    4   9
 +  2   2
```

6
```
    4   9
 +  2   6
```

7
```
    6   6
 +  2   4
```

8
```
    1   8
 +  3   5
```

9
```
    5   5
 +  1   6
```

10
```
    2   9
 +  3   4
```

11
```
    3   7
 +  5   8
```

12
```
    1   4
 +  5   7
```

13
```
    11
 +  19
```

14
```
    65
 +  29
```

15
```
    27
 +  33
```

16
```
    36
 +  16
```

▶ Quiz

Find the sum.

17
```
    25
 +  25
```

18
```
    37
 +  48
```

19
```
    56
 +  34
```

20
```
    79
 +  19
```

15 Minutes

OBJECTIVE Use addition facts to find the sum of three addends

Tell students that numbers that are added together are called addends. Explain that addends can be grouped in different ways, but the sum stays the same.

Say: **Here's an example. You can group three addends in different ways. Any way you group them will give you the same answer.**

Direct students' attention to the example at the left. Say: **Notice that both 8 and 2 are circled. They are circled to show that those two addends can be added first. The sum of 8 and 2 is 10.**

Move on to line 2. Ask: **Why is 5 added to 10?** It is the remaining addend. 5 is added to 10, which is the sum of 8 and 2.
Say: $8 + 2 + 5 = 5 + 10 = 15$.

Direct students' attention to the middle example. Say: **Notice that both 2 and 5 are circled. They are circled to show that those two addends can be added first. The sum of 2 and 5 is shown. That sum is 7.**

Move on to line 2. Ask: **Why is 8 added to 7?** It is the remaining addend. It is added to 7, which is the sum of 2 and 5.
Say: $8 + 2 + 5 = 8 + 7 = 15$.

Direct students' attention to the example at the right. Say: **Notice that if you begin with the addends 8 and 5, you will still get the final sum 15.**

TRY THESE Exercises 1–9 model the type of exercises students will find in the **Practice On Your Own** page.

- **Exercises 1–6** Horizontal addition
- **Exercises 7–14** Vertical addition

PRACTICE ON YOUR OWN Review the steps at the top of the page.

Say: **It takes three steps to add three addends.**

Step 1 Choose two addends that make an addition fact you know.

Step 2 Find the sum of those two addends.

Step 3 Find the sum of the third addend.

In Exercises 1–6, students add three numbers horizontally. In Exercises 7–14, students add numbers vertically. Remind students that both horizontal and vertical problems are solved the same way.

QUIZ Determine if students can add three numbers using addition facts they know. Success is indicated by 4 out of 6 correct responses.

Students who successfully complete the **Practice on Your Own** and **Quiz** are ready to move to the next skill.

COMMON ERRORS

- Students may add the same number twice.

- Students may not add to the sum of two addends.

Students who make more than 4 errors in the **Practice on Your Own**, or who were not successful in the **Quiz** section, may benefit from the **Alternative Teaching Strategy** on the next page.

Alternative Teaching Strategy
Model Adding 3 Numbers

15 Minutes

OBJECTIVE Use cubes to model adding 3 numbers

MATERIALS base-ten ones, paper, pencil

Ask students to fold the paper twice to divide it into four equal sections, with the folds straight across the page. Have them draw a line between the third and fourth sections.

Say: **You are going to add 5 + 3 + 7. Write each of these addends, top to bottom, in the first three sections of your paper.** Next to each addend, have students place base-ten ones equal in number to the value of the addend.

Say: **First, you will add two numbers. Choose those two numbers by looking for facts you know. For example, choose 7 and 3, which makes 10.**

Students should draw arrows from both 7 and 3 and then write the sum, 10. Have them combine the base-ten ones for 7 and 3.

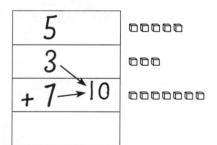

Ask: **What will you do with the addend that remains? Add it to 10.**

Have the students draw arrows from both 10 and 5 and then write the sum, 15. Have them combine the base-ten ones for 10 and 5.

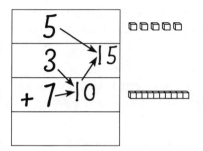

Ask: **What is the sum? 15**

Say: **5 + 3 + 7 = 15.**

Think of other problems that require adding three numbers. Have students solve them on their own using the base-ten ones.

Algebra: Add 3 Numbers

You can group three addends in different ways. The sum stays the same.

Choose two numbers to **add** first. Look for facts you know.

$(8) + (2) + 5 = \boxed{5}$
$10 + 5 = 15$

$8 + (2) + (5) = \boxed{5}$
$8 + 7 = 15$

$(8) + 2 + (5) = \boxed{5}$
$13 + 2 = 15$

 **Try These**

Circle the addends you add first. Write the sum.

1 $(2) + (7) + 3 = $ $\square$

9 + 3

2 $(8) + (5) + 6 = $ $\square$

13 + 6

3 $(2) + (6) + 6 = $ $\square$

8 + 6

4 $3 + 4 + 9 = $ $\square$

5 $1 + 6 + 3 = $ $\square$

6 $9 + 8 + 7 = $ $\square$

Go to the next side.

Practice on Your Own

Skill 9

Step 1
Look for facts you know.

$4 + 5 + 6 =$ ☐

4 plus 6 equals 10 is a fact I know. So, I'll pick 4 and 6 as my first two addends.

Step 2
Group two of the addends and find their sum.

④+ 5 +⑥= ☐
↓
10

I'll circle the 4 and the 6 to show that I'm adding them. The sum of 4 and 6 is 10.

Step 3
Add the remaining addend.

$10 + 5 = 15$

This is the same as adding 4 + 6 + 5, which is the same as adding 4 + 5 + 6. So I know that 10 + 5 equals 15.

Write the sum.

1 $7 + 3 + 4 =$ ☐   **2** $1 + 9 + 2 =$ ☐   **3** $3 + 2 + 3 =$ ☐

4 $8 + 3 + 8 =$ ☐   **5** $6 + 7 + 4 =$ ☐   **6** $3 + 6 + 8 =$ ☐

7
```
   7
   1
 + 6
 ☐
```
8
```
   5
   3
 + 5
 ☐
```
9
```
   4
   4
 + 6
 ☐
```
10
```
   9
   6
 + 4
 ☐
```

11
```
   2
   5
 + 4
 ☐
```
12
```
   1
   6
 + 9
 ☐
```
13
```
   9
   9
 + 9
 ☐
```
14
```
   5
   1
 + 8
 ☐
```

▶ **Quiz**

Write the sum.

15
```
   2
   7
 + 4
 ☐
```
16
```
   5
   5
 + 4
 ☐
```
17
```
   2
   7
 + 9
 ☐
```
18
```
   8
   3
 + 5
 ☐
```

19 $8 + 5 + 1 =$ ☐   **20** $1 + 5 + 9 =$ ☐   **21** $3 + 6 + 2 =$ ☐

Number Sense, Concepts, and Operations

Whole Number Subtraction

15 Minutes

OBJECTIVE Subtract 2-digit numbers, regrouping tens as ones

Begin by pointing to the place value labels on the subtraction exercises. Suggest that students use the labels to help them remember the value of the digits when they regroup. Explain that in this activity students are asked to subtract two 2-digit numbers.

Direct students' attention to Step 1.

Ask: **Do you have enough ones to subtract? No, 2 ones are less than 9 ones. What can you do? Regroup 4 tens as 3 tens 10 ones.**

Continue with Step 2.

Ask: **How many ones do you have after you regroup? 12 ones How many tens do you have after you regroup? 3 tens**

Look at Step 3.

Ask: **How many tens are left after you subtract? 2**

TRY THESE In Exercises 1–4, students regroup 1 ten as 10 ones.

- **Exercise 1** Regroup 2 tens as 1 ten 10 ones.

- **Exercise 2** Regroup 3 tens as 2 tens 10 ones.

- **Exercise 3** Regroup 2 tens as 1 ten 10 ones.

- **Exercise 4** Regroup 3 tens as 2 tens 10 ones.

PRACTICE ON YOUR OWN Review the example at the top of the page. Ask students to explain the subtraction and regrouping process, using the terms *ones* and *tens*.

QUIZ Determine if students know when to regroup tens as ones before they subtract the ones. Success is indicated by 3 out of 4 correct responses.

Students who successfully complete the **Practice on Your Own** and **Quiz** are ready to move on to the next skill.

COMMON ERRORS

- Students may subtract the top digit from the bottom digit instead of regrouping.

- Students may forget that they have regrouped a ten when they subtract the tens, and subtract from the original number of tens.

Students who made more than 4 errors in the **Practice on Your Own**, or who were not successful in the **Quiz** section, may benefit from the **Alternative Teaching Strategy** on the next page.

Alternative Teaching Strategy
Model 2-Digit Subtraction: Regrouping Tens as Ones

15 Minutes

OBJECTIVE Use base-ten blocks to model subtracting 2-digit numbers, regrouping tens as ones

MATERIALS base-ten blocks, place-value grid

Distribute base-ten blocks. Provide an example for students to complete using only the blocks. For example, have students find $53 - 26$. Display the exercise, then ask students to model 53 with the blocks.

Ask: **What do you subtract first? The ones, or 6 ones Can you remove 6 ones from 3 ones? No What can you do? Regroup one of the tens rods as 10 ones What do you have now? 4 tens 13 ones**

Have students remove the ones, then remove 2 tens to complete the subtraction.

Continue with another example having students verbalize the steps in the regrouping and subtraction process.

Next, have students record $42 - 19$ in a place-value grid. As they regroup and subtract with the models, have students record the result on the place-value grid.

tens	ones
4	2
− 1	9

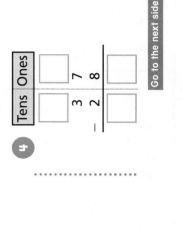

Grade 4
Skill 10

2-Digit Subtraction

Find 42 − 19 = ∎.

Step 1 Show 42 as 4 tens and 2 ones. Since 9 > 2, regroup 42 as 3 tens and 12 ones.

There are not enough ones to subtract. Regroup.

Tens	Ones
[3] 4	[12] 2
− 1	9

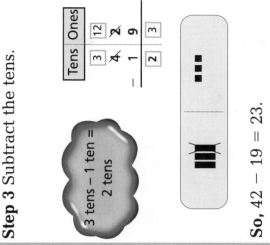

Step 2 Subtract the ones.

12 ones − 9 ones = 3 ones

Tens	Ones
[3] 4	[12] 2
− 1	9
	3

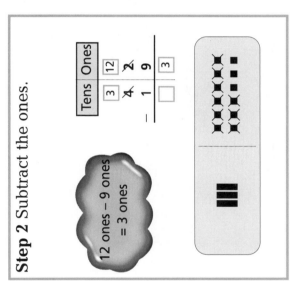

Step 3 Subtract the tens.

3 tens − 1 ten = 2 tens

Tens	Ones
[3] 4	[12] 2
− 1	9
2	3

So, 42 − 19 = 23.

Try These

Find the difference.

1

Tens	Ones
---- 4	---- 2
− 1	4

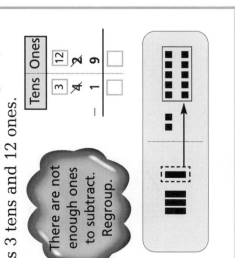

2

Tens	Ones
3	1
− 1	6

3

Tens	Ones
2	3
− 1	5

4

Tens	Ones
3	7
− 2	8

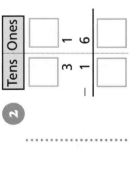

Go to the next side.

Practice on Your Own

Think: Do you need to regroup?

Tens	Ones
6̶	1̶4̶
− 4	5
☐	9

Regroup 1 ten as 10 ones.
Subtract the ones.

Tens	Ones
6̶	1̶4̶
− 4	5
2	9

Subtract the tens.

Find the difference.

1

Tens	Ones
5	13
6̶	3̶
− 4	6
☐	☐

2

Tens	Ones
☐	☐
4	5
− 2	6
☐	☐

3

Tens	Ones
☐	☐
9	2
− 3	4
☐	☐

4

Tens	Ones
☐	☐
8	0
− 3	4
☐	☐

5

☐	☐
5	4
−	8
☐	☐

6

☐	☐
6	3
− 2	7
☐	☐

7

☐	☐
8	1
− 5	4
☐	☐

8

☐	☐
9	0
− 4	6
☐	☐

9

☐	☐
3	1
−	9
☐	☐

10

☐	☐
5	7
− 4	8
☐	☐

11

☐	☐
5	0
− 2	9
☐	☐

12

☐	☐
7	1
− 3	4
☐	☐

13
```
  81
−  5
```

14
```
  47
− 18
```

15
```
  64
− 35
```

16
```
  90
− 35
```

▶ Quiz

Find the difference.

17
```
  25
−  9
```

18
```
  43
− 16
```

19
```
  72
− 38
```

20
```
  70
− 59
```

OBJECTIVE Recall fact families for addition and subtraction sums through 20

MATERIALS colored counting cubes, white counting cubes

15 Minutes

You may wish to use counting cubes to model different fact families. Remind students that addition and subtraction are inverse operations, or opposite operations that undo each other.

Have students recall that fact families have both addition and subtraction facts. Tell them that there are three numbers in a fact family.

Draw students' attention to Step 1.

Ask: **How are the two addition facts alike? They both use the same numbers.**

Ask: **How are they different? The two addends, 4 and 5, are reversed.**

Then call attention to Step 2.

Ask: **How are the subtraction facts related to the addition facts in Step 1? They use the same numbers, but they show the inverse subtraction fact. What is shown in Step 3? All four facts use the numbers 4, 5, and 9. Two facts are addition and two are subtraction.**

Explain that Step 3 shows all four facts written together to form the fact family for 4, 5, and 9.

Point out that when both addends are the same, there are only 2 number sentences in each family.

TRY THESE In Exercises 1–3, students are asked to use the numbers to write the number sentences that make a fact family.

- **Exercise 1** Write the fact family for 2, 5, and 7.

- **Exercise 2** Write the fact family for 6, 7, and 13.

- **Exercise 3** Write the fact family for 5, 10, and 15.

PRACTICE ON YOUR OWN Review the fact family for 4, 7, and 11 at the top of the page. As students complete the exercises they should see that fact families can vary. Remind students to use the visual prompts where they are provided.

QUIZ Determine if students can write fact families using the correct numbers. Success is indicated by 2 out of 3 correct responses.

Students who successfully complete the **Practice on Your Own** and **Quiz** are ready to move on to the next skill.

COMMON ERRORS

- Students may not reverse the digits to write the second addition or subtraction fact.

- Students may not begin the subtraction sentences with the greatest number.

Students who make more than two errors in the **Practice on Your Own**, or who were not successful in the **Quiz** section, may benefit from the **Alternative Teaching Strategy** on the next page.

Alternative Teaching Strategy
Model Fact Families

OBJECTIVE Use counters to model a fact family

MATERIALS two-sided counters

Provide students with a group of two-sided counters and a sheet of paper. Ask students to fold the paper, dividing it into four horizontal sections.

Tell students to show 7 counters of one color on the left side of their work area and 5 counters of the other color on the right side.

Point to each group from left to right.

Ask: **How many counters are in each group? 7 and 5**

Next, point to each group from right to left.

Ask: **How many counters in each group? 5 and 7** Explain that no matter which direction you add, the sum will be the same.

Ask: **What is the sum of 7 and 5? 12 of 5 and 7? 12**

Have students write each of these addition facts in a separate section on the paper. Then tell students they need to find the two subtraction facts.

Ask: **What is the total number of counters? 12**

Say: **Take away the 5 counters. How many are left? 7**

Then ask students to start with the 12 counters again and take away 7.

Ask: **How many are left? 5**

Have students write each subtraction fact in a separate section on the paper. Point out that each of the numbers in the fact family 5, 7, and 12 appears in each of the facts on the paper.

● ● ● ● ● ● ●   ○ ○ ○ ○ ○

| 7 + 5 = 12 |
| 5 + 7 = 12 |
| 12 − 5 = 7 |
| 12 − 7 = 5 |

Provide additional counters and have students create and write their own fact families. Remind them that they should write two addition facts and two subtraction facts, except for special cases such as 5, 5, and 10 or 2, 2, and 4. Point out that they should check to see that each number appears in each fact.

Grade 4
Skill
11

Fact Families

A **fact family** is a set of related addition and subtraction number sentences that use the same numbers.
Write the fact family for 4, 5, and 9.

Step 1 Count the shaded cubes. Then count the white cubes. Write the two addition facts.

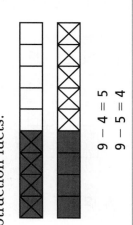

$4 + 5 = 9$
$5 + 4 = 9$

Step 2 Remove the shaded cubes from the 9 cubes. Then remove the white cubes from the 9 cubes. Write the two subtraction facts.

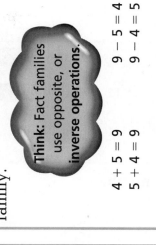

$9 - 4 = 5$
$9 - 5 = 4$

Step 3 Write the addition and subtraction facts for the fact family.

Think: Fact families use opposite, or **inverse operations.**

$4 + 5 = 9$ $9 - 5 = 4$
$5 + 4 = 9$ $9 - 4 = 5$

▲ Try These

Write the fact family for each set of numbers.

1 2, 5, 7

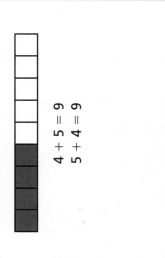

$2 + \boxed{5} = 7$ $7 - \boxed{5} = 2$
$5 + \boxed{2} = 7$ $7 - \boxed{2} = 5$

2 6, 7, 13

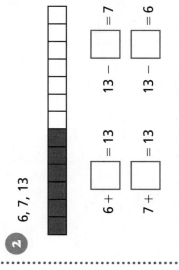

$6 + \boxed{} = 13$ $13 - \boxed{} = 7$
$7 + \boxed{} = 13$ $13 - \boxed{} = 6$

3 5, 10, 15

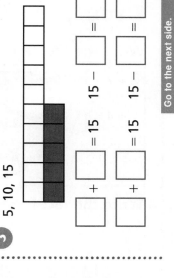

$\boxed{} + \boxed{} = 15$ $15 - \boxed{} = \boxed{}$
$\boxed{} + \boxed{} = 15$ $15 - \boxed{} = \boxed{}$

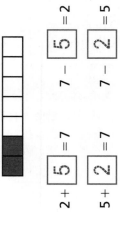

Go to the next side.

Practice on Your Own

Write the fact family for 4, 7, and 11.

$4 + 7 = 11$ 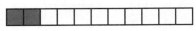 $11 - 7 = 4$

$7 + 4 = 11$ **Think:** Fact families use opposite, or inverse operations. $11 - 4 = 7$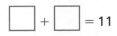

Write the fact family for each set of numbers.

1   8, 9, 17

☐ + ☐ = 17
☐ + ☐ = 17
17 − ☐ = ☐
17 − ☐ = ☐

2   2, 9, 11

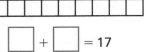

☐ + ☐ = 11
☐ + ☐ = 11
11 − ☐ = ☐
11 − ☐ = ☐

3   1, 3, 4

☐ + ☐ = ☐
☐ + ☐ = ☐
☐ − ☐ = ☐
☐ − ☐ = ☐

4   2, 4, 6

☐ + ☐ = ☐
☐ + ☐ = ☐
☐ − ☐ = ☐
☐ − ☐ = ☐

5   12, 7, 19

_____
_____
_____
_____

6   5, 5, 10

_____
_____
_____
_____

▶ Quiz

Write the fact family for each set of numbers.

7   6, 8, 14

_____
_____
_____
_____

8   7, 8, 15

_____
_____
_____
_____

9   3, 7, 10

_____
_____
_____
_____

Number Sense, Concepts, and Operations

Whole Number Multiplication

OBJECTIVE Recall multiplication facts 6 through 10

MATERIALS tiles

Begin the lesson by discussing the example at the top of the Skill. How many rows are there in the array? **6** How many tiles are in each row? **5** How many tiles are there in all? **30** What multiplication fact does the array show? **6 × 5 = 30**

Show a 7 × 4 array. Ask questions similar to those above. Have a student write the multiplication fact 7 × 4 = 28. Continue with two or three other arrays if necessary.

You may wish to provide a context for multiplying, such as: **You have 4 boxes of 8 marbles. How many marbles do you have in all? 32 What multiplication fact can you use to answer the question?** 4 × 8 = 32

TRY THESE In Exercises 1–3, students use pictorial models of arrays to write facts.

- **Exercise 1** Array for 7 × 6.
- **Exercise 2** Array for 8 × 1.
- **Exercise 3** Array for 9 × 5.

PRACTICE ON YOUR OWN Go over the example at the top of the page. Review the meaning of *row* in multiplication. Discuss why multiplying is much more efficient than counting or using repeated addition. Only the first three exercises show arrays. If students are having trouble finding the products, allow them to use tiles for some of the remaining exercises.

QUIZ Success is determined by 4 out of 5 correct responses.

Students who successfully complete the **Practice on Your Own** and **Quiz,** are ready to move on to the next skill.

COMMON ERRORS

- Students may add instead of multiplying.
- Students may recall facts incorrectly.

Students who made more than 5 errors in the **Practice on Your Own,** or who were not successful in the **Quiz** section, may benefit from the **Alternative Teaching Strategy** on the next page.

Alternative Teaching Strategy
Model Multiplication Facts to 10

20 Minutes

OBJECTIVE Use manipulatives to understand and practice multiplication facts

MATERIALS tiles, triangle flash cards

Provide a supply of tiles. Ask each student to model 3×7.

How many rows? 3

How many in each row? 7

How many in all? 21

What multiplication fact does the array show? $3 \times 7 = 21$

Repeat two or three times with different facts.

Remind students that the numbers they multiply are called *factors* and the answer is called the *product*.

If you think that the students understand the concept of multiplication, but are not recalling the facts correctly, prepare a set of

triangle flash cards. The factors are in two of the corners and the product is in the third corner. Let students work in pairs with the flash cards for a few minutes every day. Have them keep a list of the facts that give them trouble, and concentrate on those, using counters if necessary.

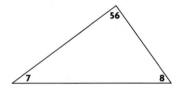

Students who do not understand what multiplication means may need further work with arrays, the number line, or equal groups.

Grade 4
Skill
12

Arrays

Use an array to multiply 6×5.

Step 1 Write the number of rows.

There are

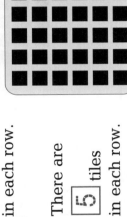

6 rows.

Step 2 Write the number of tiles in each row.

There are

5 tiles in each row.

Step 3 Multiply to find how many tiles in all.

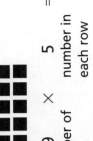

$$\underset{\substack{\text{number of}\\\text{rows}}}{6} \times \underset{\substack{\text{number in}\\\text{each row}}}{5} = \underset{\substack{\text{total}\\\text{number}\\\text{of tiles}}}{30}$$

So, $6 \times 5 = 30$.

▲ Try These

Find the product.

1

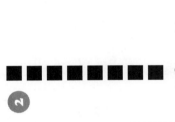

$$\underset{\substack{\text{number of}\\\text{rows}}}{7} \times \underset{\substack{\text{number in}\\\text{each row}}}{6} = \underset{\substack{\text{total}\\\text{number}\\\text{of tiles}}}{\boxed{}}$$

2

$$\underset{\substack{\text{number of}\\\text{rows}}}{8} \times \underset{\substack{\text{number in}\\\text{each row}}}{1} = \underset{\substack{\text{total}\\\text{number}\\\text{of tiles}}}{\boxed{}}$$

3

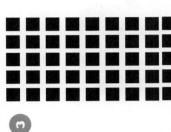

$$\underset{\substack{\text{number of}\\\text{rows}}}{9} \times \underset{\substack{\text{number in}\\\text{each row}}}{5} = \underset{\substack{\text{total}\\\text{number}\\\text{of tiles}}}{\boxed{}}$$

Go to the next side.

Practice on Your Own

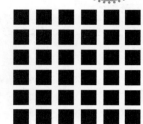

Find $6 \times 6 = \blacksquare$.

Think:
Multiply the number of rows by the number in each row to find how many in all.

6	×	6	=	36
number of rows		number in each row		total number of tiles

Find the product.

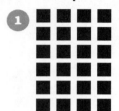 **1**

$6 \times 4 = \boxed{}$

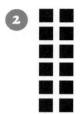 **2**

$\boxed{} \times \boxed{} = \boxed{}$

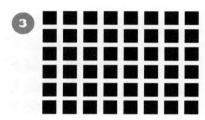 **3**

$\boxed{} \times \boxed{} = \boxed{}$

4 $7 \times 1 = \boxed{}$ **5** $7 \times 4 = \boxed{}$ **6** $7 \times 7 = \boxed{}$ **7** $7 \times 8 = \boxed{}$

8 $8 \times 2 = \boxed{}$ **9** $8 \times 5 = \boxed{}$ **10** $8 \times 8 = \boxed{}$ **11** $8 \times 9 = \boxed{}$

12 $9 \times 3 = \boxed{}$ **13** $4 \times 9 = \boxed{}$ **14** $7 \times 9 = \boxed{}$ **15** $9 \times 9 = \boxed{}$

16 $7 \times 6 = \boxed{}$ **17** $6 \times 3 = \boxed{}$ **18** $6 \times 8 = \boxed{}$ **19** $7 \times 9 = \boxed{}$

▶ Quiz

20 $7 \times 6 = \boxed{}$ **21** $5 \times 7 = \boxed{}$ **22** $6 \times 9 = \boxed{}$ **23** $9 \times 8 = \boxed{}$ **24** $6 \times 6 = \boxed{}$

20 Minutes

OBJECTIVE Write multiplication facts through 12

Demonstrate that multiplication is a "shortcut" for repeated addition.

Say: **If Jo has 5 pens, Ty has 5 pens, and Ben has 5 pens, you can add 5 + 5 + 5 to find how many pens they have in all. You can also use multiplication to save time. Adding three 5's is the same as multiplying 3 times 5.** Review with students that a multiple is the product of two numbers. Explain that they can use multiplication facts and patterns they already know to learn new facts.

Have students look at the first example.

Ask: **How can you use multiplication facts that you already know to find the product? Break apart the numbers or look for a pattern. How can you break apart 12? 11 and 1, 10 and 2, 9 and 3, 8 and 4, 7 and 5, 6 and 6**

Say: **Let's break 12 into 10 and 2.**

Ask: **Why is it helpful to use 10? It is easier to multiply a number by 10.**

Point out that the next step is to find the product of the break-apart numbers.

Ask: **What is 10 × 11? 110 What is 2 × 11? 22**

Say: **Each of these products is a part of the final product.**

Ask: **How can you find the final product? Add the part products. What is 110 + 22? 132**

Say: **So, 12 × 11 = 132.**

Repeat the procedure using the second example.

Ask: **Why are you able to use break-apart numbers to find a product? You can add parts of a product to find the whole product.**

TRY THESE In Exercises 1–4, students practice multiplying by 11 and 12.

- **Exercises 1 and 3:** Multiply by 12.

- **Exercises 2 and 4:** Multiply by 11.

PRACTICE ON YOUR OWN Review the example at the top of the page. Students practice finding products using a multiplication table.

QUIZ Determine if students can find products using a multiplication table. Success is indicated by 3 out of 4 correct responses.

Students who successfully complete **Practice on Your Own** and **Quiz** are ready to move to the next skill.

COMMON ERRORS

- Students may read the multiplication table incorrectly, not reading straight across a row or column.

- Students may add numbers instead of multiplying them.

Students who made more than 6 errors in **Practice on Your Own,** or who were not successful in the **Quiz** section, may benefit from the **Alternative Teaching Strategy** on the next page.

Alternative Teaching Strategy
Multiplication Table Through 12

20 Minutes

OBJECTIVE Model multiplication facts to find the product

MATERIALS base-ten units, base-ten rods

Distribute the base-ten units and rods.

Model 12 × 9 using base-ten units.

Say: **To multiply 12 times 9, you can break the number 12 apart into smaller numbers that are easier to multiply. One way you can model this is by using base-ten rods and units.**

Ask: **How can you use the base-ten rods and units to model the number 12? Use 1 rod and 2 units.**

Monitor students as they select 1 rod and 2 units and place them in a row.

Ask: **How can you model the multiplication fact 12 × 9? Make 9 rows of 12.** Observe students as they use base-ten rods and units to model 12 × 9.

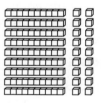

Show students that their model can be separated into a set of rods and a set of units. Have students separate their models.

Ask: **What two multiplication facts have you modeled now? 10 × 9 and 2 × 9**

Explain to students that they can rewrite the fact 12 × 9 as the sum of two facts: 10 × 9 and 2 × 9. Stress that the number of base-ten units has not changed and point out that the product will not change.

Ask: **How many base-ten rods do you have? 9 What is the value of each rod? 10 So what is the value of all of the rods? 90 How many base-ten units do you have? 18 What is the sum of the rods and the units together? 108 What does this show? The product of 12 × 9 is 108.**

Say: **So, 12 × 9 = 108.**

Grade 4
Skill 13

Multiplication Table Through 12

×	0	1	2	3	4	5	6	7	8	9	10	11	12
0	0	0	0	0	0	0	0	0	0	0	0	0	0
1	0	1	2	3	4	5	6	7	8	9	10	11	12
2	0	2	4	6	8	10	12	14	16	18	20	22	24
3	0	3	6	9	12	15	18	21	24	27	30	33	36
4	0	4	8	12	16	20	24	28	32	36	40	44	48
5	0	5	10	15	20	25	30	35	40	45	50	55	60
6	0	6	12	18	24	30	36	42	48	54	60	66	72
7	0	7	14	21	28	35	42	49	56	63	70	77	84
8	0	8	16	24	32	40	48	56	64	72	80	88	96
9	0	9	18	27	36	45	54	63	72	81	90	99	108
10	0	10	20	30	40	50	60	70	80	90	100	110	120
11	0	11	22	33	44	55	66	77	88	99	110	121	132
12	0	12	24	36	48	60	72	84	96	108	120	132	144

Use the multiplication table to find the product.

Use break-apart numbers to find
11×12.

Complete the column for 11 to
11×10.

Think: $10 \times 11 = 110$
$ 2 \times 11 = 22$
$ 12 \times 11 = \underline{10} \times 11 + \underline{2} \times 11$

So, $12 \times 11 = 132$.

Use break-apart numbers to find
12×12.

Complete the column for 12 to
10×12.

Think: $10 \times 12 = 120$
$ 2 \times 12 = 24$
$ 12 \times 12 = \underline{10} \times 12 + \underline{2} \times 12$

So, $12 \times 12 = 144$.

Try These

Use the multiplication table to find the product.

1 $10 \times 12 = \underline{120}$

2 $7 \times 11 = \underline{\hphantom{xxx}}$

3 $11 \times 12 = \underline{\hphantom{xxx}}$

4 $9 \times 11 = \underline{\hphantom{xxx}}$

Go to the next side.

Practice on Your Own

Skill 13

Use break-apart numbers to find
11×11.

Think: $10 \times 11 = 110$
$1 \times 11 = 11$
$11 \times \underline{11} = 10 \times \underline{11} + 1 \times \underline{11}$
So, $11 \times 11 = 121$.

×	0	1	2	3	4	5	6	7	8	9	10	11	12
0	0	0	0	0	0	0	0	0	0	0	0	0	0
1	0	1	2	3	4	5	6	7	8	9	10	11	12
2	0	2	4	6	8	10	12	14	16	18	20	22	24
3	0	3	6	9	12	15	18	21	24	27	30	33	36
4	0	4	8	12	16	20	24	28	32	36	40	44	48
5	0	5	10	15	20	25	30	35	40	45	50	55	60
6	0	6	12	18	24	30	36	42	48	54	60	66	72
7	0	7	14	21	28	35	42	49	56	63	70	77	84
8	0	8	16	24	32	40	48	56	64	72	80	88	96
9	0	9	18	27	36	45	54	63	72	81	90	99	108
10	0	10	20	30	40	50	60	70	80	90	100	110	120
11	0	11	22	33	44	55	66	77	88	99	110	121	132
12	0	12	24	36	48	60	72	84	96	108	120	132	144

Use the multiplication table to find the product.

1. $8 \times 7 =$ _____

2. $6 \times 9 =$ _____

3. $5 \times 8 =$ _____

4. $7 \times 7 =$ _____

5. $6 \times 6 =$ _____

6. $6 \times 12 =$ _____

7. $4 \times 12 =$ _____

8. $7 \times 9 =$ _____

9. $7 \times 11 =$ _____

10. $9 \times 9 =$ _____

11. $12 \times 12 =$ _____

12. $11 \times 8 =$ _____

13. $4 \times 11 =$ _____

14. $2 \times 12 =$ _____

15. $8 \times 8 =$ _____

16. $8 \times 12 =$ _____

17. $7 \times 8 =$ _____

18. $10 \times 10 =$ _____

19. $9 \times 11 =$ _____

20. $10 \times 11 =$ _____

▶ Quiz

Use a multiplication table to find the product.

21. $11 \times 11 =$ _____

22. $5 \times 12 =$ _____

23. $10 \times 8 =$ _____

24. $11 \times 12 =$ _____

20 Minutes

OBJECTIVE Model multiplication of a 2-digit number by a 1-digit number

MATERIALS place-value blocks

You may wish to begin by reviewing basic multiplication facts, such as $2 \times 6 = 12$, $3 \times 5 = 15$, $3 \times 7 = 21$, and so forth. Help students recall that there are different ways to model multiplication: equal groups of counters, arrays of tiles, and jumps on the number line.

Have students use place-value blocks to model the example.

Direct students' attention to Step 1. Note that 2×16 is pictured as 2 groups of 16 blocks.

Ask: **How many ones are in each group? 6 How many tens are in each group? 1**

Recall that to multiply, always begin with the ones digits. Have students look at Step 2.

Ask: **Do you need to regroup? Explain. Yes, 2 x 6 ones is 12 ones; regroup 12 ones as 1 ten 2 ones. What do you do with the regrouped ten? Put it with the other tens blocks.**

Continue with similar questioning for Step 3. Help students understand the connection between the pictorial models and the symbols that represent the multiplication.

TRY THESE Exercises 1–3 model regrouping ones as tens for multiplication. You may wish to work through each exercise with the students to make sure they understand regrouping tens as hundreds.

- **Exercise 1**   Regroup 15 ones as 1 ten 5 ones.

- **Exercise 2**   Regroup 21 ones as 2 tens 1 one, and 11 tens as 1 hundred 1 ten.

- **Exercise 3**   Regroup 16 tens as 1 hundred 6 tens.

PRACTICE ON YOUR OWN Review the examples with students. Ask them to tell the steps to find the product.

QUIZ Determine if students understand the meaning of multiplying a 2-digit number by a 1-digit number. Success is indicated by 2 out of 3 correct responses.

Students who successfully complete the **Practice on Your Own** and **Quiz** are ready to move to the next skill.

COMMON ERRORS

- Some students may write products without regrouping.

- Some students may forget to add the regrouped number.

Students who made more than 2 errors in the **Practice on Your Own**, or who were not successful in the **Quiz** section, may also benefit from the **Alternative Teaching Strategy** on the next page.

Alternative Teaching Strategy
Model Multiplication of 2-Digit Numbers

10 Minutes

OBJECTIVE Use place-value blocks to model multiplication of a 2-digit number by a 1-digit number

MATERIALS place-value blocks

Provide several exercises, such as:

2 × 14

3 × 15

4 × 18

Ask students to model the first exercise, which does not involve regrouping. Using the place-value blocks, keep the ones aligned with ones, and tens with tens.

Record the multiplication in a place-value grid on a large piece of paper.

Tens	Ones
1	4
x	2

Have students combine the ones, then the tens, to find the product.

Then ask the students to summarize the steps for multiplying.

Next ask students to model 3 × 15.

As students combine the ones, say:

Now you have 15 ones. How can 15 ones be regrouped? 1 ten 5 ones Where do you place the regrouped ten? with the other tens

Have students complete the modeling and record the multiplication in a place-value grid.

Tens	Ones
1	
1	5
x	3
4	5

The third example involves regrouping 32 ones as 3 tens 2 ones. Use similar questioning as students model the multiplication.

When you feel confident that students understand the modeling and the recording steps, have them try 3 × 17 on their own. Monitor the way they regroup with the blocks and how they record the multiplication.

Explore Multiplying 2-Digit Numbers

Find 2 × 16 = ■.

Step 1 Make 2 groups of 16.

16
× 2
____

Step 2 Combine the ones. Regroup.

1
16
× 2
____
2

2 × 6 ones = 12 ones
12 ones = 1 ten 2 ones

Step 3 Multiply the tens. Add the regrouped ten. Record the product.

1
16
× 2
____
3 2

2 × 1 ten = 2 tens
2 tens + 1 ten = 3 tens

So, 16 × 2 = 32.

Try These

Find the product.

1

2 5
3
× _____
1

3 × 5 ones = _____ ones

3 × 2 tens = _____ tens

5
7

2

3 7
3
× _____

3 × 7 ones = _____ ones

3 × 3 tens = _____ tens

3

4 0
4
× _____

4 × 0 ones = _____ ones

4 × 4 tens = _____ tens

Go to the next side.

Practice on Your Own

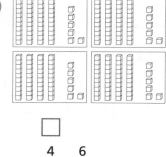

Skill 14

Find $5 \times 35 = \blacksquare$.

Think: Do I need to regroup?

5×5 ones $= 25$ ones
25 ones $= 2$ tens 5 ones
5×3 tens $= 15$ tens
15 tens $+ 2$ tens $= 17$ tens

```
  [2]
   3 5
 ×   5
 ─────
  175
```

Find the product.

1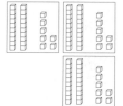

```
□
2   7
×   3
```

2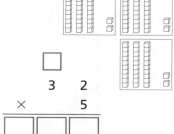

```
□
3   2
×   5
```

3

```
□
4   6
×   4
```

4
```
□
1   5
×   3
```

5
```
□
2   3
×   4
```

6
```
□
3   7
×   2
```

7
```
□
3   9
×   2
```
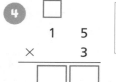

8
```
4   2
×   3
```

9
```
□
1   4
×   6
```

20 Minutes

OBJECTIVE Model and multiply a 2-digit number by a 1-digit number

MATERIALS base-ten blocks

Begin by reviewing basic multiplication facts. Then, have students use base-ten blocks to model Example 1.

Point out that in Step 1, 16×2 is pictured as 2 groups of 16 blocks.

Ask: **How many ones are in each group? 6 How many tens are in each group? 1**

Direct students to Step 2. Remind students that they always begin with the ones digits to multiply.

Ask: **Do you need to regroup? Explain. Yes, 2×6 ones is 12 ones; regroup 12 ones as 1 ten and 2 ones. What do you do with the regrouped ten? Put it with the other ten rods.**

Continue with similar questions for Step 3.

Next, direct students to Example 2. Point to the place-value labels on the grids. You may wish to have students use labels on their written work to help them remember the value of the digits when they regroup.

Ask: **What digit is in the ones place in the number 58? 8 What digit is in the ones place in the number you multiply by? 2 What is the product of 2 times 8? 16 ones Will you need to regroup? Explain. Yes, 16 ones is 1 ten 6 ones.**

Continue to ask similar questions as you work through steps 2 and 3. Point out that in this method, the 1 ten 2 ones are both written below the line. In Example 1, the ten is regrouped above the tens column.

TRY THESE Exercises 1–2 model 2-digit by 1-digit multiplication.

• **Exercise 1**   Regroup ones.

• **Exercises 2–4**   Regroup ones and tens.

PRACTICE ON YOUR OWN Review the examples at the top of the page. In Exercises 1–5 students practice regrouping. In Exercises 6–8 students will use the partial-product method to solve. Students can use either method to solve Exercises 9–19.

QUIZ Determine if students can regroup as needed and add to find the total product. Success is indicated by 4 out of 5 correct responses.

Students who successfully complete the **Practice on Your Own** and **Quiz** are ready to move to the next skill.

COMMON ERRORS

• Students may fail to regroup.

• Students may forget to add the regrouped number.

Students who made more than 5 errors in the **Practice on Your Own,** or who were not successful in the **Quiz** section, may benefit from the **Alternative Teaching Strategy** on the next page.

Alternative Teaching Strategy
Model and Record Multiplication

15 Minutes

OBJECTIVE Use base-ten blocks to model multiplying a 2-digit number by a 1-digit number, recording the results

MATERIALS base-ten blocks, at least 10 tens and 50 ones, place-value tables

You may wish to prepare and copy blank place-value tables for multiplication in advance.

100's	10's	1's
×		

Distribute the base-ten blocks. Have students model 4 × 23 and record the factors in the table.

Ask: **What is 4 times 3 ones? 12 ones Will you regroup the ones? Explain. Yes, 12 ones = 1 ten, 2 ones.**

Have students regroup and record the first partial product in the table.

100's	10's	1's
	2	3
×		4
	1	2
+		

Draw students' attention to the tens rods.

Ask: **What is 4 times 2 tens? 8 tens**

100's	10's	1's
	2	3
×		4
	1	2
+	8	0

Have students record the second partial product in the table. Then, ask a student to add to find the final product.

100's	10's	1's
	2	3
×		4
	1	2
+	8	0
	9	2

Ask: **What is the final product? 92**

Repeat the activity with other similar examples such as the following:

- 4 × 24   **96**
- 3 × 25   **75**
- 5 × 32   **160**
- 4 × 43   **172**
- 5 × 34   **170**

When students show understanding of the regrouping process, remove the base-ten blocks and have them try an exercise using only paper and pencil. Ask students to explain each step of the process as they do the multiplication.

Grade 4
Skill 15

Multiply 2-Digit Numbers

Make a model and use regrouping to find the product.

Example 1 Find $16 \times 2 = \square$.

Step 1 Model 2 groups of 16.

```
16
× 2
```

Step 2 Multiply the ones.
2×6 ones = 12 ones
Regroup the ones.

```
  1
 16
× 2
  2
```

Regroup 12 ones as 1 ten 2 ones.

Step 3 Multiply the tens.
$2 \times 1 = 2$ tens
Add the regrouped ten.

```
  1
 16
× 2
 32
```

2×1 ten = 2 tens
2 tens + 1 ten = 3 tens

So, $16 \times 2 = 32$.

Use partial products.

Example 2 Find $58 \times 2 = \square$.

Step 1 Multiply the ones.

Hundreds	Tens	Ones
	5	8
×		2
	1	6

Think:
$2 \times 8 = 16$ ones
= 1 ten 6 ones

Step 2 Multiply the tens.

Hundreds	Tens	Ones
	5	8
×		2
+ 1	0	0

Think:
$2 \times 5 = 10$ ones

Step 3 Add the products.

Hundreds	Tens	Ones
	5	8
×		2
	1	6
+ 1	0	0
1	1	6

So, $2 \times 58 = 116$.

▲ Try These

Find the product.

1 25×3

3×5 ones = $\square$ tens $\square$ ones
3×2 tens = $\square$ tens
So, $25 \times 3 = \square\square$.

2

```
 57
× 2
```

2×7 ones = $\square$ tens $\square$ ones
2×5 tens = $\square$ hundreds $\square$ tens
So, $57 \times 2 = \square\square\square$.

3
```
 42
× 7
```

4
```
 28
× 6
```

Go to the next side.

Practice on Your Own

Skill 15

3
28
× 4
112 **Think:** Do I need to regroup?

H	T	O
	3	6
×		3

 (3 × 6 ones) ← Multiply the ones.

 (3 × 3 tens) ← Multiply the tens.

← Add to find the product.

Find the product.

1
☐
37
× 2
☐☐

2
☐
15
× 5
☐☐

3
☐
26
× 4
☐☐☐

4
42
× 3

5
11
× 5

6

H	T	O
	2	2
×		4

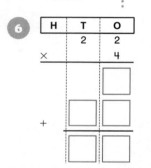

7

H	T	O
	3	4
×		5

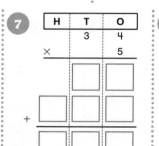

8

H	T	O
	2	4
×		7

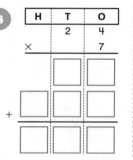

9
16
× 6

10
63
× 2

11
46
× 3

12
39
× 2

13
28
× 4

14
18
× 7

15
42
× 3

16
41
× 3

17
19
× 8

18
49
× 5

19
58
× 4

▶ Quiz

Find the product.

20
16
× 5

21
15
× 3

22
23
× 6

23
31
× 4

24
44
× 4

OBJECTIVE Use mental math to multiply by 10 and multiples of 10

Begin by reviewing basic multiplication facts with students. Review the meanings of the terms *factor* and *product*. Suggest to students that they can use basic multiplication facts and multiples of 10 to build multiplication patterns. Explain that students can use mental math to multiply greater numbers when they know basic facts and patterns.

Call students' attention to the first example of a multiplication pattern.

Ask: **What basic fact do you see?**
$5 \times 4 = 20$

Continue: **Now look at the examples that follow the basic fact. How do the second factors change? The number of zeros has increased. How has the product changed? The number of zeros has increased.**

Say: **As the number of zeros in a factor increases, the number of zeros in the product increases.**

Continue this questioning through the remainder of the pattern. Reinforce that the product of 10 and any other factor has a zero in the ones place, the product of 100 and any other factor has zeros in both the ones and tens places.

Call students' attention to the multiplication pattern. Discuss how this pattern starts with a basic fact that ends in zero.

For example:

$5 \times 4 = 20$

$5 \times 40 = 200$

$5 \times 400 = 2,000$

$5 \times 4000 = 20,000$

Point out the extra zero that comes after the product of 5×4. Be sure students understand the increasing pattern of zeros in the products.

TRY THESE Exercises 1–4 model the types of exercises students will find on the **Practice on Your Own** page.

- **Exercises 1–4** Use mental math and patterns to find products.

PRACTICE ON YOUR OWN Review the example at the top of the page. Ask students to focus on the multiplication pattern. Have them explain how to use the basic fact and multiples of 10 to build the multiplication pattern.

QUIZ Determine if students can use mental math to find the product of multiples of 10. Success is indicated by 3 out of 4 correct responses.

Students who successfully complete **Practice on Your Own** and **Quiz** are ready to move to the next skill.

COMMON ERRORS

- Students may write the wrong number of zeros in the product.

- Students may not know basic multiplication facts.

Students who make more than 4 errors in **Practice on Your Own**, or who were not successful in the **Quiz** section may benefit from the **Alternative Teaching Strategy** on the next page.

Alternative Teaching Strategy
Model Multiplication Patterns

20 Minutes

OBJECTIVE Use base-ten blocks to model multiplying by tens and multiples of 10

MATERIALS base-ten blocks: ones, tens, hundreds; paper, pencil

Begin by having students write the following:

$5 \times 1 =$ _____

$5 \times 10 =$ _____

$5 \times 100 =$ _____

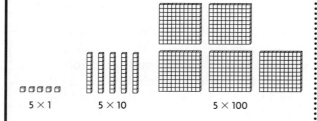

Distribute the base-ten blocks. Have the students use the blocks to model each problem.

Ask: **What is the product of 5 × 1? 5**

What is the product of 5 × 10? 50

What is the product of 5 × 100? 500

What pattern do you see? As the number of zeros in a factor increases, the number of zeros in the product increases.

Write the number sentence $5 \times 1,000 =$ _____ .

Ask: **How many zeros will be in the product? 3**

Have students write the product.

Continue the activity by asking students to write and model 2×1, 2×10, 2×100; 3×1, 3×10, 3×100. Then ask them to write and find the product of $2 \times 1,000$ and $3 \times 1,000$.

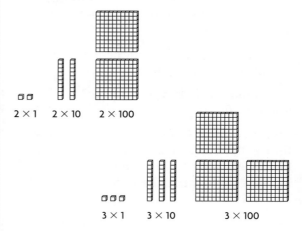

When students show an understanding of multiplying by factors of 10, have them try building multiplication patterns using only paper and pencil.

Have students write and find products for:

1×2	2×2	3×2
1×20	2×20	3×20
1×200	2×200	3×200
$1 \times 2,000$	$2 \times 2,000$	$3 \times 2,000$

You may wish to continue with similar patterns.

Multiplication Patterns

Use multiplication facts and patterns to find products.

Find 5 × 4,000.

Use mental math to multiply greater numbers when you know basic facts and patterns.

First, think of the basic multiplication fact.
Then, use a pattern to find the product.

Think: 5 × 4 = 20.

$5 \times 4 = 20$

$5 \times 40 = 200$

$5 \times 400 = 2,000$

$5 \times 4,000 = 20,000$

So, the product is 20,000.

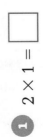

Try These

Use mental math to complete.

1 $2 \times 1 = $ ☐

$2 \times 10 = $ ☐

$2 \times 100 = $ ☐

$2 \times 1,000 = $ ☐

2 $4 \times 3 = $ ☐

$4 \times 30 = $ ☐

$4 \times 300 = $ ☐

$4 \times 3,000 = $ ☐

3 $6 \times 4 = $ ☐

$6 \times 40 = $ ☐

$6 \times 400 = $ ☐

$6 \times 4,000 = $ ☐

4 $7 \times 3 = $ ☐

$7 \times 30 = $ ☐

$7 \times 300 = $ ☐

$7 \times 3,000 = $ ☐

Go to the next side.

Practice on Your Own

Skill 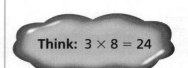 16

Multiply.
800
× 3
2,400

As the number of zeros in a factor increases, the number of zeros in the product increases.

$3 \times 8 = 24$

$3 \times 80 = 240$

$3 \times 800 = 2,400$

$3 \times 8,000 = 24,000$

Think: $3 \times 8 = 24$

3×8 hundreds = 24 hundreds

So, $3 \times 800 = 2,400$.

Use mental math to complete.

1 $6 \times 1 = \boxed{}$

$6 \times 10 = \boxed{}$

$6 \times 100 = \boxed{}$

$6 \times 1,000 = \boxed{}$

2 $3 \times 3 = \boxed{}$

$3 \times 30 = \boxed{}$

$3 \times 300 = \boxed{}$

$3 \times 3,000 = \boxed{}$

3 $5 \times 4 = \boxed{}$

$5 \times 40 = \boxed{}$

$5 \times 400 = \boxed{}$

$5 \times 4,000 = \boxed{}$

4 $9 \times 3 = \boxed{}$

$9 \times 30 = \boxed{}$

$9 \times 300 = \boxed{}$

$9 \times 3,000 = \boxed{}$

5 $6 \times 3 = \boxed{}$

$6 \times 30 = \boxed{}$

$6 \times 300 = \boxed{}$

$6 \times 3,000 = \boxed{}$

6 $7 \times 4 = \boxed{}$

$7 \times 40 = \boxed{}$

$7 \times 400 = \boxed{}$

$7 \times 4,000 = \boxed{}$

7 $8 \times 5 = \boxed{}$

$8 \times 50 = \boxed{}$

$8 \times 500 = \boxed{}$

$8 \times 5,000 = \boxed{}$

8 $5 \times 3 = \boxed{}$

$5 \times 30 = \boxed{}$

$5 \times 300 = \boxed{}$

$5 \times 3,000 = \boxed{}$

Use mental math. Write the basic fact and use a pattern to find the product.

9 7×40

10 $5 \times 1,000$

11 6×60

12 3×900

13 3×600

14 4×80

15 $2 \times 5,000$

16 4×400

 Quiz

Use mental math. Write the basic fact and use a pattern to find the product.

17 6×70

18 $2 \times 7,000$

19 8×800

20 7×700

20 Minutes

OBJECTIVE Estimate products

You may wish to begin the lesson by discussing why estimating a product is useful. Use a real-life situation. Write the following problem on the board:

Suppose there are 17 trays with 5 slices of pizza on each tray. About how many slices of pizza are there?

Say: **Do you need to know an exact amount? No; it says "about how many."**

Explain to students that when they estimate a product they find out "about how many." Review the rounding rules with students. Direct students' attention to the first example.

Ask: **What does "round to the greatest place value" mean? Round to the left-most place in the number.**

Point to the first example. Work through the rounding process for the factor 233. Review building multiplication patterns using basic multiplication facts.

Say: **Do you think the estimated product will be greater than or less than the actual product? less than Why? 200 is less than 233**

Call students' attention to the second example. Explain that compatible numbers are numbers that are easy to compute mentally.

Ask: **Is 250 a good choice for a compatible number? Yes; it is close to 233 and you can multiply 250 by 2 using mental math. Do you think the estimated product will be greater than or less than the actual product? greater than Why? 250 is greater than 233**

TRY THESE In Exercises 1–4, students use rounding or compatible numbers to estimate products.

• **Exercises 1–4** Estimate products.

PRACTICE ON YOUR OWN Review the example at the top of the page. Have a volunteer explain each of the steps in finding the estimate. Make sure students understand that when they are multiplying dollar amounts, they must write the dollar sign in front of the product.

QUIZ Determine if students can estimate products. Success is indicated by 3 out of 4 correct responses.

Students who successfully complete **Practice on Your Own** and **Quiz** are ready to move to the next skill.

COMMON ERRORS

• Students may round factors incorrectly.

• Students may use an arbitrary compatible number rather than one close to the factor it replaces.

• Students may use an incorrect number of zeros in an estimated product.

Students who make more than 4 errors in **Practice on Your Own**, or who were not successful in the **Quiz** section may benefit from the **Alternative Teaching Strategy** on the next page.

Alternative Teaching Strategy
Estimate Products on the Number Line

20 Minutes

OBJECTIVE Use a number line to estimate products

MATERIALS three number lines: one number line showing marks for ones from 10 to 20, another showing marks for tens from 200 to 300, and a third number line showing marks for hundreds from 2,000 to 3,000

Distribute the first number line. Provide students with two numbers, one that rounds up, and one that rounds down. Use 17 and 12, for example.

Ask students to find 17 on the number line. Then have students find the halfway number, 15.

Say: **You can use the halfway number to make decisions about how to round.**

Ask: **Is 17 to the left or to the right of the halfway number?** to the right

Explain that since 17 is to the right of the halfway number and closer to 20 than to 10, it rounds to 20.

Use the same questioning strategy for rounding 12. Help students understand that because 12 is to the left of the halfway number, 12 rounds down to 10.

Ask students to estimate 4×17 by rounding 17 to 20. Have students note that 4×20 can be multiplied using mental math. Reinforce that since they rounded 17 up, the estimated product will be greater than the actual product.

Point out to students that the number line can also be used to find compatible numbers.

Say: **You need to find 4×16. Look at the number line. What number close to 16 is easy to compute mentally?** 15

Ask: **Will the estimated product be greater than or less than the actual product?** less than **Why?** 15 is less than 16

Next have students estimate 3×276 and $2 \times 2,595$ using the number lines.

Repeat the activity several times. Conclude the activity by having students state the rounding rules and the definition of compatible numbers.

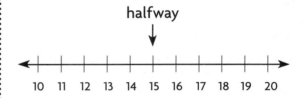

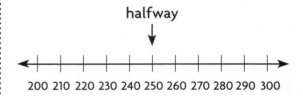

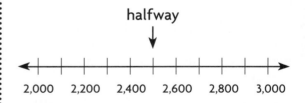

Estimate Products

Use rounding or compatible numbers to estimate 2 × 233.

Use rounding.

Step 1 Round the greater factor to the greatest place value.

$2 \times 233 \rightarrow 2 \times 200$

Step 2 Use basic facts to build multiplication patterns.

$$2 \times 2 = 4$$
$$2 \times 20 = 40$$
$$2 \times 200 = 400$$

Use compatible numbers.

Step 1 Think of a number close to 233 that is easy to compute mentally.

$2 \times 233 \rightarrow 2 \times 250$

Step 2 Multiply.

If $2 \times 25 = 50$

Then $2 \times 250 = 500$

Compatible numbers are numbers that are easy to compute mentally.

So, both 400 and 500 are reasonable estimates.

Try These

Choose the method. Estimate the product.

1 27 × 9

$27 \rightarrow \square$
$\underline{\times 9} \rightarrow \underline{\times 9}$
$\square$

2 41 × 4

$41 \rightarrow \square$
$\underline{\times 4} \rightarrow \underline{\times 4}$
$\square$

3 128 × 3

$128 \rightarrow \square$
$\underline{\times 3} \rightarrow \underline{\times 3}$
$\square$

4 412 × 2

$412 \rightarrow \square$
$\underline{\times 2} \rightarrow \underline{\times 2}$
$\square$

Go to the next side.

Practice on Your Own

Estimate $332 × 6.

$$
\begin{array}{r}
\$332 \rightarrow \quad \$300 \\
\times\,6 \rightarrow \quad \times\ \ 6 \\
\hline
\$1,800
\end{array}
$$

Think: 3 × 6 is easy to compute mentally.

So, $332 × 6 is about $1,800.

Estimate the product. Use rounding or compatible numbers.

1 $32 × 5

$$
\begin{array}{r}
\$32 \rightarrow \square \\
\times\,5 \rightarrow \times\,5 \\
\hline
\square
\end{array}
$$

2 142 × 4

$$
\begin{array}{r}
142 \rightarrow \square \\
\times\,4 \rightarrow \times\,4 \\
\hline
\square
\end{array}
$$

3 123 × 5

$$
\begin{array}{r}
123 \rightarrow \square \\
\times\,5 \rightarrow \times\,5 \\
\hline
\square
\end{array}
$$

4
$$
\begin{array}{r}
\$5.29 \rightarrow \square \\
\times\ \ 2 \rightarrow \times\,2 \\
\hline
\square
\end{array}
$$

5
$$
\begin{array}{r}
4,621 \rightarrow \square \\
\times\ \ \ 4 \rightarrow \times\,4 \\
\hline
\square
\end{array}
$$

6
$$
\begin{array}{r}
7,193 \rightarrow \square \\
\times\ \ \ 3 \rightarrow \times\,3 \\
\hline
\square
\end{array}
$$

Choose the method. Estimate the product.

7
$$
\begin{array}{r}
12 \\
\times\,6 \\
\hline
\end{array}
$$

8
$$
\begin{array}{r}
\$327 \\
\times\,3 \\
\hline
\end{array}
$$

9
$$
\begin{array}{r}
567 \\
\times\,6 \\
\hline
\end{array}
$$

10
$$
\begin{array}{r}
6,515 \\
\times\ \ \,5 \\
\hline
\end{array}
$$

11 3 × 18

12 $54 × 2

13 497 × 5

14 1,139 × 8

▶ Quiz

Choose the method. Estimate the product.

15 32 × 3

16 816 × 5

17 $1,134 × 3

18 5,825 × 4

20 Minutes

OBJECTIVE Multiply 3- and 4-digit numbers by 1-digit numbers

Students can model the example using base-ten blocks. Have students read the place-value labels in Step 1 of the first example.

Ask: **How many digits does the number 126 have? 3 What place do you multiply first? ones How many tens and ones is 12 ones? 1 ten 2 ones Where do you write the 2 ones in the product? in the ones place Where do you write the 1 ten that you regrouped? above the 2 in the tens place**

Continue to ask similar questions as you work through Steps 2 and 3.

Point out that in Step 1 of the second example, the first number has 4 digits. Discuss the place value of each digit. Remind students that the labels may help them recall the value of digits when they regroup.

Say: **Begin with the ones.**

Ask: **What is 2 × 9 ones? 18 ones Where does the regrouped ten go? in the tens column**

Next, say: **Multiply the tens in Step 2.**

Ask: **What is 2 × 6 tens? 12 tens What do you do with the ten you regrouped? Add it to the 12 tens. How many tens are there now? 13 tens How do you regroup? Regroup 13 tens as 1 hundred 3 tens. Where do you put the regrouped hundred? in the hundreds place**

Continue to work through Steps 3 and 4.

TRY THESE Exercises 1–3 provide practice multiplying 3- and 4-digit numbers by 1-digit numbers.

- **Exercise 1**   Multiply a 3-digit number, regrouping once.

- **Exercise 2**   Multiply a 3-digit number, regrouping twice.

- **Exercise 3**   Multiply a 4-digit number, regrouping twice.

PRACTICE ON YOUR OWN Review the examples at the top of the page. Students use place values to solve Exercises 1–9. In Exercises 10–17 students multiply and then add to find the products. Ask students to explain when to regroup a digit, and in what place to put the regrouped digit.

QUIZ Determine if students can multiply 3- and 4-digit numbers by 1-digit numbers. Success is indicated by 3 out of 4 correct responses.

Students who successfully complete the **Practice on Your Own** and **Quiz** are ready to move on to the next skill.

COMMON ERRORS

- Students may place the regrouped digit in the incorrect place.

- Students may not add the regrouped digit.

- Students may multiply digits in the thousands, hundreds, or tens place before multiplying the digits in the ones place.

Students who make more than 5 errors in the **Practice on Your Own**, or who were not successful in the **Quiz** section, may benefit from the **Alternative Teaching Strategy** on the next page.

Alternative Teaching Strategy
Model Multiplying 3- and 4-Digit Numbers

20 Minutes

OBJECTIVE Multiply 3-digit numbers regrouping both ones and tens

MATERIALS base-ten blocks

Distribute the base-ten blocks. You may wish to demonstrate the regrouping procedure.

Have students use the base-ten blocks to show how to regroup 14 ones as 1 ten 4 ones. Explain that the blocks were regrouped; but, the value of the number that the blocks represent is the same, since 14 ones is equal to 1 ten 4 ones.

Next, have students use the base-ten blocks to regroup 21 tens as 2 hundreds 1 ten.

Have students model 2 × 176 by showing 2 groups of 176.

Say: **Begin with the ones.**

Ask: **How many ones do you have in 2 groups of 6 ones?** 12

Say: **You have more than 9 ones.**

Ask: **When you have more than 9 in any place, what can you do? regroup How do you regroup the ones? by regrouping 12 ones as 1 ten 2 ones**

How many tens do you have in 2 groups of 7 tens? 14 What happens to the regrouped ten? It is added to the 14 tens; 14 + 1 = 15 tens. Can you regroup tens? Yes, there are more than 9 tens, so regroup 15 tens as 1 hundred 5 tens. How many hundreds are in 2 groups of 1 hundred? 2 What do you do next? Add the regrouped hundred; 2 + 1 = 3 hundreds. What is the product? 352

Working in pairs, have students repeat the modeling as they record the multiplication steps on paper. Stress the placement of the regrouped digit in the appropriate column.

Repeat modeling and recording with different numbers. Include problems multiplying 4-digit numbers. When students understand the regrouping process, have them multiply without using the base-ten blocks.

Model: 2 × 176

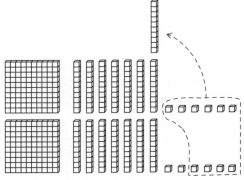

2 × 6 ones = 12 ones
12 ones = 1 ten 2 ones

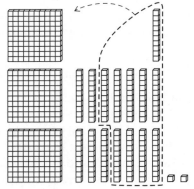

2 × 7 tens = 14 tens
14 tens + 1 ten = 15 tens
15 tens = 1 hundred 5 tens

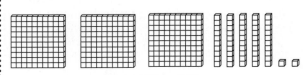

2 × 176 = 352

Grade 4
Skill 18

Multiply 3- and 4-Digit Numbers

Sometimes when you multiply, you may need to regroup.
Find 2 × 126. Estimate. 2 × 130 = 260

Step 1 Multiply the ones.
2 × 6 = 12 ones.
Regroup the 12 ones as 1 ten and 2 ones.

Hundreds	Tens	Ones
	[1]	
1	2	6
×		2
		2

Step 2 Multiply the tens.
2 × 2 tens = 4 tens.
Add the regrouped ten.
4 tens + 1 ten = 5 tens.

Hundreds	Tens	Ones
	[1]	
1	2	6
×		2
	5	2

Step 3 Multiply the hundreds.
2 × 1 hundred = 2 hundreds.
Add the regrouped hundred.

Hundreds	Tens	Ones
	[1]	
1	2	6
×		2
2	5	2

So, 2 × 126 = 252.

Find 2 × 1,169. Estimate. 2 × 1200 = 2,400.

Step 1 Multiply the ones.
Regroup the ones.

Thousands	Hundreds	Tens	Ones
	[1]	[1]	
1,	1	6	9
×			2
			8

Step 2 Multiply the tens.
Add the regrouped ten.
Regroup the tens as hundreds.

Thousands	Hundreds	Tens	Ones
	[1]	[1]	
1,	1	6	9
×			2
		3	8

Step 3 Multiply the hundreds. Add the regrouped hundred.

Thousands	Hundreds	Tens	Ones
	[1]	[1]	
1,	1	6	9
×			2
	3	3	8

Step 4 Multiply the thousands.

Thousands	Hundreds	Tens	Ones
	[1]	[1]	
1,	1	6	9
×			2
2,	3	3	8

So, 2 × 1169 = 2,338.

Try These

Find the product. Estimate to check.

1.

H	T	O
	[2]	
1	1	7
×		4
	6	8

2.

H	T	O
[1]	[1]	
2	4	4
×		3

3.

Th	H	T	O
	[1]	[1]	
1,	3	5	5
×			2

Go to the next side.

Practice on Your Own

Skill 18

Multiply. Then add to find the product. 3×452 $(3 \times 400) + (3 \times 50) + (3 \times 2)$ **So,** $3 \times 452 = 1,356$.	Multiply. Then add to find the product. $5 \times 1,164$ $(5 \times \underline{1,000}) + (5 \times \underline{100}) +$ $(5 \times \underline{60}) + (5 \times \underline{4})$ **So,** $5 \times 1,164 = 5,820$.

Find the product. Estimate to check.

1

H	T	O
☐		
1	6	3
×		2
☐	☐	☐

2

H	T	O
☐	☐	
2	3	9
×		3
☐	☐	☐

3

Th	H	T	O
	☐	☐	
1,	1	8	2
×			5
☐	☐	☐	☐

4
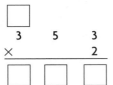

$$\begin{array}{ccc} \square & & \\ 3 & 5 & 3 \\ \times & & 2 \\ \hline \square & \square & \square \end{array}$$

5
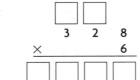

$$\begin{array}{cccc} \square & \square & & \\ 3 & 2 & 8 \\ \times & & & 6 \\ \hline \square & \square & \square & \square \end{array}$$

6
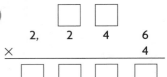

$$\begin{array}{cccc} & \square & \square & \\ 2, & 2 & 4 & 6 \\ \times & & & 4 \\ \hline \square & \square & \square & \square \end{array}$$

7

$$\begin{array}{r} 316 \\ \times \quad 2 \\ \hline \end{array}$$

8

$$\begin{array}{r} 1,246 \\ \times \quad 6 \\ \hline \end{array}$$

9

$$\begin{array}{r} 2,178 \\ \times \quad 4 \\ \hline \end{array}$$

Multiply. Find the product.

10 2×172	**11** 3×285	**12** $2 \times 2,356$	**13** $3 \times 1,275$
14 4×125	**15** 2×246	**16** 2×339	**17** 3×142

▶ **Quiz**

Find the product.

18 $\begin{array}{r} 225 \\ \times \ 3 \\ \hline \end{array}$	**19** $\begin{array}{r} 287 \\ \times \ 5 \\ \hline \end{array}$	**20** $\begin{array}{r} 1,234 \\ \times \quad 4 \\ \hline \end{array}$	**21** $\begin{array}{r} 2,285 \\ \times \quad 3 \\ \hline \end{array}$

Skill 19

Grade 4

15 Minutes

OBJECTIVE Use basic facts and patterns to multiply by multiples of 10, 100, and 1,000

Explain to students that in this lesson they are asked to multiply by multiples of 10, 100, and 1,000. Suggest that they can find a pattern and use that pattern to help them multiply.

Have students look at the first example on the page. Call their attention to the first number sentence, $3 \times 1 = 3$. Then, direct them to look at the number of zeros in the next number sentence.

Say: **One factor has a zero. How many zeros do the factors have altogether? 1 How many zeros are in the product? 1**

Repeat these questions for the next two number sentences. Guide students to identify a pattern.

Continue to ask similar questions as you work through the other examples. Have students note that each pattern begins with a basic multiplication fact, and that the pattern of increasing zeros is the same in each example.

Emphasize that they can use a basic fact and the pattern to multiply numbers by multiples of 10, 100, and 1,000.

TRY THESE In Exercises 1–4, students use a basic fact and a pattern to find products of multiples of 10, 100, and 1,000.

- **Exercise 1**   Use the basic fact 2×1.
- **Exercise 2**   Use the basic fact 7×1.
- **Exercise 3**   Use the basic fact 9×1.
- **Exercise 4**   Use the basic fact 5×1.

PRACTICE ON YOUR OWN Review the example at the top of the page. In Exercises 1–6, students use basic facts and a pattern to find products. In Exercises 7–22, students find the products of multiples of 10, 100, and 1,000.

QUIZ Determine if students can multiply by multiples of 10, 100, and 1,000. Success is indicated by 3 out of 4 correct responses.

Students who successfully complete the **Practice on Your Own** and **Quiz** are ready to move to the next skill.

COMMON ERRORS

- Students may write the incorrect number of zeros in the product when multiplying by multiples of 10, 100, and 1,000.

- Students may not know multiplication facts.

Students who make more than 6 errors in the **Practice on Your Own**, or who were not successful in the **Quiz** section, may benefit from the **Alternative Teaching Strategy** on the next page.

Alternative Teaching Strategy
Model Multiplying by Multiples of 10, 100, and 1,000

20 Minutes

OBJECTIVE Use number cards to multiply by multiples of 10, 100, and 1,000

MATERIALS index cards

Prepare sets of cards before the lesson or have students prepare their own cards. On separate cards write the numerals 1 through 9, 5 zeros (one 0 per card), and the symbols ×, =, and ,.

Distribute two sets of cards to pairs of students. Begin by displaying these multiplication sentences and reviewing the meaning of multiples of 10, 100, and 1,000.

$$6 \times 1 = 6$$
$$60 \times 10 = 600$$
$$60 \times 100 = 6,000$$
$$60 \times 1,000 = 60,000$$

Ask: **What is the basic multiplication fact? 6 × 1 = 6**

Explain that in this pattern 60 is multiplied by 10, 100, and 1,000, which are multiples of 10.

Ask: **What patterns do you see? Possible answer: As the number of zeros in the factors increases, the number of zeros in the product increases. There is the same number of zeros in the product as there is in the factors.**

Next, display 30 × 100. Have one student from each pair show the expression with the number cards.

Ask: **What basic multiplication fact will help you find the product? 3 × 1 = 3 How many zeros are in the factors? 3 How many zeros will be in the product? 3**

Have the other student in each pair remove the three zeros from the factors to show the product of 30 × 100.

Ask: **What is the product? 3,000**

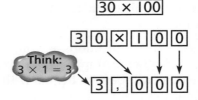

Repeat the activity for 300 × 100 and 3,000 × 100. Continue with other examples until students have internalized the pattern. Conclude the lesson by having them multiply by multiples of 10 without using the cards.

Mental Math: Multiplication Patterns

Use basic facts and patterns to help multiply by multiples of 10, 100, and 1,000.

Find a pattern of zeros.

$3 \times 1 = 3 \leftarrow$ basic fact
$3 \times 10 = 30 \leftarrow$ 1 zero
$3 \times 100 = 300 \leftarrow$ 2 zeros
$3 \times 1,000 = 3,000 \leftarrow$ 3 zeros

factors   product

The number of zeros in the products increases as the number of zeros in the factors increases.

Multiply by tens.

$4 \times 1 = 4 \leftarrow$ basic fact

$40 \times 10 = 400$
         ↑
1 zero 1 zero 2 zeros

$40 \times 100 = 4,000$
              ↑
1 zero 2 zeros 3 zeros

$40 \times 1,000 = 40,000$
                ↑
1 zero 3 zeros 4 zeros

Multiply by hundreds.

$6 \times 1 = 6 \leftarrow$ basic fact

$600 \times 10 = 6,000$
             ↑
2 zeros 1 zero 3 zeros

$600 \times 100 = 60,000$
              ↑
2 zeros 2 zeros 4 zeros

$600 \times 1,000 = 600,000$
                ↑
2 zeros 3 zeros 5 zeros

Multiply by thousands.

$8 \times 1 = 8 \leftarrow$ basic fact

$8,000 \times 10 = 80,000$
               ↑
3 zeros 1 zero 4 zeros

$8,000 \times 100 = 800,000$
                ↑
3 zeros 2 zeros 5 zeros

$8,000 \times 1,000 = 8,000,000$
                  ↑
3 zeros 3 zeros 6 zeros

▲ Try These

Use a basic fact and a pattern to find the products.

1 $2 \times 1 =$ ☐

$2 \times 10 =$ ☐

$2 \times 100 =$ ☐

$2 \times 1,000 =$ ☐

2 $7 \times 1 =$ ☐

$70 \times 10 =$ ☐

$70 \times 100 =$ ☐

$70 \times 1,000 =$ ☐

3 $9 \times 1 =$ ☐

$900 \times 10 =$ ☐

$900 \times 100 =$ ☐

$900 \times 1,000 =$ ☐

4 $5 \times 1 =$ ☐

$5,000 \times 10 =$ ☐

$5,000 \times 100 =$ ☐

$5,000 \times 1,000 =$ ☐

Go to the next side.

Practice on Your Own

Skill (19)

$2 \times 4 = 8 \leftarrow$ basic fact
$20 \times 40 = 800$
$20 \times 400 = 8,000$
$20 \times 4,000 = 80,000$

Use a basic fact and a pattern to multiply by multiples of 10, 100, or 1,000.

Use a basic fact and a pattern to find the products.

1 $1 \times 1 = \boxed{}$

$10 \times 10 = \boxed{}$

$10 \times 100 = \boxed{}$

$10 \times 1,000 = \boxed{}$

2 $2 \times 2 = \boxed{}$

$20 \times 20 = \boxed{}$

$20 \times 200 = \boxed{}$

$20 \times 2,000 = \boxed{}$

3 $4 \times 4 = \boxed{}$

$40 \times 40 = \boxed{}$

$40 \times 400 = \boxed{}$

$40 \times 4,000 = \boxed{}$

4 $8 \times 10 = \boxed{}$

$80 \times 100 = \boxed{}$

$80 \times 1,000 = \boxed{}$

5 $3 \times 20 = \boxed{}$

$30 \times 20 = \boxed{}$

$30 \times 200 = \boxed{}$

6 $4 \times 50 = \boxed{}$

$40 \times 50 = \boxed{}$

$400 \times 50 = \boxed{}$

Use a basic fact and a pattern to find the products.

7
$$\begin{array}{r} 10 \\ \times\ 6 \\ \hline \end{array}$$

8
$$\begin{array}{r} 40 \\ \times\ 6 \\ \hline \end{array}$$

9
$$\begin{array}{r} 300 \\ \times\ 9 \\ \hline \end{array}$$

10
$$\begin{array}{r} 5,000 \\ \times\ 5 \\ \hline \end{array}$$

11
$$\begin{array}{r} 20 \\ \times\ 20 \\ \hline \end{array}$$

12
$$\begin{array}{r} 600 \\ \times\ 100 \\ \hline \end{array}$$

13
$$\begin{array}{r} 8,000 \\ \times\ 10 \\ \hline \end{array}$$

14
$$\begin{array}{r} 2,000 \\ \times\ 100 \\ \hline \end{array}$$

15 $100 \times 7 =$

16 $30 \times 300 =$

17 $7 \times 500 =$

18 $400 \times 600 =$

19 $90 \times 6 =$

20 $7,000 \times 20 =$

21 $800 \times 4,000 =$

22 $50 \times 700 =$

▶ Quiz

Use a basic fact and a pattern to find the product.

23 $10 \times 9 =$

24 $60 \times 60 =$

25 $2,000 \times 7 =$

26 $800 \times 80 =$

15 Minutes

OBJECTIVE Use multiplication properties to find the products of two or more factors

Begin by explaining to students that multiplication properties can help them recall multiplication facts.

Direct students' attention to the explanation and example of the Commutative Property. Explain how the arrays help show how the two multiplication facts are related.

Say: **Look at the first array. How many rows are there? 2 How many tiles are in each row? 5 What multiplication fact does the array show?** $2 \times 5 = 10$

Repeat the questions for the second array. Then, ask students to look at the two multiplication sentences.

Ask: **How are they alike? The product is the same. How are they different? The order of factors is different.**

For the Associative Property, explain that the parentheses group the factors in two different ways. Point out to students how one way may make it easier to find the product.

As you work through the Identity Property and the Zero Property, ask: **How can these properties help you multiply? Possible response: Knowing the Identity Property and Zero Property allows me to build all the facts for 1 and 0.**

TRY THESE In Exercises 1–4, students compete a multiplication sentence using each of the properties.

- **Exercise 1**   Commutative Property
- **Exercise 2**   Associative Property
- **Exercise 3**   Identity Property
- **Exercise 4**   Zero Property

PRACTICE ON YOUR OWN Review the examples at the top of the page. Help students see that the multiplication properties can help them multiply. Advise students to check their work as they complete the page. Exercises 1–3 have students identify the property used. Students complete Exercises 4–6 to show the multiplication property. Exercises 7–15 have the students find the product and name the property used.

QUIZ Determine if students know the multiplication properties. Success is indicated by 4 out of 6 correct responses.

Students who successfully complete the **Practice on Your Own** and **Quiz** are ready to move to the next skill.

COMMON ERRORS

- Students may confuse the Commutative and Associative Properties.

- Students may multiply incorrectly.

Students who make more than 4 errors in the **Practice on Your Own**, or who were not successful in the **Quiz** section may benefit from the Alternative Teaching Strategy on the next page.

15 Minutes

Alternative Teaching Strategy
Model Multiplication Properties

OBJECTIVE Use multiplication properties to help find products of two or more factors

MATERIALS 40 tiles for each pair of students

You may wish to have students work in pairs.

Distribute tiles.

Explain to students that knowing multiplication properties can make multiplying easier. Ask students to show

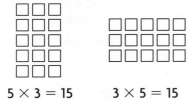

$5 \times 3 = 15$ $3 \times 5 = 15$

5 rows of 3.
Then have them show 3 rows of 5.

Have students write a multiplication sentence for each array. Point out to students that their arrays model the Commutative Property.

Ask: **If 5 × 3 = 15, then does 3 × 5 = 15? yes How do you know? Possible response: Both arrays have 15 tiles. How does this model the Commutative Property? Possible response: The Commutative Property states that you can multiply two factors in any order and get the same product. Since the factors—3 and 5—are the same for both multiplication sentences, the product is the same, too.**

Have students suggest other factors. Repeat the activity several times.

To model the Associative Property, have students write the following:

$$(2 \times 4) \times 3 = 2 \times (4 \times 3)$$

Have them show three 2 by 4 arrays to model the first expression. Then have them model the second expression by showing two arrays of 4 by 3.

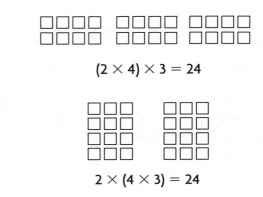

$(2 \times 4) \times 3 = 24$

$2 \times (4 \times 3) = 24$

Repeat this activity several times until students understand that they can change the grouping of factors without changing the product.

You can also use arrays to show the Identity Property. Then, demonstrate the Zero Property by showing, for example, why 3 groups of 0 or 0 groups of 3 will result in 0 as the product.

When students demonstrate an understanding of the multiplication properties, have them show the properties using number sentences only.

Multiplication Properties

Use multiplication properties to help you find products of two or more factors.

Commutative Property
You can multiply two factors in any order and the product remains the same.

$2 \times 5 = 10$ $5 \times 2 = 10$

So, if you know that $2 \times 5 = 10$, then you also know that $5 \times 2 = 10$.

Associative Property
You can group factors in different ways and the product remains the same. Use parentheses ( ) to group the factors you multiply first.

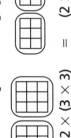

$2 \times (3 \times 3) = (2 \times 3) \times 3$
$2 \times 9 = 6 \times 3$
$18 = 18$

So, $2 \times (3 \times 3)$ can be grouped as $(2 \times 3) \times 3$, and the product remains the same.

Identity Property
The product of 1 and any other number is that number.

$1 \times 5 = 5$
$5 \times 1 = 5$

Zero Property
The product of 0 and any number is 0.

$0 \times 4 = 0$
$4 \times 0 = 0$

Try These

Complete to show each multiplication property.

1 Commutative Property

$3 \times 4 = \square \times 3$

2 Associative Property

$(2 \times 4) \times 3 = \square \times (4 \times 3)$

3 Identity Property

$8 \times \square = 8$

4 Zero Property

$\square \times 6 = 0$

Go to the next side.

Practice on Your Own

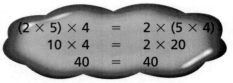

Commutative Property	Associative Property
 $4 \times 6 = 24$ $6 \times 4 = 24$	$(2 \times 5) \times 4 \quad = \quad 2 \times (5 \times 4)$ $10 \times 4 \quad = \quad 2 \times 20$ $40 \quad = \quad 40$
So, $4 \times 6 = 6 \times 4$.	**So,** $(2 \times 5) \times 4 = 2 \times (5 \times 4)$.

Name the multiplication property.

1 $7 \times 0 = 0$

_____ Property

2 $4 \times 8 = 32$
$8 \times 4 = 32$

_____ Property

3 $2 \times (3 \times 5) =$
$(2 \times 3) \times 5$

_____ Property

Complete to show the multiplication property.

4 Identity Property

$2 \times \square = 2$

5 Associative Property

$(5 \times 2) \times 6 =$
$\square \times (\square \times \square)$

6 Commutative Property

$6 \times \square = 42$
$\square \times 6 = 42$

Find the product. Name the property you used.

7 $3 \times (2 \times 6)$

8 1×0

9 3×8
8×3

10 3×0

11 5×1

12 $2 \times (5 \times 3)$

13 6×5
5×6

14 $(4 \times 3) \times 6$

15 13×1

▶ **Quiz**

Find the product. Name the property you used.

16 10×1

17 $3 \times (4 \times 5)$

18 2×4
4×2

19 7×1

20 0×9

21 $7 \times (4 \times 2)$

Number Sense, Concepts, and Operations

Whole Number Division

OBJECTIVE Form equal groups to divide

MATERIALS counters

15 Minutes

Begin by asking students for different ways of dividing 6 counters into smaller equal size groups. Demonstrate with the counters as students suggest forming 2 groups of 3, 3 groups of 2, or 6 groups of 1. Point out that for each situation, the smaller groups each had the same number of counters.

Direct the students' attention to the first example.

Ask: **What does it mean to form equal groups? The groups all have the same number in them. How many triangles are there? 8 How many equal groups do you have to form? 2 How many triangles are in each group? 4 Can one group have 6 triangles and the other group have 2 triangles? No, the groups have to be equal.**

Continue to ask similar questions as you work through the next example.

TRY THESE Exercises 1–3 model the type of exercises students will find on the **Practice on Your Own** page.

* **Exercise 1** Form 2 groups of 3.

* **Exercise 2** Form 2 groups of 5.

* **Exercise 3** Form 3 groups of 3.

PRACTICE ON YOUR OWN Review the example at the top of the page. Ask students to explain each step in dividing the 8 squares into 4 equal groups.

QUIZ Determine if students know how to form equal groups. Success is determined by 2 out of 3 correct responses.

Students who successfully complete the **Practice on Your Own** and **Quiz** are ready to move on to the next skill.

COMMON ERRORS

* Students may form unequal groups.

* Students may confuse the number of groups with how many are in each group.

Students who made more than 2 errors in the **Practice on Your Own**, or who were not successful in the **Quiz** section, may benefit from the **Alternative Teaching Strategy** on the next page.

Alternative Teaching Strategy
Model the Meaning of Division

OBJECTIVE Use counters to model the meaning of division

MATERIALS counters

Explain why it is necessary to be able to divide a group of objects equally. You may wish to relate it to a real life example:

Suppose you and 2 friends want to share equally 12 crackers with peanut butter.

Ask: **How many people will be sharing crackers? 3**

Distribute the counters. Have the students start by using the counters to model the 12 crackers.

Ask: **How many groups of crackers do you want to make? 3**

Have students draw three circles to represent the three groups. Then direct the students to start by putting one counter in each circle. Have them repeat this until all of the counters are gone.

Ask: **Does each group have an equal number of counters? Yes How many counters are in each group? 4 counters**

Repeat this activity with similar examples. Ask the students to tell you each time how many are in each group and how many groups there are. Have them use the word *equal* when discussing the number in each group.

12 crackers

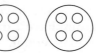

3 groups of 4
12 ÷ 3 = 4

Meaning of Division

Grade 4
Skill
21

When you separate a large group into smaller equal groups, you are dividing.

Find the number in each group.
There are 8 triangles in all.

△△△△△△△△

Divide the 8 triangles into 2 equal groups.

△△△△ △△△△

So, there are 4 triangles in each group.

Find the number of equal groups.
There are 12 triangles in all.

△△△△△△△△△△△△

Divide the 12 triangles into groups of 3 triangles.

△△△ △△△ △△△ △△△

So, there are 4 groups.

▲ Try These

Complete.

1

[ ]

_____ in all

_____ in each group

_____ groups

2

[ ]

_____ in all

_____ in each group

_____ groups

3

[ ]

_____ in all

_____ in each group

_____ groups

Go to the next side.

Practice on Your Own

Skill 21

Think:
There are 8 squares in all.
There are 4 equal groups.
There are 2 squares in each group.

□□ □□ □ □□

. . . .

Complete.

1 □□ □□ □□
☐ in all
☐ in each group
☐ groups

2 □□□□ □□□□
☐ in all
☐ in each group
☐ groups

3 □□□□□□ □□□□□□
☐ in all
☐ in each group
☐ groups

Find the number in each group.

4 Divide 10 circles into 2 equal groups.
○○○○○
○○○○○
☐ in each group

5 Divide 12 circles into 4 equal groups.
○○○○○○
○○○○○○
☐ in each group

6 Divide 15 circles into 5 equal groups.
○○○○○
○○○○○
○○○○○
☐ in each group

Find the number of groups.

7 Divide 10 squares into groups of 5 squares.
□□□□□
□□□□□
☐ groups

8 Divide 14 squares into groups of 2 squares.
□□□□□□□
□□□□□□□
☐ groups

9 Divide 16 squares into groups of 4 squares.
□□□□□□□□
□□□□□□□□
☐ groups

▶ Quiz

Complete.

10 □□□□□□□□□
☐ in all   ☐ groups
☐ in each group

11 Divide the 14 triangles into 2 equal groups.
△△△△△△△
△△△△△△△
☐ in each group

12 Divide the 14 circles into groups of 7 circles.
○○○○○○○
○○○○○○○
☐ groups

15 Minutes

OBJECTIVE Relate multiplication and division facts through 5

MATERIALS counters

Begin the lesson by recalling the definitions of multiplication and division. You may wish to review the terms *factor, product, divisor, dividend,* and *quotient.*

Point out that multiplication and division are opposite, or *inverse,* operations. One undoes the other or can be used to prove the other.

Call students' attention to the first model, the number line. Ask: **How many jumps are there? 2 How many spaces are in each jump? 4 What multiplication fact is shown? 2 × 4 = 8**

Call students' attention to the second number line. Ask: **What is the starting number? 8 How many jumps are there? 2 How many spaces are in each jump? 4 What division fact is shown? 8 ÷ 2 = 4**

Discuss the next two models similarly.

Ask: **How many groups [or rows] are there? 3 [2] How many are in each group [or row]? 4 [5] How many are there in all? 12 [10] How many do you start with? 12 [10] How many groups [or columns] do you separate them into? 3 [5] How many are there in each group [column]? 4 [2]**

You may wish to give each student a handful of counters and have them illustrate these related multiplication and division facts:

$3 \times 4 = 12$, and $12 \div 3 = 4$
$2 \times 5 = 10$, and $10 \div 2 = 5$

TRY THESE In Exercises 1–3, students use models to find a related multiplication or division equation.

- **Exercise 1**   Use a number line.

- **Exercise 2**   Use equal groups.

- **Exercise 3**   Use an array.

PRACTICE ON YOUR OWN Review the example at the top of the page. Check that students understand the multiplication table and see the inverse relationship between multiplication and division. Exercises 1–3 provide students with visuals to find the related fact. Exercises 4–6 require students to find facts without visuals. Exercises 7–14 ask students to find the product or quotient.

QUIZ You may want to allow students to draw a number line, an array, or equal sets of objects if they need help. Success is indicated by 3 out of 4 correct responses.

Students who successfully complete **Practice on Your Own** and **Quiz** are ready to move on to the next skill.

COMMON ERRORS

- Students may have difficulty finding related facts.

- Students may not know multiplication and division facts.

Students who make more than 4 errors in the **Practice on Your Own**, or who were not successful in the **Quiz** section, may benefit from the **Alternative Teaching Strategy** on the next page.

Alternative Teaching Strategy
Model Multiplication and Division

20 Minutes

OBJECTIVE Use models to show that multiplication and division are inverse operations

MATERIALS counters, construction paper, paper and pencil

Distribute a handful of counters to each student. Say a multiplication fact, for example, 5 × 2. Ask students to illustrate the fact by arranging their counters into an array of 5 groups of 2. They may find the total by repeated addition 2 + 2 + 2 + 2 + 2, or by counting. Have students record the number sentence that corresponds to the fact: 5 × 2 = 10.

Discuss how the array can show both multiplication and division. Explain that multiplication and division are opposite, or *inverse* operations. One undoes the other.

Demonstrate how to push apart the 5 rows of 2 and describe the result. Say: **I divided the 10 counters into 5 equal groups. Each group has 2 counters, so 10 ÷ 5 = 2.**

Provide students with large pieces of construction paper and have them make an equal-group work mat by folding the paper into thirds vertically and then into thirds horizontally.

Call out different equal groups. For example, say: **Show me three groups of two.** Have students verbalize the result. Students should be able to say that they made 3 groups of 2 counters and the total number is 6.

Work in the same way to have students show division. Say: **Show me 6 divided into 3 equal groups.** Again, have students verbalize the result. Students should be able to say that they separated 6 counters into 3 groups of 2 counters.

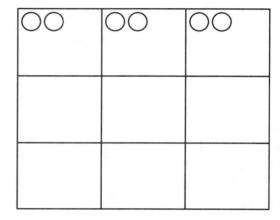

Continue in a similar way with other multiplication and division facts through 5. Have students record the multiplication or division fact for each model they complete. As students complete the models, continue to stress that multiplication and division are opposite, or inverse operations.

To check for understanding, display an expression such as 4 × 3. Ask students to describe how they would model this multiplication fact and a related division fact.

Grade 4
Skill 22

Multiply and Divide Facts Through 5

You can use different models to show that multiplication and division are inverse operations.

Use a number line.

Start at 0 and make 2 jumps of 4 to land at 8.

2 jumps × 4 spaces per jump = 8 in all

Start at 8 and take 2 jumps of 4 back to 0.

8 in all ÷ 2 jumps = 4 spaces per jump

Use equal groups.

Make 3 groups of 4 sticks to get 12 sticks.

3 groups × 4 sticks = 12 in all

Separate 12 sticks into 3 groups to get 4 in each group.

12 in all ÷ 3 groups = 4 sticks per group

Use an array.

Make 2 rows of 5 blocks to make 10 blocks.

2 rows × 5 blocks = 10 in all

Divide 10 blocks into 5 columns to get 2 in each column.

10 in all ÷ 5 columns = 2 blocks per column

Try These

Find a related multiplication or division equation.

1

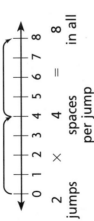

2 × 6 = 12

12 ÷ ☐ = ☐

2

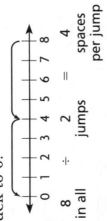

16 ÷ 4 = 4

☐ × ☐ = ☐

3

2 × 3 = 6

☐ ÷ ☐ = ☐

Go to the next side.

Practice on Your Own

Think: Look across row 6 and down column 4 to find the product 24.

$$6 \times 4 = 24$$

Think: Find 24 by looking down column 4. Then look left to find the quotient 6.

$$24 \div 4 = 6$$

×	0	1	2	3	4	5	6	7	8	9
0	0	0	0	0	0	0	0	0	0	0
1	0	1	2	3	4	5	6	7	8	9
2	0	2	4	6	8	10	12	14	16	18
3	0	3	6	9	12	15	18	21	24	27
4	0	4	8	12	16	20	24	28	32	36
5	0	5	10	15	20	25	30	35	40	45
6	0	6	12	18	24	30	36	42	48	54

Find a related multiplication or division equation.

1 $5 \times 2 = 10$

$\Box \div \Box = \Box$

0 1 2 3 4 5 6 7 8 9 10

2 $9 \div 3 = 3$

$\Box \times \Box = \Box$

3 $20 \div 5 = 4$

$\Box \times \Box = \Box$

4 $15 \div 3 = 5$

$\Box \times \Box = \Box$

5 $2 \times 8 = 16$

$\Box \div \Box = \Box$

6 $2 \times 7 = 14$

$\Box \div \Box = \Box$

Find the product or quotient.

7 $4 \times 5 = \Box$

8 $25 \div 5 = \Box$

9 $30 \div 5 = \Box$

10 $4 \times 6 = \Box$

11 $5 \times 7 = \Box$

12 $24 \div 3 = \Box$

13 $3 \times 9 = \Box$

14 $36 \div 4 = \Box$

▶ Quiz

Find the product or quotient.

15 $18 \div 3 = \Box$

16 $5 \times 9 = \Box$

17 $4 \times 8 = \Box$

18 $40 \div 5 = \Box$

OBJECTIVE Break apart numbers to make them easier to multiply.

MATERIALS centimeter grid paper, scissors

Remind students that you can break apart numbers to make them easier to multiply.

Direct students' attention to Step 1. Have them use grid paper to draw a rectangle that is 4 units wide and 7 units long. Tell them to think of the area as 4 × 7.

Ask: **Is there an easier way to find this product?** Yes, we can break apart the numbers so they're easier to multiply.

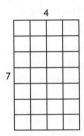

Direct students' attention to Step 2. Now have them cut apart the rectangle to make two arrays for the products they know.

Ask: **What is the factor 4 now?** 2 + 2

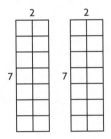

Direct students' attention to Step 3.

Ask: **What is the product of each of these smaller rectangles (2 × 7)?** 2 × 7 = 14 Tell students to add the two products of the rectangles together to find the sum.

Ask: **Now, what is 4 × 7?** 28 Discuss with students why this is much easier than counting up all the squares on the grid paper.

TRY THESE Exercises 1–4 guide students through the different strategies for solving multiplication and division problems.

- **Exercise 1**   Think of the inverse.
- **Exercise 2**   Use the Order Property.
- **Exercise 3**   Use a pattern.
- **Exercise 4**   Use the *break apart* strategy.

PRACTICE ON YOUR OWN Review the example at the top of the page. Remind students they have several strategies from which to choose to solve the problems.

QUIZ Determine if students can find products and quotients. Success is indicated by 6 out of 8 correct responses.

Students who successfully complete the **Practice on Your Own** and **Quiz** are ready to move to the next skill.

COMMON ERRORS

- Students may add instead of multiply.

- Students may count correctly.

Students who made more than 4 errors in the **Practice on Your Own**, or who were not successful in the **Quiz** section, may benefit from the **Alternative Teaching Strategy** on the next page.

Alternative Teaching Strategy
Use Arrays to Review Multiplication and Division Facts Through 10

20 Minutes

OBJECTIVE Use arrays to review multiplication and division facts through 10

MATERIALS mini-dot stickers, index cards

Some individualization is necessary for this lesson.

Note which facts were difficult for students on the **Practice on Your Own** page.

Have students use mini-dot stickers to create arrays for the missed facts on index cards. Help them write the entire fact families—both multiplication and division—on the cards.

For example:

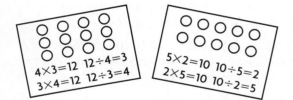

Have students review their cards with the group by displaying them.

Ask: **How many rows are there? 3 rows How many dots are in each row? 4 Based on these factors, how many dots are there in all? Explain. 12; 3 × 4 = 12** Then ask them to read the four multiplication and division facts for the array.

Note: You may wish to provide grid paper instead of index cards for students who might have difficulty lining up the dots to create arrays.

Invite students to review all the facts with which they are having difficulty, and then use these cards to help them with other multiplication and division facts through 10.

Multiply and Divide Facts Through 10

Use arrays and the *break apart* strategy to find 4×7.

Step 1
Draw a rectangle that is 4 units wide and 7 units long. Think of the area as 4×7. Use grid paper to find 4×7.

4

7

Step 2
Cut apart the rectangle to make two arrays for products you know.

2   2

7   7

The factor 4 is now 2 plus 2.

Step 3
Find the sum of the products of the two smaller rectangles.

$2 \times 7 = 14$
$2 \times 7 = 14$
$14 + 14 = 28$

So, $4 \times 7 = 28$.

▲ Try These

Find the product or quotient using each strategy.

1 Think of the inverse.
What is $27 \div 9$?

Think: $\square \times 9 = 27$

So, $27 \div 9 = \square$.

2 Use the Order Property.
What is 4×5?

Think: $5 \times 4 = \square$

So, $4 \times 5 = 5 \times 4 = \square$.

3 Use a pattern.
What is 8×6?

Think: $8 \times 3 = 24$, so I can count on from 24 for the remaining 3 times.

Count: 24 . . . $\square$, $\square$, $\square$.

So, $8 \times 6 = \square$.

4 Use the *break apart* strategy.
What is 6×5?

Think: $5 = 2 + 3$

$6 \times 2 = \square$ and $6 \times 3 = \square$

$6 \times 5 = \square + \square$

So, $6 \times 5 = \square$.

Go to the next side.

Practice on Your Own

Skill 23

What is 9×5?

Think: $5 = 2 + 3$

$9 \times 2 = 18$ and $9 \times 3 = 27$,

$9 \times 5 = 18 + 27$

So, $9 \times 5 = 45$.

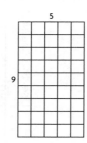
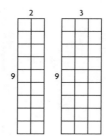

Show how arrays can be used to find the product.

1 $3 \times 8 = \square$

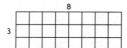

2 $6 \times 9 = \square$

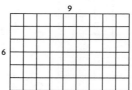
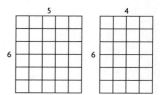

Find the product or quotient. Show the strategy you need.

3 $10 \times 9 = \square$ **4** $6 \times 3 = \square$ **5** $4 \times 8 = \square$ **6** $8 \times 7 = \square$

7 $8 \times 8 = \square$ **8** $7 \times 3 = \square$ **9** $6 \times 7 = \square$ **10** $5 \times 9 = \square$

11 $5 \times 5 = \square$ **12** $8 \times 4 = \square$ **13** $8 \times 5 = \square$ **14** $56 \div 8 = \square$

15 $50 \div 10 = \square$ **16** $90 \div 10 = \square$ **17** $72 \div 9 = \square$ **18** $36 \div 4 = \square$

▶ Quiz

Find the product or quotient. Show the strategy you need.

19 $7 \times 5 = \square$ **20** $8 \times 8 = \square$ **21** $8 \times 10 = \square$ **22** $7 \times 9 = \square$

23 $10 \times 4 = \square$ **24** $40 \div 8 = \square$ **25** $24 \div 6 = \square$ **26** $28 \div 4 = \square$

15 Minutes

OBJECTIVE Practice division facts through 10

You may wish to have students model the steps in the lesson with counters.

Ask a student to explain the meaning of division and how it relates to multiplication. Guide students to understand that since multiplication is the inverse, or opposite, of division, multiplication facts can be used to help them with division facts.

Call students' attention to the first example.

Ask: **What multiplication fact can help you find 24 ÷ 8? 8 × 3 = 24**

Emphasize the idea that $24 \div 8 = 3$ because $8 \times 3 = 24$.

Ask: **How can you show the division with counters? Separate 24 counters into 8 equal groups.**

Invite students to look at the model.

Ask: **How many counters are there in all? 24 How many groups are there? 8 What does the 3 represent? the number of counters in each group**

Continue with similar questions for $40 \div 10$. Make sure students understand that when they divide, they separate a total number into equal groups.

TRY THESE In Exercises 1–3, students use models to help them find quotients.

- **Exercise 1**   Divide by 4.
- **Exercise 2**   Divide by 6.
- **Exercise 3**   Divide by 7.

PRACTICE ON YOUR OWN Review the examples at the top of the page. In Exercises 1–8, students show equal groups for division facts and find the quotient. In Exercises 9–20, students find the quotients without referring to models.

QUIZ Determine if students know division facts through 10. Success is indicated by 3 out of 4 correct responses.

Students who successfully complete the **Practice on Your Own** and **Quiz** are ready to move to the next skill.

COMMON ERRORS

- Students may not know division facts and may use an incorrect fact to find a quotient.

- Students may add or multiply instead of dividing.

Students who make more than 6 errors in the **Practice on Your Own**, or who were not successful in the **Quiz** section, may benefit from the **Alternative Teaching Strategy** on the next page.

Alternative Teaching Strategy
Model Division Facts

15 Minutes

OBJECTIVE Use models to practice
division facts

MATERIALS paper plates, counters

Have students form small groups. Distribute
paper plates and counters.

Have students put 4 counters on each of
6 plates.

Ask: **What multiplication fact does the
model represent?** $4 \times 6 = 24$

Have students gather the counters together,
and then model $24 \div 6$.

Explain that $4 \times 6 = 24$ and $24 \div 6 = 4$
are *related multiplication and division facts*.
If students know that $4 \times 6 = 24$, then they
also know that $24 \div 6 = 4$.

Continue with examples for other facts. For
each example, encourage students to think of
a multiplication fact that can help them find
the quotient.

As students show understanding, provide less
guidance. Conclude by having students try
some exercises without using models. The
goal is to have students use related fact
strategies to divide symbolically.

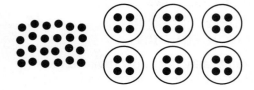

$$4 \times 6 = 24$$
$$24 \div 6 = 4$$

Practice Division Facts

There are many ways to find the quotient. One way is to use counters.

$24 \div 8 = \square.$

Step 1
Show 24 counters.

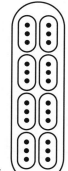

Think: 8 times what number equals 24?

Step 2
Put the counters into 8 equal groups.

Step 3
Record the division fact.

$24 \div 8 = 3$

So, $24 \div 8$ equals 3.

$40 \div 10 = \square.$

Step 1
Show 40 counters.

Think: 10 times what number equals 40?

Step 2
Put the counters into 10 equal groups.

Step 3
Record the division fact.

$40 \div 10 = 4$

So, $40 \div 10$ equals 4.

Try These

Find the quotient.

1

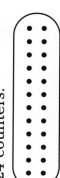

$4 \div 4 = \square$

2

$18 \div 6 = \square$

3

$35 \div 7 = \square$

Go to the next side.

Intervention • Skills IN105

Practice on Your Own

Another way to find the quotient is to think about fact families.

Find 56 ÷ 7.

Fact family for 7, 8, 56

factor		factor		product		divisor		divisor		quotient
7	×	8	=	56		56	÷	8	=	7
8	×	7	=	56		56	×	7	=	8

So, 56 ÷ 8 = 7.

Find the quotient.

1 10 ÷ 5 = □

2 15 ÷ 3 = □

3 20 ÷ 4 = □

4 21 ÷ 3 = □

Write a division sentence for each.

5 ___ ÷ ___ = ___

6 ___ ÷ ___ = ___

7 ___ ÷ ___ = ___

8 ___ ÷ ___ = ___

Find the quotient.

9 14 ÷ 2 = □

10 □ = 18 ÷ 9

11 12 ÷ 6 = □

12 27 ÷ □ = 3

13 54 ÷ □ = 9

14 35 ÷ 5 = □

15 □ = 42 ÷ 7

16 48 ÷ 6 = □

17 □ = 50 ÷ 10

18 63 ÷ □ = 9

19 64 ÷ □ = 8

20 81 ÷ 9 = □

▶ **Quiz**

Find the quotient.

21 6 ÷ 6 = □

22 12 ÷ 4 = □

23 45 ÷ 5 = □

24 72 ÷ 9 = □

OBJECTIVE Divide by 1-digit divisors, with remainders in the quotient

MATERIALS counters

15 Minutes

You may wish to have students model the example with counters.

When students have formed the 4 groups of 6, have them observe that they could form 4 equal groups, but 1 counter is left over. Note that, sometimes when they divide there will be some counters left over. This is called the *remainder*.

Connect Steps 1–3 to the modeling just completed.

For Step 2, ask: **What number shows the total number of counters? 25 What number tells how many counters are in each group? 6 What number tells how many equal groups? 4 What is the remainder? 1**

TRY THESE In Exercises 1–4, students should circle groups to show each division.

- **Exercise 1** Circle groups of 4 with 2 left over.

- **Exercise 2** Circle groups of 3 with 2 left over.

- **Exercise 3** Circle groups of 5 with 1 left over.

- **Exercise 4** Circle groups of 4 with 2 left over.

PRACTICE ON YOUR OWN Review the example at the top of the page. Note that the example has a two-digit quotient. Emphasize that the "multiply, subtract" step is followed twice. Point out also that the remainder is always less than the divisor. You may wish to give another similar example, such as $44 \div 3$.

Exercise 9 has a two-digit quotient; monitor students' work to provide help if necessary.

QUIZ Determine if students can divide by 1-digit divisors, with remainders in the quotient. Success is determined by 2 out of 3 correct responses.

Students who successfully complete the **Practice on Your Own** and **Quiz** are ready to move to the next skill.

COMMON ERRORS

- Students may forget to record the remainder.

- In divisions where the quotient is greater than 9, students may not finish the final step, and may record a remainder that is greater than the divisor.

Students who made more than 2 errors in the **Practice on Your Own**, or who were not successful in the **Quiz** section, may benefit from the **Alternative Teaching Strategy** on the next page.

Alternative Teaching Strategy
Model Division with Remainders

15 Minutes

OBJECTIVE Use tiles and arrays to understand division with remainders

MATERIALS square tiles, or counters; triangular flash cards

Students may need to take a step back in building understanding. Begin the activity by having students work with an exercise that does not have a remainder, for example $30 \div 5$.

Distribute the tiles. Demonstrate how to form an array of rows and columns with the tiles.

$30 \div 5 = 6$

Observe with the students that there are 6 rows of 5 tiles. All the rows have an equal number. If necessary, have students try several exercises similar to this one before moving on to modeling division with remainders.

Now ask students to model $27 \div 5$. They will discover that they cannot complete an array. There are 5 rows of 5 tiles with two left over.

$27 \div 5 = 5r2$

Continue with other examples.

When students demonstrate understanding of equal groups and remainders, have students record the division symbolically.

If you find that students cannot remember division facts, give a short daily review. You may have pairs of students work together with flash cards. Triangular flash cards are simple to make and useful.

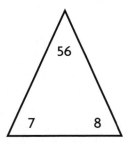

Grade 4
Skill

Divide with Remainders

Sometimes when you divide counters into equal groups, you may have some counters left over. The number left over is called the **remainder**.
Find $25 \div 6$.

Divide 25 counters into groups of 6.

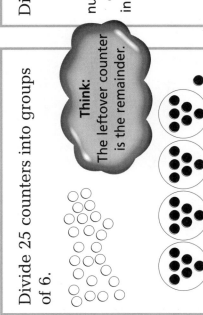

Think:
The leftover counter is the remainder.

Divide.

$$\begin{array}{r} 4 \leftarrow \text{number of groups} \\ 6\overline{)25} \leftarrow \text{number of} \\ \underline{-24} \quad \text{counters} \\ 1 \leftarrow \text{remainder} \end{array}$$

number of counters in a group

Write the remainder next to the quotient.

$$\begin{array}{r} 4\ \text{r1} \leftarrow \text{quotient and} \\ 6\overline{)25} \qquad \text{remainder} \\ \underline{-24} \\ 1 \end{array}$$

► Try These

Divide the counters into equal groups to find the quotient and remainder.

1

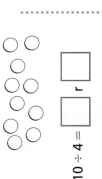

$10 \div 4 = \boxed{}\ \text{r}\ \boxed{}$

2

$8 \div 3 = \boxed{}\ \text{r}\ \boxed{}$

3

$16 \div 5 = \boxed{}\ \text{r}\ \boxed{}$

4

$22 \div 4 = \boxed{}\ \text{r}\ \boxed{}$

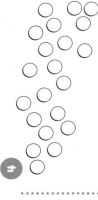
Go to the next side.

Practice on Your Own

Skill 25

Find 35 ÷ 2.

```
  17 r1
2)35
 − 2
  15
 − 14
   1
```

Think: Make 2 equal groups.

So, 35 ÷ 2 = 17 r1.

Divide the counters into groups to find the quotient and remainder.

1

13 ÷ 3 = ☐ r ☐

2

28 ÷ 5 = ☐ r ☐

3

17 ÷ 7 = ☐ r ☐

4

☐ r ☐
6)37
− ☐
☐

5

☐ r ☐
4)21
− ☐
☐

6

☐ r ☐
8)26
− ☐
☐

Find the quotient and remainder.

7 5)21

8 6)44

9 7)75

 Quiz

Find the quotient and remainder.

10 9)28

11 3)32

12 9)56

OBJECTIVE Divide whole numbers by 1-digit divisors

You may wish to review multiplication facts to 9. Review the words *dividend*, *divisor*, and *quotient*. Remind students that *remainder* means the part that is left over or is not used.

Have students look at the example.

Say: **To divide, always start with the greatest place value.**

Ask: **What is the greatest place value? tens Can 5 go into 7? yes So, what is the first step in the division? 7 tens ÷ 5 How many times does 5 go into 7? 1 What is the place value of the 1 in the quotient? tens** Stress the importance of keeping place values aligned properly.

Ask: **What do you do next? Multiply 1 by 5 and subtract the product from 7.** Stress the importance of comparing the difference with the divisor. Point out that if the difference is greater than the divisor, then the quotient is too small.

Say: **The next step is to bring down the ones.** Demonstrate how to bring down the digit.

Ask: **What do you do now? 28 ÷ 5 What happens next? Multiply 5 by 5 and subtract the product from 28. What is the difference? 3 Can 5 be divided into 3? no**

Say: **So, 3 is the remainder.**

Explain to students that they can use the phrase "**d**addy, **m**ommy, **s**ister, **b**rother" to help them remember to **d**ivide, **m**ultiply, **s**ubtract, and then **b**ring down.

Remind students to write the remainder next to the quotient. Show students how to check the answer by multiplying the quotient times the divisor, and adding the remainder.

TRY THESE Exercises 1–4 provide students with practice in dividing by 1-digit divisors.

- **Exercises 1–4:** Divide a whole number by a 1-digit divisor.

PRACTICE ON YOUR OWN Review the example at the top of the page. The exercises provide practice dividing by 1-digit divisors with and without leaving a remainder.

QUIZ Determine if students can divide by a 1-digit divisor. Success is indicated by 4 out of 6 correct responses.

Students who successfully complete **Practice on Your Own** and **Quiz** are ready to move to the next skill.

COMMON ERRORS

- Students may be unsure of basic multiplication, addition, or subtraction facts and have difficulty dividing properly.

- Students may not work neatly and bring down digits incorrectly.

Students who made more than 3 errors in **Practice on Your Own**, or who were not successful in the **Quiz** section, may benefit from the **Alternative Teaching Strategy** on the next page.

Alternative Teaching Strategy
Modeling Division by 1-Digit Divisors

OBJECTIVE Model dividing by
1-digit divisors

MATERIALS base-ten units, base-ten rods

Distribute the base-ten rods and units to each student. Have students model 76 ÷ 3 using base-ten rods and units.

Say: **Model 76 using your rods and units.** Allow time for students to perform the task. Check students' models.

Say: **Now, separate the tens from the ones.**

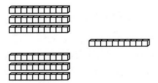

Say: **To divide, start with the tens. Since you are dividing by 3, divide your tens into groups of 3.**

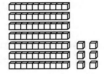

Ask: **How many groups did you make? 2 How many rods are left over? 1**

Say: **Exchange the rod for 10 units. Add these units to the 6 units you already have.**

Ask: **How many units are there now? 16**

Say: **Now divide the units into groups of 3.**

Ask: **How many groups can you make? 5 How many units are left over? 1**

Say: **When you divided, you made 2 groups of tens and 5 groups of ones.**

Ask: **What number does that make? 25 How many units did you have left over? 1 What does that unit represent? remainder**

Say: **So, 76 ÷ 3 = 25 r1.**

Grade 4
Skill 26

Division Procedures

Divide 78 by 5. Write 78 ÷ 5 or 5)78.

Step 1 Divide the 7 tens.

$$\begin{array}{r} 1 \\ 5\overline{)78} \\ -5 \\ \hline 2 \end{array}$$

Divide. 7 ÷ 5
Multiply. 1 × 5
Subtract. 7 − 5
Compare. 2 < 5

The difference, 2, must be less than the divisor, 5.

Step 2 Bring down the 8 ones.

$$\begin{array}{r} 1 \\ 5\overline{)78} \\ -5\downarrow \\ \hline 28 \end{array}$$

Step 3 Divide the 28 ones.

$$\begin{array}{r} 15\ r3 \\ 5\overline{)78} \\ -5 \\ \hline 28 \\ -25 \\ \hline 3 \end{array}$$

Divide. 28 ÷ 5
Multiply. 5 × 5
Subtract. 28 − 25
Compare. 3 < 5

Write the remainder next to the quotient.

Check

$$\begin{array}{r} 15 \\ \times 5 \\ \hline 75 \\ + 3 \\ \hline 78 \end{array}$$

quotient
divisor

remainder
dividend

Try These

Divide and check.

1 4)63 15 r3

2 7)89

3 73 ÷ 3

4 8)94

Go to the next side.

Practice on Your Own

Skill 26

Divide 65 by 4. Write 65 ÷ 4 or 4)65.

Step 1 Divide the 6 tens.	**Step 2** Bring down the 5 ones.	**Step 3** Divide the 25 ones.	**Check**
$\begin{array}{r} 1 \\ 4\overline{)65} \\ -4 \\ \hline 2 \end{array}$ Divide. 6 ÷ 4 Multiply. 1 × 4 Subtract. 6 − 4 Compare. 2 < 4	$\begin{array}{r} 1 \\ 4\overline{)65} \\ -4\downarrow \\ \hline 25 \end{array}$	$\begin{array}{r} 16\,r1 \\ 4\overline{)65} \\ -4\downarrow \\ \hline 25 \\ -24 \\ \hline 1 \end{array}$ Divide. 25 ÷ 4 Multiply. 6 × 4 Subtract. 25 − 24 Compare. 1 < 4	$\begin{array}{r} 16 \\ \times\ 4 \\ \hline 64 \\ +\ 1 \\ \hline 65 \end{array}$ quotient divisor remainder dividend
The difference, 2, must be less than the divisor, 4.		Write the remainder next to the quotient.	

Divide and check.

1 4)67

2 5)81

3 3)75

4 8)92

5 3)57

6 6)80

7 93 ÷ 6

8 71 ÷ 5

9 55 ÷ 2

▶ Quiz

Divide and check.

10 7)99

11 4)59

12 3)94

13 76 ÷ 5

14 70 ÷ 4

15 89 ÷ 6

15 Minutes

OBJECTIVE Estimate a quotient by using compatible numbers

Before beginning, give a brief review of compatible numbers. Display this division: $28 \div 5$.

Say: **Think of as many facts as you can that are close to this expression. Possible answers: $25 \div 5$, $27 \div 3$, $28 \div 4$, and $30 \div 5$**

Observe with students that they can find these quotients using mental math. Then have students decide which of the facts they listed might give an estimated quotient close to the actual quotient. Work with the students to find the actual quotient, then compare the quotients from the facts they chose to the result. Note that the facts students chose are compatible numbers.

Direct students' attention to the example. Note that numbers compatible with 4 are numbers that 4 divides evenly, such as 8, 12, or 16.

Ask: **What compatible number can you use to estimate the quotient $38 \div 4$? Try 36. It is close to 38 and 4 divides 36 evenly. $36 \div 4 = 9$. The compatible numbers are 36 and 4.**

How do compatible numbers help you estimate the quotient? They are easy to divide.

Students should know that they can use basic multiplication and division facts to help find compatible numbers.

TRY THESE Exercises 1–3 prompt students as they estimate quotients using compatible numbers.

- **Exercise 1**   Compatible numbers 27, 3.
- **Exercise 2**   Compatible numbers 48, 6.
- **Exercise 3**   Compatible numbers 54, 9.

PRACTICE ON YOUR OWN Work through the example with students. Have them identify the compatible numbers. Explain that 90 is one number close to 94 that is divisible by 9.

QUIZ Determine if students know how to use compatible numbers to estimate a quotient. Success is determined by 2 out of 3 correct responses.

Students who successfully complete the **Practice on Your Own** and **Quiz** are ready to move on to the next skill.

COMMON ERRORS

- Students may not know basic multiplication and division facts.

- Students may not use the closest compatible numbers to the actual numbers, which results in an estimate that may be too high or too low.

Students who made more than 2 errors in the **Practice on Your Own**, or who were not successful in the **Quiz** section, may benefit from the **Alternative Teaching Strategy** on the next page.

Alternative Teaching Strategy
Choose Compatible Numbers

15 Minutes

OBJECTIVE Estimate a quotient by using compatible numbers

MATERIALS large index cards

Prepare a card with a division sentence and at least four cards with division facts that are close to the division sentence.

Display a card, for example, $40 \div 6 = \square$. Then explain to the students that they are to estimate the quotient using compatible numbers. Remind them that compatible numbers are numbers close to the actual numbers. Compatible numbers are easier to divide because they divide evenly.

$$40 \div 6 = \square$$

$$42 \div 6 = \square \qquad 40 \div 5 = \square$$

$$36 \div 6 = \square \qquad 48 \div 6 = \square$$

Have students look at the cards with the close facts and choose the fact they think is closest to $40 \div 6 = \square$. Then have them divide 40 by 6 and compare the actual quotient to the quotients of the close facts. **$40 \div 6 = 6r4$ and $42 \div 6 = 7$ are the closest.** Point out that $42 \div 6 = 7$ is closest because the divisor remains the same and the dividend was increased by only 2.

Repeat this activity several times with other division sentences and close facts until the students are able to estimate without the fact cards. Have students note that although there could be more than one estimate, the closest estimate is preferable.

$$40 \div 6 = 6r4$$
$$42 \div 6 = 7 \quad \leftarrow \textbf{closest}$$
$$40 \div 5 = 8$$
$$36 \div 6 = 6$$
$$48 \div 6 = 8$$

Estimate Quotients

You can estimate a quotient by using **compatible numbers**.

> **Compatible numbers** are numbers close to the actual numbers and can be divided evenly.

Estimate $38 \div 4 = \blacksquare$.

Think: 36 is close to 38.
36 can be divided evenly by 4.

$$38 \div 4 = \blacksquare$$

$$36 \div 4 = 9 \quad \text{—— compatible numbers}$$

So, $38 \div 4$ is about 9.

Estimate $34 \div 8 = \blacksquare$.

Think: 34 is close to 32.
32 can be divided evenly by 8.

$$34 \div 8 = \blacksquare$$

$$32 \div 8 = 4 \quad \text{—— compatible numbers}$$

So, $38 \div 8$ is about 4.

Try These

Estimate the quotient. Use compatible numbers.

1 $28 \div 3 = \blacksquare$

> **Think:** 27 is close to 28. 27 can be divided evenly by 3.

$27 \div 3 = \boxed{9}$

So, $28 \div 3$ is about $\boxed{}$.

2 $47 \div 6 = \blacksquare$

> **Think:** 48 is close to 47. 48 can be divided evenly by 6.

$\boxed{} \div \boxed{} = \boxed{}$

So, $47 \div 6$ is about $\boxed{}$.

3 $52 \div 9 = \blacksquare$

> **Think:** 52 is close to 54. 54 can be divided evenly by 9.

$\boxed{} \div \boxed{} = \boxed{}$

So, $52 \div 9$ is about $\boxed{}$.

Go to the next side.

Practice on Your Own

Estimate: $94 \div 9 = \blacksquare$.

$$90 \div 9 = 10$$

compatible numbers

Think:
90 is close to 94,
90 can be divided evenly by 9.

So, $94 \div 9$ is about $\boxed{10}$.

Estimate. Use compatible numbers.

1 $25 \div 6 = \blacksquare$.

Think:
24 is close to 25,
24 can be divided evenly by 6.

$\boxed{} \div 6 = \boxed{}$

compatible numbers

So, $25 \div 6$ is about $\boxed{}$.

2 $70 \div 8 = \blacksquare$.

Think:
72 is close to 70,
72 can be divided evenly by 8.

$\boxed{} \div 8 = \boxed{}$

compatible numbers

So, $70 \div 8$ is about $\boxed{}$.

3 $52 \div 5 = \blacksquare$

$\boxed{} \div \boxed{} = \boxed{}$

So, $52 \div 5$ is about $\boxed{}$.

4 $47 \div 7 = \blacksquare$

$\boxed{} \div \boxed{} = \boxed{}$

So, $47 \div 7$ is about $\boxed{}$.

5 $66 \div 8 = \blacksquare$

$\boxed{} \div \boxed{} = \boxed{}$

So, $66 \div 8$ is about $\boxed{}$.

6 $84 \div 9$ is about $\boxed{}$.

7 $61 \div 7$ is about $\boxed{}$.

8 $41 \div 6$ is about $\boxed{}$.

▶ Quiz

Estimate. Use compatible numbers.

9 $32 \div 6$ is about $\boxed{}$.

10 $58 \div 9$ is about $\boxed{}$.

11 $73 \div 8$ is about $\boxed{}$.

OBJECTIVE Use strategies to place the first digit in the quotient; divide

Begin the lesson by recalling that the answer to a division problem is called the *quotient*.

Call students' attention to Step 1. Point out that students can use one of two strategies to decide where to place the first digit in the quotient. The first strategy shown is *estimate*.

Say: **You need to find 125 ÷ 5. You can estimate to find where to place the first digit in the quotient.**

Explain how to estimate the quotient using a number that is easy to divide mentally, such as 100 or 200. 100 ÷ 5 = 20, and 200 ÷ 5 = 40, so the first digit is placed in the tens place.

Call students' attention to the second strategy in Step 1, *use place value*.

Ask: **What number is being divided? 125 What number will you divide by? 5 If you begin dividing with the left-most digit in 125, what will you divide first? 1 Is that digit greater than the divisor? No, 1 < 5.**

Point out that since 1 < 5, students should begin dividing with the 12 tens.

Ask: **How many whole groups of 5 are in 12? 2 Where do you place the 2 in the quotient? in the tens place**

Work through Steps 2 and 3, emphasizing the "divide, multiply, subtract, compare" steps used in dividing. Have students pay special attention to the compare step, noting that if the remainder is greater than the divisor, they continue dividing.

TRY THESE Exercises 1–4 model the types of exercises students will encounter on the **Practice on Your Own** page.

- **Exercises 1–2** 2-digit dividends, no remainders

- **Exercises 3–4** 3-digit dividends, no remainders

PRACTICE ON YOUR OWN Review the example at the top of the page. Remind students that they can either estimate or use place value to place the first digit of the quotient in the hundreds place. Exercises 1–3 provide students with division charts to help them divide. Exercises 4–12 provide practice in dividing 2- and 3-digit dividends.

QUIZ Determine if students can tell where to place the first digit. Determine if students can set up the division correctly, aligning digits as they divide. Success is indicated by 4 out of 6 correct responses.

Students who successfully complete the **Practice on Your Own** and **Quiz** are ready to move to the next skill.

COMMON ERRORS

- Students may write the digits of the quotient in the wrong place.

- Students may forget to subtract before bringing down the next digit in the dividend.

- Students may multiply or subtract incorrectly.

Students who make more than 2 errors in the **Practice on Your Own**, or who were not successful in the **Quiz** section, may benefit from the **Alternative Teaching Strategy** on the next page.

Alternative Teaching Strategy
Model Placing the First Digit and Division

⟨20 Minutes⟩

OBJECTIVE Use base-ten blocks to model placing the first digit and division

MATERIALS base-ten blocks

You may wish to begin by asking students to suggest a possible real-life situation for dividing 34 by 2. (Possible responses: number of students in each of 2 buses, the cost of each of 2 shirts)

Write the division on the board for students to copy on their papers.

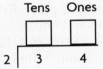

Distribute the base-ten blocks.

Ask: **Into how many groups are you dividing 34? 2 groups How many tens blocks can you put in each of 2 groups? 1 each**

Pay special attention to the process of deciding where to place the first digit in the quotient.

Ask: **Where do you record the 1 ten in each group in the division? above the 3 in the tens place**

Say: **You have 1 ten and 4 ones left. What do you need to do next to the ten block to divide the blocks evenly between the two groups? Regroup the leftover ten as 10 ones.**

Ask: **How many ones do you have now? 14 Can you divide 14 ones evenly between the 2 groups? yes How many ones does each group have? 7 Where do you record the 7 ones? above the 4 in the ones place**

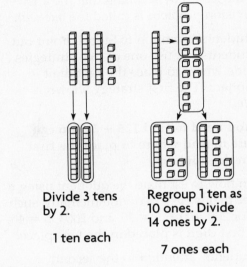

Divide 3 tens by 2.

1 ten each

Regroup 1 ten as 10 ones. Divide 14 ones by 2.

7 ones each

So, 34 ÷ 2 = 17.

Repeat the activity for exercises with 3-digit dividends. Be sure to vary the placement of the first digit. When the students show an understanding of the division process, collect the base-ten blocks and have them try an exercise using only paper and pencil. Ask students to tell you each step as they complete the division.

Grade 4
Skill 28

Place the First Digit

Find $5\overline{)125}$. Use strategies to place the first digit in the quotient.

Step 1

Decide whether to estimate or use place value to place the first digit in the quotient.

Estimate to place the first digit.

Think: $5\overline{)100}$ or $5\overline{)200}$
         20   40

So, the first digit is in the tens place.

Or

Use place value to place the first digit.

Think: Look at the hundreds. $1 < 5$, so look at the tens. $12 > 5$, so use 12 tens.

So, place the first digit in the tens place.

Step 2

Divide the 12 tens.

Hundreds	Tens	Ones
	2	
5)1	2	5
− 1	0	
	2	

Divide. $5\overline{)12}$
Multiply. 5×2
Subtract. $12 - 10$
Compare. $2 < 5$

Step 3

Bring down the ones.
Divide the 25 ones.

Hundreds	Tens	Ones
	2	5
5)1	2	5 →
− 1		5
	2	5
	− 2	5
		0

Divide. $5\overline{)25}$
Multiply. 5×5
Subtract. $25 - 25$
Compare. $0 < 5$

There is no remainder.
So, $125 \div 5 = 25$.

▲ Try These

Tell where to place the first digit. Then divide.

1 $2\overline{)16}$

Tens	Ones
	6
2)1	
−	

2 $4\overline{)64}$

Tens	Ones
	4 →
4)6	
−	

3 $3\overline{)219}$

Hundreds	Tens	Ones
		9 →
3)2	1	
−		

4 $2\overline{)172}$

Hundreds	Tens	Ones
	7	2 →
2)1		
−		

Go to the next side.

Practice on Your Own

Skill 28

Find 2)329.

Think: Decide where to place the first digit in the quotient. 3 > 2, so place the first digit in the hundreds place.

Hundreds	Tens	Ones
1	6	4
2)3	2	9
− 2	↓	
1	2	
− 1	2	
0	9	
	8	
	1	

Remember:
Bring down the ones.
Multiply. $2 \times 4 = 8$
Subtract. $9 − 8$
Compare. $1 < 2$

So, $329 \div 2 = 164$ r1.

Tell where to place the first digit. Then divide.

1 3)63

Tens	Ones
☐	☐
3)6	3
− ☐	↓
☐	
	− ☐
	☐

2 6)138

Hundreds	Tens	Ones
	☐	☐
6)1	3	8
− ☐		↓
	☐	☐
	− ☐	☐
		☐

3 4)269

Hundreds	Tens	Ones	
	☐	☐	r ☐
4)2	6	9	
− ☐	☐	↓	
	☐	☐	
	− ☐	☐	
		☐	

4 4)18

5 6)72

6 3)642

7 65 ÷ 5

8 155 ÷ 3

9 847 ÷ 7

10 537 ÷ 6

11 885 ÷ 5

12 252 ÷ 8

▶ Quiz

Tell where to place the first digit. Then divide.

13 33 ÷ 3

14 216 ÷ 2

15 162 ÷ 5

16 992 ÷ 8

17 357 ÷ 4

18 588 ÷ 6

15 Minutes

OBJECTIVE Divide dividends that contain zeros.

Begin by reviewing strategies to place the first digit in the quotient. Suggest to students that the placement of the first digit also helps them predict the total number of digits in the quotient.

Direct students' attention to the first step. Ask: **Where is the first digit in both estimates? the hundreds place How many digits are in each estimate? 3 How many digits will be in the quotient? 3**

Work through Step 2, reviewing the "divide, multiply, subtract, compare" steps used in dividing.

Direct students' attention to Step 3. Point out that since $3 > 0$, you write a zero in the quotient.

Say: **You bring down 0 tens.**
Ask: **How many whole groups of 3 are in 0? 0 How do you place the 0 in the quotient? above the 0 in the tens place**

Work through Step 4. Have students explain each step as they divide.

TRY THESE Exercises 1–4 model the type of exercises students will find on the **Practice on Your Own** page.

• **Exercises 1–4** Divide 3-digit dividends and place zeros in the quotient.

PRACTICE ON YOUR OWN Review the example at the top of the page. Exercises 1–3 provide long division prompts to help students divide. Exercises 4–12 ask students to divide without prompts.

QUIZ Determine if students can divide dividends that have zeros and place zeros in quotients. Success is indicated by 4 out of 6 correct responses.

Students who successfully complete the **Practice on Your Own** and **Quiz** are ready to move to the next skill.

COMMON ERRORS

• Students may write the digits of the quotient in the wrong place.

• Students may forget to place a zero in the ones or tens place in the quotient.

• Students may multiply or subtract incorrectly.

Students who made more than 3 errors in the **Practice on Your Own**, or who were not successful in the **Quiz** section, may benefit from the **Alternative Teaching Strategy** on the next page.

Alternative Teaching Strategy
Model Zeros in Division

15 Minutes

OBJECTIVE Use base-ten blocks to model zeros in division

MATERIALS base-ten blocks: ones, tens, hundreds

Have students work in pairs. One student models the exercise with the base-ten blocks, while the other student records the exercise on paper.

Write a division exercise on the board for students to copy.

For example:

Hundreds	Tens	Ones
☐	☐	☐

5)6   0   0

Distribute the base-ten blocks. Have students use the blocks to model the exercise.

Ask: **Into how many groups are you dividing 600? 5 How many hundreds blocks can you put in each of 5 groups? 1 each Where do you record the 1 hundred in each group in the division? above the 6 in the hundreds place How many blocks are left? 100 What do you need to do to divide the 100 blocks evenly between 5 groups? Regroup the leftover hundred as 10 tens.**

Ask: **How many tens do you have now? 10 Can you divide 10 tens evenly between the 5 groups? yes How many tens does each group have? 2 Where do you record the 2 tens? above the 0 in the tens place How many blocks are left? 0 What do you need to record in the ones place to complete the division? 0**

Repeat for exercises with zeros in different places in the dividend and quotient. Have partners switch roles with each new exercise. When students show an understanding of zeros in division, collect the base-ten blocks and have them try an exercise using only paper and pencil.

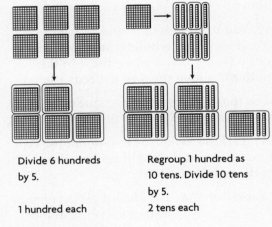

Divide 6 hundreds by 5.

1 hundred each

Regroup 1 hundred as 10 tens. Divide 10 tens by 5.

2 tens each

So, $600 \div 5 = 120$.

Grade 4
Skill
29

Zeros in Division

Find 3)309.

Step 1: Estimate to place the first digit in the quotient.

Think: $\dfrac{100}{3)300}$ or $\dfrac{200}{3)600}$

So, place the first digit in the hundreds place.

Step 2: Divide the 3 hundreds.

Hundreds	Tens	Ones
1	☐	☐

$$
\begin{array}{r}
1 \\
3)\overline{3\;0\;9} \\
-\,3 \\
\hline
0
\end{array}
$$

Divide 3)3.
Multiply 3 × 1.
Subtract 3 − 3.
Compare 0 < 3.

Step 3: Bring down the 0 tens. Divide the 0 tens.

Hundreds	Tens	Ones
1	0	☐

$$
\begin{array}{r}
1\;0 \\
3)\overline{3\;0\;9} \\
-\,3 \\
\hline
0\;0 \\
- \\
\hline
0
\end{array}
$$

Step 4: Bring down the 9 ones. Divide the 9 ones.

Hundreds	Tens	Ones
1	0	3

$$
\begin{array}{r}
1\;0\;3 \\
3)\overline{3\;0\;9} \\
-\,3 \\
\hline
0\;0 \\
- \\
\hline
0\;9 \\
-\,9 \\
\hline
0
\end{array}
$$

3 > 0, so write a zero in the quotient.

▲ Try These

Divide.

1 2)208

Hundreds	Tens	Ones
☐	0	8

$$2)\overline{2\,0\,8}$$

2 4)804

Hundreds	Tens	Ones
☐	0	4

$$4)\overline{8\,0\,4}$$

3 5)509

Hundreds	Tens	Ones	r
☐	0	9	☐

$$5)\overline{5\,0\,9}$$

4 6)607

Hundreds	Tens	Ones	r
☐	0	7	☐

$$6)\overline{6\,0\,7}$$

Go to the next side.

Practice on Your Own   Skill 29

Find 4)320.

Think: Decide where to place the first digit. Look at the hundreds. 3 < 4, so look at the tens. 32 > 4, so use 32 tens.

Hundreds	Tens	Ones
	8	0
4)3	2	0
− 3	2	
	0	0
	−	0
		0

Bring down the ones.

Think: 4 > 0, so place a zero in the ones place in the quotient. Multiply 4 × 0 = 0. Subtract 0 − 0. Compare 0 < 4.

Divide and check.

1 3)360

Hundreds	Tens	Ones
☐	☐	☐
3)3	6	0
− ☐	↓	
☐	☐	
−	☐	↓
	☐	☐
	−	☐
		☐

2 5)200

Hundreds	Tens	Ones
	☐	☐
5)2	0	0
− ☐	☐	↓
	☐	☐
	−	☐
		☐

3 3)810

Hundreds	Tens	Ones
☐	☐	☐
3)8	1	0
− ☐	↓	
☐	☐	
− ☐	☐	↓
	☐	☐
	−	☐
		☐

Divide and check.

4 6)120

5 5)250

6 3)320

7 800 ÷ 4 =

8 408 ÷ 4 =

9 930 ÷ 3 =

10 670 ÷ 3 =

11 909 ÷ 3 =

12 750 ÷ 5 =

▶ **Quiz**

Divide and check.

13 300 ÷ 6 =

14 630 ÷ 6 =

15 50 ÷ 5 =

16 608 ÷ 3 =

17 420 ÷ 6 =

18 907 ÷ 3 =

15 Minutes

OBJECTIVE Use basic facts and patterns to find quotients mentally

As you begin, you may want to remind students that as the number of zeros in the dividend increases, the number of zeros in the quotient also increases.

Begin the lesson by writing:

$6{,}400 \div 8 = \square$

Remind students that they can use basic facts and patterns to find this quotient mentally.

Ask: **What division fact do you see in this equation?** $64 \div 8 = 8$ Write this equation on the board above the original equation. Ask: **What is the difference between these two equations? There are two zeros following the dividend in $6{,}400 \div 8$. What pattern can you use to help you find the quotient? If the number of zeros in the dividend is increased by 2 zeros, the number of zeros in the quotient will be increased by 2 zeros. Using this pattern, what is the answer to $6{,}400 \div 8 = \square$?** 800

TRY THESE Exercises 1–4 provide practice in using basic facts and patterns to find quotients.

- **Exercises 1–2** The number of zeros in the dividend and the quotient increased by one.

- **Exercises 3–4** The number of zeros in the dividend and the quotient increased by two.

PRACTICE ON YOUR OWN Review the examples at the top of the page. As students work through the examples, ask them to name the basic facts they will use and the patterns made by the zeros.

QUIZ Determine if students can use basic facts and patterns to find quotients mentally. Success is indicated by 6 out of 8 correct responses.

Students who successfully complete **Practice on Your Own** and **Quiz** are ready to move to the next skill.

COMMON ERRORS

- Students may use the wrong basic fact.

- Students may count the zeros in the quotients of basic facts as zeros to be added.

Students who make more than 5 errors in **Practice on Your Own**, or who were not successful in the **Quiz** section may benefit from the **Alternative Teaching Strategy** on the next page.

Alternative Teaching Strategy
Model Mental Math Division Patterns

OBJECTIVE Model using basic facts and patterns to find quotients mentally

MATERIALS chart paper, index cards, tape

You may want to give students a tip to remember the parts of a division problem.

The divid<u>end</u> is on the *end*.
Just as an act<u>or</u> does the acting in a show, a divis<u>or</u> does the dividing in the problem. The <u>quotient</u> is the answer.

On a piece of chart paper, write *30 ÷ 6 =*. Leave about 4 inches between each number and symbol. Then write a zero on each of ten index cards.

Ask: **What is the quotient 30 ÷ 6? 5**
Point out to students that the dividend in this equation has a zero in the ones place. Next, put a zero card after 30 to make 300.

Ask: **What is the dividend now? 300**
Underline 30 on the chart paper and explain that this number was part of the original basic fact. Ask: **By how many zeros did I increase the 30? 1 Using our division pattern, by how many zeros will I increase the quotient? 1**

Write these equations on the chart, underlining the original dividend of 30 in each:

$$\underline{30} \div 6 = \underline{}$$
$$\underline{300} \div 6 = \underline{}$$
$$\underline{3000} \div 6 = \underline{}$$

$$30 \quad \div \quad 6 \quad = \quad 5$$
$$30\boxed{0} \quad \div \quad 6 \quad = \quad 5\boxed{0}$$
$$30\boxed{0}\boxed{0} \div \quad 6 \quad = \quad 5\boxed{0}\boxed{0}$$

Point out that because the original basic fact had a zero in the dividend, the number of zeros in the dividend and quotient will not be the same. Explain that this happens *only* with division facts in which the dividend has a zero in ones place.

Write this equation on the chart:

$$40 \div 8 = \square$$

Ask students to solve the problem and write the answer. Then place a zero card behind the 40 to make 400. Ask: **Using our division pattern, what is the quotient? 50** Place a zero card after the 5 to demonstrate. Then place another zero to the dividend to make 4,000. Ask a volunteer to use a zero card to change the quotient to fit the pattern.

Repeat with other division equations that may or may not have a zero in the dividend.

Grade 4
Skill 30

Mental Math: Division Patterns

Find $5,600 \div 7 = \square$.

Step 1 Use a basic fact.

dividend		divisor		quotient
56	÷	7	=	8

Think: What is the basic fact?

Step 2 Use patterns.

dividend		divisor		quotient
56	÷	7	=	8
560	÷	7	=	80
5,600	÷	7	=	800

two zeros ↗   ↖ two zeros

Step 3 Find the quotient mentally.

dividend		divisor		quotient
5,600	÷	7	=	800

As the number of zeros in the dividend increases, the number of zeros in the quotient also increases.

▶ Try These

Use a basic division fact and patterns to write each quotient.

1 $420 \div 6 = \square$

dividend		divisor		quotient
42	÷	6	=	7
420	÷	6	=	☐

2 $350 \div 7 = \square$

dividend		divisor		quotient
35	÷	7	=	☐
350	÷	7	=	☐

3 $3,600 \div 6 = \square$

dividend		divisor		quotient
36	÷	6	=	☐
360	÷	6	=	☐
3,600	÷	6	=	☐

4 $2,700 \div 3 = \square$

dividend		divisor		quotient
27	÷	3	=	☐
270	÷	3	=	☐
2,700	÷	3	=	☐

Go to the next side.

Practice on Your Own

Skill 30

Find $1,800 \div 6 = \square$.

Use a basic division fact and the pattern of zeros to find the quotient.

Think:
$18 \div 6 = 3$

Think:
As the number of zeros in the dividend increases, the number of zeros in the quotient also increases.

Use a basic division fact and patterns to write each quotient.

1 $2,400 \div 8 = \square$

$24 \div 8 = \square$
$240 \div 8 = \square$
$2,400 \div 8 = \square$

2 $300 \div 5 = \square$

$30 \div 5 = \square$
$300 \div 5 = \square$

3 $54,000 \div 9 = \square$

$54 \div 9 = \square$
$540 \div 9 = \square$
$5,400 \div 9 = \square$
$54,000 \div 9 = \square$

4 $15,000 \div 3 = \square$

$15 \div 3 = \square$
$150 \div 3 = \square$
$1,500 \div 3 = \square$
$15,000 \div 3 = \square$

5 $1,600 \div 4 = \square$

$16 \div 4 = \square$
$160 \div 4 = \square$
$1,600 \div 4 = \square$

6 $180 \div 6 = \square$

$18 \div 6 = \square$
$180 \div 6 = \square$

Divide mentally. Write the basic division fact and the quotient.

7 $45,000 \div 9 = \square$

8 $2,100 \div 7 = \square$

9 $2,800 \div 4 = \square$

10 $320 \div 4 = \square$

11 $1,200 \div 2 = \square$

12 $63,000 \div 9 = \square$

13 $400 \div 5 = \square$

14 $4,900 \div 7 = \square$

15 $560 \div 8 = \square$

16 $8,100 \div 9 = \square$

17 $64,000 \div 8 = \square$

18 $91,000 \div 10 = \square$

▶ Quiz

Use a basic division fact and patterns to write each quotient.

19 $4,800 \div 6 = \square$

20 $36,000 \div 6 = \square$

21 $20,000 \div 10 = \square$

22 $480 \div 8 = \square$

23 $2,700 \div 9 = \square$

24 $25,000 \div 5 = \square$

25 $180 \div 3 = \square$

26 $45,000 \div 5 = \square$

Number Sense, Concepts, and Operations

Fractions

15 Minutes

OBJECTIVE Count parts of a whole

MATERIALS (optional) fraction strips

You may wish to begin the lesson by reviewing how to model a fraction. Display a fraction strip for 1 third and have students tell you the fraction and write it as shown below.

$$\frac{1}{3}$$ ← parts shaded
← number of equal parts in the whole

Review the meaning of numerator and denominator. Then, direct the students' attention to the rectangle in Model A.

Ask: **Into how many equal parts is the whole figure divided? 4 How many parts are shaded? 1 What fraction shows that just one part is shaded?** $\frac{1}{4}$ **What if 4 out of 4 parts were shaded, then what fraction shows 4 out of 4 parts shaded?** $\frac{4}{4}$

Direct students' attention to Model B.

Ask: **As the number of shaded parts increases, what do you notice about the number of equal parts or the denominator? The number stays the same.**

Then have students name each fraction, explaining that they are counting by fourths.

TRY THESE In these three exercises students count parts of a whole step-by-step.

• **Exercise 1** One part shaded.

• **Exercise 2** Two parts shaded.

• **Exercise 3** Three parts shaded.

PRACTICE ON YOUR OWN Review the example at the top of the page. Have students identify the numerator 3 and denominator 5.

QUIZ Make sure students can distinguish the parts from the whole, and can represent the fraction correctly. Success is determined by 2 out of 3 correct responses.

Students who successfully complete the **Practice on Your Own** and **Quiz** are ready to move on to the next skill.

COMMON ERRORS

• Students may confuse the numerator and the denominator.

• Students may compare shaded and unshaded parts to each other, and record the fraction as part-to-part relationship.

Students who made more than 2 errors in the **Practice on Your Own**, or were not successful in the **Quiz** section, may benefit from the **Alternative Teaching Strategy** on the next page.

Alternative Teaching Strategy
Count Parts of a Whole

20 Minutes

OBJECTIVE Count parts of a whole

MATERIALS Fraction strips for the fractions: $\frac{0}{5}, \frac{1}{5}, \frac{2}{5}, \frac{3}{5}, \frac{4}{5}, \frac{5}{5}$

Make corresponding fraction flash cards. Prepare sets of flash cards for other fractions.

Before beginning, review with the class how to model a fraction. Review the meaning of numerator and denominator.

Then distribute a set of shaded figures to the students. Have them arrange the figures in order, from no parts shaded to all parts shaded.

Distribute the corresponding fractions. Have them match fractions and figures. $\frac{0}{5}, \frac{1}{5}, \frac{2}{5}, \frac{3}{5}, \frac{4}{5}, \frac{5}{5}$

Repeat the activity with other fraction sets. Then take out some of the figures or flash cards and have students identify which are missing.

Finally, use only the flash cards to encourage students to count fractions in symbolic form only.

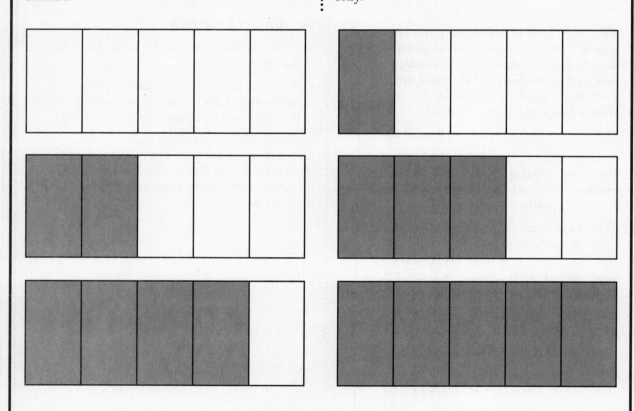

Grade 4
Skill 31

Parts of a Whole

You can write a fraction to show how many parts of a whole are shaded.

Model A

The whole figure is divided into 4 equal-size parts.

1 of **4** parts are shaded.

So, 1 fourth of the whole is shaded.

part shaded ⟶ $\frac{1}{4}$
parts in the whole ⟶

Model B

You can use a pattern to write fractions for the shaded part of a whole.

Model				
Parts Shaded	0	1	2	3	4
Number of Equal Parts	4	4	4	4	4
Fraction	$\frac{0}{4}$	$\frac{1}{4}$	$\frac{2}{4}$	$\frac{3}{4}$	$\frac{4}{4}$

Try These

Complete to show part of a whole.

1

☐ out of ☐ parts shaded

☐ ⟵ parts shaded
☐ ⟵ parts in the whole

2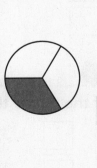

☐ out of ☐ parts shaded

☐ ⟵ parts shaded
☐ ⟵ parts in the whole

3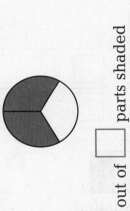

☐ out of ☐ parts shaded

☐ ⟵ parts shaded
☐ ⟵ parts in the whole

Go to the next side.

Practice on Your Own

Think:

The whole is divided into
5 equal parts.

3 out of **5** parts are shaded.

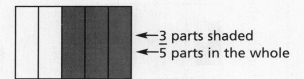

←3 parts shaded
←5 parts in the whole

Complete. Show the part of the whole that is shaded.

Model						
1 Parts Shaded						
2 Number of Equal Parts						
3 Fraction						

4 ☐/☐ ←parts shaded / ←parts in whole

5 ☐/☐ ←parts shaded / ←parts in whole

6 ☐/☐ ←parts shaded / ←parts in whole

7 ☐/☐

8 ☐/☐

9 ☐/☐

▶ Quiz

Show the part of the whole that is shaded.

10 ☐/☐

11 ☐/☐

12 ☐/☐

OBJECTIVE Count parts of a set

MATERIALS (optional) two-color counters

15 Minutes

You may wish to have students represent Model A and Model B with two-color counters.

Ask students to count the number of parts in Model A. 5 Verify that they recognize the parts as the encircled figures. Have students confirm that each part is 1 fifth of the set. Then have them count by fifths: 1 fifth, 2 fifths, and so forth.

Ask: **How many fifths make a whole set? 5 If no parts of the set are shaded, how many fifths is that? 0 fifths If one part is shaded, how many fifths is that? 1 fifth**

Recall that the numerator of the fraction represents the number of parts being considered, and the denominator represents the number of parts in the whole set.

As you work through Model B with the students, ask: **In the pattern, what number in the fraction stays the same? The denominator Why? because the number of parts in the whole set does not change What number changes? the numerator, because the number of parts being considered changes**

TRY THESE Exercises 1–3 show a pattern of thirds of the set. The sentence, for example,

_____ out of _____ **parts are shaded,**

helps students keep track of the number of parts and reinforce part-to-set concepts.

PRACTICE ON YOUR OWN Review the example at the top of the page with students. You may wish to have them represent the parts with counters. Ask student to count from 1 sixth to 6 sixths.

Exercises 1–3 provide a pattern for the students to complete. Exercises 4–6 are not patterned, however, students are supported with cued fraction boxes. Exercises 7–9 provide an opportunity for students to record fractions without written cues.

QUIZ Determine if students recognize that the numerator counts the number of parts being considered. Success is determined by 2 out of 3 correct responses.

Students who successfully complete the **Practice on Your Own** and the **Quiz** are ready to move to the next skill.

COMMON ERRORS

- Students may write the numerator correctly, but may write the number of figures in one part as the denominator.

- Students may count parts correctly, but record the number of parts being considered as the denominator and name the numerator as 1.

Students who made more than 2 errors in **Practice on Your Own**, or were not successful in the **Quiz** section, may benefit from the **Alternative Teaching Strategy** on the next page.

Alternative Teaching Strategy
Count Parts of a Set

⏱ 20 Minutes

OBJECTIVE Use concrete models to represent and count parts of a set

MATERIALS 2-color counters (or construction paper cut into small squares), construction paper student-made workmats

Have students use construction paper or notebook paper to make workmats for 3, 4, 5, 6, . . . parts in a set.

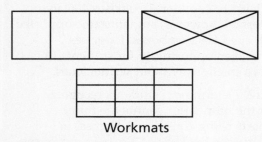

Workmats

Begin with the mat for thirds. Distribute a set of counters to each student and have the students use 6 of the counters.

Ask the students to make 3 equal sets using the counters and the workmats. Have them tell you the number of parts and orally count: 1 third, 2 thirds, 3 thirds.

Next, have students remove the counters, and now partition 12 counters into 3 equal sets. Have them count by thirds again.

Ask students to show $\frac{1}{3}$ by turning the counters in 1 part to the second color.

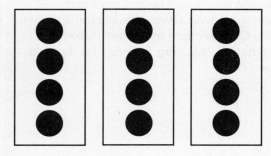

Count: 1 third, 2 thirds, 3 thirds

Repeat the activity for fourths or fifths. Each time have students count using the fraction name: 1 fourth, 2 fourths, 3 fourths, 4 fourths.

After students have completed several examples in this way, have them draw a picture of a set of 15 figures separated into 5 parts. Ask students to write the fractions to represent 1 of 5 parts, 2 of 5 parts, and so on.

As a culminating activity, show these fractions:

$$\frac{\square}{5} \quad \frac{\square}{8} \quad \frac{\square}{9}$$

Have students tell you the number of parts in a set with each denominator, then count to tell the fractions for each set (e.g., 1 fifth, 2 fifths, 3 fifths, . . .).

Grade 4
Skill
32

Parts of a Set

You can write a fraction to show how many parts of a set are shaded.

Model A
There are 5 parts in this set.

0 of 5 parts are shaded.

parts shaded ⟶ $\dfrac{0}{5}$
number of parts in the set ⟶

Model B
You can use a pattern to write fractions for the shaded parts.

Model					
Parts Shaded	0	1	2	3	4	5
Number of Parts	5	5	5	5	5	5
Fraction	$\dfrac{0}{5}$	$\dfrac{1}{5}$	$\dfrac{2}{5}$	$\dfrac{3}{5}$	$\dfrac{4}{5}$	$\dfrac{5}{5}$

▲ Try These

Complete to show how many parts are shaded.

1

□ out of □ parts are shaded.

□ ⟵ parts shaded
□ ⟵ number of parts in the set

2

□ out of □ parts are shaded.

□ ⟵ parts shaded
□ ⟵ number of parts in the set

3

□ out of □ parts are shaded.

□ ⟵ parts shaded
□ ⟵ number of parts in the set

Go to the next side.

Practice on Your Own

Skill 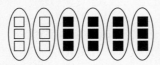 **32**

Think: There are 6 parts in this set.

4 out of **6** parts are shaded.

parts shaded ——→ 4
number of parts ——→ 6

- -

Complete to show how many parts are shaded.

Model					
1 Parts Shaded					
2 Number of Parts					
3 Fraction	⬚/⬚	⬚/⬚	⬚/⬚	⬚/⬚	⬚/⬚

Complete to show how many parts are shaded.

4 ⬚ ← parts shaded ⬚ ← parts in the set

5 ⬚ ← parts shaded ⬚ ← parts in the set

6 ⬚ ← parts shaded ⬚ ← parts in the set

7 ⬚/⬚   **8** ⬚/⬚   **9** ⬚/⬚

▶ Quiz

Complete to show how many parts are shaded.

10 ⬚/⬚   **11** ⬚/⬚   **12** ⬚/⬚

OBJECTIVE Write equivalent fractions and recognize when a fraction is in simplest form

It may be helpful to begin by reviewing the terms *numerator, denominator,* and *equivalent* with students. Then, have students read the example.

Say: **Look at the first way to find an equivalent fraction.**

Ask: **What was done to create an equivalent fraction? A different fraction bar was used to show the same amount. How could you find other equivalent fractions? by lining up fraction bars of other values to show the same amount**

Point out that there is another way to find equivalent fractions. Discuss with students that multiplying or dividing a number by 1 does not change the value of the number. Review fractions that are equivalent to 1.

Ask: **How is an equivalent fraction found in the first example? by multiplying the numerator and denominator by the same number, 2 How is the equivalent fraction found in the second example? by dividing the numerator and denominator by the same number, 2**

Make sure that students understand that multiplying or dividing by $\frac{2}{2}$ (or any other fraction with the same numerator and denominator) is the same as multiplying or dividing by 1. The value of the fraction does not change.

Explain to students that one way fractions are written in simplest form is by dividing the numerator and denominator by the same number. Stress the importance of checking to make sure that the fraction cannot be divided further.

TRY THESE Exercises 1–3 provide students with the opportunity to write equivalent fractions and to write a fraction in simplest form.

- **Exercises 1–3:** Write equivalent fractions and write fractions in simplest form.

PRACTICE ON YOUR OWN Review the examples at the top of the page to help students write equivalent fractions and to write fractions in simplest form. Explain to students that multiplication can always be used to create equivalent fractions. Division can be used only if the fraction is not in simplest form.

QUIZ Determine if students can write equivalent fractions. Success is indicated by 3 out of 4 correct responses.

Students who successfully complete **Practice on Your Own** and **Quiz** are ready to move to the next skill.

COMMON ERRORS

- Students may multiply or divide only the numerator or denominator of the fraction.

- Students may not divide by the greatest common factor when writing a fraction in simplest form.

Students who made more than 3 errors in **Practice on Your Own**, or who were not successful in the **Quiz** section, may benefit from the **Alternative Teaching Strategy** on the next page.

Alternative Teaching Strategy
Model Equivalent Fractions

15 Minutes

OBJECTIVE Use models to create equivalent fractions

MATERIALS two-color counters

Model two fractions equivalent to $\frac{6}{8}$.

Draw 8 circles and shade 6 of them.

Say: **There are 8 circles and 6 of them are shaded. So, $\frac{6}{8}$ of them are shaded. The denominator represents how many circles there are in all. The numerator represents how many circles are shaded. Now use the two-color counters to model $\frac{6}{8}$.**

Say: **You can also create equivalent fractions by multiplying the numerator and denominator by the same number.**

Ask: **If you multiply the denominator by 2, how many counters should you have? 16 If you multiply the numerator by 2, how many should be a different color? 12**

Say: **Use your counters to model the fraction.**

Have students create a new model so that both fractions are shown.

Ask: **What fraction is modeled? $\frac{12}{16}$**

Say: **Sometimes, you can create equivalent fractions by dividing. Look at the original fraction, $\frac{6}{8}$.**

Ask: **What number can be used to divide both the numerator and denominator? 2 If you divide the denominator by 2, how many counters do you need to show? 4 If you divide the numerator by 2, how many counters do you need to show? 3** Have students model this equivalent fraction with counters. Check that students have the three correct models.

Ask: **What fraction is modeled? $\frac{3}{4}$**

Say: **Now, look at the three fractions that are modeled on your desk. Each of these is equivalent to the others.**

So, $\frac{6}{8}$ is equivalent to $\frac{12}{16}$ and $\frac{3}{4}$.

Say: **You can also create equivalent fractions by lining up fraction lines.**

Ask: **What should your fraction line be divided into to model $\frac{6}{8}$? eighths How many eighths do you need? 6 If you line up a fraction line divided into sixteenths, how many will be the same amount as 6 one-eighths? 12 How many one-fourths will you need to show the same amount? 3**

Have students make the fraction lines.

Say: **So, $\frac{6}{8}$ is equivalent to $\frac{3}{4}$ and $\frac{12}{16}$.**

Equivalent Fractions

Find equivalent fractions for $\frac{4}{6}$.

One Way

Step 1 Line up fraction bars to show $\frac{4}{6}$.

$\frac{1}{6}$	$\frac{1}{6}$	$\frac{1}{6}$	$\frac{1}{6}$

Step 2 Then line up other fraction bars that show the same amount as $\frac{4}{6}$.

$\frac{1}{6}$	$\frac{1}{6}$	$\frac{1}{6}$	$\frac{1}{6}$
$\frac{1}{3}$		$\frac{1}{3}$	
$\frac{1}{12}\ \frac{1}{12}$	$\frac{1}{12}\ \frac{1}{12}$	$\frac{1}{12}\ \frac{1}{12}$	$\frac{1}{12}\ \frac{1}{12}$

Fractions that line up with $\frac{4}{6}$ are equivalent to $\frac{4}{6}$.

So, $\frac{2}{3}$ and $\frac{8}{12}$ are equivalent to $\frac{4}{6}$.

Another Way

Multiply the numerator and denominator by the same number.
Try 2.

$$\frac{4}{6} = \frac{4 \times 2}{6 \times 2} = \frac{8}{12}$$

So, $\frac{8}{12}$ is equivalent to $\frac{4}{6}$.

Divide the numerator and denominator by the same number.
Try 2.

$$\frac{4}{6} = \frac{4 \div 2}{6 \div 2} = \frac{2}{3}$$

So, $\frac{2}{3}$ is equivalent to $\frac{4}{6}$.

Simplest Form

If you continue to divide until 1 is the only number that can be divided into the numerator and the denominator evenly, you find the fraction in **simplest form**.
Try 2.

$$\frac{4}{6} = \frac{4 \div 2}{6 \div 2} = \frac{2}{3}$$

Now the only number that can be divided into the numerator and denominator of $\frac{2}{3}$ evenly is 1.

So, the simplest form of $\frac{4}{6}$ is $\frac{2}{3}$.

Try These

Write two equivalent fractions for each. Then write the fraction in simplest form.

1

$\frac{1}{4}$	$\frac{1}{4}$	$\frac{1}{4}$	$\frac{1}{4}$
$\frac{1}{8}$	$\frac{1}{8}$	$\frac{1}{8}$	$\frac{1}{8}$
$\frac{1}{8}$	$\frac{1}{8}$	$\frac{1}{8}$	$\frac{1}{8}$

2 $\frac{8}{24}$

3 $\frac{6}{18}$

Go to the next side.

Practice on Your Own

Find an equivalent fraction for $\frac{2}{5}$. Since you cannot divide, multiply to find an equivalent fraction.

Try 2. $\frac{2}{5} = \frac{2 \times 2}{5 \times 2} = \frac{4}{10}$

So, $\frac{4}{10}$ is equivalent to $\frac{2}{5}$.

Find the simplest form of $\frac{4}{16}$.

Try 4. Divide the numerator and denominator by 4.

$$\frac{4}{16} = \frac{4 \div 4}{16 \div 4} = \frac{1}{4}$$

So, the simplest form of $\frac{4}{16}$ is $\frac{1}{4}$.

Write two equivalent fractions for each. Then write the fraction in simplest form.

1

$\frac{1}{8}$	$\frac{1}{8}$	$\frac{1}{8}$	$\frac{1}{8}$	$\frac{1}{8}$	$\frac{1}{8}$

2

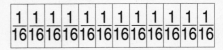

3 $\frac{5}{25}$ **4** $\frac{2}{8}$ **5** $\frac{12}{15}$ **6** $\frac{1}{6}$

7 $\frac{5}{30}$ **8** $\frac{4}{8}$ **9** $\frac{24}{36}$ **10** $\frac{8}{40}$

11 $\frac{1}{4}$ **12** $\frac{21}{28}$ **13** $\frac{8}{12}$ **14** $\frac{2}{6}$

▶ Quiz

Write two equivalent fractions for each. Then write in simplest form.

15 $\frac{6}{8}$ **16** $\frac{2}{12}$ **17** $\frac{3}{9}$ **18** $\frac{8}{48}$

15 Minutes

OBJECTIVE Rename fractions and compare mixed numbers

It will be helpful to review the terms **numerator** and **denominator** before beginning this lesson. Remind students that a fraction represents a part of a whole.

Ask students to look at the example in the first box.

Say: **A mixed number is made up of a whole number and a fraction. Which whole number is shown here? 1 Which fraction bar is used? $\frac{1}{4}$ How many $\frac{1}{4}$-bars are there? 3**

Ask: **What mixed number can we write for this picture? $1\frac{3}{4}$**

Now say: **In the second box, two mixed numbers are compared on the number line. Which two whole numbers is $2\frac{2}{3}$ between? 2 and 3 Which two whole numbers is $3\frac{1}{4}$ between? 3 and 4 Which mixed number is to the right? $3\frac{1}{4}$. So $3\frac{1}{4}$ is greater than $2\frac{2}{3}$.**

Ask students to look at the third box.

Say: **The fraction $\frac{17}{5}$ is renamed using division. Which part becomes the numerator of the mixed number? the remainder Which part is the whole number? the quotient**

TRY THESE In Exercises 1–3, students practice the types of activities they will find in the **Practice on Your Own** section.

- **Exercise 1**   Write a mixed number from a picture.

- **Exercise 2**   Compare mixed numbers using a number line.

- **Exercise 3**   Rename an improper fraction as a mixed number using division.

PRACTICE ON YOUR OWN Review the examples at the top of the page. Stress that mixed numbers consist of a whole number added to a fraction. Students should be able to convert between mixed numbers and improper fractions.

QUIZ Determine if students can successfully rewrite improper fractions as mixed numbers and then compare them. Success is indicated by 2 out of 3 correct responses.

Students who successfully complete the **Practice on Your Own** and **Quiz** are ready to move to the next skill.

COMMON ERRORS

- Students will compare improper fractions by comparing only the numerators.

- Students will use the incorrect parts of the division problem to create a mixed number.

Students who made more than 2 errors in the **Practice on Your Own**, or who were not successful in the **Quiz** section, may benefit from the **Alternative Teaching Strategy** on the next page.

Alternative Teaching Strategy
Model and Compare Mixed Numbers

OBJECTIVE Model and compare mixed numbers

Compare $\frac{9}{2}$ and $\frac{10}{4}$.

Draw 5 circles on the chalkboard and ask students to do the same on a sheet of paper.

Say: **Now divide each circle in half by drawing a line through it. Color in 9 of the halves.**

Ask: **How many whole circles are colored? 4 How many halves are left over? 1 How can we write this as a mixed number? $4\frac{1}{2}$**

Now say: **Draw 3 more circles. Divide these circles in fourths. Color in 10 of the fourths.** Stress to students that they should complete one circle before moving to the next while they are coloring.

Ask: **How many whole circles are colored now? 2 How many fourths are left over? 2**

What mixed number can be written to show this? $2\frac{2}{4}$ or $2\frac{1}{2}$ If students say $2\frac{2}{4}$, show them that $\frac{2}{4}$ can be written in simplest form as $\frac{1}{2}$.

Now say: **Let's compare the two mixed numbers we have written. What is the whole number in $4\frac{1}{2}$? 4 What is the whole number in $2\frac{1}{2}$? 2 Compare the whole numbers. Which is greater? 4**

Say: **Since $4 > 2$, we can say that $4\frac{1}{2} > 2\frac{1}{2}$.**

Grade 4
Skill 34

Mixed Numbers

Write a mixed number for the picture.

$\frac{1}{4}$	$\frac{1}{4}$	$\frac{1}{4}$
$\frac{1}{4}$	$\frac{1}{4}$	$\frac{1}{4}$
$\frac{1}{4}$	$\frac{1}{4}$	$\frac{1}{4}$
$\frac{1}{4}$	$\frac{1}{4}$	$\frac{1}{4}$

There is one whole-bar and three $\frac{1}{4}$-bars.

So, the mixed number is $1\frac{3}{4}$.

Compare $2\frac{2}{3}$ and $3\frac{1}{4}$ using a number line.

$3\frac{1}{4}$ is to the right of $2\frac{2}{3}$, so $3\frac{1}{4} > 2\frac{2}{3}$.

Rewrite $\frac{17}{5}$ as a mixed number.

Divide 17 by 5 to find the whole number. Then use the remainder to write the fractional part.

$$\text{denominator} \rightarrow 5\overline{)17} \quad \begin{array}{l} 3 \leftarrow \text{whole number} \\ -15 \\ \hline 2 \leftarrow \text{numerator} \end{array}$$

So, $\frac{17}{5}$ can be rewritten as $3\frac{2}{5}$.

Try These

1 Write a mixed number for the picture.

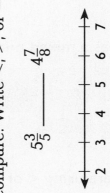

_____

2 Compare. Write $<$, $>$, or $=$.

$5\frac{3}{5}$ _____ $4\frac{7}{8}$

3 Rename $\frac{23}{6}$ as a mixed number.

Divide. $6\overline{)23}$ Then rewrite. $\dfrac{\square}{\square}$

$\square\overline{)23}$
$-\square\square$

_____

Go to the next side.

Practice on Your Own

Write a mixed number.	Compare $3\frac{1}{8}$ __ $4\frac{1}{5}$.	Write $\frac{11}{5}$ as a mixed number.
There are 3 whole-bars. There is 1 $\frac{1}{2}$-bar. **So,** the mixed number is $3\frac{1}{2}$.	Place the mixed numbers on the number line. 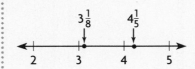 $4\frac{1}{5}$ is to the right of $3\frac{1}{8}$, so $4\frac{1}{5} > 3\frac{1}{8}$.	Divide. $\begin{array}{r} 2 \\ 5\overline{)11} \\ -10 \\ \hline 1 \end{array}$ **So,** $\frac{11}{5}$ can be rewritten as $2\frac{1}{5}$.

Write as a mixed number.

1  _____

2  _____

Compare using < or >.

3 $3\frac{1}{4}$ _____ $4\frac{1}{5}$

4 $1\frac{7}{8}$ _____ $2\frac{1}{7}$

5 $5\frac{2}{3}$ _____ $3\frac{2}{5}$

Write as a mixed number.

6 $\frac{12}{5}$ _____

7 $\frac{17}{8}$ _____

8 $\frac{7}{2}$ _____

▶ Quiz

9 Write the mixed number. 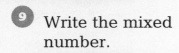 _____	**10** Compare. $5\frac{4}{5}$ _____ $6\frac{1}{2}$	**11** Rewrite $\frac{25}{3}$ as a mixed number. _____

15 Minutes

OBJECTIVE Write fractions with denominators of 10 and 100.

MATERIALS decimal squares

Begin by reminding students that when a whole is divided into equal parts, each part is a fraction of the whole.

Direct students' attention to the first example.

Ask: **Into how many equal parts is the square divided?** 10 **What fraction does one part represent?** $\frac{1}{10}$ **How many parts are shaded?** 2 **What fraction of the square is shaded?** $\frac{2}{10}$

Continue to ask similar questions as you work through the next two examples. You may wish to display decimal squares as you work through the next examples.

Point out that for each example, the same size square was divided into equal parts. Note that the tenths parts are larger than the hundredths parts.

TRY THESE Exercises 1–3 model the type of exercises students will find on the **Practice on Your Own** page.

- **Exercise 1** Fraction with a denominator of 10.

- **Exercise 2** Fraction with a denominator of 100.

- **Exercise 3** Equivalent fractions.

PRACTICE ON YOUR OWN Review the example at the top of the page. Ask students to explain how they know the models have the same amount shaded. **The region or area for $\frac{5}{10}$ is the same size as the area for $\frac{50}{100}$.**

QUIZ Determine if the students can identify the correct name for each denominator, can write fractions for tenths and hundredths, and can recognize equivalent fractions. Success is determined by 2 out of 3 correct responses.

Students who successfully complete the **Practice on Your Own** and **Quiz** are ready to move on to the next skill.

COMMON ERRORS

- Students may count the wrong number of shaded parts or count the parts that are not shaded.

- Students may write the correct numerator, but write the number of unshaded parts as the denominator.

- Students may write all denominators as 10 or as 100 without regard to the number of the parts in the model.

Students who made more than 3 errors in the **Practice on Your Own**, or who were not successful in the **Quiz** section, may benefit from the **Alternative Teaching Strategy** on the next page.

Alternative Teaching Strategy
Model Fractions with Denominators of 10 and 100

15 Minutes

OBJECTIVE Use decimal squares to represent fractions with denominators of 10 and 100.

MATERIALS decimal squares, paper

Distribute the decimal squares.

Have students separate them into two piles. One pile has squares divided into 10 equal parts and the other pile has squares that are divided into 100 equal parts.

Say: **Find the square that would represent the fraction $\frac{3}{10}$.**

Ask: **Into how many equal parts is the square divided? 10 Does this number represent the numerator or denominator of the fraction? denominator How many parts out of 10 are shaded? 3 out of 10 parts**

Say: **Then this number represents the numerator of the fraction.**

Have students record the fraction.

Continue with the square for 30 hundredths.

Say: **Find a square divided into 100 equal parts with the same area shaded as $\frac{3}{10}$.**

After the students have found the square, Ask: **How many parts out of 100 are shaded? 30 out of 100 parts**

What fraction does this square show? $\frac{30}{100}$

Have students record the fraction to the right of $\frac{3}{10}$.

Explain that the two fractions are equal. Ask students to show this by writing an equal sign between $\frac{3}{10}$ and $\frac{30}{100}$.

Repeat this activity with similar examples. As the students select squares, have them tell you the fraction name.

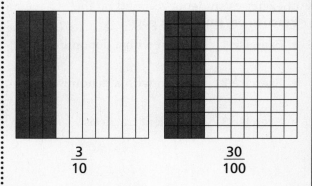

$$\frac{3}{10}$$ $$\frac{30}{100}$$

Grade 4
Skill
35

Read and Write Fractions

A fraction is a number that names part of a whole.

Fractions with Denominators of 10

The whole is divided into 10 equal parts. Each part is one tenth.

2 out of 10 parts are shaded.

Read: two tenths

Write: $\dfrac{2}{10}$ ← parts shaded
       ← parts in the whole

Fractions with Denominators of 100

The whole is divided into 100 equal parts. Each part is one hundredth.

20 out of 100 parts are shaded.

Read: twenty hundredths

Write: $\dfrac{20}{100}$ ← parts shaded
       ← parts in the whole

Equivalent Fractions

Equivalent fractions name the same amount.

Compare the shaded parts of the models. They are the same size.

$$\frac{2}{10} = \frac{20}{100}$$

So, $\frac{2}{10}$ and $\frac{20}{100}$ are equivalent fractions.

▲ Try These

Complete.

1

Read: _____ tenth

Write: $\dfrac{\square}{\square}$ ← parts shaded
       ← parts in the whole

2

Read: _____ hundredths

Write: $\dfrac{\square}{\square}$ ← parts shaded
       ← parts in the whole

3

Complete to show equivalent fractions.

$$\frac{\square}{\square} = \frac{\square}{\square}$$

Go to the next side.

Practice on Your Own

Think:
The models have the same amount shaded. So, the fractions are equivalent.

$$\frac{5}{10} = \frac{50}{100}$$

five tenths = fifty hundredths

Write a fraction for each.

1 three tenths

☐
―
☐

2 9 tenths

☐
―
☐

3 twenty-five hundredths

☐
―
☐

4 ninety hundredths

☐
―
☐

Complete to show equivalent fractions.

5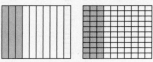

$$\frac{3}{10} = \frac{\boxed{}}{100}$$

6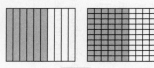

$$\frac{6}{10} = \frac{\boxed{}}{100}$$

7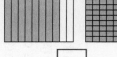

$$\frac{8}{10} = \frac{\boxed{}}{100}$$

8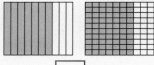

$$\frac{7}{10} = \frac{\boxed{}}{100}$$

9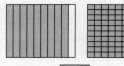

$$\frac{9}{10} = \frac{\boxed{}}{100}$$

10

$$\frac{10}{10} = \frac{\boxed{}}{100}$$

▶ Quiz

11 Write a fraction for seven tenths.

☐
―
☐

12 Write a fraction for seventy-five hundredths.

☐
―
☐

13 Complete to show equivalent fractions.

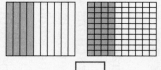

$$\frac{4}{10} = \frac{\boxed{}}{100}$$

Number Sense, Concepts, and Operations

Decimals

20 Minutes

OBJECTIVE Relate decimals to money

You may wish to begin the lesson by discussing with students why money is written using decimals. Explain that the amounts shown to the right of the decimal point represent parts of a dollar.

Direct students' attention to the first example.

Ask: **How many dimes are in 1 dollar? 10 What part or fraction of a dollar is 1 dime? $\frac{1}{10}$ You write $\frac{1}{10}$ of a dollar as $0.10.**

How many pennies are in 1 dollar? 100 What fraction of a dollar is 1 penny? $\frac{1}{100}$ How do you write $\frac{1}{100}$ of a dollar as a decimal? $0.01

Point out the relationship between decimal notation and money notation in the next example.

You may wish to show students the expanded form of 15 hundredths and 15 cents so students understand the meaning of the digits in each place.

$$0.15 = 0.10 + 0.05$$

$$\$0.15 = \$0.10 + \$0.05$$

TRY THESE Exercises 1–3 model the type of exercises students will find on the **Practice on Your Own** page.

• **Exercises 1–3** Write amounts written in money notation as a number of dimes and pennies, then as tenths and hundredths.

PRACTICE ON YOUR OWN Review the example at the top of the page. Ask students to explain how dimes and tenths are related. Help students understand that 1 dime is $\frac{1}{10}$ of a dollar.

QUIZ Determine if students can write amounts of money using money notation. Success is determined by 2 out of 3 correct responses.

Students who successfully complete the **Practice on Your Own** and **Quiz** are ready to move on to the next skill.

COMMON ERRORS

• Students may write 1 penny as $0.1 thinking of it as 1 tenth of a dime.

• Students may forget to write the dollar sign.

Students who made more than 2 errors in the **Practice on Your Own**, or who were not successful in the **Quiz** section, may benefit from the **Alternative Teaching Strategy** on the next page.

Alternative Teaching Strategy
Model Relating Decimals to Money

20 Minutes

OBJECTIVE Model amounts of money and use money notation

MATERIALS play money (dollars, dimes, and pennies)

Distribute the play money. Display the dollar and ask the students to show you an equivalent amount using the dimes. Observe that 10 dimes or 10 tenths equal 1 dollar. Have students set aside 9 of the dimes.

Ask: **What part of a dollar is still showing?** $\frac{1}{10}$ Record the amount as $0.10.

Have students add 2 more dimes to the 1 on their desks.

Ask: **Now, what part of a dollar is represented?** $\frac{3}{10}$ **How would you write that using money notation?** **$0.30** Recall that this amount is read as 30 cents.

Now have students show an amount equivalent to 1 dollar using pennies. As students count the pennies, suggest that they arrange them in rows of 10. Observe that 100 pennies or 100 hundredths equal 1 dollar.

Have students move one penny aside.

Ask: **What part of a dollar does 1 penny represent?** $\frac{1}{100}$ of a dollar

Ask: **How would you write that using money notation?** **$0.01**

If students have trouble showing this, display a place-value table and record the amount in the table.

Continue building the connection between pennies and hundredths through amounts to 9 cents. When students have demonstrated understanding, work with amounts such as $0.24, $0.85, $1.10, $1.05, and $1.17.

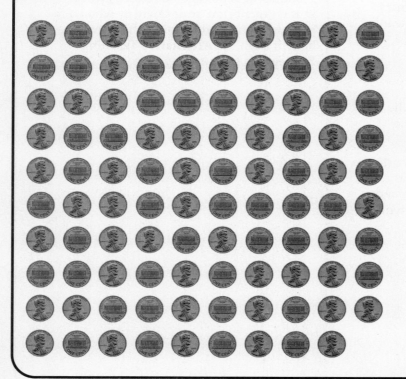

↑ 1 hundredth of 1 dollar
$0.01

Grade 4
Skill 36

Decimals and Money

Write amounts of money using decimals.

Dimes and Pennies
Here are some ways to think about dimes and pennies.

10 dimes = 1 dollar   100 pennies = 1 dollar
1 dime = 1 tenth of a dollar   1 penny = 1 hundredth of a dollar

$\frac{1}{10}$ of a dollar → $\frac{1}{100}$ of a dollar

0.1 of a dollar → 0.01 of a dollar or $0.01

$0.10

You can see that a dime and a tenth show $\frac{1}{10}$ of 100.
A penny and a hundredth show $\frac{1}{100}$ of 100.

Use a Place Value Chart
Use the place value chart to understand the meaning of $0.15 and 0.15.

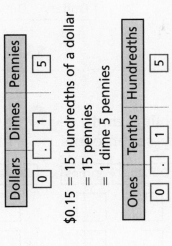

Dollars	Dimes	Pennies
0	. 1	5

$0.15 = 15 hundredths of a dollar
= 15 pennies
= 1 dime 5 pennies

Ones	Tenths	Hundredths
0	. 1	5

0.15 = 15 hundredths
= 1 tenth 5 hundredths

▲ Try These

Complete.

1

Dollars	Dimes	Pennies
0	. 4	7

$0.47 = ☐ dimes ☐ pennies

= ☐ tenths ☐ hundredths

2

Dollars	Dimes	Pennies
0	. 6	2

$0.62 = ☐ dimes ☐ pennies

= ☐ tenths ☐ hundredths

3

Dollars	Dimes	Pennies
0	. 2	3

$0.23 = ☐ dimes ☐ pennies

= ☐ tenths ☐ hundredths

Go to the next side.

Practice on Your Own

Skill 36

Think:
Use a place-value chart to write the money amount.

three dollars and forty-seven cents

Dollars	Dimes	Pennies
3	4	7

$3.47

Complete.

1 one dollar and eighty-four cents

Dollars	Dimes	Pennies
☐	☐	☐

$☐ . ☐ ☐

2 two dollars and twenty-seven cents

Dollars	Dimes	Pennies
☐	☐	☐

$☐ . ☐ ☐

3 two dollars and fifty-two cents

Dollars	Dimes	Pennies
☐	☐	☐

$☐ . ☐ ☐

4 three dollars and thirty-six cents

Dollars	Dimes	Pennies
☐	☐	☐

$☐ . ☐ ☐

5 five dollars and eight cents

Dollars	Dimes	Pennies
☐	☐	☐

$☐ . ☐ ☐

6 three cents

Dollars	Dimes	Pennies
☐	☐	☐

$☐ . ☐ ☐

Write the decimal.

7 one dollar and nineteen cents

$☐ . ☐ ☐

8 two dollars and five cents

$☐ . ☐ ☐

9 thirty-nine cents

$☐ . ☐ ☐

▶ Quiz

Write the decimal.

10 two dollars and eighty-two cents

$☐ . ☐ ☐

11 one dollar and eighteen cents

$☐ . ☐ ☐

12 fourteen cents

$☐ . ☐ ☐

OBJECTIVE Model decimals for tenths and hundredths

MATERIALS decimal squares

15 Minutes

Begin by pointing to the place-value labels on the place-value chart. Explain that any place value to the right of the decimal point ends in *ths*. Also recall that places to the right of the decimal point are less than 1.

Direct students' attention to the first example. Explain that the model represents a whole. It is not divided into parts. Point out that 1 can be written as a decimal: 1.0. The zero in the tenths place shows that there are no tenths.

Have students look at the model for tenths and compare it to the square for 1. Although they are the same size and shape, the tenths model is divided into 10 equal parts, one part is written as 0.1 to show that there are no ones and only 1 tenth. Continue in the same way for the example for hundredths.

TRY THESE Exercises 1–4 model the type of exercises students will find on the **Practice on Your Own** page.

- **Exercises 1–2** Write decimals for tenths.

- **Exercises 3–4** Write decimals for hundredths.

PRACTICE ON YOUR OWN Review the example at the top of the page. Work with students to compare the two models. Help students understand that 8 hundredths is a very small part of the whole and that 8 tenths is close to 1.

QUIZ Determine if students know the difference between tenths and hundredths. Success is determined by 2 out of 3 correct responses.

Students who successfully complete the **Practice on Your Own** and **Quiz** are ready to move on to the next skill.

COMMON ERRORS

- Students may write tenths in the tens place or may write tenths two places to the right of the decimal point.

- Students may write a decimal such as 3 hundredths as 0.300.

Students who made more than 2 errors in the **Practice on Your Own**, or who were not successful in the **Quiz** section, may benefit from the **Alternative Teaching Strategy** on the next page.

Alternative Teaching Strategy
Model Decimals (Tenths and Hundredths)

15 Minutes

OBJECTIVE Use decimal squares to model decimals

MATERIALS decimal squares

Begin by writing the following on the board for the students.

ones	.	tenths
0	.	6

Ask: **What does the zero in the ones place mean?** there are no ones **What does the digit 6 represent?** 6 tenths

Explain that the decimal separates ones from tenths and hundredths.

In the number six tenths, what does the tenths mean? The whole is divided into 10 equal parts

What does the six represent in the number six tenths? There are 6 out of 10 parts being considered.

Distribute the decimal squares. Ask students to find a decimal square that matches 0.6. Have students confirm that the square they chose represents 6 tenths. Students should be able to say that the whole is divided into 10 parts and 6 out of 10 parts are shaded.

Repeat this activity with similar examples. Each time, have the students use the place-value names when reading the numbers.

Grade 4
Skill 37

Relate Fractions and Decimals

Use decimal squares to model decimal numbers.

> A decimal uses place value and a decimal point to show values less than one.

This model represents one whole or 1.

ones	.	tenths
1	.	0

← decimal point

Read: one
Write: 1.0

The whole is divided into 10 equal parts.
1 of 10 equal parts of a whole is one tenth.
1 out of **10** equal parts is shaded. **So,** one tenth is shaded.

ones	.	tenths
0	.	1

Read: one tenth
Write: 0.1

The whole is divided into 100 equal parts.
1 of 100 equal parts of a whole is one hundredth.
1 out of **100** equal parts is shaded.
So, one hundredth is shaded.

ones	.	tenths	hundredths
0	.	0	1

Read: one hundredth
Write: 0.01

▲ Try These

Write how many parts are shaded. Write the decimal two ways.

1
| 3 | out of | 10 | parts shaded |

Read: _____ tenths
Write: _____ . _____

2
_____ out of _____ parts shaded

Read: _____ tenths
Write: _____ . _____

3
_____ out of _____ parts shaded

Read: _____ hundredths
Write: _____ . _____

4
_____ out of _____ parts shaded

Read: _____ hundredths
Write: _____ . _____

Go to the next side.

Practice on Your Own

Skill 37

8 out of 10 equal parts are shaded.

ones	.	tenths
0	.	8

Read: eight tenths

Write: 0.8

8 out of 100 equal parts are shaded.

ones	.	tenths	hundredths
0	.	0	8

Read: eight hundredths

Write: 0.08

Write how many parts are shaded. Write the decimal two ways.

1 ☐ out of ☐ parts shaded.

Read: ☐ tenths

Write: ☐ . ☐

2 ☐ out of ☐ parts shaded.

Read: ☐ tenths

Write: ☐ . ☐

3 ☐ out of ☐ parts shaded.

Read: ☐ tenths

Write: ☐ . ☐

4 Read: ☐ hundredths

Write: ☐ . ☐ ☐

5 Read: ☐ hundredths

Write: ☐ . ☐ ☐

6 Read: ☐ hundredths

Write: ☐ . ☐ ☐

Write the decimal for the shaded part.

7 ☐ . ☐

8 ☐ . ☐

9 ☐ . ☐

▶ Quiz

Write the decimal for the shaded part.

10 ☐ . ☐

11 ☐ . ☐ ☐

12 ☐ . ☐ ☐

OBJECTIVE Read and write decimal place value to thousandths

MATERIALS place-value charts

You may wish to review how a place-value chart can help students determine the value of the digits in a decimal number.

Direct students' attention to Step 1.

Explain that thousandths are smaller parts than hundredths. Ask students to identify the digits that are in the ones, tenths, hundredths, and thousandths positions.

Continue with Step 2. Guide students to understand that the value of a digit can be determined by its position in the number.

Ask: **What is the value of the digit 3? 3 thousandths or 0.003 What fraction represents this digit?** $\frac{3}{1,000}$

Repeat these steps with the digits 6 and 5. (6 hundredths or 0.06; $\frac{6}{100}$) (5 tenths or 0.5; $\frac{5}{10}$)

In Step 3, show students how place value relates to the denominator of the fraction. For thousandths, the denominator will always be 1,000.

TRY THESE Exercises 1–3 model the type of exercises students will find on the **Practice on Your Own** page.

- **Exercises 1–3** Students write decimals as fractions.

PRACTICE ON YOUR OWN Review the examples at the top of the page. Go over with students how to write numbers in the different forms. Exercises 1–8 ask students to write decimals as fractions. Exercises 9–16 have students write fractions as decimals. Exercises 17–20 have students use a place-value chart to find the value of a digit. In Exercises 21–23, students write the decimals two other ways.

QUIZ Determine if students can write the decimal as a fraction. Success is indicated by 3 out of 4 correct responses.

Students who successfully complete the **Practice on Your Own** and **Quiz** are ready to move to the next skill.

COMMON ERRORS

- Students may confuse positions on the place-value chart.

- Students may have difficulty understanding the value of 0.

- Students may not understand how to write a decimal as a fraction.

Students who make more than 7 errors in the **Practice on Your Own,** or who were not successful in the **Quiz** section may benefit from the **Alternative Teaching Strategy** on the next page.

Alternative Teaching Strategy
Read and Write Decimal Place Value

10 Minutes

OBJECTIVE Read and write decimal place value to thousandths

MATERIALS place-value charts, paper

Students work in pairs for this activity. Distribute a place-value chart to each pair. You may want to have students identify the ones, decimal point, tenths, hundredths, and thousandths columns on the place-value chart.

Explain to students that they will use the charts to practice writing decimals in words.

Write the number 0.243 on paper.
Ask: **What digit is in the ones place? 0**
You may want to point out that the remaining three digits follow the decimal point and are numbers less than one.
Ask: **What digit is in the tenths place? 2 hundredths place? 4 thousandths place? 3**

Guide students to understand that 2 tenths 4 hundredths 3 thousandths is the same as 0.243.

Ones	.	Tenths	Hundredths	Thousandths
0	.	2	4	3

Discuss with students how to write a decimal in words. Point to the 2, 4, and 3 on the place value chart and ask: **What number do these three digits make? 243** Tell them that first they will write this number in words. Since the zero is to the left of any other digit, they can disregard it.

Say: **Now find the place on the chart that is the farthest to the right of the decimal point.** Ask: **What number is farthest to the right? 3 What place is the 3 in? the thousandths** Explain that this last place tells them the last word they will write.

On paper, write: **two hundred forty-three thousandths.** Retrace the steps that led to finding each of the parts of this word form.

Repeat the activity with other examples.

Grade 4
Skill
38

Decimals to Thousandths

If one hundredth were divided into ten equal parts, each part would represent one *thousandth*.

You can use a place-value chart to help you understand thousandths.

Write 0.563 as a fraction.

Step 1
Use a place-value chart.

Ones	.	Tenths	Hundredths	Thousandths
0	.	5	6	3

Step 2
Write the value of each digit.

The value of the 5 is 5 tenths or $\frac{5}{10}$.

The value of the 6 is 6 hundredths or $\frac{6}{100}$.

The value of the 3 is 3 thousandths or $\frac{3}{1,000}$.

Step 3
Write the decimal as a fraction.

$$0.563 = \frac{563}{1,000}$$

Try These

Write each decimal as a fraction.

1 0.294

Ones	.	Tenths	Hundredths	Thousandths
0	.	2	9	4

2 0.107

Ones	.	Tenths	Hundredths	Thousandths
	.			

3 0.006

Ones	.	Tenths	Hundredths	Thousandths
	.			

Go to the next side.

Practice on Your Own

Skill 38

Standard Form	Word Form	Expanded Form	Fraction
0.379	three hundred seventy-nine thousandths	0.3 + 0.07 + 0.009	$\frac{379}{1,000}$
0.046	forty-six thousandths	0.04 + 0.006	$\frac{46}{1,000}$
0.008	eight thousandths	0.008	$\frac{8}{1,000}$

Write each decimal as a fraction.

1 0.906   **2** 0.112   **3** 0.002   **4** 0.306

5 0.007   **6** 0.551   **7** 0.604   **8** 0.843

Write each fraction as a decimal.

9 $\frac{89}{1,000}$ **10** $\frac{781}{1,000}$ **11** $\frac{4}{1,000}$ **12** $\frac{161}{1,000}$

13 $\frac{3}{1,000}$ **14** $\frac{121}{1,000}$ **15** $\frac{334}{1,000}$ **16** $\frac{25}{1,000}$

Use a place-value chart to write the value of the digit 4 in each decimal.

17 0.134   **18** 0.402   **19** 0.645   **20** 0.049

Write the number two other ways.

21 $\frac{15}{1,000}$ **22** five hundred six thousandths   **23** 0.819

 **Quiz**

Write each decimal as a fraction.

24 0.001   **25** 0.865   **26** 0.071   **27** 0.129

Measurement

15 Minutes

OBJECTIVE Tell time to the minute by counting minutes after and before the hour

MATERIALS large analog clock

You may wish to use a large clock to model the lesson. Point out the hour and minute hands.

Direct students' attention to the clock in Example A. Point out that the clock shows that it is after 10 o'clock.

Say: **To read the actual time, what can you do? Count the minutes from 12 to the minute hand.**

Explain that since it takes five minutes for the minute hand to move from number to number, they can count by fives to the 4, and then count by ones to the minute hand. After the students have counted aloud, say: **You have counted 23 minutes. What is the time? 23 minutes after 10 or 10:23**

Direct students' attention to the clock in Example B. Explain that when the minute hand passes the 6, it may be easier to tell time *before* the hour. Point out that the clock shows that it is not yet 7 o'clock.

Ask: **To read the time, how can you count the minutes before the hour? Start at the 12 and count back by fives to 10 and then count one more to the minute hand. You counted 11 minutes before the hour. What time is it? 11 minutes before 7**

Have students count the minutes after the hour and note that 11 minutes before 7 is also 6:49. Explain that digital clocks show time in minutes after the hour.

TRY THESE Exercises 1–4 model writing the time before and after the hour in this order:

- **Exercise 1**   Time before the hour
- **Exercises 2–4**   Time after the hour

PRACTICE ON YOUR OWN Review the two examples at the top of the page. Ask students to explain the two ways to tell time that are shown. Ask which time would a digital clock show.

QUIZ Determine if students know how to count the number of minutes before and after the hour. Success is determined by 2 out of 3 correct responses.

Students who successfully complete the **Practice on Your Own** and **Quiz** are ready to move to the next skill.

COMMON ERRORS

- Students may be unable to distinguish between the hour and minute hands.

- Students may count too many or too few "fives."

- Students may confuse time before the hour and time after the hour.

Students who made more than 2 errors in the **Practice on Your Own**, or who were not successful in the **Quiz** section, may benefit from the **Alternative Teaching Strategy** on the next page.

Alternative Teaching Strategy
Model Telling Time to the Minute

OBJECTIVE Use a clock to tell time before and after the hour

MATERIALS analog clocks, paper, pencil

If necessary, familiarize the students with the clock. Point out the hour and minute hands and the minute marks that are between the numbers.

Explain to the students that they will be counting the minutes to tell the time.

Begin by having students use the clocks to model telling time to the hour, half hour, and quarter hour. Then show 9:18 on the clock, pointing out that since the time is after 9 o'clock, they count the minutes from the 12 to the minute hand.

Students may recall that since there are 5 minutes between each number, they can count by fives to the 3. Then they can count by ones to the minute hand. Have them record the time as 18 minutes after nine, or 9:18. Have students recall that on a digital clock, the time is displayed as 9:18.

Repeat the activity for 8:42. Have students model the time by counting minutes after the hour. Then recall that when the minute hand passes the six, they can also tell the time by counting the minutes before the next hour. Have them count back by fives from the 12 to the 9 and then by ones to the minute hand. Then have them record the time three ways:

> 42 minutes after 8
> 18 minutes before 9
> 8:42

Ask which time is displayed on a digital clock.

Continue with other examples of time before and after the hour. Pay attention to students who have difficulty counting by fives and then ones, or get confused when switching from time after the hour to time before the hour.

When students show an understanding of how to tell time to the minute, have them stop modeling the time and tell time from your clock only.

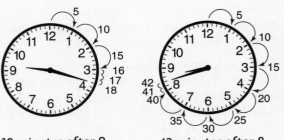

18 minutes after 9
9:18

42 minutes after 8
8:42

18 minutes before 9
8:42

Tell Time

Read the time.

Example A

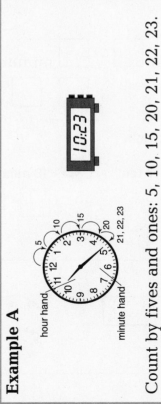

Count by fives and ones: 5, 10, 15, 20, 21, 22, 23.
The time is 23 minutes after 10 or 10:23.

Example B

Count back from 12 by fives and ones: 5, 10, 11.
The time is 11 minutes before 7 or 6:49.

 **Try These**

Count by fives and ones. Write the time.

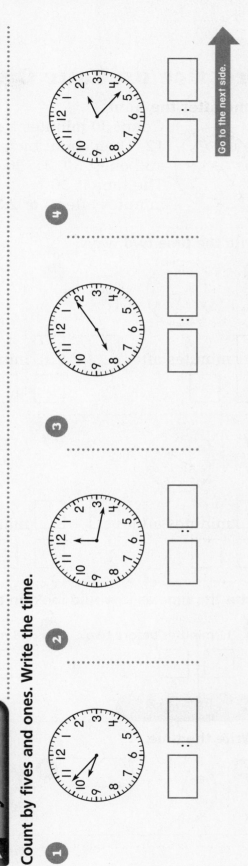

1

2

3

4

Go to the next side.

Practice on Your Own

Skill 39

Time after the hour

Count 30 minutes from 12. Then count by fives and ones: 30, 35, 36. The time is 36 minutes after 2 or 2:36.

Time before the hour

Count by fives and ones back from 12: 5, 10, 15, 20, 21, 22, 23, 24. The time is 24 minutes before 3 or 2:36.

- -

Write the time two ways.

1 ☐ minutes after ☐

☐ : ☐

2 ☐ minutes before ☐

☐ : ☐

3 ☐ minutes after ☐

☐ : ☐

4 ☐ minutes after ☐

☐ : ☐

5 ☐ minutes after ☐

☐ : ☐

6 ☐ minutes before ☐

☐ : ☐

Write the time as it would look on a digital clock.

7 11 minutes before two

☐ : ☐

8 18 minutes after ten

☐ : ☐

9 18 minutes before seven

☐ : ☐

▶ Quiz

Write the time.

10 ☐

11 ☐

12 ☐

OBJECTIVE Use a calendar

Begin the skill by reviewing the meaning of ordinal numbers and practicing some examples. Generate the following table from students' responses to questions like: **How do you say the ordinal number for 3? third How do you write it in a date? 3rd**

	Say	Write
1	first	1st
2	second	2nd
3	third	3rd
4	fourth	4th
5	fifth	5th
6	sixth	6th
7	seventh	7th
8	eighth	8th
9	ninth	9th
10	tenth	10th

As students read through the skill, ask them to point to each date on the calendar. Then have them use ordinal numbers to describe other days of the month. Ask them to find other information such as: **How many Mondays are there in April? 5 If swim meets are on Mondays and Fridays, how many meets will there be in April? 9**

Students need to understand that the spaces in a calendar represent days belonging to other months. So, there are only 4 Tuesdays in April, not 5.

TRY THESE Exercises 1–3 give students practice in getting information from a calendar.

- **Exercises 1 and 2** Use ordinal numbers to describe days of the month.

- **Exercises 3 and 4** Use the calendar to find information about days of the month.

PRACTICE ON YOUR OWN Review the material at the top of the page. Alert stu-dents to the fact that they will need to write dates using ordinal numbers. For example, for the first Saturday of December, write December 5th, not December 5.

QUIZ Success is determined by 2 out of 3 correct responses.

Students who successfully complete the **Practice on Your Own** and **Quiz** are ready to move to the next skill.

COMMON ERRORS

- Students may count spaces representing days from other months as belonging to the month they are looking at. For example, there are 5 Wednesdays in December but only 4 Mondays.

Students who made more than 4 errors in the **Practice on Your Own**, or who were not successful in the **Quiz** section, may benefit from the **Alternative Teaching Strategy** on the next page.

Alternative Teaching Strategy
Hands-On: Use a Calendar

20 Minutes

OBJECTIVE Use a calendar

MATERIALS 9 × 12-inch copies of April calendar shown in Skill 64

Give out copies of the April calendar. Have students cover or fold the calendar page so that only the first week of April is visible.

Have students use ordinal numbers to describe the days of the first week only. For example, ask them to name the first day of the week, the second, and so on. Then repeat, this time mixing up the order.

Next, have students describe the dates of the first week. They should be able to tell you that April 5th is a Thursday, April 2nd a Monday, and so on.

Tell students to next look at the complete calendar for April. Ask them a variety of questions about the rest of the month, such as:

What is the fourth Friday of April? April 27th Which day of the week is April 11th? Wednesday How many Wednesdays are in the month? 4

You might also ask students to circle all the Tuesdays, put a square around every other Monday, a triangle around the first and last Fridays, or to cross out all the Saturdays.

APRIL

Sunday	Monday	Tuesday	Wednesday	Thursday	Friday	Saturday
1	2	3	4	5	6	7
8	9	10	11	12	13	14
15	16	17	18	19	20	21
22	23	24	25	26	27	28
29	30					

Conclude the activity by having students write in dates of after–school or weekend activities, appointments, or events of their own. Have them describe the dates of their activities using ordinal numbers.

Dates on a Calendar

You can use **ordinal numbers** to describe days on a calendar. Ordinal numbers tell the order or position of things.

The table shows some ordinal numbers.

SAY	WRITE
first	1st
second	2nd
third	3rd
fourth	4th
fifth	5th
sixth	6th
seventh	7th
eighth	8th
ninth	9th
tenth	10th

APRIL

Sun	Mon	Tue	Wed	Thu	Fri	Sat
1	2	3	4	5	6	7
8	9	10	11	12	13	14
15	16	17	18	19	20	21
22	23	24	25	26	27	28
29	30					

Use ordinal numbers to describe dates on the calendar.

The *first* Saturday is April 7th.
The *fourth* Monday is April 23rd.

April 13th is a Friday.
April 25th is a Wednesday.

Here is some other information you can find on the calendar.

- There are four Fridays in April.

- If baseball practices are on Tuesdays and Thursdays, there will be 8 practices in April.

Try These

Use the April calendar above. Use ordinal numbers where you can. Complete.

1. April 17th is the [ ] Tuesday of the month.

2. The [ ] Sunday is April 1st.

3. Which day of the week is April 12th? [ ]

4. How many Tuesdays are in the month? [ ]

Go to the next side. ➤

Practice on Your Own

DECEMBER						
Sun	Mon	Tue	Wed	Thu	Fri	Sat
		1	2	3	4	5
6	7	8	9	10	11	12
13	14	15	16	17	18	19
20	21	22	23	24	25	26
27	28	29	30	31		

> December 3 is the *first* Thursday of the month.

MONTHS OF THE YEAR			
January	31 days	July	31 days
February	28 days	August	31 days
March	31 days	September	30 days
April	30 days	October	31 days
May	31 days	November	30 days
June	30 days	December	31 days

> October is the *tenth* month.

Use the December calendar. Write the date.

1 first Saturday
_____

2 third Wednesday
_____

3 fourth Monday
_____

4 fifth Wednesday
_____

Answer the questions.

5 What day of the week is December 21st?
_____

6 How many Tuesdays are in the month of December?
_____

7 If you circled all the Mondays and Wednesdays in December, how many dates would be circled? _____

8 Write an ordinal number for the last day of December. _____

9 Name the fifth month of the year.
_____

10 What is the date of the third Tuesday of December?
_____

11 What is the month after January?
_____

12 Which month comes before September?
_____

13 How many months are in one year?
_____

▶ Quiz

14 What day of the week is December 12th?
_____

15 What date is the fourth Saturday of December?
_____

16 Name the eleventh month of the year.
_____

20 Minutes

OBJECTIVE Measure objects to the nearest inch and half-inch

MATERIALS inch rulers

Begin by pointing out to students that one inch is about the length from the tip of the thumb to the first joint.

Have students look at the inch ruler in the first picture. Point out the inch marks and numbers.

Say: **Notice how one end of the pencil is lined up with the zero mark on the ruler.**

Have students trace the dashed line from the pencil point down to the ruler.

Ask: **Between which two inch marks on the ruler is the other end of the pencil?** 2 in. and 3 in. **Which inch mark is closer, the 2-inch mark or the 3-inch mark?** 2-in. **So, what is the length of the pencil to the nearest inch?** 2 inches

Direct students' attention to the next picture. Explain that the marks between the inch marks are half-inch marks. Have students find the $\frac{1}{2}$-inch mark and the $1\frac{1}{2}$-inch mark.

Have students trace the dotted line from the pencil point down to the ruler.

Ask: **Between which marks on the ruler is the other end of the pencil?** between the $\frac{1}{2}$-inch and the 1-inch marks **Is the end of the pencil closer to the $\frac{1}{2}$-inch mark or the 1-inch mark?** closer to the 1-inch mark

TRY THESE Exercises 1–2 have inch rulers in place. Dashed lines help students measure each pencil to the nearest inch or half-inch.

- **Exercise 1** Length to the nearest inch.

- **Exercise 2** Length to the nearest half-inch.

PRACTICE ON YOUR OWN Review the example at the top of the page. Suggest to students that they use the dashed line to see where the pencil point would be on the ruler.

Ask: **Between which two marks does the dashed line fall on the ruler?** between the $2\frac{1}{2}$-inch mark and the 2-inch mark

QUIZ Determine if students can use a ruler to measure to the nearest inch or half-inch. Success is indicated by 2 out of 2 correct responses.

Students who successfully complete the **Practice on Your Own** and **Quiz** are ready to move on to the next skill.

COMMON ERRORS

- Students may confuse inch and half-inch marks.

- Students may record the next whole inch when they write a length to the nearest half-inch.

Students who made more than 2 errors in the **Practice on Your Own**, or who were not successful in the **Quiz** section, may benefit from the **Alternative Teaching Strategy** on the next page.

Alternative Teaching Strategy
Use Inch Rulers to Measure

20 Minutes

OBJECTIVE Use inch rulers to measure objects to the nearest inch and half-inch

MATERIALS inch rulers with inch and half-inch marks, paper, small objects

You may wish to have students work in pairs. Distribute rulers and have students draw a line segment that is three inches long.

Emphasize starting the line at the end of the ruler and ending the line at the 3-inch mark. Encourage students to be as accurate as possible. Have students exchange papers to check each other's work.

Now have each student use the ruler to draw a line segment whose length falls between any two inch marks. Have partners exchange papers and measure each other's line segment.

To guide students, say: **This line segment does not end precisely on an inch mark. You can measure the line segment to the nearest inch.**

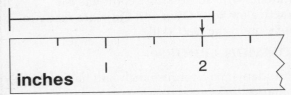

This line is 2 inches long, to the nearest inch.

Then ask: **To which inch mark on the ruler is the end of the line segment nearest? 2 inch**

Have students record the nearest inch and then compare that measurement with their partner's.

Point out the half-inch intervals on the ruler. Suggest that the students draw a line segment that is three and one-half inches long, and have partners check each other's work.

Then have students draw a line segment whose length falls between 2 and $2\frac{1}{2}$ inches.

Say: **This line segment does not end exactly on an inch mark or on a half-inch mark. Which inch mark or half-inch mark is closest to the end of the line segment? Check students' work.**

Repeat the activity several times until students demonstrate competence with measuring to the nearest inch and half inch. Then let student pairs measure small objects in the classroom. Partners can check each other's results.

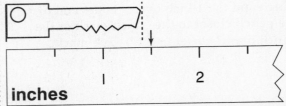

This key is $1\frac{1}{2}$ inches long, to the nearest half inch.

Grade 4
Skill 41

Length: Customary Units

The inch (in.) is a customary unit of length. Use the inch to measure small objects.

Find the length of the pencil to the nearest inch.

inches 1   2   3

Think: Line up one end of the object with the end of the ruler. Then measure.

The length is closer to 2 inches than to 3 inches.

So, to the nearest inch, the pencil is 2 in. long.

Find the length of the pencil to the nearest half-inch.

inches 1   2

The length is closer to 1 inch than to $\frac{1}{2}$ inch. So, to the nearest half-inch, the pencil is 1 in. long.

Try These

1 Measure to the nearest inch.

inches 1   2

[   ] inches

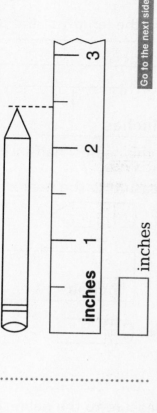

2 Measure to the nearest half-inch.

inches 1   2   3

[   ] inches

Go to the next side.

Practice on Your Own

Skill 41

Find the length of the pencil to the nearest half-inch.

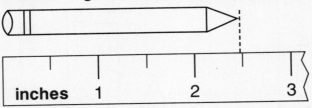

Think:
Line up one end of the object
with the end of the ruler.
Then measure.

To the nearest half-inch, the pencil is $2\frac{1}{2}$ in.

Measure to the nearest inch.

1 [ ] inches

2 [ ] inches

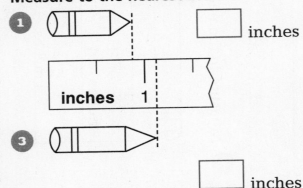

3 [ ] inches

4 [ ] inches

Measure to the nearest half-inch.

5 [ ] inches

6 [ ] inches

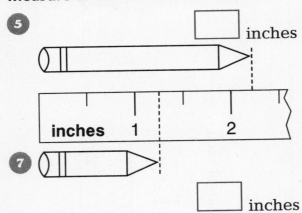

7 [ ] inches

8 [ ] inches

▶ Quiz

9 Measure to the nearest inch.

[ ] inches

10 Measure to the nearest half-inch.

[ ] inches

OBJECTIVE Measure to the nearest centimeter

MATERIALS centimeter rulers

Begin by recalling that a centimeter (cm) is a metric unit of length used to measure small objects. Have students look closely at the metric ruler on the page. Point out where the ruler begins on the left.

Direct students' attention to the first example.

Emphasize how the ruler is lined up with the left end of the pencil.

Point out that the dashed line comes down from the very tip of the pencil to the ruler at a point between 8 cm and 9 cm.

Ask: **What is the length of the pencil to the nearest centimeter? 9 cm How did you decide? Possible response: The dashed line marks a point on the ruler that is closer to the 9-cm mark than to the 8-cm mark.**

Confirm for students that, in this case, the nearest centimeter is to the right of the point marked by the dashed line.

Ask similar questions as students measure the second pencil.

TRY THESE In Exercises 1–3, students measure the lengths of pencils to the nearest centimeter. Metric rulers are in place on the page and dashed lines are provided to help students measure.

* **Exercises 1–3** Measure to the nearest centimeter. The nearest cm is to the right of the dashed line.

PRACTICE ON YOUR OWN Review the example with students. Help students focus on deciding whether the nearest centimeter is to the right or to the left of the pencil point. **to the right, 7 cm**

Exercises 1–4 Students measure lengths to the nearest centimeter with cues in place.

QUIZ Determine if students can measure an object to the nearest centimeter. Success is indicated by 2 out of 2 correct responses.

Students who successfully complete the **Practice on Your Own** and **Quiz** are ready to move on to the next skill.

COMMON ERRORS

* Students may not align the ruler precisely at the left end and thus measure inaccurately.

* Students may mistakenly believe that the nearest centimeter mark is always to the right of the pencil point.

Students who made more than 1 error in the **Practice on Your Own**, or who were not successful in the **Quiz** section, may benefit from the **Alternative Teaching Strategy** on the next page.

Alternative Teaching Strategy
Measure Objects to the Nearest Centimeter

20 Minutes

OBJECTIVE Measure objects to the nearest centimeter

MATERIALS centimeter ruler, paper clips (3.2 cm long), small objects, and paper

Distribute materials and instruct students to look closely at the metric ruler. Point out where the ruler begins. **Some metric rulers begin at the very edge of the ruler; others have a small space and then a mark to label the beginning. Tell students that this is the** *zero mark*, **even if it is not labeled 0.**

Discuss any questions students might have about the centimeter ruler and measuring.

Then call students' attention to the length of one centimeter. Ask students to point to the 1 cm mark on the ruler. Have them measure the width of one of their fingers; ask them to see which finger fits most easily between the beginning of the ruler and the one centimeter mark.

Now, have students measure the length of a paper clip to its nearest centimeter.

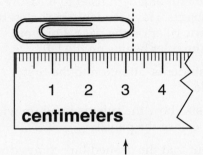

Say: **Line up one end of end of the paper clip with the zero mark on the ruler. Look at the other end. Between which two centimeter marks is that end? 3 cm and 4 cm Is it closer to the 3 or to the 4 on the ruler? closer to the 3**

Repeat this activity using several small objects such as a large paper clip, eraser, key, or crayon. Monitor students as they work and have them compare their results.

When students have demonstrated sufficient competence, have them work independently to measure small objects around the classroom.

Grade 4
Skill 42

Length: Metric Units

A centimeter (cm) is a metric unit of length. Use the centimeter to measure small objects.

Find the length of the pencil to the nearest centimeter.

centimeters
1 2 3 4 5 6 7 8 9 10

So, to the nearest centimeter, the pencil is 9 cm.

Think: Line up one end of the object with the end of the ruler. Then measure.

Find the length of the pencil to the nearest centimeter.

centimeters
1 2 3 4 5 6 7

So, to the nearest centimeter, the pencil is 6 cm.

Try These

Measure each pencil to the nearest centimeter.

1

centimeters
1 2 3

☐ centimeters

2

centimeters
1 2 3 4

☐ centimeters

3

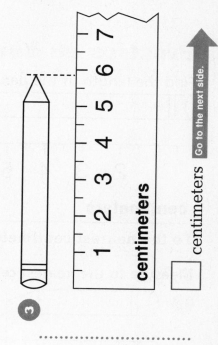

centimeters
1 2 3 4 5 6 7

☐ centimeters

Go to the next side.

Name _____   Skill _____

Practice on Your Own

Skill 42

Find the length of the pencil to the nearest centimeter.

Think: Line up one end of the object with the end of the ruler. Then measure.

1 2 3 4 5 6 7
centimeters

To the nearest centimeter, the pencil is 7 centimeters.

Measure to the nearest centimeter.

1
1 2 3 4
centimeters
[ ] centimeters

2
1 2 3 4 5 6
centimeters
[ ] centimeters

3
1 2 3 4
centimeters
[ ] centimeters

4
1 2 3 4 5
centimeters
[ ] centimeters

Quiz

Measure to the nearest centimeter.

5
1 2 3
centimeters
[ ] centimeters

6
1 2 3 4 5 6
centimeters
[ ] centimeters

IN184 Intervention • Skills

15 Minutes

OBJECTIVE Find the perimeter of a figure

Begin by reviewing the definition of perimeter as the distance around a figure. Explain that the number of units around a figure can be counted to find the perimeter.

As students look at the first figure, say: **This figure has 4 sides, each side is 1 unit long. Count the units to find the perimeter.** 4 units

For the second figure ask: **How many sides does the figure have? 4 Count the units. What is the perimeter of the figure? 12 units**

Then ask: **How can you find the perimeter without counting each unit? Count the units on each side of the figure and find the sum.**

Discuss how this method is easier and more accurate, especially when the perimeters are greater or the figures more complex.

TRY THESE Exercises 1–3 model the types of exercises students will find on the **Practice on Your Own** page.

- **Exercise 1**   Figure with 4 sides.

- **Exercise 2**   Figure with 4 sides.

- **Exercise 3**   Figure with 6 sides.

PRACTICE ON YOUR OWN Review the example at the top of the page. Ask students how many sides the figure has, and how many addends are in the addition sentence. Remind students to check the number of sides and the number of addends as they work through the page.

QUIZ Determine if students understand that to find perimeter they count the units on each side of the figure and find the sum. Success is indicated by 2 out of 3 correct responses.

Students who successfully complete the **Practice on Your Own** and **Quiz** are ready to move on to the next skill.

COMMON ERRORS

- Students may not count the number of units correctly.

- Students may not include all the sides in the calculation.

- Students may not add correctly.

Students who made more than 2 errors in the **Practice on Your Own**, or who were not successful in the **Quiz** section, may benefit from the **Alternative Teaching Strategy** on the next page.

Alternative Teaching Strategy
Use Models to Find Perimeter

15 Minutes

OBJECTIVE Find the perimeter of a figure using grid paper

MATERIALS tiles, centimeter grid paper

Students may benefit from working in pairs or small groups. Explain that the activity is about finding perimeter. Explain that perimeter is the distance around a figure.

Using tiles, form a 3 × 5 unit rectangle. Then point out that to find the perimeter of the tile figure, you count the number of units around the outside of the figure. Demonstrate how the side of a tile represents a unit, and count each side of a corner unit as one unit each. Have students count the units as you point to each unit.

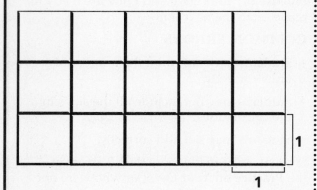

Distribute the grid paper. Have students draw a 5 × 4 unit rectangle. Have students count the units to find the perimeter.

What is the perimeter? 18 units

Then suggest that they can count the units on each side and add them to find the perimeter.

How many units are on each side? 5, 4, 5, 4

What addition sentence can you write?
5 + 4 + 5 + 4 = 18 units

Repeat the activity with similar examples.

Caution students to check that they have counted the units correctly, included all the sides in their addition, and added correctly.

When the students show understanding of how to find the perimeter, have each student outline a figure on the grid paper and exchange figures with another student. After they have found the perimeter, have students describe their methods.

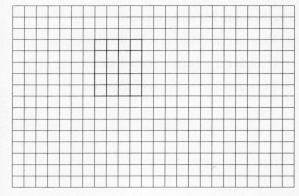

Grade 4
Skill 43

Perimeter

The **perimeter** is the distance around a figure. To find the perimeter, count the number of units around the figure.

Each side of the square tile has a length of 1 unit.

1 unit

1 unit

The perimeter is 4 units.

Count the units on each side.

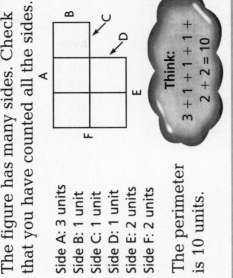

Think:
4 + 2 + 4 + 2 = 12

Side A: 4 units
Side B: 2 units
Side C: 4 units
Side D: 2 units

The perimeter is 12 units.

The figure has many sides. Check that you have counted all the sides.

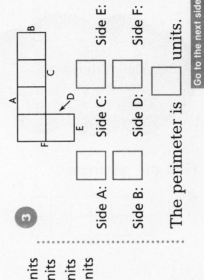

Think:
3 + 1 + 1 + 1 +
2 + 2 = 10

Side A: 3 units
Side B: 1 unit
Side C: 1 unit
Side D: 1 unit
Side E: 2 units
Side F: 2 units

The perimeter is 10 units.

▶ Try These

Complete.

1

Side A: 3 units
Side B: 2 units
Side C: 3 units
Side D: 2 units

The perimeter is ☐ units.

2

Side A: 3 units
Side B: 4 units
Side C: 3 units
Side D: 4 units

The perimeter is ☐ units.

3

Side A:
Side B:
Side C:
Side D:
Side E:
Side F:

The perimeter is ☐ units.

Go to the next side.

Practice on Your Own

Think:
Count the units
on each side.
$3 + 3 + 3 + 3 = 12$

Side A: 3 units
Side B: 3 units
Side C: 3 units
Side D: 3 units

The perimeter is 12 units.

Find the perimeter.

1

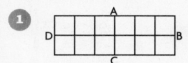

A: ☐ units

B: ☐ units

C: ☐ units

D: ☐ units

Perimeter: ☐ units

2

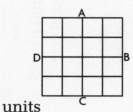

A: ☐ units

B: ☐ units

C: ☐ units

D: ☐ units

Perimeter: ☐ units

3

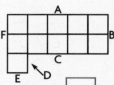

A: ☐ units   E: ☐ units

B: ☐ units   F: ☐ units

C: ☐ units

D: ☐ units

Perimeter: ☐ units

4

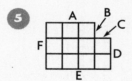

Perimeter: ☐ units

5

Perimeter: ☐ units

6

Perimeter: ☐ units

▶ Quiz

Find the perimeter.

7

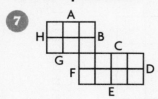

Perimeter: ☐ units

8

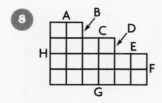

Perimeter: ☐ units

9

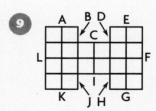

Perimeter: ☐ units

15 Minutes

OBJECTIVE Find area by counting square units

You may wish to begin by reviewing that the area is the number of square units needed to cover a flat surface. Suggest that students think of each square as 1 square unit. Explain that they are going to count the square units to find the area of a figure.

Direct students to the first figure. **To find the area of this figure, count the number of square units you see. What is the area of the figure? 4 square units**

Ask students to explain how they counted. Some may count the square units one by one. Others may see 2 rows of 2 units and add 2 and 2. Some may multiply 2 by 2. Remind students to count carefully, perhaps marking each unit as they count.

Continue in a similar way as you work through the remaining figures. Remind students that their answers are given in square units.

TRY THESE Exercises 1–3 model the types of exercises students will find on the **Practice on Your Own** page.

- **Exercise 1** 6 squares, 6 square units.
- **Exercise 2** 6 squares, 6 square units.
- **Exercise 3** 8 squares, 8 square units.

PRACTICE ON YOUR OWN Review the example at the top of the page. Ask students to explain why the area of this figure is 6 square units. Then caution students to read the directions carefully as they complete the page.

QUIZ Determine if students understand that area is the number of square units needed to cover a flat surface, and that to find area they need to count the square units in the figure. Success is determined by 2 out of 3 correct responses.

Students who successfully complete the **Practice on Your Own** and **Quiz** are ready to move on to the next skill.

COMMON ERRORS

- Students may count incorrectly.
- Students may have difficulty realizing that figures with different shapes may have the same area.
- Students may not remember that area is measured in square units.

Students who made more than 2 errors in the **Practice on Your Own**, or who were not successful in the **Quiz** section, may benefit from the **Alternative Teaching Strategy** on the next page.

Alternative Teaching Strategy
Use Models to Find Area

15 Minutes

OBJECTIVE Find area by counting tiles

MATERIALS tiles, several large, different size rectangles and squares that can be completely and precisely covered with tiles

Have students work in pairs or small groups. Distribute materials. Display a large square piece of paper.

Review that area is the number of square units needed to cover a flat surface. Explain to the students that they can use square tiles to find the area of the square.

Then demonstrate how to place the tiles so the square is entirely covered. Have students count the tiles and give the area in square units.

Then distribute the other rectangles and squares. Have students find the area of each figure, noting how many rows of tiles it took to cover the figure and how many tiles were in each row.

When students show an understanding of how to find area, ask if they think two figures can have different shapes, but the same area. Have students use the same number of tiles to make a figure on paper and trace it. Then discuss and compare the figures they traced.

To extend the activity, you may wish to have students outline squares and rectangles on grid paper, and then find each area.

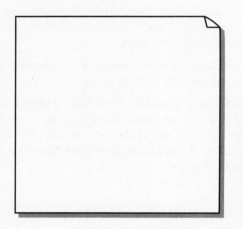

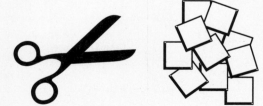

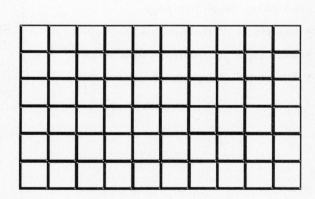

The area is 60 square units.

Grade 4
Skill 44

Area

Count the square units to find the area.

Area is the number of square units needed to cover a flat surface.

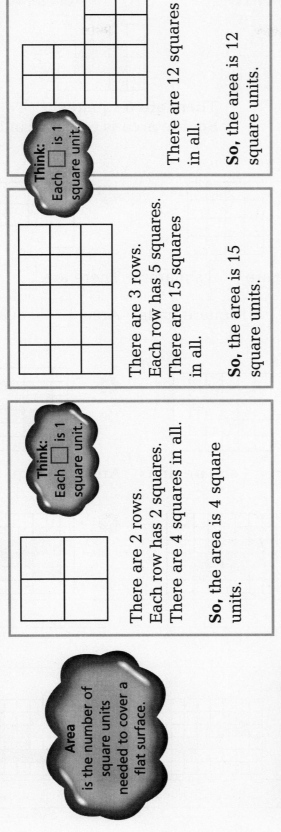

Think: Each ☐ is 1 square unit.

There are 2 rows.
Each row has 2 squares.
There are 4 squares in all.

So, the area is 4 square units.

There are 3 rows.
Each row has 5 squares.
There are 15 squares in all.

So, the area is 15 square units.

Think: Each ☐ is 1 square unit.

There are 12 squares in all.

So, the area is 12 square units.

Try These

Find the area.

1

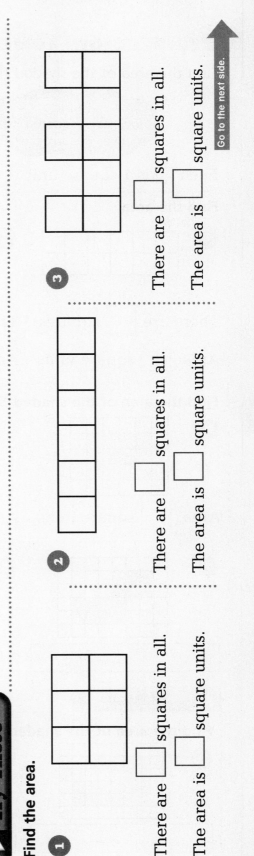

There are ☐ squares in all.

The area is ☐ square units.

2

There are ☐ squares in all.

The area is ☐ square units.

3

There are ☐ squares in all.

The area is ☐ square units.

Go to the next side.

Practice on Your Own

Find the area of the shaded figure.

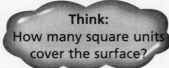

Think:
How many square units cover the surface?

Each ☐ is 1 square unit.

There are **6** squares.
So, the area is 6 square units.

Find the area.

1 There are ☐ squares.

Area: ☐ square units

2 There are ☐ squares.

Area: ☐ square units

3 There are ☐ squares.

Area: ☐ square units

Find the area of the shaded figure.

4 Area: ☐ square units

5 Area: ☐ square units

6 Area: ☐ square units

7

8

9

▶ Quiz

Find the area of the shaded figure.

10

11

12

Geometry and Spatial Sense

20 Minutes

OBJECTIVE Identify lines, points, line segments, rays, and angles

Begin the lesson by suggesting that certain terms help describe figures in geometry.

Review the definition of each term with students. You may wish to draw each figure on the board as you discuss its attributes.

Emphasize that a right angle is a special angle that forms a square corner. If you wish, distribute index cards and have students use them to model a square corner as you review the different types of angles.

Instruct students to hold the square corner of the index card against the right angle.

Say: **The right angle is the same as a square corner.**

Ask: **What are other things that have square corners or right angles? Possible answers: notebook paper, desk top**

Call students' attention to the example of an acute angle.

Ask: **How can you tell that the angle is less than a right angle? The opening between the rays is less than the opening between the rays for a right angle.**

Call students' attention to the example of an obtuse angle.

Ask: **How can you tell that the angle is more than a right angle? The opening between the rays is greater than the opening between the rays for a right angle.**

TRY THESE In Exercises 1–4 students identify figures.

- **Exercise 1**   Identify a point.
- **Exercise 2**   Identify a line segment.
- **Exercise 3**   Identify a ray.
- **Exercise 4**   Identify a line.

PRACTICE ON YOUR OWN Review the examples at the top of the page with students. Ask students to describe each figure in their own words. Exercises 1–4 are similar to those in **Try These**. In Exercises 5–8, students are asked to draw certain figures. In Exercises 9–11, students use a piece of paper to identify angles. In Exercises 12–14, students complete a table identifying the number of line segments, angles, and right angles in various geometric figures.

QUIZ Determine if students can identify figures. Success is indicated by 3 out of 4 correct responses.

Students who successfully complete the **Practice on Your Own** and **Quiz** are ready to move to the next skill.

COMMON ERRORS

- Students may confuse terms.
- Students may not recognize angles when they are shown in different positions.

Students who make more than 4 errors in the **Practice on Your Own**, or who were not successful in the **Quiz** section, may benefit from the **Alternative Teaching Strategy** on the next page.

Alternative Teaching Strategy
Draw Geometric Figures

15 Minutes

OBJECTIVE Identify and draw lines, points, line segments, rays, and angles

MATERIALS for each student: straightedge or ruler, 5 index cards

Begin the lesson by reviewing the terms *line, point, line segment, ray,* and *angle*.

As you discuss each term, have students work individually to draw the figure. Instruct students to use the straightedge or ruler to draw the figure on one side of an index card. Have students write the name of the figure on the back of the card.

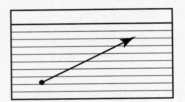

Have students work in pairs and use index cards to review the terms. Students should take turns holding up index cards and quizzing their partners.

You may wish to extend this activity by having students quiz each other with the "term" side of their index cards. One student holds up a card with the name of a figure. The partner draws that figure on a sheet of paper. Students take turns quizzing each other.

Line Segments and Angles

Special terms are used to describe figures in geometry.

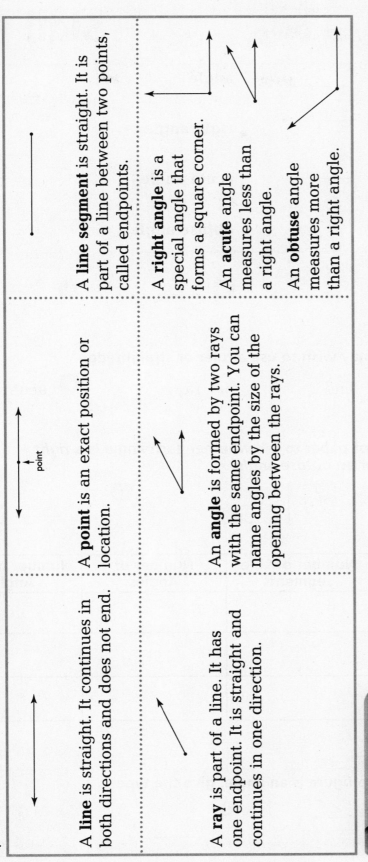

A **line** is straight. It continues in both directions and does not end.

A **ray** is part of a line. It has one endpoint. It is straight and continues in one direction.

A **point** is an exact position or location.

point

An **angle** is formed by two rays with the same endpoint. You can name angles by the size of the opening between the rays.

A **line segment** is straight. It is part of a line between two points, called endpoints.

A **right angle** is a special angle that forms a square corner.

An **acute** angle measures less than a right angle.

An **obtuse** angle measures more than a right angle.

Try These

Name each figure.

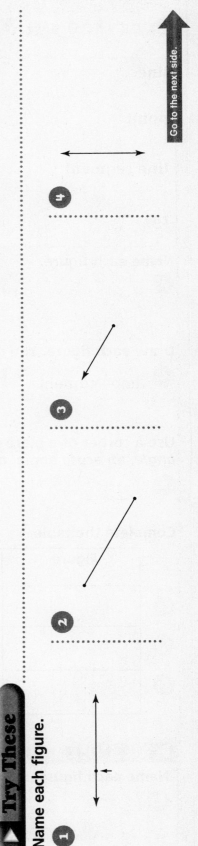

1

2

3

4

Go to the next side.

Practice on Your Own

line	↔	angle	
point	← • →	right angle	
line segment	•——•	acute angle	
ray	• →	obtuse angle	

Name each figure.

1.
2.
3.
4.

. . . .

Draw each figure. You may wish to use a ruler or straightedge.

5. line segment
6. line
7. ray
8. acute angle

. . . .

Use a corner of a piece of paper to tell whether each angle is a *right angle*, an *acute angle*, or an *obtuse angle*.

9.
10.
11.

Complete the table.

	Figure	Number of Line Segments	Number of Angles	Number of Right Angles
12	○			
13	□			
14	◺			

▶ **Quiz**

Name each figure. If the figure is an angle, give the type.

15.
16.
17.
18.

15 Minutes

OBJECTIVE Identify right angles, acute angles, and obtuse angles; then measure angles

MATERIALS protractor

You may start the lesson by using two sheets of paper to model types of angles. Remind students that an angle is formed when two rays meet at the same endpoint. Point out that the size of an angle is determined by the size of the opening between the rays.

Explain to students that they are asked to classify right, acute, and obtuse angles.

Direct students' attention to the first example, a right angle. Recall that in a right angle the rays meet and form a square corner. Have students measure the angle and see that a right angle measures 90°.

Ask: **Where can you find right angles or square corners? Possible answers: where floors or ceilings meet walls, windows**

Have students study the acute and obtuse angles. Explain that once they identify a right angle, they can use it to see if other angles are greater than or less than the right angle. Then they can measure the angles.

Ask: **How can you tell if an angle measures less than a right angle? The opening between the rays is less than 90°. What is this type of angle? an acute angle How can you tell if an angle measures greater than a right angle? The opening between the rays is greater than 90°. What is this type of angle? an obtuse angle**

TRY THESE Exercises 1–4 prepare students for the types of exercises they will find on the **Practice on Your Own** page.

- **Exercise 1**   Acute
- **Exercise 2**   Obtuse
- **Exercise 3**   Right
- **Exercise 4**   Right

PRACTICE ON YOUR OWN Review the examples. In Exercises 1–6 students measure and classify angles. Ask volunteers to explain why they classify each angle as right, acute, or obtuse.

QUIZ Determine if students can measure and classify angles. Success is indicated by 2 out of 3 correct responses.

Students who successfully complete the **Practice on Your Own** and **Quiz** are ready to move to the next skill.

COMMON ERRORS

- Students may not recognize angles that are shown in different positions.

- Students may confuse the terms *acute* and *obtuse.*

- Students may place the protractor incorrectly when measuring an angle.

Students who made more than 2 errors in the **Practice on Your Own,** or who were not successful in the **Quiz** section, may benefit from the **Alternative Teaching Strategy** on the next page.

Alternative Teaching Strategy
Use Models to Classify Angles

OBJECTIVE Identify right angles, acute angles, and obtuse angles using an index card

MATERIALS drawings of right angles, acute angles, and obtuse angles in different positions; index cards; angle model

Prepare angle drawings and an angle model prior to the lesson. For the angle model, fasten the ends of two strips of tag board with a fastener.

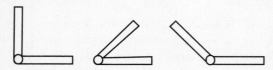

Begin the lesson by showing students the angle model and demonstrating how the strips stand for the rays of an angle. Explain how they can form different angles by increasing or decreasing the size of the opening between the rays.

Review with students the definitions of an angle, a right angle, an acute angle, and an obtuse angle. Use an index card and the model to show each type of angle. Change the position of the model to show these angles in several different positions.

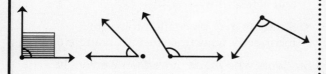

Distribute the angle drawings and index cards. Suggest that students find a right angle on the paper by fitting the square corner of the index card into the angle drawing.

Ask: **How do you know that the angle is a right angle? The square corner of the card fits the angle. One ray is along the bottom of the card, and the other ray is along the side of the card.**

Then, have students find a right angle in a different position. Have them explain why this angle is also a right angle.

Continue the activity by asking students to find acute angles and obtuse angles on the paper. Remind students that they can compare these angles to a right angle to determine if their measures are greater than or less than a right angle. Be sure students can identify acute and obtuse angles in different positions.

When students show the ability to identify angles without the index card, ask them to draw an example of each type of angle.

Then, conclude the lesson by having them explain how they know whether the angle is a right angle, an acute angle, or an obtuse angle.

Grade 4
Skill 46

Classify and Measure Angles

Two rays with the same endpoint form an **angle**.
The endpoint is called the vertex. The unit used for measuring angles is a degree (°).
An angle is classified according to the size of the opening between its rays.

Right Angle

A right angle measures 90°. A right angle forms a square corner.

Acute Angle

An acute angle measures **less than** a right angle. It measures greater than 0° and less than 90°.

Obtuse Angle

An obtuse angle measures **greater than** a right angle. It measures greater than 90° and less than 180°.

Try These

Name each angle. Write *right, acute,* or *obtuse.*

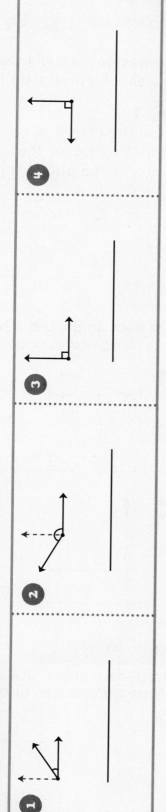

1. _____

2. _____

3. _____

4. _____

Go to the next side.

Practice on Your Own

A **protractor** is a tool used to measure the size of an angle.
The scale of a protractor is marked from 0° to 180°.

Step 1	Step 2	Step 3
Place the center of the protractor on the vertex of the angle.	Line up the center point and 0° mark on the protractor with one ray of the angle.	Read the measure of the angle where the other ray passes through the scale.

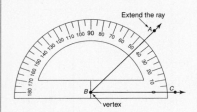 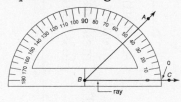 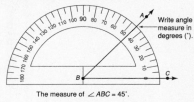

The measure of ∠ABC = 45°.

Trace each angle. Use a protractor to measure the angle.
Write *right, acute,* or *obtuse.*

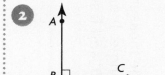 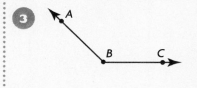

① B A C _____

② A B C _____

③ A B C _____

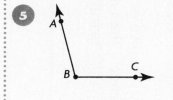 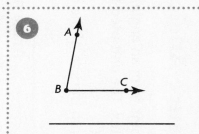

④ A B C _____

⑤ A B C _____

⑥ A B C _____

▶ Quiz

Trace each angle. Use a protractor to measure the angle.
Write *right, acute,* or *obtuse.*

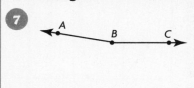 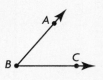 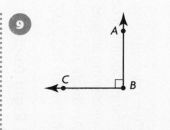

⑦ A B C _____

⑧ A B C _____

⑨ A C B _____

20 Minutes

OBJECTIVE Identify plane figures: circles, triangles, rectangles, and squares

Begin by having students count the sides and angles of models of plane figures. As they manipulate the models, point out that a polygon is a closed plane figure with straight sides. Remind them that a closed figure begins and ends at the same point and that an open figure does not begin and end at the same point.

Reinforce the concept of closed figures by shading examples of closed and open figures.

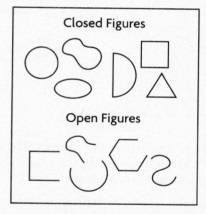

Have students name any figures they recognize. Then ask them to name some objects that have the same shapes as the figures on the page, for example: coins, windows, sheets of paper, and traffic signs.

Ask a student to read the definition of each figure. Ask: **Which plane figure is formed by a curved line? the circle** Emphasize that a circle has no sides and no angles. Ask: **How are the three figures in Example B alike? They all have three sides and three angles. How are they different? They are different sizes.**

Next discuss Examples C and D.

Ask: **Which plane figures have four sides and four angles? squares and rectangles How is a square different from a rectangle? Only squares have four equal sides.**

TRY THESE In Exercises 1–4, students circle the figure that matches the name.

- **Exercise 1**   Square
- **Exercise 2**   Circle
- **Exercise 3**   Rectangle
- **Exercise 4**   Triangle

PRACTICE ON YOUR OWN Review the closed plane figures at the top of the page. Exercises 1–8 ask students to match a plane figure with its name. Exercises 9–12 allow students to write the number of sides and angles of each plane figure and then name the figure. Before students complete the exercises, remind them to make sure the figure they choose is a closed figure, and that it has the correct number of sides and angles.

QUIZ Determine if students can identify plane figures based on their attributes. Success is indicated by 3 out of 4 correct responses.

Students who successfully complete the **Practice on Your Own** and **Quiz** are ready to move to the next skill.

COMMON ERRORS

- Students may confuse square figures with rectangles.

- Students may not recognize a plane figure that is rotated.

- Students may not recognize all types of triangles–equilateral, isosceles, and scalene.

Students who made more than 3 errors in the **Practice on Your Own**, or who were not successful in the **Quiz** section, may benefit from the **Alternative Teaching Strategy** on the next page.

Alternative Teaching Strategy
Use Models to Identify Plane Figures

15 Minutes

OBJECTIVE Identify plane figures: circles, triangles, rectangles, and squares

MATERIALS pre-cut squares and rectangles, construction paper, scissors

Distribute the pre-cut figures.

Have students look at the squares and rectangles. Point out the square and tell students that all four sides are equal and all the angles are right angles.

To demonstrate this idea, have students fold the squares diagonally, corner to corner, and see that the edges of the square match exactly.

Next, have students fold the rectangles diagonally, corner to corner, and show that the edges do not match. Remind students that all sides of a rectangle are not equal. Then, have students fold the figure in half to show that opposite sides of a rectangle are equal.

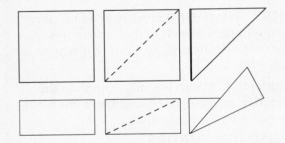

Give students construction paper and have them draw a large triangle and cut it out. Choose two students' triangles to compare and point out that although they may look different, all triangles have three sides and three angles. Hold one model in various positions to demonstrate.

Ask: **Is it still a triangle? yes**

Continue with other plane figures. The goal is to have students identify the plane figures by recognizing their attributes.

Conclude the lesson by having each student draw one figure and explain its attributes to the group.

Plane Figures

A **plane figure** is a flat figure that lies in one plane. It can be an open or closed figure. A **closed** plane figure begins and ends at the same point.

Example A
A **circle** is a plane figure that has no sides. It is made up of points that are the same distance from the center point. A circle is a plane figure that has no angles.

circles

Example B
A **triangle** is a plane figure with 3 sides and 3 angles.

triangles

Example C
A **rectangle** is a plane figure with opposite sides that are equal and 4 right angles.

rectangles

Example D
A **square** is a plane figure with 4 equal sides and 4 right angles.

squares

Try These

Circle the figure that matches the name.

1 square

a.
b.
c.

2 circle

a.
b.
c.

3 rectangle

a.
b.
c.

4 triangle

a.
b.
c.

Go to the next side.

Practice on Your Own

Skill (47)

Circles, triangles, rectangles, and squares are closed plane figures.

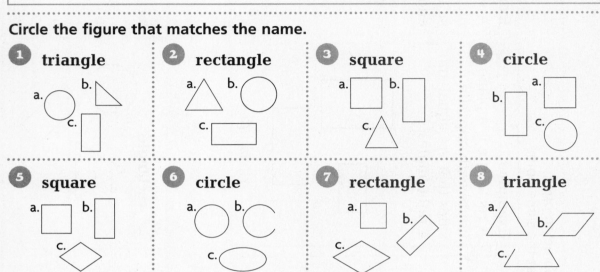

| circle | triangle | rectangle | square |

Circle the figure that matches the name.

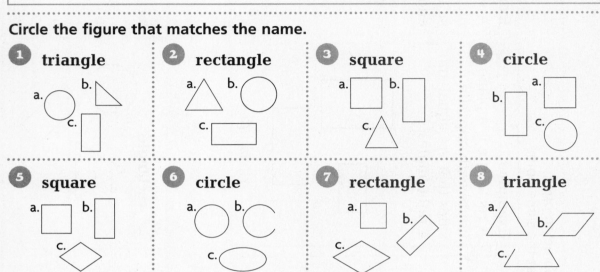

1 triangle
2 rectangle
3 square
4 circle

5 square
6 circle
7 rectangle
8 triangle

Write the number of sides and angles each figure has. Then name the figure.

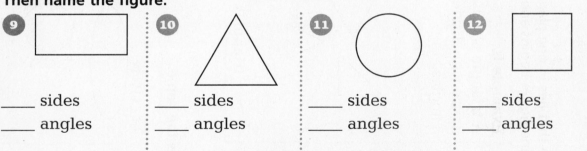

9
____ sides
____ angles
_____

10
____ sides
____ angles
_____

11
____ sides
____ angles
_____

12
____ sides
____ angles
_____

▶ **Quiz**

Write the number of sides and angles each figure has. Write the name of each figure.

13
____ sides
____ angles
_____

14
____ sides
____ angles
_____

15
____ sides
____ angles
_____

16
____ sides
____ angles
_____

OBJECTIVE Name and compare types of quadrilaterals

Begin by reminding students that quadrilaterals are polygons with 4 sides and 4 angles. Then suggest that they can name and sort different types of quadrilaterals by looking at their sides and angles.

Call students' attention to the figures at the top of the page.

Help them identify what characteristics make each type of quadrilateral different from the others.

Ask: **How is a parallelogram different from a rhombus? A parallelogram has 2 pairs of equal sides. A rhombus has 4 equal sides. How is a rhombus different from a square? A rhombus does not have any right angles. A square has 4 right angles.**

Continue with similar questions until all types of quadrilaterals have been discussed.

Then help students identify what characteristics make different types of quadrilaterals alike.

Ask: **How is a parallelogram like a rhombus? Both are quadrilaterals; they both have 2 pairs of parallel sides. How is a rhombus like a square? Both are quadrilaterals; they both have 2 pairs of parallel sides and 4 equal sides.**

Help students understand that a trapezoid is a unique quadrilateral in that it has 1 pair of parallel sides.

TRY THESE In **Exercises 1–4,** students write as many names for each quadrilateral as they can.

PRACTICE ON YOUR OWN Review the names of the quadrilaterals at the top of the page. Be sure students can identify each type.

QUIZ Determine if students can name and compare types of quadrilaterals.

Success is indicated by 3 out of 4 correct responses.

Students who successfully complete the **Practice on Your Own** and **Quiz** are ready to move to the next skill.

COMMON ERRORS

- Students may confuse quadrilaterals that look similar, such as squares and rhombuses or rectangles and parallelograms.

- Students may not recognize right angles.

Students who make more than 1 error in the **Practice on Your Own,** or who were not successful in the **Quiz** section may benefit from the **Alternative Teaching Strategy** on the next page.

Alternative Teaching Strategy
Use Questions to Sort Quadrilaterals

30 Minutes

OBJECTIVE Name and sort quadrilaterals using a sorting tree

MATERIALS index cards, markers

Students can benefit from using questions to compare different figures.

Explain to students that they can ask questions to help them sort different types of quadrilaterals. Tell them that a classification key is a tool that helps them ask useful questions.

Distribute index cards and markers to students. On the first index card, have students write the definition of a quadrilateral:

Quadrilateral:
A polygon with 4 sides and 4 angles is a quadrilateral.

On the next five cards, students should write questions and answers that help them sort the different types of quadrilaterals.

1. *Does the quadrilateral have any parallel sides?*
   Yes—Go to Question 2.
   No—It is a quadrilateral.

2. *Does the quadrilateral have 2 pairs of parallel sides?*
   Yes—Go to Question 3.
   No—The quadrilateral is a trapezoid.

3. *Does the quadrilateral have 4 equal sides?*
   Yes—Go to Question 4.
   No—Go to Question 5.

4. *Does the quadrilateral have 4 right angles?*
   Yes—The quadrilateral is a square.
   No—The quadrilateral is a rhombus.

5. *Does the quadrilateral have 4 right angles?*
   Yes—The quadrilateral is a rectangle.
   No—The quadrilateral is a parallelogram.

Explain to students that the stack of index cards with questions and identifying characteristics makes up a classification key for quadrilaterals. Show them how to lay out the cards in order to read them.

Demonstrate how to use the key. Draw a parallelogram on the board.

Say: **I ask myself the first question:** *Does the quadrilateral have any parallel sides?* **Yes, it does. I go to the second question:** *Does the quadrilateral have 2 pairs of parallel sides?* **Yes it does, I go to the third question:** *Does the quadrilateral have 4 equal sides?* **No, it does not, so I go to the fifth question:** *Does the quadrilateral have 4 right angles?* **No, so it is a parallelogram. To check, I read the parallelogram card to make sure the quadrilateral fits the description.**

Continue with similar examples. Draw additional quadrilaterals on the board. Then have students use their keys to name each quadrilateral.

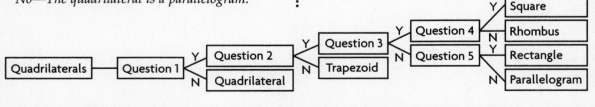

Grade 4
Skill 48

Quadrilaterals

A quadrilateral is a polygon with 4 sides and 4 angles.
There are different types of quadrilaterals.

All quadrilaterals have 4 sides and 4 angles.

Parallelogram

2 pairs of parallel sides
2 pairs of equal sides

Rectangle

2 pairs of parallel sides
2 pairs of equal sides
4 right angles

Rhombus

2 pairs of parallel sides
4 equal sides

Square

2 pairs of parallel sides
4 equal sides
4 right angles

Trapezoid

1 pair of parallel sides
angles may be different sizes

Try These

Write as many names for each quadrilateral as you can.

1 ⋯⋯⋯ 2 ⋯⋯⋯ 3 ⋯⋯⋯ 4

Go to the next side.

Practice on Your Own

You can name and sort quadrilaterals by looking at their sides and angles.

Quadrilateral
polygon with 4
sides and 4 angles

Trapezoid
one pair of parallel
sides and size of
angles not always
the same.

Parallelogram
2 pairs of parallel sides
2 pairs of equal sides

Rhombus
2 pairs of
parallel sides
4 equal sides

Rectangle
2 pairs of parallel sides
2 pairs of equal sides
4 right angles

Square
2 pairs of parallel sides
4 equal sides
4 right angles

For 1–5, use quadrilaterals to the right.

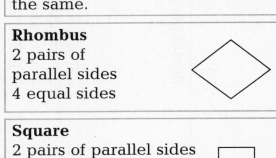

1. Which quadrilaterals have 4 right angles?

2. Which quadrilaterals have no right angles?

3. Which quadrilaterals have 2 pairs of parallel sides?

4. How are quadrilateral B and quadrilateral C alike?

5. Describe the sides and angles of quadrilateral E. What are the names for it?

Quiz

6. Describe the sides and angles of this quadrilateral. What are the names for it?

7. Write as many names for this quadrilateral as you can.

8. Describe the sides and angles of the figure in Exercise 7.

9. Which of the quadrilaterals shown in Exercises 1–5 has only two parallel sides?

OBJECTIVE Identify and draw polygons

15 Minutes

Begin by reviewing the definition of a polygon. Remind students that a *closed figure* is a figure that begins and ends at the same point.

Review the definitions of sides and angles. Point out that students may recognize some of the polygons, but may not recognize some of the others. Tell students that any closed figure with straight sides is a polygon, even if the sides are not the same length. Explain that a polygon with sides that are the same length and angles that are the same measure are *regular* polygons, and that polygons with sides of different lengths and angles of different measures are *not regular*.

Call students' attention to the first example.

Ask: **How many sides does a triangle have? 3 How many angles? 3 How are the two triangles alike? They have the same number of sides and angles. How are they different? Possible answer: Each side of the triangle on the left is the same length. It is a regular polygon. Each side of the triangle on the right is different. It is not regular.**

Repeat the questions as students examine each plane figure.

Explain that polygons are named by the number of sides and angles. You may wish to point out how the prefixes in the names suggest the number of sides and angles.

Prefix	Meaning
tri	three
quadri	four
penta	five
hexa	six
octa	eight

TRY THESE Exercises 1–4 prepare students for identifying and drawing the types of polygons they will encounter in the **Practice on Your Own** section.

- **Exercise 1**   Identify a quadrilateral.
- **Exercise 2**   Identify a triangle.
- **Exercise 3**   Identify a pentagon.
- **Exercise 4**   Identify a hexagon.

PRACTICE ON YOUR OWN Review the process of using dot paper to draw a regular polygon or a polygon that is not regular. Ask students to explain why each figure is regular or not regular. Exercises 1–6 ask students to identify the polygon and tell whether it is regular or not regular. Exercises 7–9 instruct students to connect the points to identify the regular or not regular polygon.

QUIZ Determine if students can name the polygon and identify it as regular or not regular. Success is indicated by 3 out of 4 correct responses.

Students who successfully complete the **Practice on Your Own** and **Quiz** are ready to move to the next skill.

COMMON ERRORS

- Students may count the number of sides or angles incorrectly.

- Students may not remember the correct name of the polygon.

- Students may connect points to make a random figure that is not a polygon.

Students who make more than 2 errors in the **Practice on Your Own**, or who were not successful in the **Quiz** section, may benefit from the **Alternative Teaching Strategy** on the next page.

Alternative Teaching Strategy
Use Models to Draw Polygons

OBJECTIVE Use models to draw polygons

MATERIALS several examples of each type of polygon, regular and not regular; markers; dot paper

Begin the lesson by reviewing with students the definition of a polygon as a closed figure with straight sides.

Have students trace a regular, or equilateral, triangle. Suggest that they use markers to draw each side of the triangle in a different color. Then have students count and record the number of sides and angles in the triangle.

3 sides

3 angles

Ask: **How many sides does a triangle have? 3 How many angles does a triangle have? 3**

Distribute examples of other regular polygons for students to trace. Have them repeat the counting process. Continue the activity with quadrilaterals, pentagons, hexagons, and octagons. You may also wish to remind students that a regular quadrilateral is also named a *square*.

When students show understanding, introduce some polygons that are not regular. Have students trace these polygons, counting and recording the number of sides and angles of each one.

Guide students to use their results to verify that polygons are named by the number of sides or angles they have, and that while the sides of a regular polygon are all the same length, the sides of a polygon that is not regular have different lengths.

You may wish to extend the lesson by asking students to work in pairs. Without the aid of models, have students use pencils and dot paper to draw polygons that are regular and polygons that are not regular.

Polygons

A **polygon** is a closed plane figure with straight sides. A polygon is named by the number of sides or angles it has. In a **regular polygon,** all the sides have equal length and all the angles have equal measure.

Triangle	**Quadrilateral**	**Pentagon**	**Hexagon**	**Octagon**
3 sides, 3 angles	4 sides, 4 angles	5 sides, 5 angles	6 sides, 6 angles	8 sides, 8 angles
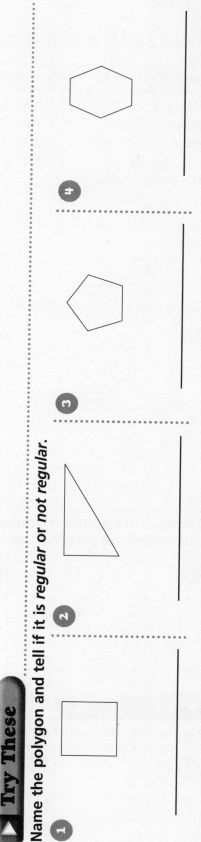				
regular not regular	regular not regular	regular not regular	regular not regular	regular not regular

▲ Try These

Name the polygon and tell if it is *regular* or *not regular.*

1 ....

2 ....

3 ....

4 ....

Go to the next side.

Practice on Your Own

Skill 49

Use dot paper to draw a regular polygon.		Draw a polygon that is not regular.	
Step 1 Mark three points that are all the same distance apart.	**Step 2** Connect the three points to form a triangle.	**Step 1** Mark three points that are not the same distance apart.	**Step 2** Connect the three points to form a triangle.

Name the polygon and tell if it is *regular* or *not regular*.

1 _____

2 _____

3 _____

4 _____

5 _____

6 _____

Connect the points to make a polygon. Name the polygon. Tell whether it is *regular* or *not regular*.

7 _____

8 _____

9 _____

▶ **Quiz**

Name the polygon and tell whether it is *regular* or *not regular*.

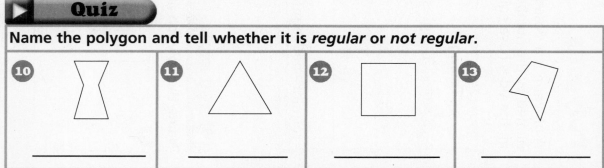

10 _____

11 _____

12 _____

13 _____

OBJECTIVE Identify lines of symmetry

Begin the skill by reminding students that if they fold a figure in half along a line so that both parts match, the fold is a line of symmetry.

Call students' attention to Model A.

Ask: **How many lines of symmetry does the trapezoid have? 1 How do you know? Possible answer: I can fold the figure in half once and the parts will match.**

Call students' attention to Model B.

Ask: **How many lines of symmetry does the rectangle have? 2 How do you know? Possible answer: I can fold the figure in half two ways and the parts will match.**

For Model C, ask: **Do the two parts match? No** Help students understand that matching parts should have the same size and shape. So, the line shown on the circle is not a line of symmetry.

TRY THESE Exercises 1–3 prompt students to match the part on each side of the dashed line to determine if the line is a line of symmetry.

- **Exercise 1** Line of symmetry

- **Exercise 2** Not a line of symmetry

- **Exercise 3** Line of symmetry

PRACTICE ON YOUR OWN Review the examples at the top of the page. Have students identify which lines in each figure are lines of symmetry. Make sure they justify their responses. In Exercises 1–6, students tell whether or not the line is a line of symmetry. In Exercises 7–9, students draw the line(s) of symmetry.

QUIZ Determine if students are able to identify a line of symmetry in a figure. Success is indicated by 2 out of 3 correct responses.

Students who successfully complete the **Practice on Your Own** and **Quiz** are ready to move to the next skill.

COMMON ERRORS

- Students may identify a line that does not divide the figure into two matching parts as a line of symmetry.

- Students may not recognize that a figure has more than one line of symmetry.

Students who make more than 3 errors in the **Practice on Your Own**, or who were not successful in the **Quiz** section, may benefit from the **Alternative Teaching Strategy** on the next page.

Alternative Teaching Strategy
Use Models to Identify Lines of Symmetry

15 Minutes

OBJECTIVE Fold figures to identify one or more lines of symmetry

MATERIALS dot paper, scissors

Remind students that when they fold a figure along a line of symmetry, both parts match.

Provide students with the dot paper. Have them outline and cut out a 5-by-5 square.

Say: **Begin by folding the square in half from top to bottom.**

Ask: **Do both parts match? yes Does the square have at least one line of symmetry? yes**

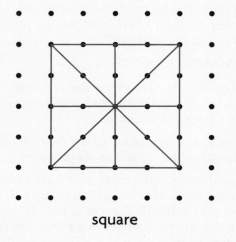

square

As students find the lines of symmetry, have them trace those lines on the dot paper.

Ask: **Suppose you fold the square in half from one corner to the opposite corner. Is the fold line a line of symmetry? yes**

Guide students as they discover the two diagonal lines of symmetry for the square.

Repeat this activity for a 4-by-6 rectangle.

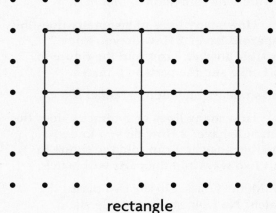

rectangle

When students show an understanding of lines of symmetry in a square and rectangle, have them look for lines of symmetry in an equilateral triangle (3) and a parallelogram (0). Each time ask students to explain how they know if a figure has a line of symmetry.

Symmetry

A line of symmetry is an imaginary line that divides a figure into two congruent parts. If you fold a figure along a line of symmetry, both halves match. A figure can have one or more lines of symmetry, or no lines of symmetry.

Model A

1 line of symmetry

The two parts match.

Model B

2 lines of symmetry

The parts match for each line.

Model C

0 lines of symmetry

The two parts do not match.

▲ Try These

Tell if the dashed line is a line of symmetry. Write *yes* or *no*.

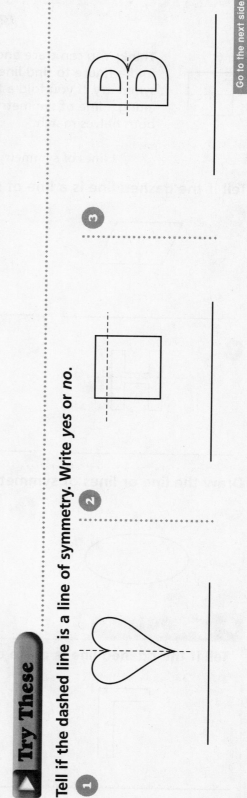

1

2

3

Go to the next side.

Practice on Your Own

 Think: You can trace and fold a figure to find lines of symmetry. If you fold a figure along a line of symmetry, both halves match.

4 lines of symmetry

 Think: A figure can have 1 line of symmetry, more than one line of symmetry, or no lines of symmetry.

0 lines of symmetry

Tell if the dashed line is a line of symmetry. Write *yes* or *no*.

1

2

3 _____

4

5

6

Draw the line or lines of symmetry.

7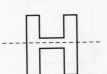

8

9 _____

▶ **Quiz**

Tell if the dashed line is a line of symmetry. Write *yes* or *no*.

10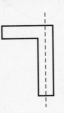

11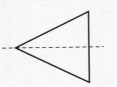

12

_____   _____   _____

Skill  51

Grade 4

Congruent Figures

OBJECTIVE Identify congruent figures

MATERIALS 2 congruent triangles, 2 congruent rectangles *15 Minutes*

Begin by reminding students that congruent figures have the same size and shape.

As students look at the first model, say: **Look at the size and shape of the figures. Are these figures the same size?** Yes **Are they the same shape?** Yes

Explain that because they are the same size and the same shape, they are congruent.

Have students look at the second model.

Say: **Look at the figures. Are they the same shape?** No **How do you know? The figures are not the same shape. One is a rectangle and one is a triangle.**

For the third model, say: **The figures are the same shape. Are they congruent?** No, **the triangles are the same shape but they are not the same size.**

Display the congruent triangles, laying one upon the other to show that they are the same size and shape. Rotate the triangle.

Ask: **Are the triangles still congruent?** Yes, **they are still the same size and shape.**

Show the congruent rectangles in different positions and ask the same question. Remind students that congruent figures are the same size and shape, but are in different positions.

TRY THESE In Exercises 1–4 students look at size, shape, and position to test for congruence.

- **Exercise 1**   Different shape.
- **Exercises 2 and 4**   Different position.
- **Exercise 3**   Different size.

PRACTICE ON YOUR OWN Review the examples at the top of the page. Have students explain why the figures in the first model are congruent, and those in the second are not congruent.

QUIZ Determine if students can select congruent figures, and that they understand position does not affect congruency. Success is determined by 2 out of 3 correct responses.

Students who successfully complete the **Practice on Your Own** and **Quiz** are ready to move on to the next skill.

COMMON ERRORS

- Students may neglect to check both size and shape when determining congruency.

- Students may have difficulty determining if figures are congruent when they are in different positions.

Students who made more than 2 errors in the **Practice on Your Own**, or who were not successful in the **Quiz** section, may benefit from the **Alternative Teaching Strategy** on the next page.

Alternative Teaching Strategy
Model Congruent Figures

OBJECTIVE Use models to show congruent figures

MATERIALS a template of various sized squares, a template of various sized rectangles, a template of various sized triangles, tracing paper

Display the templates for each plane figure and have students name the plane figure. Emphasize that the figures on each template are the same shape but different sizes.

Distribute the templates and tracing paper. Direct students to trace a square. Then have students trace a triangle.

Ask: **Are your traced figures the same shape? No**

Explain that the traced figures cannot be congruent because congruent figures have the same shape and size.

Then, have each student choose a figure from a template and trace it. When tracings are complete, ask: **Are your traced figure and the figure on the template the same size and shape? Yes**

Explain that because the traced figure and the template are the same size and shape, they are congruent figures.

Have students trace several more figures. Choose a tracing and a figure on the template with the same shape but different size.

Ask: **These figures have the same shape. Are they congruent? No How do you know? They are different sizes.**

As students demonstrate an understanding of congruence, have them pick a template and a tracing and tell whether they are congruent. Have students explain why they are or are not congruent.

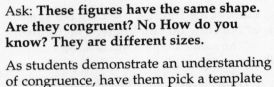

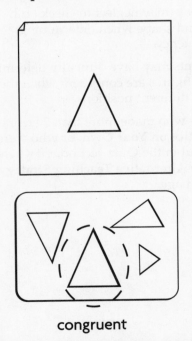

congruent

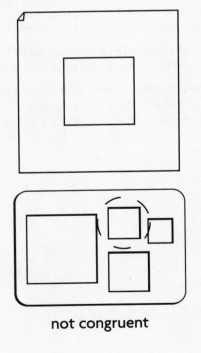

not congruent

Congruent Figures

Figures that are the same shape and the same size are **congruent**.

Congruent	Not Congruent	Not Congruent

Congruent

These squares are the same size and the same *shape*.

squares

They are congruent.

Not Congruent

These figures are *not* the same shape.

rectangle   triangle

They are **not** congruent.

Not Congruent

These triangles are the same shape but *not* the same size.

triangles

They are **not** congruent.

▲ Try These

Answer the questions about the figures. Write yes or no.

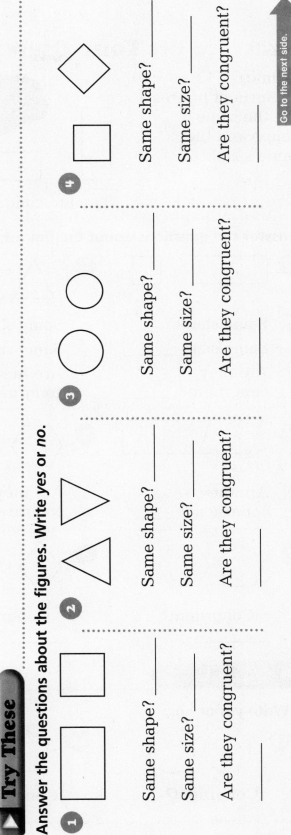

1

Same shape? _____

Same size? _____

Are they congruent? _____

2

Same shape? _____

Same size? _____

Are they congruent? _____

3

Same shape? _____

Same size? _____

Are they congruent? _____

4

Same shape? _____

Same size? _____

Are they congruent? _____

Go to the next side.

Practice on Your Own

Skill (51)

Think:
Congruent figures are the same *shape* and the same *size*.

Remember:
Figures do not have to be in the same position to be congruent.

They are congruent.   They are **not** congruent.

....

Answer the questions about the figures. Write *yes* or *no*.

1

Same shape? _____
Same size? _____
Are they congruent? _____

2

Same shape? _____
Same size? _____
Are they congruent? _____

3

Same shape? _____
Same size? _____
Are they congruent? _____

....

4

Are they congruent? _____

5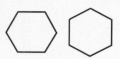

Are they congruent? _____

6

Are they congruent? _____

....

7

Congruent?
_____

8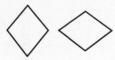

Congruent?
_____

9

Congruent?
_____

▶ **Quiz**

Write *yes* or *no*.

10

Congruent?
_____

11

Congruent?
_____

12

Congruent?
_____

15 Minutes

OBJECTIVE Identify slides, flips, and turns

MATERIALS pattern blocks (optional)

Begin the lesson by suggesting to students that a plane figure can be moved in different ways. Tell them that when you move a plane figure, you can *slide*, *flip*, or *turn* it.

You may wish to have students model the motions with pattern blocks as you work through the lesson.

Call students' attention to each of the diagrams. In turn, ask them to describe the motion used to move the figure.

Ask: **What motion do you use to** *slide* **the figure? Move the figure in a straight line. What motion do you use to** *flip* **the figure? Flip the figure over a line. How does the hexagon to the left of the dotted line compare to the hexagon to the right of the dotted line? They look the same, but they point in opposite directions. What motion do you use to** *turn* **the figure? Spin or rotate the figure around a point.**

To assess understanding, you may wish to ask students to describe how they use slides, flips, and turns to move real-world objects.

Guide students to understand that sliding, flipping, or turning a figure does not change its shape or size. The only thing that changes is the location of the figure.

TRY THESE In Exercises 1–3, students tell what kind of motion was used to move a plane figure.

• **Exercise 1**   Identify a slide.

• **Exercise 2**   Identify a turn.

• **Exercise 3**   Identify a flip.

PRACTICE ON YOUR OWN Review the examples at the top of the page with students. Suggest that they compare each pair of drawings carefully to determine what type of motion was used to move the figure. Exercises 1–9 ask students to tell what kind of motion was used to move the figure.

QUIZ Determine if students can identify plane figures as a slide, flip, or turn. Success is indicated by 4 out of 6 correct responses.

Students who successfully complete the **Practice on Your Own** and **Quiz** are ready to move to the next skill.

COMMON ERRORS

• Students may confuse flipping with turning and vice versa.

• Students may think that the size or shape of a plane figure changes when they slide, flip, or turn it.

Students who make more than 2 errors in the **Practice on Your Own**, or who were not successful in the **Quiz** section, may benefit from the **Alternative Teaching Strategy** on the next page.

Alternative Teaching Strategy
Draw Slides, Flips, and Turns

15 Minutes

OBJECTIVE Identify slides, flips, and turns

MATERIALS pattern blocks, spiral-bound notebook (optional)

Have students work in pairs for this activity.

Review with students the motions used to move a plane figure and the terms that describe the motions.

Hold up a pattern block, such as a trapezoid.

Ask: **What is the name of this figure? trapezoid** Trace the trapezoid on the board. Then ask: **What motion will I use to *slide* the trapezoid? Move it in a straight line.** Slide the trapezoid, and then draw an arrow to indicate the movement. Trace the trapezoid in its new location.

Trace another trapezoid on the board.

Ask: **What motion will I use to *flip* the trapezoid? Flip it over a line.** Draw a dotted line, flip the trapezoid over it, and trace the trapezoid in its new location.

Students may benefit from seeing a figure flipped in a different context. Draw a trapezoid with a heavy marker on the left-hand page in a spiral-bound notebook. Make sure the figure bleeds through the page. Model a flip by flipping the page so that the figure shows on the right-hand side of the notebook. Indicate that the dotted lines shown in the flips in this lesson are like the spiral binding of the notebook.

Trace another trapezoid on the board.

Ask: **What motion will I use to *turn* the trapezoid? Spin or rotate it around a point.** Rotate the trapezoid, and trace the trapezoid in its new location. Draw an arrow to indicate the turning motion.

Ask volunteers to label each drawing. Repeat with other plane figures.

When students show understanding, distribute pattern blocks to partners. One partner selects a pattern block, traces it, and passes the paper to his or her partner. While the first partner looks away, the other partner slides, flips, or turns the pattern block, and traces the block in its new location. The drawing is passed back to the first partner, who must identify the movement as a *slide*, *flip*, or *turn*, and label the drawing. Students take turns selecting pattern blocks and making the first tracing.

Conclude the lesson by having pairs show drawings that represent each type of motion.

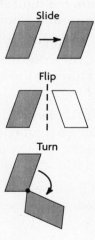

Slide

Flip

Turn

Grade 4
Skill 52

Slides, Flips, and Turns

Three different ways to move a plane figure are a *slide*, a *flip*, and a *turn*.

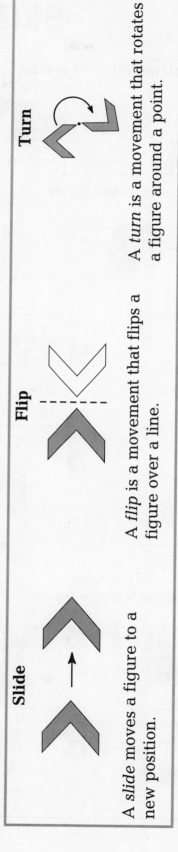

Slide	Flip	Turn

A *slide* moves a figure to a new position.

A *flip* is a movement that flips a figure over a line.

A *turn* is a movement that rotates a figure around a point.

◢ Try These

Tell what kind of motion was used to move each plane figure. Write *slide*, *flip*, or *turn*.

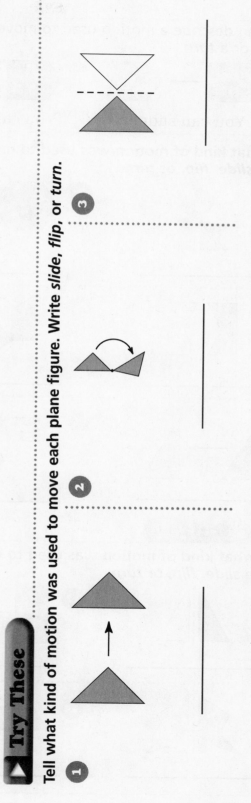

1 _____

2 _____

3 _____

Go to the next side.

Practice on Your Own

Skill 52

You can describe a motion used to move a plane figure as a *slide*, a *flip*, or a *turn*.

 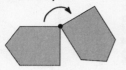 

You can slide it.   You can flip it.   You can turn it.

Tell what kind of motion was used to move each plane figure.
Write *slide*, *flip*, or *turn*.

1
_____

2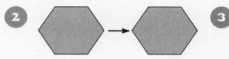
_____

3
_____

4
_____

5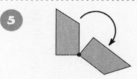
_____

6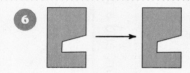
_____

7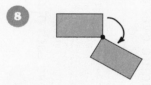
_____

8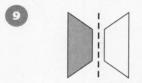
_____

9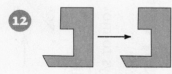
_____

Quiz

Tell what kind of motion was used to move each plane figure.
Write *slide*, *flip*, or *turn*.

10
_____

11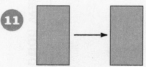
_____

12
_____

13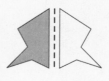
_____

14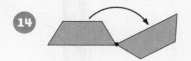
_____

15
_____

OBJECTIVE Identify solid figures by the number of faces, edges, and vertices, or by a curved surface

MATERIALS classroom objects that look like geometric solids, or large pictures of figures

15 Minutes

Begin the lesson by pointing out each solid figure and its name. Review the definitions of *face*, *edge*, and *vertex*. Be sure to clarify that the plural of *vertex* is *vertices*. Have students find the faces, edges, and vertices of several classroom objects.

Then, call students' attention to the rectangular prism. Have them identify the 6 faces, 12 edges, and 8 vertices.

Follow the same procedure for the cube.

Then ask students to find and number the faces, edges, and vertices on the square pyramid.

Now direct students' attention to the sphere.

Ask: **How many faces does the sphere have? 0 Edges? 0 Vertices? 0 Why doesn't the sphere have any faces, edges, or vertices? It has no flat surfaces.**

TRY THESE Exercises 1–3 provide visual prompts to help students name the solid.

- **Exercise 1**   Square pyramid
- **Exercise 2**   Cube
- **Exercise 3**   Sphere

PRACTICE ON YOUR OWN Review the examples at the top of the page. Ask students to explain how they know that these are solid figures. Ask students to compare the attributes of some of the different figures. Exercises 1–3 provide visual prompts that guide students to name different solid figures. In Exercises 4–6, students must identify the figure's name.

QUIZ Determine if students can identify three solid figures and their attributes. Success is indicated by 2 out of 3 correct responses.

Students who successfully complete the **Practice on Your Own** and **Quiz** are ready to move to the next skill.

COMMON ERRORS

- Students may miscount the faces, edges, and vertices of a solid figure.

- Students may use incorrect vocabulary.

- Students may forget that only prisms and pyramids have faces, edges, and vertices.

Students who make more than 2 errors in the **Practice on Your Own**, or who were not successful in the **Quiz** section, may benefit from the **Alternative Teaching Strategy** on the next page.

Alternative Teaching Strategy
Use Models to Identify Solid Figures

15 Minutes

OBJECTIVE Use models to identify solid figures

MATERIALS models of solids, figures, and small, multi-colored sticky notes

Students work in pairs for this activity. One partner labels each attribute with a sticky note, while the other counts and records the number of sticky notes used. Partners take turns labeling each model and recording the number of faces, edges, and vertices.

Distribute the models of solid figures and the small, multi-colored sticky notes. Instruct students to start with the rectangular prism.

First, tell students to use one color of sticky notes (for example, blue) to label all of the *faces* on the rectangular prism.

Ask: **How many faces does a rectangular prism have? 6**

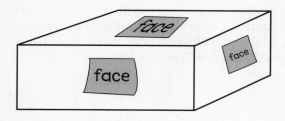

Then suggest students use another color of sticky notes (for example, yellow) to label all of the *edges* of the rectangular prism.

Ask: **How many *edges* does the rectangular prism have? 12**

Finally, tell students to use a third color of sticky notes to label all of the *vertices* of the rectangular prism.

Ask: **How many *vertices* does the rectangular prism have? 8**

Repeat the activity for the cube.

Ask: **How are the rectangular prism and the cube alike? They have the same number of faces, edges, and vertices. How are they different? Possible answer: All of the faces on the cube are the same size and the same shape. On the rectangular prism, only the faces opposite each other are the same size and same shape.**

Repeat this activity for the rest of the geometric models.

Ask: **What sort of test could you do to find out if one of these solid figures is a curved surface? See if it can roll.**

Conclude the activity by asking students to compare and contrast different figures.

Grade 4
Skill
53

Solid Figures

Some solid figures can be described by the number of faces, edges, and vertices they have.

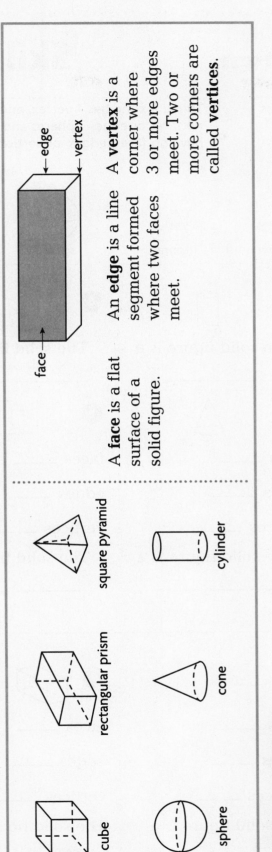

A **face** is a flat surface of a solid figure.

An **edge** is a line segment formed where two faces meet.

A **vertex** is a corner where 3 or more edges meet. Two or more corners are called **vertices**.

cube   rectangular prism   square pyramid

sphere   cone   cylinder

▶ Try These

Name the solid figure.

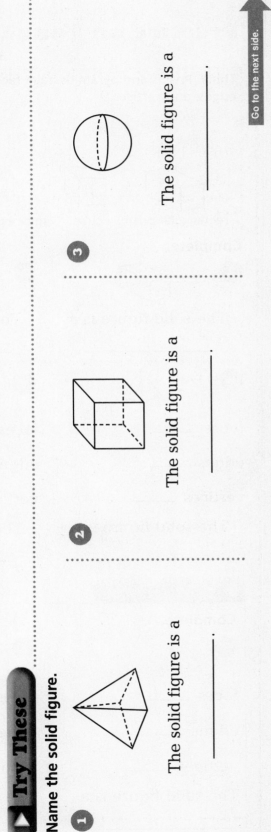

1 The solid figure is a _____

2 The solid figure is a _____

3 The solid figure is a _____

Go to the next side.

Intervention • Skills IN229

Practice on Your Own

Skill 53

Think: Prisms and pyramids have faces, edges, and vertices.

rectangular prism   cube   square pyramid

Think: A cone has 1 vertex, and no faces or edges. Spheres and cylinders have no faces, edges, or vertices.

cone   sphere   cylinder

Complete.

1

The solid figure is a _____.

2

The solid figure is a _____.

3

The solid figure is a _____.

4

faces _____

edges _____

vertices _____

The solid figure is a _____.

5

faces _____

edges _____

vertices _____

The solid figure is a _____.

6

faces _____

edges _____

vertices _____

The solid figure is a _____.

▶ Quiz

Complete.

7

faces _____

edges _____

vertices _____

The solid figure is a _____.

8

faces _____

edges _____

vertices _____

The solid figure is a _____.

9

faces _____

edges _____

vertices _____

The solid figure is a _____.

Algebraic Thinking, Patterns, and Functions

15 Minutes

OBJECTIVE Find missing addends

You may wish to have students use counters to represent mathematical sentences.

Call students' attention to the first example, $6 + \_\_\_ = 15$. Have students identify the known addend and the sum.

Have students model the sentence using counters. Then, ask one student to write the addition sentence on the board: $6 + 9 = 15$.

Write the subtraction sentence $15 - 6 = \_\_\_$. Have students model the sentence using counters. Then ask one student to write the subtraction sentence on the board: $15 - 6 = 9$.

Ask: **What happens to the sum when the addition sentence is rewritten as a subtraction sentence? The sum becomes the number to subtract from.**

Link the modeling activity to the steps for finding the missing addend.

TRY THESE Exercises 1–4 prepare students for the types of exercises they will encounter in the **Practice on Your Own** section.

• **Exercises 1–4** Find the missing addend.

PRACTICE ON YOUR OWN Review the example at the top of the page. Have students identify the known addend, missing addend, and sum in each number sentence: $7 + \_\_\_ = 20$ and $20 - 7 = \_\_\_$.

MATERIALS counters

QUIZ Determine if students can use a related subtraction sentence to find a missing addend.

Success is indicated by 3 out of 4 correct responses.

Students who successfully complete the **Practice on Your Own** and **Quiz** are ready to move to the next skill.

COMMON ERRORS

• Students may not know basic facts for addition and subtraction, and thus write an incorrect addend.

• Students may have difficulty changing the order of numbers when they write subtraction sentences from addition sentences.

Students who make more than 7 errors in the **Practice on Your Own**, or who were not successful in the **Quiz** section may benefit from the **Alternative Teaching Strategy** on the next page.

Alternative Teaching Strategy
Model Missing Addends with Cubes

15 Minutes

OBJECTIVE Find missing addends

MATERIALS connecting cubes of different colors, prepared index cards with related addition and subtraction sentences written on each

Distribute at least 10 of each color of the connecting cubes, and index cards with related addition and subtraction sentences, such as 9 + ___ = 13 and 13 − ___ = 4 written on them.

Have students model the known addend with cubes of one color. Then have them count on with cubes of a second color to find the missing addend.

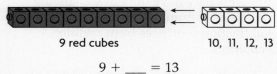

9 red cubes   10, 11, 12, 13

$$9 + \underline{\quad} = 13$$
$$9 + 4 = 13$$

Ask students to use the cubes to represent the subtraction sentence they would write to find the missing addend.

$$13 - 9 = 4$$

Repeat this activity several times. Encourage students to use the connecting cubes to model each addition and subtraction sentence on the index cards.

You may wish to extend the activity by including index cards with exercises such as 3 + ___ = 4 + 3. Help the students model finding the sum on the right side of the equation, using two different colors of connecting cubes. Then have them work as before, modeling the known addend and counting on to find the missing addend.

Repeat with similar equations several times. Ask students to share any patterns they find.

Grade 4
Skill
54

Missing Addends

Think of an addition fact or a related subtraction fact to find the missing addend.

Think: $6 + 9 = 9 + 6$.
Addends may be added in any order without changing their sum.

Think about an addition fact to find $6 + \underline{\quad} = 15$.

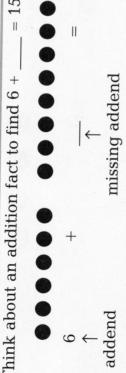

$$6 + \underset{\underset{\text{missing addend}}{\uparrow}}{\underline{\quad}} = \underset{\underset{\text{sum}}{\uparrow}}{15}$$

Use a related subtraction fact to find $6 + \underline{\quad} = 15$.

$$\underset{\underset{\text{sum}}{\uparrow}}{15} - \underset{\underset{\text{addend}}{\uparrow}}{6} = \underset{\underset{\text{missing addend}}{\uparrow}}{\underline{\quad}}$$

So, $6 + 9 = 15$.

▲ Try These

Find the missing addends.

1 $7 + \underline{?} = 13$

$\underset{\underset{\text{sum}}{\uparrow}}{13} - \underset{\underset{\text{addend}}{\uparrow}}{7} = \underset{\underset{\text{missing addend}}{\uparrow}}{6}$

$7 + \underline{\quad} = 13$

2 $\underline{?} + 8 = 17$

$\underset{\underset{\text{sum}}{\uparrow}}{17} - \underset{\underset{\text{addend}}{\uparrow}}{8} = \underset{\underset{\text{missing addend}}{\uparrow}}{\underline{\quad}}$

$\underline{\quad} + 8 = 17$

3 $6 + \underline{?} = 8 + 6$
   $6 + \underline{?} = 14$

$\underset{\underset{\text{sum}}{\uparrow}}{14} - \underset{\underset{\text{addend}}{\uparrow}}{6} = \underset{\underset{\text{missing addend}}{\uparrow}}{\underline{\quad}}$

$6 + \underline{\quad} = 8 + 6$

4 $\underline{?} + 3 = 3 + 9$
   $\underline{?} + 3 = \underline{\quad}$

$\underset{\underset{\text{sum}}{\uparrow}}{\underline{\quad}} - \underset{\underset{\text{addend}}{\uparrow}}{3} = \underset{\underset{\text{missing addend}}{\uparrow}}{\underline{\quad}}$

$\underline{\quad} + 3 = 3 + 9$

Go to the next side.

Practice on Your Own

Skill 54

Find 7 + ____ = 20.

7	+	__	=	20
↑		↑		↑
addend		missing addend		sum

Think: Use a related subtraction fact to find a missing addend.

Rewrite the subtraction sentence.

20	−	7	=	__
↑		↑		↑
sum		addend		missing addend

20 − 7 = 13

Write the missing addend. 7 + <u>13</u> = 20

Remember:
7 + 13 = 20
13 + 7 = 20

Find the missing addend.

1 8 + ? = 15
15 − 8 = ____
8 + ____ = 15

2 ? + 3 = 14
14 − 3 = ____
____ + 3 = 14

3 7 + ? = 16
16 − 7 = ____
7 + ____ = 16

4 4 + ? = 5 + 4
4 + ? = 9
9 − 4 = ____
4 + ____ = 9

5 6 + 5 = 5 + ?
11 = 5 + ?
11 − 5 = ____
5 + ____ = 11

6 6 + ? = 13 + 6
6 + ? = 19
19 − 6 = ____
6 + ____ = 19

Find the missing addend.

7 6 + __ = 17

8 __ + 6 = 6 + 8

9 4 + __ = 22

10 __ + 8 = 8 + 8

11 7 + __ = 6 + 7

12 __ + 5 = 5 + 8

13 12 + __ = 17

14 __ + 4 = 17

15 __ + 5 = 14

16 7 + 3 = 3 + __

17 12 = __ + 8

18 9 + 6 = __ + 9

19 14 = 10 + __

20 6 + 2 = __ + 6

21 11 = __ + 7

22 8 + 3 = 3 + __

▶ Quiz

Find the missing addend.

23 __ + 8 = 12

24 6 + __ = 18

25 __ + 7 = 10

26 2 + __ = 16

20 Minutes

OBJECTIVE Extend number patterns using addition and subtraction

Review the definition of a pattern. Have students look at Example 1. Explain that the task is to examine the series of numbers that the blocks represent to see if they can discover the pattern. Then they will use the pattern to find the next number.

Ask: **What numbers are represented by the base-ten blocks? 350, 300, 250, and 200 Are the numbers increasing or decreasing? decreasing**
Say: **When the numbers decrease, the pattern may be a subtraction pattern.**
Ask: **What number do you subtract from 350 to get 300? 50 What number do you subtract from 300 to get 250? 50 What do you think is the rule for the pattern? Subtract 50.**

Point out that once they know the rule, they can extend the pattern to find the next number.
Ask: **From which number should you subtract 50, to continue the pattern? the last number, 200. What is the next number that will continue the pattern? 150**

Repeat the procedure to help to guide students through the next two examples. Help them to identify the rule for each pattern so that they can extend the pattern.

TRY THESE Exercises 1–3 provide practice extending a pattern.

* **Exercises 1–2** Use addition to extend a pattern.

* **Exercise 3** Use subtraction to extend a pattern.

PRACTICE ON YOUR OWN Review the examples at the top of the page. Make sure students understand that they should look at whether the numbers in the pattern are increasing or decreasing. This tells them whether the pattern is an addition pattern or a subtraction pattern. Then, they can identify the rule and extend the pattern.

QUIZ Determine if students can extend number patterns involving addition or subtraction. Success is indicated by 3 out of 4 correct responses.

Students who successfully complete **Practice on Your Own** and **Quiz** are ready to move to the next skill.

COMMON ERRORS

* Students may not understand how to find the rule and add 1 to extend the pattern.

* Students may understand the pattern, but add or subtract incorrectly.

* Students may apply the correct rule, but may add to or subtract from the wrong number in the pattern.

Students who make more than 3 errors in **Practice on Your Own**, or who were not successful in the **Quiz** section may benefit from the **Alternative Teaching Strategy** on the next page.

Alternative Teaching Strategy
Model Finding Number Patterns

20 Minutes

OBJECTIVE Use counters to model patterns for addition and subtraction

MATERIALS counters

Students may benefit from working in small groups. Distribute the counters and explain to students that they will use the counters to find and continue a number pattern.

Have students arrange counters in groups of 2, 5, 8, 11, 14, and 17. Ask students to look carefully at the groups. Students may note that the number of counters in the groups increases. Suggest that since the number of counters increases, the pattern may be an addition pattern.

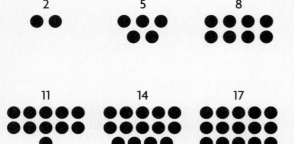

Say: **There are two counters in the first group.**
Ask: **How many more counters do you need to make 5 counters for the second group? 3 How many more counters than 5 do you need to make 8 counters? 3 How many more than 8 to make 11? 3**
Say: **Each group has 3 more counters than the last group.**
Ask: **What rule do you see for the pattern? Add 3.**

Discuss with students how they can find the number of counters for the group that comes next. Explain that they can add 3 counters to the last group of 17 counters. So, the next group will have 20 counters.

Repeat the activity with a subtraction pattern. Help students to find the pattern, write the rule, and find the next number.

When students show an understanding of both addition and subtraction patterns with counters, have them find number patterns using numbers only.

Number Patterns

Predict the number in each pattern. A **pattern** is an ordered set of numbers or objects. The order helps you predict what will come next.

Example 1

The numbers decrease by 50, so the next number would be 200 – 50, or 150.

Example 2

21, 31, 41, 51, 61

The numbers increase by 10. The next number will be 61 + 10, or 71.

Example 3

85, 80, 75, 70, 65

The numbers decrease by 5. The next number will be 65 – 5, or 60.

Try These

Predict the next number in each pattern.

1.

2.

3. 27, 22, 17, 12, _____

Go to the next side.

Practice on Your Own

Skill 55

Predict the next number in each pattern.

Example 1	Example 2
7, 9, 11, 13, 15	28, 24, 20, 16
The numbers increase by 2. The next number will be 15 + 2, or 17.	The numbers decrease by 4. The next number will be 16 − 4, or 12.

Predict the next number in each pattern.

1 10, 15, 20, 25, _____

2 123, 121, 119, 117, _____

3 64, 68, 72, 76, _____

4 118, 114, 110, 106, _____

5 114, 111, 108, 105, _____

6 233, 236, 239, 242, _____

7 120, 130, 140, 150, _____

8 300, 400, 500, 600, _____

9 200, 195, 190, 185, _____

10 153, 143, 133, 123, _____

11 144, 132, 120, 108, _____

12 97, 94, 91, 88, _____

▶ Quiz

Write the next number in the pattern.

13 262, 252, 242, 232, _____

14 306, 303, 300, 297, _____

15 180, 200, 220, 240, _____

16 795, 800, 805, 810, _____

20 Minutes

OBJECTIVE Recognize and extend number patterns by using a rule

Begin by reminding students that a pattern is an ordered set of numbers or objects. Suggest to students that they can write rules to describe number patterns.

Call students' attention to Example 1 on the page. Help them see the pattern.

Ask: **What does the table show? the total number of plates on different numbers of tables How many plates are on 1 table? 5 How many are on 2? 10 How many are on 3? 15 What is the pattern? For every table added, there are 5 more plates.**

Invite students to state the rule for the pattern in their own words. Make sure that they understand that the rule *Multiply the number of tables by 5* describes this pattern.

Ask: **How many plates are on 5 tables? How do you know?** *25 plates; 5 × 5 = 25*

Call students' attention to Example 2 and ask similar questions to help them see the pattern. Invite students to state the rule for the pattern in their own words. Make sure that they understand that the rule *Multiply the number of pies by 7* describes this pattern.

Ask: **How does the table help you find a rule for the pattern? Possible response: The table shows the numbers in an organized way so the pattern is clear.**

TRY THESE In Exercises 1–3, students write a rule to describe a number pattern.

- **Exercise 1**   Multiply by 4.
- **Exercise 2**   Multiply by 2.
- **Exercise 3**   Multiply by 3.

PRACTICE ON YOUR OWN Review the example at the top of the page. Be sure students understand they should first identify the pattern and then write a rule that describes that pattern.

QUIZ Determine if students can recognize and extend number patterns by using a rule. Success is indicated by 3 out of 4 correct responses.

Students who successfully complete the **Practice on Your Own** and **Quiz** are ready to move to the next skill.

COMMON ERRORS

- Students may have difficulty recognizing a pattern.

- Students may have difficulty identifying the rule to extend the pattern.

- Students may not know multiplication facts.

Students who made more than 2 errors in the **Practice on Your Own**, or who were not successful in the **Quiz** section, may benefit from the **Alternative Teaching Strategy** on the next page.

Alternative Teaching Strategy
Use Models to Find a Rule

20 Minutes

OBJECTIVE Use base-ten blocks to show number patterns and find rules

MATERIALS base-ten blocks, paper

You may wish to have students work in pairs. One student models the number pattern with blocks, while the other student records each step with paper and pencil.

Write the following table on the board.

Quarts of Juice	1	2	3	4	5	6
Oranges (pounds)	5	10	15	20	25	☐

Distribute the base-ten blocks. Have one partner model the numbers in the table.

Have the other partner record:

$1 \times \underline{\hspace{1cm}} = 5$

$2 \times \underline{\hspace{1cm}} = 10$

$3 \times \underline{\hspace{1cm}} = 15$

$4 \times \underline{\hspace{1cm}} = 20$

$5 \times \underline{\hspace{1cm}} = 25$

Have students examine the base-ten block models and the incomplete multiplication sentences.

Ask: **What pattern do you see?**

Students may note that the number 5 is missing in each multiplication sentence, and that for each new column in the model, the number of blocks increases by 5.

Help students recognize that the table shows the same pattern. For every quart of juice, there are 5 pounds of oranges. Thus, for 2 quarts of juice, there are 2×5, or 10 pounds of oranges.

Invite students to state the rule for the pattern in their own words. Make sure that they understand that the rule *Multiply the number of quarts of juice by 5* describes this pattern.

Ask: **How many pounds of oranges are needed to make 6 quarts of juice?**
30; $6 \times 5 = 30$

Repeat modeling and recording number patterns until students are confident they are able to recognize and describe patterns.

Find a Rule

Look for a pattern. Write a rule.

Example 1
How many plates are on 5 tables?

Think: 1 table has 5 plates. 2 tables have 10 plates.

Tables	1	2	3	4	5
Plates	5	10	15	20	☐

Pattern: The number of plates equals the number of tables times 5.

Rule: Multiply the number of tables by 5.
Since $5 \times 5 = 25$, there are 25 plates on 5 tables.

Example 2
How many apples are needed for 6 pies?

Think: 1 pie has 7 apples. 2 pies have 14 apples.

Pies	1	2	3	4	5	6
Apples	7	14	21	28	35	☐

Pattern: The number of apples equals the number of pies times 7.

Rule: Multiply the number of pies by 7.
Since $6 \times 7 = 42$, then 42 apples are needed for 6 pies.

▲ Try These

Write a rule for each table. Then complete the table.

1

Ostriches	1	2	3	4	5	6
Toes	4	8	12	16	☐	☐

Rule: _____

2

Beds	1	2	3	4	5	6
Pillows	2	4	6	8	☐	☐

Rule: _____

3

Plants	1	2	3	4	5	6
Leaves	3	6	9	12	☐	☐

Rule: _____

Go to the next side.

Practice on Your Own

How many raisins are in 7 cookies?

Think: Look for a pattern.

Pattern: The number of raisins equals the number of cookies times 6.

Think: Write a rule.

Cookies	2	3	4	5	6	7
Raisins	12	18	24	30	36	42

Rule: Multiply the number of cookies by 6.

Since $7 \times 6 = 42$, there are 42 raisins in 7 cookies.

Write a rule for each table. Then complete the table.

1

Boxes	1	2	3	4	5	6
Blocks	9	18	27			

Rule: _____

_____

2

Dollars	1	2	3	4	5	6
Nickels	20	40	60			

Rule: _____

_____

3

Cabinets	3	4	5	6	7	8
Drawers	9	12	15			

Rule: _____

_____

4

Flowers	2	3	4	5	6	7
Petals	16	24	32			

Rule: _____

_____

5

Rooms	4	5	6	7	8	9	10
Rugs	16	20	24				

Rule: _____

_____

6

Bicycles	5	6	7	8	9	10	11
Tires	10	12	14				

Rule: _____

_____

▶ Quiz

Write a rule for each table. Then complete the table.

7

Teams	3	4	5	6	7	8	9
Players	30	40	50				

Rule: _____

_____

8

Cartons	1	2	3	4	5	6	7
Eggs	12	24	36				

Rule: _____

_____

9

Shirts	3	4	5	6	7	8	9
Buttons	15	20	25				

Rule: _____

_____

10

Tins	1	2	3	4	5	6	7
Sardines	15	30	45				

Rule: _____

_____

Skill 57 Grade 4

20 Minutes

OBJECTIVE Find missing factors

Explain to the students that they are going to find the missing factor in a multiplication sentence. Point out the multiplication table. Suggest that when they do not remember a multiplication fact, they can use the multiplication table to help them find missing factors.

You may wish to familiarize the students with the table. Explain that there are factors in the left-most column, and factors in the top row. Where the row of one factor meets the column of another, they can find the product of those factors.

Then direct students' attention to the steps in the skill.

Say: **What do you already know about the multiplication fact? One factor is 4 and the product is 20.**

Ask students to find the row for the factor, 4, and look across until they find the product, 20.

Ask: **When you look up the column to the top, what factor do you find? 5 The multiplication table shows that $4 \times 5 = 20$. So, what is the missing factor? 5**

TRY THESE In Exercises 1–3, students find the missing factor step by step.

- **Exercise 1**   Multiplication fact for 3
- **Exercise 2**   Multiplication fact for 7
- **Exercise 3**   Multiplication fact for 8

PRACTICE ON YOUR OWN Review the example at the top of the page. Ask a volunteer to explain how to use the multiplication table to find the missing factor.

QUIZ Determine if students understand the relationship between the factors and the product, and can use one factor and the product to find a missing factor. Success is determined by 2 out of 3 correct responses.

Students who successfully complete the **Practice on Your Own** and **Quiz** are ready to move to the next skill.

COMMON ERRORS

- Students may not understand how to use the multiplication table.

- Students may have trouble tracking a row or column, and thus write an incorrect factor as a missing factor.

Students who made more than 5 errors in the **Practice on Your Own**, or who were not successful in the **Quiz** section, may benefit from the **Alternative Teaching Strategy** on the next page.

Alternative Teaching Strategy
Model Finding Missing Factors

20 Minutes

OBJECTIVE Find missing factors using arrays

MATERIALS counters or tiles

Prepare multiplication sentences on cards that show missing factors. Begin with products of 30 or less. Be sure to provide missing factors in both positions in the multiplication sentence.

Distribute the counters. Have students choose a card. Point out that the number sentences they have chosen show a missing factor. Explain that they already know one factor and the product. Suggest that they can use what they know to discover the missing factor.

Demonstrate how to use an array to find the missing factor for the multiplication sentence.

$$4 \times \square = 24.$$

○ ○ ○ ○ ○ ○
○ ○ ○ ○ ○ ○
○ ○ ○ ○ ○ ○
○ ○ ○ ○ ○ ○

$$4 \times 6 = 24$$

Explain that the product represents the total number of counters to use. Have students count out 24 counters.

Then point out that they can make 4 rows of counters using all 24 counters. The number of counters in each row will be the other factor. There are 6 counters in a row. So, $4 \times 6 = 24$.

Repeat the activity for $\square \times 6 = 18$. Suggest they make rows of 6 with the 18 counters. The number of rows will be the missing factor. There are 3 rows. So, $3 \times 6 = 18$.

$$\square \times 6 = 18.$$

○ ○ ○ ○ ○ ○
3 ○ ○ ○ ○ ○ ○
○ ○ ○ ○ ○ ○

$$3 \times 6 = 18$$

Continue the activity by having students choose other cards. When the students understand how to find a missing factor using arrays, give them more counters and have them work with greater products.

Grade 4
Skill
57

Algebra: Missing Factors

Use a multiplication table to find missing factors.

Find $4 \times \blacksquare = 20$.

factors ⟍ product

Think: 4 times what number is 20?

Step 1 Find the row for the factor, 4.
Look **across** the row. Find the product, 20.

Step 2 Look **up** the column.
Find the missing factor. It is 5.

Step 3 Complete the multiplication sentence.

$4 \times \mathbf{5} = 20$
factor — row
factor — column
product — row × column

Multiplication Table

column ↓

×	0	1	2	3	4	5	6	7	8	9
0	0	0	0	0	0	0	0	0	0	0
1	0	1	2	3	4	5	6	7	8	9
2	0	2	4	6	8	10	12	14	16	18
3	0	3	6	9	12	15	18	21	24	27
4	0	4	8	12	16	20	24	28	32	36
5	0	5	10	15	20	25	30	35	40	45
6	0	6	12	18	24	30	36	42	48	54
7	0	7	14	21	28	35	42	49	56	63
8	0	8	16	24	32	40	48	56	64	72
9	0	9	18	27	36	45	54	63	72	81

Factors →

row →

Try These

Use the multiplication table to find the missing factors.

1 $3 \times \blacksquare = 9$

Product: ☐

Row Factor: ☐   Product: ☐

Missing Factor: ☐

$3 \times$ ☐ $= 9$

2 $7 \times \blacksquare = 42$

Product: ☐

Row Factor: ☐   Product: ☐

Missing Factor: ☐

$7 \times$ ☐ $= 42$

3 $8 \times \blacksquare = 24$

Product: ☐

Row Factor: ☐   Product: ☐

Missing Factor: ☐

$8 \times$ ☐ $= 24$

Go to the next side. ↑

Practice on Your Own

Skill 57

Find ■ × 7 = 21.

Think:
Find the column for 7.
Look **down** the column to 21.
Look **left across** the row to 3.
The missing factor is 3.

×	0	1	2	3	4	5	6	7	8	9
0	0	0	0	0	0	0	0	0	0	0
1	0	1	2	3	4	5	6	7	8	9
2	0	2	4	6	8	10	12	14	16	18
3	0	3	6	9	12	15	18	21	24	27
4	0	4	8	12	16	20	24	28	32	36
5	0	5	10	15	20	25	30	35	40	45
6	0	6	12	18	24	30	36	42	48	54
7	0	7	14	21	28	35	42	49	56	63
8	0	8	16	24	32	40	48	56	64	72
9	0	9	18	27	36	45	54	63	72	81

$$3 \times 7 = 21$$
row × column = product

Use the multiplication table to find the missing factors.

1 ■ × 2 = 8
Column Factor: ☐
Product: ☐
Missing Factor: ☐
☐ × 2 = 8

2 ■ × 5 = 30
Column Factor: ☐
Product: ☐
Missing Factor: ☐
☐ × 5 = 30

3 ■ × 9 = 54
Column Factor: ☐
Product: ☐
Missing Factor: ☐
☐ × 9 = 54

4 ☐ × 4 = 20

5 6 × ☐ = 30

6 ☐ × 4 = 36

7 6 × ☐ = 18

8 ☐ × 7 = 28

9 8 × ☐ = 48

▶ Quiz

Use the multiplication table to find the missing factors.

10 ☐ × 8 = 72

11 6 × ☐ = 12

12 3 × ☐ = 15

13 ☐ × 9 = 45

14 ☐ × 3 = 24

15 5 × ☐ = 35

16 4 × ☐ = 16

17 7 × ☐ = 42

18 ☐ × 4 = 32

19 8 × ☐ = 64

20 ☐ × 7 = 63

21 8 × ☐ = 56

OBJECTIVE Locate points on a coordinate grid, first quadrant only

Read together the description of the miner's map at the top of the page. Examine the grid.

Ask: **What do the numbers across the bottom of the grid and up the side remind you of? two number lines, one horizontal and the other vertical At which point do the lines meet? 0**

Focus on the term *ordered pair*. Examine the grid closely. Point out that all the places marked with symbols can be found by naming ordered pairs. This might be a good time to look at the legend and read the names and symbols of all the places that can be located.

Help students trace the path to the miner's cabin. For point (3, 2), show them how to first move their finger 3 spaces to the right. Then they move 2 spaces up.

Ask: **Where do I start? at 0 What does the first number tell you? Move 3 spaces right. the second number? Move 2 spaces up.**

Emphasize the importance of the order of the numbers in the ordered pair. Ask students to find (2, 3). Contrast the location of this point to that of (3, 2).

TRY THESE Exercises 1–3 require students to identify places located at various points on the grid.

- **Exercise 1** Move right 1, up 1.

- **Exercise 2** Move right 5, up 4.

- **Exercise 3** Move right 2, up 4.

- **Exercise 4** Move right 4, up 5.

PRACTICE ON YOUR OWN Before students begin the exercises, examine together the map of the state park. Study the legend. Review the term *ordered pair*. Stress care in moving right first, then up. Remind students to always start at point 0.

QUIZ Determine if students know how to use ordered pairs to locate points on a grid. Success is determined by 2 out of 3 correct responses.

Students who successfully complete the **Practice on Your Own** and **Quiz** are ready to move to the next skill.

COMMON ERRORS

- Students may move up first, then right.

- Students may forget to start at point 0.

Students who made more than 2 errors in **Practice on Your Own**, or who were not successful in the **Quiz** section, may benefit from the **Alternative Teaching Strategy** on the next page.

Alternative Teaching Strategy
Locate Points on a Coordinate Grid

20 Minutes

OBJECTIVE Locate points on a coordinate grid

MATERIALS grids, marked as shown below

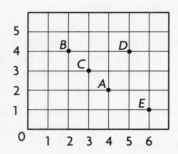

Distribute grids. Tell students they will use the ordered pair (4, 2) to locate a point on the grid.

Ask: **Where should you start? point 0 In which direction should you move first? right How many spaces? 4**

Observe students as they move across 4 spaces, using their finger as a guide. You may have them draw an arrow as shown on the miner's map. Have them stop and check that they are at the right point so far.

Ask: **In which direction should you move next? up How many spaces? 2**

Observe as they move up 2 spaces, again using a finger or an arrow to guide them. Have them name the letter, A, at point (4, 2).

Give students the ordered pairs for the rest of the points on the grid. Students can work in pairs, checking each other as they name the letters at the points.

Working in pairs, one student can mark another point, for example F, given the ordered pair (1,1) and ask the partner to name the letter at that point (1, 1).

Ordered Pairs

The horizontal and vertical lines on the map are called a **grid**. An **ordered pair** of numbers like (**3,2**) names a point on a grid. You can use ordered pairs to locate points on a grid.

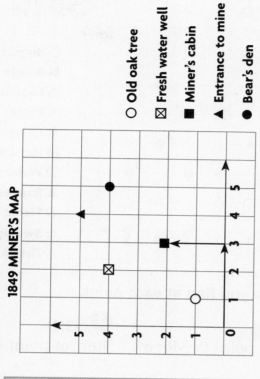

1849 MINER'S MAP

○ Old oak tree
⊠ Fresh water well
■ Miner's cabin
▲ Entrance to mine
● Bear's den

Look at the map. Name the place at point (3,2).

Step 1 Start at point 0 on grid.

Step 2 The first number in the ordered pair tells you how many spaces to move to the right. Move 3 spaces to the right.

Step 3 The second number tells you how many spaces to move up. Move up 2 spaces.

So, the miner's cabin is located at point (3,2).

▲ Try These

Use the map above. Name the place you find at each point.

1 (1,1)
Start at point 0. Move ☐ spaces to the right.
Move ☐ spaces up.
The place at point (1,1) is _____.

2 (5,4)
Start at point 0. Move ☐ spaces to the right.
Move ☐ spaces up.
The place at point (5,4) is _____.

3 (2,4)
Start at point 0. Move ☐ spaces to the right.
Move ☐ spaces up.
The place at point (2,4) is _____.

4 (4,5)
Start at point 0. Move ☐ spaces to the right.
Move ☐ spaces up.
The place at point (4,5) is _____.

Go to the next side.

Practice on Your Own

Skill 58

Think:
The ordered pair (4,3) means move **4 spaces to the right** and then move **3 spaces up**.
Remember: Start at 0. Look at the map of the state park. Name the place at point (4,3). The place at point (4,3) is **Campsite A.**

○ **Bicycle Rack**
■ **Bridge**
△ **Lookout Tower**
✕ **Eagle's Nest**
● **Campsite A, B, & C**
⊠ **Nature Center**
☐ **Water Fall**
▲ **Ranger's Cabin**
⊗ **Picnic Tables**
≈ **Swimming Hole**
△ **First Aid Station**

Use the map above. Name the place you find at each point.

1 (1,1)
Start at point 0. Move ☐ spaces to the right.
Move ☐ spaces up.
Place: _____

2 (1,3)
Start at point 0. Move ☐ spaces to the right.
Move ☐ spaces up.
Place: _____

3 (3,2)
Start at point 0. Move ☐ spaces to the right.
Move ☐ spaces up.
Place: _____

---

4 (2,4)
Move ☐ spaces to the right.
Move ☐ spaces up.
The place at point (2,4): _____

5 (4,5)
Move ☐ spaces to the right.
Move ☐ spaces up.
The place at point (4,5): _____

6 (5,2)
Move ☐ spaces to the right.
Move ☐ spaces up.
The place at point (5,2): _____

▶ Quiz

Use the map above. Name the place you find at each point.

7 (4,1)
Place: _____

8 (2,1)
Place: _____

9 (5,0)
Place: _____

15 Minutes

OBJECTIVE Find the value of numerical and algebraic expressions involving parentheses

Begin by reading aloud the definition of *expression*. Direct students' attention to Example 1. Have students name the numbers and operations in the expression.

Mention that the first step in finding the value of an expression that has parentheses is to do the operation within the parentheses.

Ask: **What is the operation within the parentheses? addition What is the sum of 10 + 2? 12 What do we do with the 5? Subtract it from the sum, 12. So, what is the value of the expression (10 + 2) − 5? 7**

Have students compare the two expressions in Example 2. Point out that the expressions are very similar, but the parentheses are not in the same place. Explain to students that even though the numbers may be the same, changing the placement of the parentheses can change the value of the expression. Have students compare the first steps in finding the value of each of the two expressions.

Then, direct students to Example 3. Point out that the expression describes the sum of a known number and an unknown number. A variable is used to stand for the unknown number. Ask: **Is there a value for this expression? no Why not? There isn't enough information; we don't know what number the variable stands for.**

Direct students' attention to the value, 5, for the variable x.

Guide them as they observe the addition to find the value of the expression. Emphasize that the value of the expression will change if the value of the variable changes.

TRY THESE Exercises 1–4 model the types of exercises students will find on the **Practice on Your Own** page.

- **Exercises 1–2** Students find the value of the expression.

- **Exercises 3–4** Students replace the variable with a value to find the value of the expression.

PRACTICE ON YOUR OWN Review the examples at the top of the page. Point out that for Exercises 1–9, students find the value of each expression. In Exercises 10–18, students substitute numbers for variables, and then find the value of the expression.

QUIZ Determine if students can find the value of an expression with parentheses and variables. Success is indicated by 3 out of 4 correct responses.

Students who successfully complete the **Practice on Your Own** and **Quiz** are ready to move to the next skill.

COMMON ERRORS

- Students may forget to do the operation within the parentheses first.

Students who make more than 5 errors in the **Practice on Your Own**, or who were not successful in the **Quiz** section may benefit from the **Alternative Teaching Strategy** on the next page.

Alternative Teaching Strategy
Modeling Expressions with Parentheses

20 Minutes

OBJECTIVE Use connecting cubes to model expressions with parentheses

MATERIALS connecting cubes

Begin by passing out at least 9 connecting cubes to each student. Have them connect 6 cubes and place them on the desk. Write the expression (6 − 2) + 3 on the board. Mention that it is an expression and not a number sentence because there is no equal sign.

Remind students that to find the value of an expression with parentheses, you must do the operation in the parentheses first. Ask: **What part of the expression is in parentheses? 6 − 2 What do you have to do to find the value of 6 − 2? Subtract 2 from 6.**

Point out that the cubes stand for the number 6 in the expression. Have students model 6 − 2 by taking away 2 connecting cubes, then have students count the cubes that are left.

Ask: **So, what is the value of the first part of the expression, 6 − 2? 4** On the board, draw an arrow to show that 6 minus 2 is 4. Do not use an equal sign.

Ask: **What is the next step in finding the value of the expression? Add 4 and 3. How can we show 4 + 3 with the connecting cubes? Link a set of 3 cubes to the 4 you already have.** Have students model the rest of the expression with the cubes. Count the total. Ask: **So, what is the value of the expression (6 − 2) + 3? 7**

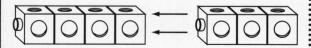

Next, mention that the value of the expression may change if the parentheses are moved. To illustrate, rewrite the expression on the board so that it reads 6 − (2 + 3).

Ask: **How is this expression the same as the first expression? The numbers and operations are in the same order. How is it different? The parentheses are in different places. If we want to find the value of this expression, what is the first step? Do the operation in parentheses first. What is the total of 2 + 3? 5** Have students model 2 + 3 using their counting cubes.

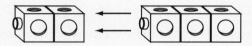

Rewrite the expression on the board, replacing 2 + 3 with 5. Point out that after doing the operation in parentheses, the expression now reads 6 − 5. Have students model the expression with their cubes. Ask: **How can we show the subtraction using the cubes? Take away 5 from the set of 6.** Have students take away 5 cubes and count the number of cubes left to find the value of the expression.

Ask: **What is the difference? 1 So how did the value of the expression change when the parentheses were moved? The value of the expression changed from 7 to 1.**

Make sure that students understand that the only thing that changed in the last expression was the placement of the parentheses. Repeat the exercise with other expressions, if needed.

Expressions

An **expression** has numbers and operation signs. It does not have an equal sign. Find the value of the expression.

Example 1

$(10 + 2) - 5$
→
$12 - 5$
→
7

Think: First, add 10 and 2. Then, subtract 5 from 12.

So, $(10 + 2) - 5$ is 7.

Example 2

$(9 - 5) + 2$ $9 - (5 + 2)$
→   →
$4 + 2$ $9 - 7$
→   →
6 2

Expressions with the same numbers and operations can have different values depending on where you place parentheses.

Think: Parentheses tell which operation to do first.

So, $(9 - 5) + 2$ is 6 but $9 - (5 + 2)$ is 2.

Example 3

A **variable** is a letter or symbol that can stand for any number you don't know.

Known number   Unknown number
→   →
3 $+$ x

The expression showing the total is $3 + x$.
To find the value of an expression with a variable, replace the variable with its value.

$3 + x$ Replace x with 5.
→
$3 + 5$ Add 3 and 5.
→
8

So, the value of the expression is 8.

▲ Try These

Find the value of the expression.

1 $(6 + 2) + 4$
    $\boxed{8} + 4$
    $\boxed{}$

2 $(6 - 4) + 2$
    $\boxed{} + 2$
    $\boxed{}$

Find the value of the expression if $x = 4$.

3 $6 - (x + 2)$
    $6 - (\boxed{} + 2)$
    $6 - \boxed{}$

4 $10 + (x - 1)$

Go to the next side.

Practice on Your Own

Skill 59

Example 1

Find the value of 7 − (x + 2) if x = 3.

7 − (x + 2)   Replace x with 3.
   ↓
7 − (3 + 2)   Add 3 and 2.
     ↓
  7 − 5   Subtract 5 from 7.
   ↓
   2

So, the value of the expression is 2.

Example 2

Find the value of a + (b − 3) if a = 9 and b = 7.

a + (b − 3)   Replace a with 9 and b with 7.
↓   ↓
9 + (7 − 3)   Subtract 3 from 7.
     ↓
  9 + 4   Add 9 and 4.
   ↓
   13

So, the value of the expression is 13.

Find the value of each expression.

1 (8 − 5) + 1

2 15 − (4 + 8)

3 (15 − 4) + 8

4 (4 + 2) + 5

5 14 − (3 + 6)

6 (11 − 3) + 7

7 13 + (7 − 4)

8 5 + (9 + 2)

9 (17 − 5) − 3

Find the value of the expression if a = 3 and b = 5.

10 a − 1 + 7
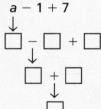

11 (b + 6) − 2
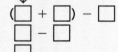

12 4 + (a + b)

4 + (☐ + ☐)
4 + ☐
☐

13 (b + 3) − 5

14 (2 + a) − b

15 6 + (b − a)

16 b − 4 + 9

17 (a + 5) + b

18 (a − 2) + b

▶ Quiz

Find the value of the expression. For 21–22, find the value of the expression if x = 6.

19 7 − (4 + 1)

20 (9 − 5) + 4

21 (5 + 4) − x

22 14 − (2 + x)

OBJECTIVE Evaluate numerical expressions; solve equations containing variables by using mental math

Students can use connecting cubes to model the examples.

Ask: **What does *c* represent in Example 1? the amount Henry spent on each car Can you figure out what that amount is at first? Why or why not? No, there isn't enough information. You don't know how much money he spent. What number does *c* stand for? 5**

Tell students that once you know the value of the variable, you can replace the variable with that value and evaluate the expression. Remind students that an expression does not have an equal sign.

Ask: **What is the value of 3 × *c* if *c* is 5? 15**

Direct students to Example 2. Point out that the problem can be written as an equation instead of an expression.

Ask: **What does *a* represent? the total amount Henry spent**

Make sure students see the relationship between the variables and the information in the original problem. Point out that they can use mental math and their knowledge of multiplication facts to solve the equations.

TRY THESE Exercise 1–4 prepare students for the types of exercises they will find on the **Practice on Your Own** page.

- **Exercises 1–4** Students find the value of an expression.

PRACTICE ON YOUR OWN Review the examples at the top of the page. In Exercises 1–4, students evaluate expressions. Point out that for Exercises 5–6, students write a numerical expression to describe the word problem. Then, in Exercises 7–8, students write an equation that describes the word problem, including a variable to stand for the missing information. Have students use mental math to solve the equations in Exercises 9–11.

QUIZ Determine if students can evaluate expressions and solve an equation with variables. Success is indicated by 3 out of 4 correct responses.

Students who successfully complete the **Practice on Your Own** and **Quiz** are ready to move to the next skill.

COMMON ERRORS

- Students may incorrectly identify the unknown information that a variable represents.

- Students may perform the wrong operation.

Students who made more than 3 errors in the **Practice on Your Own**, or who were not successful in the **Quiz** section, may benefit from the **Alternative Teaching Strategy** on the next page.

Alternative Teaching Strategy
Modeling Equations with Variables

15 Minutes

OBJECTIVE Use connecting cubes to model expressions and equations with variables

MATERIALS connecting cubes

Begin by distributing connecting cubes. Mention to students that a variable can stand for any number. Write on the board the equation $3 \times 2 = d$.

Ask: **Can you find the value of d? yes How do you know? The equation gives you the numbers and the operation you need to solve the problem.**

Have students make 3 sets of 2 connecting cubes and place them on their desks. Point out that the 3 sets of 2 cubes now illustrate the equation.

Have students refer to the equation on the board.

Say: **The operation in this expression is multiplication, which is joining together equal sets.**

Ask: **How can we show that with the connecting cubes? by connecting them** Have students connect the cubes and count the total. **6**

Write beneath the first equation $3 \times 2 = 6$. Draw an arrow from d to 6.

Say: **So, the variable in the equation $3 \times 2 = d$ stands for the number 6.**

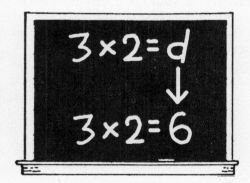

Next, write on the board $12 \div r = 4$.

Ask: **Is there enough information to find the value of r? yes**

Have students make a single set of 12 connecting cubes and place them on their desk.

Ask: **What happens to the 12 in the equation? It is divided into groups.**

Ask: **According to the equation, how many cubes will be in each group after we have divided the 12 into equal groups? 4**

Have students make groups of 4 connecting cubes from the set of 12 cubes.

Ask: **How many equal groups of 4 did you make from the 12? 3**

Say: **I'll write that as $12 \div 3 = 4$.** Write the equation below $12 \div r = 4$.

Ask: **What is the value of r? 3**

Write the following on the board:

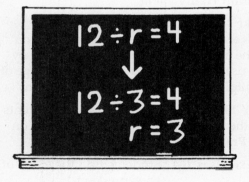

Repeat the activity with new multiplication and division equations involving variables, gradually increasing the values until students must use mental math instead of connecting cubes to solve the equations.

Grade 4
Skill 60

Expressions with Variables

A **variable** can stand for any number. An **equation** is a number sentence that shows two amounts are equal.

Example 1 Expressions with Variables

Write and evaluate an expression with a variable.

Henry bought 3 toy cars. Each car cost the same amount. How much money did he spend?

number of cars × price of each car
$\rightarrow$ $\rightarrow$
3   c

Think: The variable c stands for the price of the car.

Suppose Henry paid $5 for each car.

3 × c
$\rightarrow$ $\rightarrow$
3 × 5
15

Think: replace c with 5 since he paid $5 for each car.

So, Henry paid $15 for 3 toy cars.

Example 2 Equations with Variables

Write an equation to represent unknown information.

Henry bought 3 toy cars. How much money did he spend if each toy car cost $5.00?

3 cars multiplied by 5 dollars is the total amount spent.
$\rightarrow$ $\rightarrow$ $\rightarrow$ $\rightarrow$
3   ×   5   =   a

An amount spent on each car multiplied by 3 cars is $15.
$\rightarrow$ $\rightarrow$ $\rightarrow$
c   ×   3   =   15

A number of cars bought multiplied by $5 is $15.
$\rightarrow$ $\rightarrow$ $\rightarrow$
b   ×   5   =   15

Try These

Find the value of the expression.

1 5 × p if p = 10

5 × 10 = **50**

2 4 × s if s = 5

s = ☐
4 × s = ☐

3 54 ÷ c if c = 9

54 ÷ ☐ = ☐

4 40 ÷ y if y = 8

40 ÷ ☐ = ☐

Go to the next side.

Practice on Your Own

Skill 60

Example 1
Write an expression that matches the words.
Ben builds some bookcases. He uses 8 boards in each bookcase.

$b \times 8$ Variable b represents the unknown number.

Evaluate the expression for $b = 9$.

$$b \quad \times \quad 8$$
$$\downarrow$$
$$9 \quad \times \quad 8$$
$$\downarrow$$
$$72$$

So, Ben uses 72 boards for 9 bookcases.

Example 2
Write an equation with a variable.
Milo plants 4 equal rows of trees. If he plants 32 trees altogether, how many trees are in each row?

$4 \times t = 32$ Variable t represents the unknown number.

Use mental math to solve the equation. **Think:** 4 times what number equals 32?

$4 \times 8 = 32$ Replace t with 8.
The value of t is 8.
So, there are 8 trees in each row.

Find the value of the expression.

1 $4 \times b$ if $b = 6$ **2** $9 \times d$ if $d = 3$ **3** $24 \div h$ if $h = 6$ **4** $45 \div y$ if $y = 5$

_____   _____   _____   _____

Write an expression that matches the words.

5 25 t-shirts divided into a number of piles

6 A number of peppers on each of 7 plates.

Write an equation for each. Choose a variable for the unknown. Tell what the variable represents.

7 150 bricks divided equally among 30 model forts is the number of bricks in each fort.

8 A number of soup cans in each of 4 boxes is the total of 20 soup cans.

Use mental math to solve each equation. Check your work.

9 $55 \div a = 11$
$\square \div \square = \square$
$a = \square$

10 $m \times 6 = 42$
$\square \times \square = \square$
$m = \square$

11 $12 \times b = 48$
_____
$b = $ _____

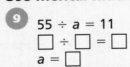
Quiz

Find the value of the expression.

12 $5 \times c$ if $c = 8$

13 $56 \div k$ if $k = 8$

14 $n \div 8 = 5$

15 $5 \times w = 30$

_____   _____ $n = $ _____ $w = $ _____

Data Analysis and Probability

OBJECTIVE Read a pictograph

Begin by recalling that a pictograph uses pictures to show and compare data. Explain that the title on the graph tells what the pictograph is about.

Ask: **What is the title of the pictograph? Favorite Winter Sports**

As students read the second step, explain that the key is an important part of the pictograph. Point out that the key may be different for different graphs, so students should pay close attention to what each symbol represents. Once they know what one symbol stands for, students can use skip counting to count the number of votes. Point out that sometimes a half picture is used.

Ask: **If a whole symbol stands for two votes, what does a half symbol stand for? one vote How many votes are there for ice skating? three**

Next, read Step 3. Have students find the sport with the most votes. Tell them to skip count by two, and then add 1 for the half symbol to find the total number of votes.

Ask: **How do you find the number of votes for skiing? Skip count first, 2, 4, 6, 8 and then add 1. 8 + 1 = 9; 9 votes.**

TRY THESE In Exercises 1–5 students answer questions about the pictograph.

- **Exercise 1** Title
- **Exercise 2** The total for one topping
- **Exercise 3** The topping with the most votes
- **Exercise 4** How many more of one topping than another
- **Exercise 5** The total votes

PRACTICE ON YOUR OWN Review the parts of a pictograph and read the key in the example at the top of the page. Ask students to find the number of votes for each drink. Caution them to read the sentences carefully.

QUIZ Determine if students know how to use a pictograph, interpret the key, and answer questions about the data. Success is indicated by 3 out of 4 correct responses.

Students who successfully complete **Practice on Your Own** and **Quiz** are ready to move on to the next skill.

COMMON ERRORS

- Students may forget to use the key, and simply count the symbols for each item as representing 1.

- Students may count half symbols as whole symbols.

Students who made more than 1 error in the **Practice on Your Own**, or who were not successful in the **Quiz** section, may benefit from the **Alternative Teaching Strategy** on the next page.

Alternative Teaching Strategy
Make and Use a Pictograph

20 Minutes

OBJECTIVE Make a pictograph and use it to compare data

MATERIALS centimeter grid paper, pencils, markers

Have students work in pairs or small groups. Explain that you will display data about dogs and together students will show that data in a pictograph.

Prepare a tally table that shows the results of a survey about the breed of dog most people prefer. Have students choose a title and decide what symbol to use, for example, a dog biscuit. Then discuss the key. Suggest that each symbol represent two votes.

Ask: **If we use one symbol for every two votes, how will you show the key?** 1 dog biscuit = 2 votes **There are 11 votes for Boxers. How many whole symbols will you show?** 5 **How many votes does that represent?** 10 **How will you show the eleventh vote?** with a half symbol

DOG	NUMBER OF VOTES
Collie	4
Boxer	11
German Shepherd	14
Irish Setter	8
Terrier	2

Have students complete the pictograph by drawing the appropriate number of symbols for each breed of dog.

When students have completed the pictograph, discuss the graph by asking questions such as: **What does the title tell you?** what the pictograph is about **What does the key show?** 1 symbol = 2 votes **How many types of dogs are in the survey?** 5

Remind students to skip count by twos to find the total number of votes.

Ask: **Which type of dog has the most votes?** German Shepherd

As students show an understanding of how to read the graph, continue with questions that require computation, such as: **How many more students voted for Boxers than for Irish Setters?** 3 **If six more students voted for Collies, how many votes would Collies have in all?** 10 **How would you show that on the pictograph?** Draw 5 dog biscuits.

FAVORITE DOGS	
Collie	🦴🦴
Boxer	🦴🦴🦴🦴🦴
German Shepherd	🦴🦴🦴🦴🦴🦴🦴
Irish Setter	🦴🦴🦴🦴
Terrier	🦴

Key: 🦴 = 2 Votes

Use a Pictograph

Which sport has the most votes?

Step 1 Find the title.

This is the title: Favorite Winter Sports

Favorite Winter Sports

skiing	✳ ✳ ✳ ✳
ice skating	✳
sledding	✳ ✳
ice fishing	✳ ✳

Key: Each ✳ = 2 votes.

A pictograph uses pictures to show and compare information.

Step 2 Read the key.

The key shows what each picture in the graph represents.

Each picture represents 2 votes.

Key: Each ✳ = 2 votes.

So, skip-count by two to find the number of votes for each sport.

Step 3 Find the sport with the most votes.

Skiing has the most pictures.

Skiing: ✳ ✳ ✳ ✳

If ✳ = 2 votes, then ✱ = 1 vote.

2, 4, 6, 8, **9**

Skiing has the most votes. It has 9.

Try These

Read the pictograph. Answer the questions.

Favorite Pizza Toppings

cheese	🍅 🍅 🍅
peppers	🍅 🍅 🍅
mushrooms	🍄
broccoli	🥦 🥦

Key: Each 🍅 =4 votes

If 🍅 equals 4 votes,
then 🥦 equals 2 votes.

1 What is the title of the pictograph?

2 How many students voted for the broccoli topping?

3 Which topping was the most popular?

4 How many more students voted for peppers than cheese?

5 How many students voted in all?

Go to the next side. →

Practice on Your Own

Skill 61

Favorite Juice Drinks	
apple	🥛🥛
cranberry	🥛
fruit	🥛🥛🥛🥛🥛
grape	🥛🥛🥛🥛
mango	🥛🥛
Key: Each 🥛 =4 votes.	

The graph is about **favorite juice drinks.**

Each picture represents **4 votes.**

A half picture represents **2 votes.**

The flavor with the fewest votes is **cranberry.**

....

Read the pictograph. Answer the questions.

Books Read This Month	
Tamika	📖📖📖📖📖
Julio	📖📖📖📖
Suki	📖📖📖📖📖📖
Jamal	📖📖📖
Key: Each 📖 = 2 books.	

1 What is the title of the pictograph?

_____

2 How many books does each picture represent?

☐

3 How many books does a half picture represent? ☐

4 Who read the most books? ☐ How many? ☐

Favorite Games	
board	👤👤👤👤
video	👤👤👤👤
puzzle	👤👤👤
tag	👤
Key: Each 👤 = 10 students	

5 How many students voted for each type of game?

board games ☐   video games ☐

puzzles ☐   tag games ☐

▶ Quiz

Read the pictograph. Answer the questions.

Number of Books Read	
mysteries	📖📖📖
novels	📖📖📖📖
biographies	📖📖📖📖
poetry	📖📖
Key: Each 📖 = 8 books read	

6 How many students read biographies? ☐

7 How many books were read in all? ☐

8 How many more students read novels than mysteries? ☐

9 If 4 more students read mysteries, how many pictures would there be for mysteries? ☐

25 Minutes

OBJECTIVE Count tally marks in a tally table and make a frequency table

Begin by pointing out the tally table. Tell students that the marks in the table are called tally marks. They are used to keep track of information that is counted. One mark represents one piece of data. Tally marks are grouped by fives. When adding the fifth mark, draw it across the other four marks. This represents a group of five. If there are single marks also, add them to the five to find the total.

Ask: **How many people chose popcorn as a favorite snack? 6 How many chose pretzels? 4 Why do the tally marks for popcorn look different from the others? Possible answer: There is a group of five tally marks and one more tally mark.**

Next, point out the frequency table. A frequency table uses numbers to show how often something happens. Tell students that this is where they will record the information from the tally table. Point out that the frequency table uses numbers instead of tally marks. The numbers make it easier to do calculations with the data or draw graphs.

Ask: **How are the tables the same? They show the same data; they have the same title and labels How are the tables different? One has tally marks and the other has numbers**

TRY THESE In Exercises 1–4, students use a tally table to answer questions.

- **Exercise 1** Count tally marks in a tally table and write the numbers in the frequency table.

- **Exercises 2–4** Use frequency table to answer questions.

PRACTICE ON YOUR OWN Explain that after a tally table is used to complete a frequency table, the data can be used to answer questions. Then have students complete the frequency tables and answer the questions.

QUIZ Determine if students know how to count tally marks, complete a frequency table, and answer questions about the data. Success is indicated by 3 out of 4 correct responses.

Students who successfully complete the **Practice on Your Own** and **Quiz** are ready to move on to the next skill.

COMMON ERRORS

- Students may count the tally marks incorrectly, forgetting to count a group as five.

- Students may read the data incorrectly when answering questions.

- Students may not understand what information they need to answer the question.

Students who made more than 1 error in the **Practice on Your Own**, or who were not successful in the **Quiz** section, may benefit from the **Alternative Teaching Strategy** on the next page.

Alternative Teaching Strategy
Use Models and Tallies to Make Frequency Tables

20 Minutes

OBJECTIVE Use models to make a tally table and a frequency table

MATERIALS paper bag and 35 colored cubes for each pair, paper, pencils

You may wish to have students work in pairs. Draw a tally table and list the colors of the cubes. Demonstrate how to choose a cube from the bag, and record the color on the tally table with a tally mark.

Explain that when the fifth cube of any color is picked, the tally mark is drawn at an angle to group the five marks. Show how the tally marks are counted.

Have one student pick 20 cubes out of the bag, and return them to the bag, as the partner records the results on the tally table.

When the tally table is complete, draw a frequency table. Recall that a frequency table uses numbers to show how often something happens, or in this activity, how often cubes of each color were picked. Have students count the tally marks and write each total in the frequency table.

Point out that it is easier to use the numbers in the frequency table to compare the data about the cubes.

Ask simple questions such as: **Which color cube was picked most often? How many blue cubes were picked? red cubes? green cubes? Which color was picked the least?**

Have students switch roles and repeat the activity until about thirty tally marks are in the table. Have students create a frequency table with the data.

Discuss the data in the frequency table. Ask questions about the data. Have students point to where they found the answer on the table as the questions are asked.

As the students show understanding, ask questions that require calculating with numbers from two or more rows of the table, such as: **How many red and blue cubes were picked? How many more blue cubes than green cubes were picked?**

Cubes We Picked	
Color	Tallies
Red	~~IIII~~ IIII
Green	~~IIII~~ III
Blue	III

Cubes We Picked	
Color	Frequency
Red	9
Green	8
Blue	3

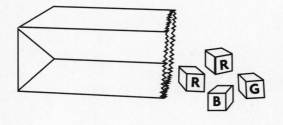

Use Data from a Survey

Use the tally table to make a frequency table.

Step 1 Read the tally table.

Favorite Snacks

Type	Number
Popcorn	ⲧⲧⲧⲧ Ⅰ
Pretzels	Ⅰ Ⅰ Ⅰ Ⅰ
Peanuts	Ⅰ Ⅰ Ⅰ

Remember:
In a tally table, tally marks (/) are used to record data.
ⲧⲧⲧⲧ = 5

Step 2 Make a frequency table.

Count the tally marks for each snack. Record the numbers in the frequency table.

Favorite Snacks

Type	Frequency
Popcorn	6
Pretzels	4
Peanuts	3

Try These

Complete the frequency.

1 Count the tally marks for each pet.

Favorite Pet

Type	Number
Dog	ⲧⲧⲧⲧ
Cat	ⲧⲧⲧⲧ Ⅰ
Fish	Ⅰ Ⅰ Ⅰ Ⅰ
Bird	Ⅰ Ⅰ

Favorite Pet

Type	Frequency
Dog	
Cat	
Fish	
Bird	

Answer the questions.

2 How many chose a cat as a favorite pet?

3 How many more chose cat than chose fish?

4 Which pet was chosen least often?

Go to the next side.

Practice on Your Own

Skill 62

Answer the questions.

Balls Sold	
Type	Number
Football	I I I I
Basketball	⊥⊥⊤
Soccer	⊥⊤⊤ I I

Balls Sold	
Type	Frequency
Football	4
Basketball	5
Soccer	7

How many more basketballs than footballs were sold? | I |

Remember:
A frequency table is a table that uses numbers to show how often something happens.

How many balls were sold altogether? | 16 |

Complete the frequency table. Answer the questions.

Flowers Planted	
Type	Number
Tulip	I I I I
Daisy	⊥⊤⊤ I I
Rose	⊥⊤⊤
Mum	I I

1

Flowers Planted	
Type	Frequency
Tulip	4
Daisy	
Rose	5
Mum	2

2 How many tulips were planted?

3 How many daisies and roses were planted?

4 How many tulips and mums were planted?

5 Which flower was planted most often?

▶ Quiz

Complete the frequency table. Answer the questions.

Pairs of Shoes Sold	
Day	Number
Mon.	I I
Tues.	⊥⊤⊤ I I I
Wed.	I I I
Thur.	⊥⊤⊤ I

Pairs of Shoes Sold	
Day	Frequency
Mon.	2
Tues.	
Wed.	
Thur.	6

6 How many pairs of shoes were sold on Wednesday?

7 How many pairs of shoes were sold on Monday?

8 How many more pairs of shoes were sold on Tuesday than Monday?

9 How many pairs of shoes were sold altogether?

20 Minutes

OBJECTIVE Read and interpret bar graphs

Begin by pointing to the title of the bar graph and the labels on the side and bottom of the graph. Explain to students that the length of the bars will aid them in making comparisons quickly and easily.

Call attention to the title and labels on the horizontal and vertical axes of the bar graph.

Ask: **What is this bar graph about? the color of students' shoes What are the shoe colors? blue, white, brown, black**

Continue by saying: **The bottom or horizontal labels on the graph represent the scale. It has numbers that represent numbers of students. How many students does 1 space represent? 1 student**

TRY THESE Exercises 1–3 model the type of exercises students will find on the **Practice on Your Own** page.

- **Exercises 1–2** Read and interpret the bar graph.

- **Exercise 3** Use the information from the bar graph to solve a comparison problem.

PRACTICE ON YOUR OWN Begin by explaining to the students that another way to show the information on a bar graph is to have the bars go up. Review with the students the title of the bar graph and the labels on the side and bottom of the graph. Also discuss the interval on this graph: each space represents 2 students.

QUIZ Determine if students can read and interpret bar graphs. Then use the information on the bar graph to solve problems. Success is indicated by 2 out of 3 correct responses.

Students who successfully complete the **Practice on Your Own** and **Quiz** are ready to move on to the next skill.

COMMON ERRORS

- Students may not read all of the information, such as the title, labels and numbers, found on a bar graph.

- Students may interpret the scale incorrectly.

Students who made more than 2 errors in the **Practice on Your Own**, or were not successful in the **Quiz** section, may benefit from the **Alternative Teaching Strategy** on the next page.

Alternative Teaching Strategy
Make a Bar Graph

20 Minutes

OBJECTIVE Making and labeling a vertical bar graph and using the information on the bar graph to solve problems

MATERIALS copies of a 5-column, 10-row grid

Explain to the students that they will be making a vertical bar graph that will record their favorite colors.

Have students name 5 favorite colors. Begin with the left column and have students label each *column* at the bottom of the grid with one color.

Ask: **What could you label the columns? colors**

Then help students decide on a reasonable interval for the scale. Record these numbers to the left of the grid. Explain that these numbers tell how many votes.

Ask: **What could you label the scale? number of votes What would be an appropriate title for the graph? favorite colors**

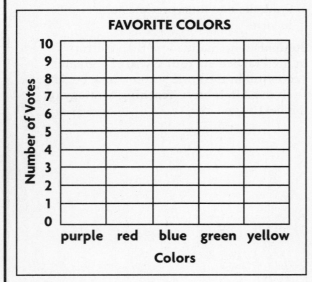

Explain that students will now gather and record information on their graph.

Ask: **Who chooses purple as their favorite color?** Students shade in one box for each vote above the word *purple*.

Repeat this procedure for each color listed.

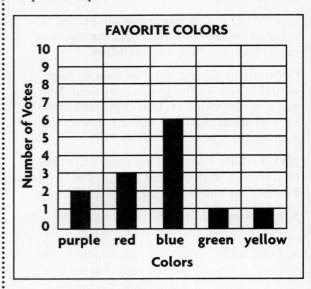

Ask: **How many more students chose blue than red for their favorite color?**

Ask questions about the information on the bar graph. Then have students work in pairs to create problems from the information on the graph. Write each problem on a 5 × 8 card, then write the answer on the back of the card. Students work back and forth asking questions off the cards. If there is more than one pair of students working on this exercise, have the pairs exchange cards.

Bar Graphs

Bar graphs use bars to show data. This is a **horizontal** bar graph. The bars go across.

The graph at the right shows how many students wore each color shoes.

Read the graph.

• What shoe colors does the graph show?
The graph shows blue, white, brown, and black.

• How many students wore blue shoes?
The bar for blue stops at 2. **So**, 2 students wore blue shoes.

• How many students altogether were counted?
Add to find the number of students.

2	+	4	+	6	+	10	=	22
blue shoes		white shoes		brown shoes		black shoes		students counted

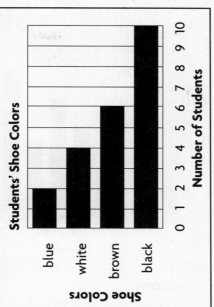

Students' Shoe Colors

Shoe Colors: blue, white, brown, black

Number of Students: 0 1 2 3 4 5 6 7 8 9 10

▲ Try These

Use the graph above to answer the questions.

1 How many students wore brown shoes?

[ ]

2 Which color shoe did most students wear?

[   ]

3 How many more students wore brown shoes than white?

[ ] − [ ] = [ ]
brown shoes   white shoes   answer

Go to the next side.

Practice on Your Own

Skill **63**

This is a **vertical** bar graph.
It has bars that go up.

- The graph shows students' favorite fruit.
- The scale shows that each space stands for 2 votes. The bar for pears stops halfway between 4 and 8.

The halfway number between 4 and 8 is 6.

So, 6 students voted for pears.

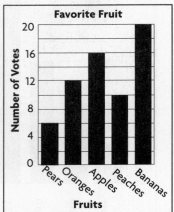

Use the graph above to answer the questions.

1 How many votes were for oranges?

2 Which fruit had the fewest votes?

3 Which fruit had the most votes?

4 How many more votes were there for oranges than pears?

5 How many votes were there for peaches?

6 Were there more votes for apples or oranges?

7 How many students voted for pears or oranges?

8 How many students voted for bananas or apples?

9 How many students voted for oranges or peaches?

 **Quiz**

Use the graph above to answer the questions.

10 How many more votes were there for apples than peaches?

11 How many students voted for apples or oranges?

12 How many votes were there altogether?

OBJECTIVE Identify parts of a bar graph

Read about the *title* and then ask: **Where do you find the title of the bar graph? above the graph** Have students point to that part of the graph. **Why is the title so important? Possible response: Without the title it's difficult to understand what the graph is about.**

Read about the *labels* and then have students locate each label on the graph.

Point out to students how the *scale* helps them read the number each bar shows. Explain that the scale on a bar graph can have intervals of any number, for example, two, three, five, ten, and so forth. Point out that on this graph not every line is labeled. Help students understand that each space represents 1 bird, and that the first line after zero is 1; likewise, the line just after 2 is 3.

Once students have reviewed all the parts of this graph,

Ask: **Why are the bars different lengths? There are different numbers of each bird: A longer bar means a greater number of birds; a shorter bar means fewer birds. Were there more cardinals than bluebirds at the bird feeder? There were more cardinals. How do you know? The bar for *cardinal* stops at the line for 2, the bar for *bluebird* stops at the line for 1; so, according to the graph, there were 2 cardinals and just 1 bluebird. Were there more goldfinches than robins at the bird feeder? There were just as many goldfinches as robins. How do you know? The bars are the same length; each bar shows 4 birds.**

TRY THESE In Exercises 1–4 students answer questions about the parts of a bar graph.

- **Exercise 1** Identify the title.
- **Exercise 2** Identify the left label.
- **Exercise 3** Identify the bottom label.
- **Exercise 4** Identify the scale.

PRACTICE ON YOUR OWN Use the example at the top of the page to review parts of a graph. Explain that bar graphs can be vertical or horizontal. Have students use the data on the graph at the top of the page to answer the questions.

QUIZ Determine if students can identify parts of a graph and understand what each part shows. Success is indicated by 2 out of 3 correct responses.

Students who successfully complete the **Practice on Your Own** and **Quiz** are ready to move to the next skill.

COMMON ERRORS

- Students may have trouble reading the number that a bar shows, especially when the line for the interval is not labeled.

- Students may be able to name parts of a graph, but not understand what they represent.

Students who made more than 2 errors in the **Practice on Your Own**, or who were not successful in the **Quiz** section, may benefit from the **Alternative Teaching Strategy** on the next page.

Alternative Teaching Strategy
Draw Parts of a Bar Graph

OBJECTIVE Draw a bar graph and label its parts

MATERIALS Centimeter grid paper, pencils, markers

Draw a bar graph with the students. Start by listing the results of a survey about students' favorite subject in school:

math	12
art	8
science	10
social studies	7

Distribute materials to the students and have them draw the two axes of the bar graph. Ask students what title the graph should have. Have them write the title.

Decide whether the graph will be horizontal (numbers on the bottom; bars extend from left to right) or vertical (numbers on left side; bars extend up). Then have students decide on labels.

Together decide on a scale. Guide students to understand that since most of the numbers are even, the scale can show intervals of 2.

Ask: **Between which two even numbers is 7? 6 and 8 Where will the bar for 7 end? halfway between 6 and 8**

Have students draw the bars for each subject. When students have completed the graph, review the parts of the graph and why they are necessary.

Ask: **At which number does the bar for science stop? 10 What does the bar for math tell us? Twelve students chose math as their favorite subject.**

Continue by having each student make up a question to ask and choose another student to give the answer.

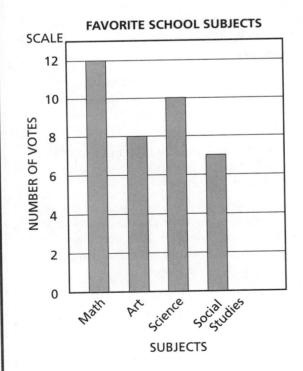

FAVORITE SCHOOL SUBJECTS

Make Bar Graphs

A **bar graph** uses bars to show data.

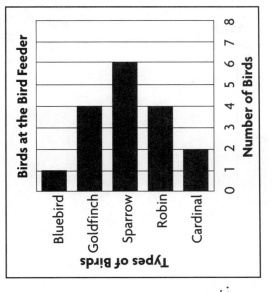

Birds at the Bird Feeder

Types of Birds

Bluebird
Goldfinch
Sparrow
Robin
Cardinal

Number of Birds
0 1 2 3 4 5 6 7 8

Identify the parts of a bar graph.

• Look at the title. It tells what the graph is about.
  The title is "Birds at the Bird Feeder."

• Look at the labels. There are two of them.
  The label on the left side is "Types of Birds."
  The label at the bottom is "Number of Birds."

• Find the scale. It has numbers that tell you the number
  each bar shows.
  The numbers on the scale are 0, 1, 2, 3, 4, 5, 6, 7, 8.
  One space stands for one bird.

• Compare the bars. Each bar tells how many birds were
  at the feeder.
  The bar for robins stops at 4. **So**, there were 4 robins at the feeder.
  The bar for bluebirds stops at 1. **So**, 1 bluebird was at the feeder.

◣ Try These

Use the graph to answer the questions.

Favorite Breakfast Food

Types of Foods

Cereal
Eggs
Pancakes
Fruit and Yogurt
Waffles

Number of Students
0 2 4 6 8 10

1 What is the title?

2 What is the left label?

3 What is the bottom label?

4 What are the numbers on the scale?

Go to the next side.

Practice on Your Own

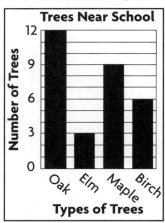

Think:
The bar graph shows how many trees are near school.

Use the graph above to answer the questions.

1 What is the title?

2 What is the bottom label?

3 What is the left label?

4 What part of the graph tells what the graph is about?

5 What do the bars show?

6 At what number does the bar for elm trees stop?

7 What part of the graph tells you that there are 9 maple trees?

8 At what number does the bar for birch trees stop?

9 How many trees do two spaces show?

▶ Quiz

Use the graph above to answer the questions.

10 What part of the graph shows that there are 3 elms?

11 Where do you find the names of the trees?

12 What part of the graph are the numbers?

OBJECTIVE Identify possible outcomes of an event

MATERIALS Coins, such as a penny and a dime; two spinners, one divided into 4 equal parts, another divided into 4 unequal size parts; number cube labeled 1–6

15 Minutes

Begin by demonstrating the possible outcomes when tossing or flipping a coin. Ask the students to name the possible outcomes. **two: heads, tails** Introduce the term *equally likely* to be used when the possible outcomes have the same chances of happening.

Direct students' attention to the example for Tossing a Penny. You may wish to have the students look at a penny while they are discussing the possible outcomes.

For the second example, emphasize that all the parts must be of *equal size* for the outcomes to be equally likely. You may wish to demonstrate on the two spinners.

Point out that on the second spinner the parts are not equal size so the outcomes for each part are not equally likely.

Direct the students' attention to the example for Tossing Two Coins. You may wish to have the students look at each coin and name the outcomes for each.

TRY THESE In Exercises 1–3, all of the outcomes are equally likely.

* **Exercise 1**   2 possible outcomes
* **Exercise 2**   3 possible outcomes
* **Exercise 3**   4 possible outcomes

PRACTICE ON YOUR OWN Review the example at the top of the page. You may wish to show a cube so students can see all of its sides. In Exercises 1–3, students use prompts to determine the number of possible outcomes. In Exercises 4–6, students list all possible outcomes without prompts.

QUIZ Determine if the students can list all the possible outcomes for each event. Success is determined by 2 out of 3 correct responses.

Students who successfully complete the **Practice on Your Own** and **Quiz** are ready to move on to the next skill.

COMMON ERRORS

* Student may write the possible outcome for a coin or a cube as 1, because there is one coin or cube.

* Students may think that because a quarter is larger than a penny, the outcomes for tossing both coins are not equally likely.

Students who made more than 2 errors in the **Practice on Your Own**, or who were not successful in the **Quiz** section, may benefit from the **Alternative Teaching Strategy** on the next page.

Alternative Teaching Strategy
Identify Possible Outcomes

15 Minutes

OBJECTIVE Use an event to identify all possible outcomes and make a table

MATERIALS same size blocks: 4 red, 4 blue cubes, 2 yellow; paper bags labeled A, B

Place 2 red and 2 blue blocks in each paper bag.

Students can work in pairs for this activity. One student draws a block from bag A, while the other student records the result in a table. Next, the student draws a block from bag B and the other student records the result in the table. The students take turns. Have the students use both paper bags and record all possible outcomes. Remind them not to put back any of the blocks into the bags.

Ask: **What were the possible outcomes when you used bag A? red, blue What were the possible outcomes when you used bag B? red, blue What were the possible outcomes when you took out a block from each bag? red, blue; red, red; blue, blue; blue, red When you use two blocks, one red and one blue, what are the only possible outcomes? red, blue**

Place the 2 red and 2 blue blocks back into bag A and bag B. Add a yellow cube to each bag and have students determine the possible outcomes. **red, blue; red, yellow; red, red; blue, red; blue, yellow; blue, blue; yellow, red; yellow, blue; yellow, yellow.**

Possible Outcomes

A *possible outcome* is something that has the chance of happening.
Two outcomes are **equally likely** if they have the same chance of happening.

Example A Tossing a Penny
There are only 2 sides on a penny.

heads   tails

There are 2 possible outcomes for tossing a penny, heads (H) or tails (T).

So, it is equally likely the coin will land on heads or tails.

Example B Spinning a Spinner
There are 4 equal size parts on the spinner.

There are 4 possible outcomes for spinning the spinner: red, blue, yellow or green.

Since the 4 parts are the same size, the chance is equally likely for spinning red, blue, yellow or green.

Example C Tossing Two Coins
There are 2 coins. Each coin has 2 sides.

heads   tails   heads   tails

There are 4 possible outcomes for tossing 2 coins: heads-heads, heads-tails, tails-heads, tails-tails.

Try These

Write the possible outcomes for each event.

1 Tossing a dime

2 Spinning the spinner

_____

_____

3 Tossing a nickel and a penny

Go to the next side.

Practice on Your Own

The sides on the cube are labeled 1, 2, 3, 4, 5, 6.

There are 6 possible outcomes for tossing the cube: 1, 2, 3, 4, 5, and 6.

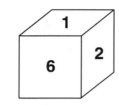

Skill 65

Think:
It is equally likely that you will toss a 1, 2, 3, 4, 5, or 6.

Write the possible outcomes for each event.

1 Tossing a cube labeled A, B, C, D, E, F

_____ , _____,

_____ , _____,

_____ , _____

2 Tossing a quarter and a dime

_____

_____

_____

_____

3 Spinning the spinner

_____, _____,

_____, _____

4 Pulling a shape from this box

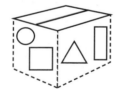

_____

5 Tossing a number cube numbered 7, 8, 9, 10, 11, 12

_____

6 Pulling 2 marbles from a bag of 2 orange marbles and 2 blue marbles

_____

▶ **Quiz**

Write the possible outcomes for each event.

7 Spinning the spinner

_____

8 Tossing a dime and a penny

_____

9 Tossing a cube labeled E, F, G, H, I, J

_____

15 Minutes

OBJECTIVE Determine whether an event is certain or impossible

Begin by defining an event as something that happens.

Direct the students' attention to the first example. Emphasize that a certain event is one that will always happen.

Ask: **What is an example of a certain event? Possible response: The sun will rise tomorrow.**

As you work through the example for Certain Events, ask: **Suppose I pull out a button from the bag, will the button be blue? No. How do you know? There are only gray buttons in the bag.**

Continue: **So, every time I pull out a button, what color will it be? Gray. Will this event *always* happen? Yes.**

Conclude by pointing out that events which will always happen are *certain events*.

Direct students' attention to the example for Impossible Events.

Ask: **Can I spin a 1? Yes. Can I spin a 2? Yes. Can I spin a 3? No. Why not? There is no 3 on the spinner. Can I say that spinning a 3 on this spinner will never happen? Yes.**

Conclude by saying that events that can never happen are impossible events.

Explain that to determine whether an event is certain or impossible, students can ask themselves, "Will this event always happen?" and "Will this event never happen?"

TRY THESE Exercises 1 and 2 model the type of exercises students will find on the **Practice on Your Own** page.

• **Exercise 1** Impossible event

• **Exercise 2** Certain event

PRACTICE ON YOUR OWN Review the definitions of *certain* and *impossible* events. Discuss the examples at the top of the page. Have students explain why each event is certain or impossible.

QUIZ Determine if students can identify events as either certain or impossible. Success is determined by 2 out of 2 correct responses.

Students who successfully complete the **Practice on Your Own** and **Quiz** are ready to move on to the next skill.

COMMON ERRORS

• Students may not think spinning a spinner or pulling a figure from a bag is an event, and may conclude that it is impossible to happen.

Students who made more than 2 errors in the **Practice on Your Own**, or who were not successful in the **Quiz** section, may benefit from the **Alternative Teaching Strategy** on the next page.

Alternative Teaching Strategy
Model Certain and Impossible Events

15 Minutes

OBJECTIVE Use coins to model certain and impossible events

MATERIALS play money: pennies, nickels, quarters, small plastic bags

Recall that a certain event is something that will always happen.

Put a few pennies in a small plastic bag. Have students take turns pulling out one coin, and then putting it back in the bag. When all of the students have had a turn, ask: **Will we always pull out a penny? Yes. Why? There are only pennies in the bag.**

Continue: **Can we call this event certain? Yes. Why? Because the event will always happen or it is certain to happen.**

Display a bag of nickels. Ask students if they can pull a penny from the bag. When they say they cannot, ask: **Will we ever pull out a penny from this bag? No. Why not? There are no pennies in the bag. Can we call pulling out a penny an impossible event? Yes. Why? It will never happen. It is impossible.**

Confirm for students: **That's right. It's impossible to pull a penny out of this bag.**

Continue the activity by having students plan certain or impossible events. For example, suggest that one student make the event of pulling a quarter out of the bag a certain event. **Student puts only quarters in a bag.** Than have the next student make that same event impossible. **Student puts any coins but quarters in a bag.**

Probability

An **event** is something that happens. An event can be **certain** or **impossible**.

Certain Events
An event is **certain** if it will always happen.

Here is a bag of gray buttons.

It is **certain** that if you pull out a button, it will be gray.

How do you know?
There are only gray buttons in the bag.

Impossible Events
An event is **impossible** if it will never happen.

Here is a spinner showing the numbers 1 and 2.

It is **impossible** to spin a 3.

How do you know?
There is not a number 3 on the spinner.

▲ Try These

Write whether the event is *certain* or *impossible*.

1. pulling a triangle out of the box

   _____

   How do you know?

   _____

2. spinning a 3

   _____

   How do you know?

   _____

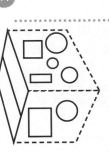

Go to the next side.

Practice on Your Own

Skill 66

Think:
An event is *certain* if it will always happen.

This event is **certain**:

Pulling a blue cube from a bag of blue cubes

This event is **impossible**:

Think:
An event is *impossible* if it will never happen.

Pulling a red cube from a bag of yellow cubes.

Write *certain* or *impossible* for each event.

1 spinning an even number

_____

How do you know?

_____

2 picking the letter A

_____

How do you know?

_____

3 pulling a yellow marker from a box of red markers

_____

How do you know?

_____

4 pulling a nickel from a bag of nickels

_____

How do you know?

_____

5 spinning an odd number on a spinner numbered 6, 8, 10, and 12

_____

6 spinning an even number on a spinner numbered 2, 4, 6, 8

_____

Quiz

Write *certain* or *impossible* for each event.

7 pulling a dime from a bag of pennies and nickels

_____

8 spinning a number less than 5 on a spinner with sections numbered 2, 3, and 4

_____

Skill 1 — Grade 4

Place Value: 4-Digit Numbers

Write the value of each digit in the number 1,275.

Step 1 Use a place value chart.

TH	H	T	O
1	2	7	5

Step 2 Write the value of each digit.

The value of the 1 is 1 thousand or 1,000.
The value of the 2 is 2 hundreds or 200.
The value of the 7 is 7 tens or 70.
The value of the 5 is 5 ones or 5.

Step 3 Use place value words to write the number.

1 thousand, 2 hundreds 7 tens 5 ones = 1,275

▶ Try These

Write the value of each digit.

1 7,569

TH	H	T	O
7	5	6	9

The value of the 7 is [7] thousands or [7,000]
The value of the 5 is [5] hundreds or [500]
The value of the 6 is [6] tens or [60]
The value of the 9 is [9] ones or [9]

[7] thousands [5] hundreds [6] tens [9] ones
= **7,569**

2 6,403

TH	H	T	O
6	4	0	3

The value of the 6 is [6] thousands or [6,000]
The value of the 4 is [4] hundreds or [400]
The value of the 0 is [0] tens or [0]
The value of the 3 is [3] ones or [3]

[6] thousands [4] hundreds [0] tens [3] ones
= **6,403**

Go to the next side.

Practice on Your Own — Skill 1

Example:
Write the value of each digit of the number 2,063.

TH	H	T	O
2	0	6	3

The value of the 2 is 2 thousands or 2,000.
The value of the 0 is 0 hundreds or 0.
The value of the 6 is 6 tens or 60.
The value of the 3 is 3 ones or 3.
2 thousands 0 hundreds 6 tens 3 ones = **2,063**

Write the value of each digit.

1 3,079

TH	H	T	O
3	0	7	9

The value of 3 is [3] thousands or [3,000]
The value of 0 is [0] hundreds or [0]
The value of 7 is [7] tens or [70]
The value of 9 is [9] ones or [9]

2 7,503

TH	H	T	O
7	5	0	3

The value of 7 is [7] thousands or [7,000]
The value of 5 is [5] hundreds or [500]
The value of 0 is [0] tens or [0]
The value of 3 is [3] ones or [3]

3 8,290

TH	H	T	O
8	2	9	0

The value of 8 is [8] thousands or [8,000]
The value of 2 is [2] hundreds or [200]
The value of 9 is [9] tens or [90]
The value of 0 is [0] ones or [0]

4 6,100

TH	H	T	O
6	1	0	0

The value of 6 is [6] thousands or [6,000]
The value of 1 is [1] hundred or [100]
The value of 0 is [0] tens or [0]
The value of 0 is [0] ones or [0]

▶ Quiz

Write the value of the underlined digit.

5 4,066 [4,000]

6 2,078 [70]

Skill 2 — Grade 4

Benchmark Numbers

Benchmark numbers are useful numbers such as 10, 25, 50, and 100. They help you estimate about how much or how many without counting.

Example A
Choose a benchmark number. Tell about how many squares will cover the figure.
Look at the figure. Choose 10. Estimate.

Think: About 3 groups of 10 will cover the figure.

10 + 10 + 10 = 30

So, about 30 squares will cover the figure.

Example B
Choose a benchmark number. Tell about how many squares will cover the figure.
Look at the figure.

Choose 25.

Estimate.

Think: About 3 groups of 25 will cover the figure.

25 + 25 + 25 = 75

So, about 75 squares will cover the figure.

▶ Try These

Use the benchmark number to estimate. Tell about how many squares will cover the figure.

1 About [4] groups of 10 will cover the figure.
About [40] squares will cover the figure.

2 About [2] groups of 25 will cover the figure.
About [50] squares will cover the figure.

3 About [2] groups of 50 will cover the figure.
About [100] squares will cover the figure.

Go to the next side.

Practice on Your Own — Skill 2

About 4 groups of 100 will cover the figure.

100 + 100 + 100 + 100 = 400

So, about 400 squares will cover the figure.

Think: Use benchmark numbers to estimate.

Use benchmark numbers to estimate. Tell about how many squares cover the figure.

1 Benchmark number: [10]
Estimate: [50] squares

2 Benchmark number: [100]
Estimate: [200] squares

3 Benchmark number: [50]
Estimate: [150] squares

4 Benchmark number: [50]
Estimate: [150] squares

5 Benchmark number: [25]
Estimate: [75] squares

6 Benchmark number: [10]
Estimate: [20] squares

▶ Quiz

Use benchmark numbers to estimate. Tell about how many squares cover the figure.

7 Benchmark number: [10]
Estimate: [30] squares

8 Benchmark number: [25]
Estimate: [50] squares

9 Benchmark number: [50]
Estimate: [150] squares

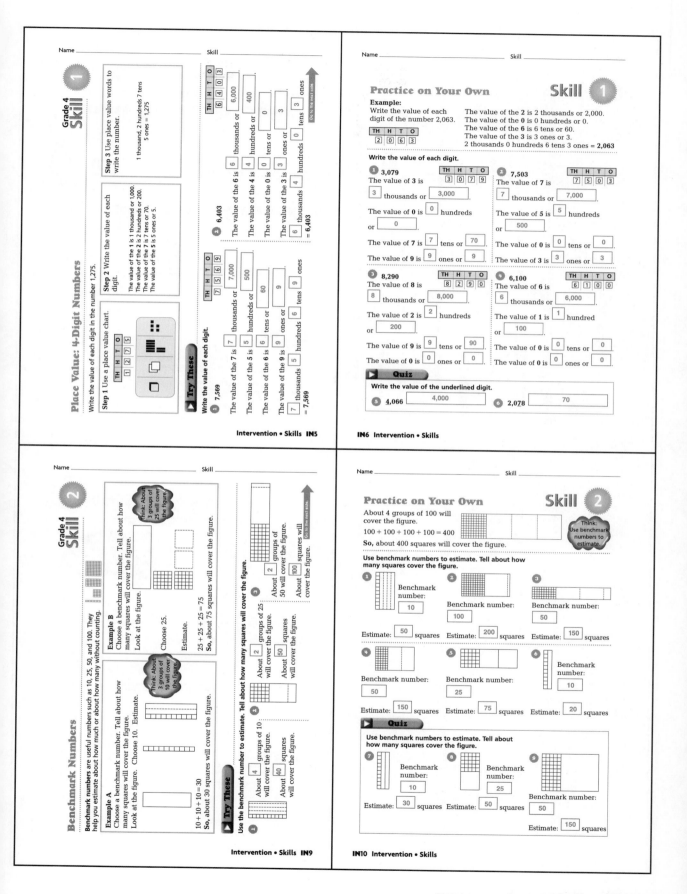

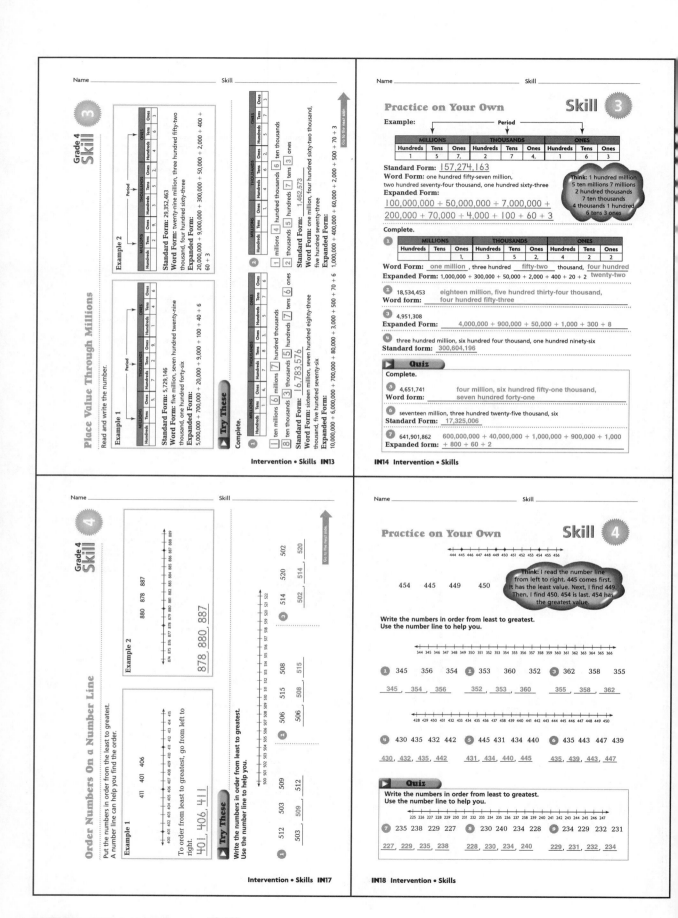

Grade 4 — Skill 3

Place Value Through Millions

Read and write the number.

Example 1

MILLIONS			THOUSANDS			ONES		
Hundreds	Tens	Ones	Hundreds	Tens	Ones	Hundreds	Tens	Ones
		5,	7	2	9,	1	4	6

Standard Form: 5,729,146
Word Form: five million, seven hundred twenty-nine thousand, one hundred forty-six
Expanded Form:
5,000,000 + 700,000 + 20,000 + 9,000 + 100 + 40 + 6

Example 2

MILLIONS			THOUSANDS			ONES		
Hundreds	Tens	Ones	Hundreds	Tens	Ones	Hundreds	Tens	Ones
	2	9,	3	5	2,	4	6	3

Standard Form: 29,352,463
Word Form: twenty-nine million, three hundred fifty-two thousand, four hundred sixty-three
Expanded Form:
20,000,000 + 9,000,000 + 300,000 + 50,000 + 2,000 + 400 + 60 + 3

▶ Try These

Complete.

1

MILLIONS			THOUSANDS			ONES		
Hundreds	Tens	Ones	Hundreds	Tens	Ones	Hundreds	Tens	Ones
	1	ten millions	6	millions	7	hundred thousands		
	8	ten thousands	3	thousands	5	hundreds	7	tens	6	ones

Standard Form: 16,783,576
Word Form: sixteen million, seven hundred eighty-three thousand, five hundred seventy-six
Expanded Form:
10,000,000 + 6,000,000 + 700,000 + 80,000 + 3,000 + 500 + 70 + 6

2

| 1 | millions | 4 | hundred thousands | 6 | ten thousands |
| 2 | thousands | 5 | hundreds | 7 | tens | 3 | ones |

Standard Form: 1,462,573
Word Form: one million, four hundred sixty-two thousand, five hundred seventy-three
Expanded Form:
1,000,000 + 400,000 + 60,000 + 2,000 + 500 + 70 + 3

Go to the next side. →

Intervention • Skills **IN13**

Practice on Your Own — Skill 3

Example:

← Period →								
MILLIONS			**THOUSANDS**			**ONES**		
Hundreds	Tens	Ones	Hundreds	Tens	Ones	Hundreds	Tens	Ones
1	5	7,	2	7	4,	1	6	3

Standard Form: 157,274,163
Word Form: one hundred fifty-seven million, two hundred seventy-four thousand, one hundred sixty-three
Expanded Form:
100,000,000 + 50,000,000 + 7,000,000 + 200,000 + 70,000 + 4,000 + 100 + 60 + 3

> **Think:** 1 hundred million 5 ten millions 7 millions 2 hundred thousands 7 ten thousands 4 thousands 1 hundred 6 tens 3 ones

Complete.

1

MILLIONS			THOUSANDS			ONES		
Hundreds	Tens	Ones	Hundreds	Tens	Ones	Hundreds	Tens	Ones
		1,		3	5	2,	4	2	2

Word Form: one million , three hundred fifty-two thousand, four hundred twenty-two
Expanded Form: 1,000,000 + 300,000 + 50,000 + 2,000 + 400 + 20 + 2

2 18,534,453
Word form: eighteen million, five hundred thirty-four thousand, four hundred fifty-three

3 4,951,308
Expanded Form: 4,000,000 + 900,000 + 50,000 + 1,000 + 300 + 8

4 three hundred million, six hundred four thousand, one hundred ninety-six
Standard form: 300,604,196

▶ Quiz

Complete.

5 4,651,741 four million, six hundred fifty-one thousand, seven hundred forty-one
Word form:

6 seventeen million, three hundred twenty-five thousand, six
Standard Form: 17,325,006

7 641,901,862 600,000,000 + 40,000,000 + 1,000,000 + 900,000 + 1,000
Expanded form: + 800 + 60 + 2

IN14 Intervention • Skills

Grade 4 — Skill 4

Order Numbers On a Number Line

Put the numbers in order from the least to greatest.
A number line can help you find the order.

Example 1

← 400 401 402 403 404 405 406 407 408 409 410 411 412 413 414 415 →

411   401   406

To order from least to greatest, go from left to right.

401, 406, 411

Example 2

← 874 875 876 877 878 879 880 881 882 883 884 885 886 887 888 889 →

880   878   887

878, 880, 887

▶ Try These

Write the numbers in order from least to greatest.
Use the number line to help you.

← 500 501 502 503 504 505 506 507 508 509 510 511 512 513 514 515 516 517 518 519 520 521 522 →

1 512   503   509
503, 509, 512

2 506   515   508
506, 508, 515

3 514   520   502
502, 514, 520

Go to the next side. →

Intervention • Skills **IN17**

Practice on Your Own — Skill 4

← 444 445 446 447 448 449 450 451 452 453 454 455 456 →

454   445   449   450

> **Think:** I read the number line from left to right. 445 comes first. It has the least value. Next, I find 449. Then, I find 450. 454 is last. 454 has the greatest value.

Write the numbers in order from least to greatest.
Use the number line to help you.

← 344 345 346 347 348 349 350 351 352 353 354 355 356 357 358 359 360 361 362 363 364 365 366 →

1 345   356   354
345, 354, 356

2 353   360   352
352, 353, 360

3 362   358   355
355, 358, 362

← 428 429 430 431 432 433 434 435 436 437 438 439 440 441 442 443 444 445 446 447 448 449 450 →

4 430 435 432 442
430, 432, 435, 442

5 445 431 434 440
431, 434, 440, 445

6 435 443 447 439
435, 439, 443, 447

▶ Quiz

Write the numbers in order from least to greatest.
Use the number line to help you.

← 225 226 227 228 229 230 231 232 233 234 235 236 237 238 239 240 241 242 243 244 245 246 247 →

7 235 238 229 227
227, 229, 235, 238

8 230 240 234 228
228, 230, 234, 240

9 234 229 232 231
229, 231, 232, 234

IN18 Intervention • Skills

Grade 4 — Skill 5

Order Numbers

Write these numbers in order from greatest to least: 3,927; 3,101; and 3,762.

Step 1
Line up the numbers by place-value. Look at the digit in the place-value position on the left first. Compare the thousands.

3,927
3,101
3,762
↑

All the thousands are the same.

Step 2
Now look at the next place-value position. Compare the hundreds.

3,927
3,101
3,762
↑

The hundreds places are not the same.

Step 3
Write the numbers in order from greatest to least.

Think: The number with 9 in the hundreds place is the greatest. The number with 1 in the hundreds place is the least.

9 > 7 > 1

So, the order from greatest to least is 3,927 > 3,762 > 3,101.

▲ Try These

Write these numbers in order from greatest to least.

② 2,957; 7,968; 4,960
7,968 > 4,960 > 2,957

④ 4,999; 4,001; 4,500
4,999 > 4,500 > 4,001

⑦ 3,700; 3,750; 3,735
3,750 > 3,735 > 3,700

③ 1,987; 2,897; 3,789
3,789 > 2,897 > 1,987

⑤ 9,500; 9,249; 9,350
9,500 > 9,350 > 9,249

⑧ 8,877; 8,887; 8,899
8,899 > 8,887 > 8,877

⑥ 7,898; 8,000; 1,999
8,000 > 7,898 > 1,999

⑥ 5,877; 5,787; 5,699
5,877 > 5,787 > 5,699

⑨ 6,728; 6,705; 6,753
6,753 > 6,728 > 6,705

Go to the next side.

Practice on Your Own — Skill 5

Write these numbers in order from least to greatest: 59,712; 52,085; 56,436.

First, line up the numbers by place-value. Compare the ten thousands.
59,712
52,085
56,436
The digits in ten thousands place are the same.

Next, look at the digits in the next place-value position to the right. Compare the thousands.
59,712
52,085
56,436
The thousands are different.

Order the numbers in thousands place from least to greatest.

2 < 6 < 9

So, the order from least to greatest is
52,085 < 56,436 < 59,712.

Write the numbers in order from least to greatest.

① 88,727; 99,545; 63,258
63,258 < 88,727 < 99,545

④ 75,656; 75,156; 75,428
75,156 < 75,428 < 75,656

② 52,759; 55,865; 51,917
51,917 < 52,759 < 55,865

⑤ 85,443; 87,489; 86,416
85,443 < 86,416 < 87,489

③ 94,976; 94,388; 94,095
94,095 < 94,388 < 94,976

⑥ 23,564; 51,215; 34,111
23,564 < 34,111 < 51,215

Write the numbers in order from greatest to least.

⑦ 31,532; 51,594; 61,626
61,626 > 51,594 > 31,532

⑩ 27,256; 35,512; 48,064
48,064 > 35,512 > 27,256

⑧ 70,388; 78,036; 73,805
78,036 > 73,805 > 70,388

⑪ 54,095; 54,121; 54,292
54,292 > 54,121 > 54,095

⑨ 77,564; 77,878; 77,901
77,901 > 77,878 > 77,564

⑫ 33,222; 35,420; 34,911
35,420 > 34,911 > 33,222

▶ Quiz

Write the numbers in order from least to greatest.

⑬ 34,824; 44,873; 24,256
24,256 < 34,824 < 44,873

⑭ 51,402; 58,321; 50,693
50,693 < 51,402 < 58,321

⑮ 64,875; 64,737; 64,949
64,737 < 64,875 < 64,949

Write the numbers in order from greatest to least.

⑯ 93,872; 13,012; 33,792
93,872 > 33,792 > 13,012

⑰ 12,587; 15,576; 16,525
16,525 > 15,576 > 12,587

⑱ 10,872; 10,974; 10,716
10,974 > 10,872 > 10,716

Grade 4 — Skill 6

Round to Nearest 10 and 100

Round 1,463 to the nearest ten using a number line.

1,460   1,463   1,465   1,470

1,463 is closer to 1,460 than to 1,470.

1,463 rounded to the nearest ten is 1,460.

Round 1,463 to the nearest hundred.

1,400   1,450   1,463   1,500

1,463 is closer to 1,500 than to 1,400.

1,463 rounded to the nearest hundred is 1,500.

To round to the nearest **ten**, look at the digit in the ones place. If the digit is less than 5, the digit to be rounded stays the same.

3 < 5

digit to be rounded → ones place
1, 4 6 3

1,463 rounded to the nearest ten is 1,460.

To round to the nearest **hundred**, look at the digit in the tens place. If the digit is 5 or greater, the digit to be rounded increases by 1.

6 > 5

digit to be rounded → tens place
1, 4 6 3

1,463 rounded to the nearest hundred is 1,500.

① Use rounding rules. Round 1,617 to the nearest hundred.

The digit in the tens place is [1].

1, 6 1 7   The digit to be rounded is [6].

1,617 rounded to the nearest hundred is [1,600].

▲ Try These

Complete.

① Use a number line. Round 126 to the nearest ten.

120   125   126   130

126 is closer to [130] than to [120].

126 rounded to the nearest ten is [130].

Go to the next side.

Practice on Your Own — Skill 6

Round 259 to the nearest hundred.

Number Line
259

200   250   300

Look at the number line.
259 is closer to 300 than to 200.

Rounding Rules
To round to the nearest hundred, look at the tens digit.

tens digit
2 5 9

If the digit is 5 or greater, the digit to be rounded increases by 1. If the digit is less than 5, the digit to be rounded stays the same.

So, 259 rounded to the nearest hundred is 300.

Round to the nearest ten.

① 646
640   645   650
646 to the nearest ten is [650]

② 1,987
1,980   1,985   1,990
1,987 to the nearest ten is [1,990]

Use rounding rules to round the numbers to the nearest hundred.

③ 380   ↓   3 8 0
380 rounded to the nearest hundred is [400].

④ 1,794   ↓   1, 7 9 4
1,794 rounded to the nearest hundred is [1,800].

Round to the place of the underlined digit.

⑤ 4_6_2
460

⑥ 6,9_2_7
6,930

⑦ _2_65
300

⑧ 3,_8_78
3,900

▶ Quiz

Round to the place of the underlined digit.

⑨ 5_8_6
590

⑩ 9,0_3_8
9,040

⑪ _6_30
600

⑫ 5,_6_83
5,700

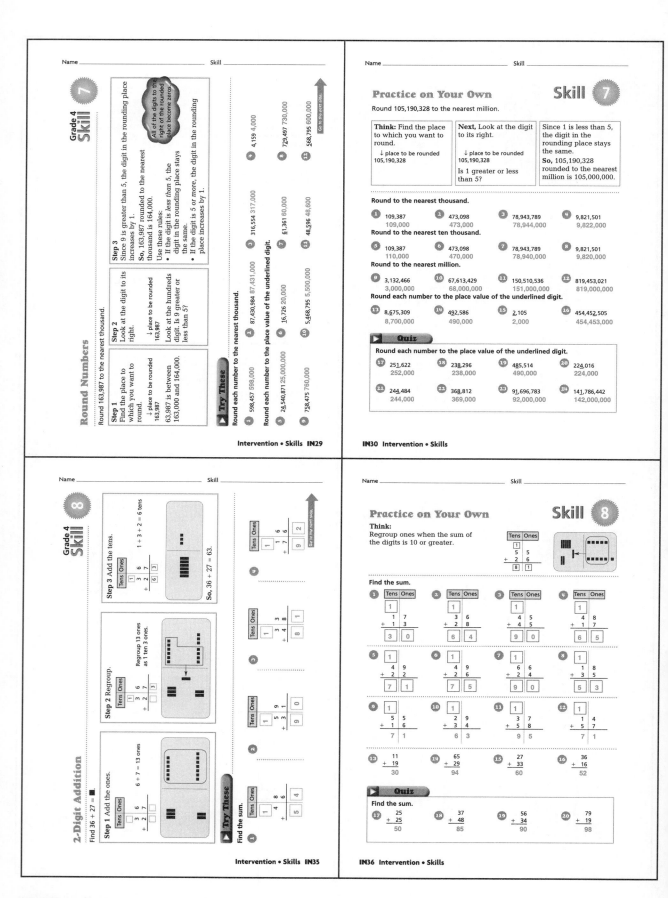

Grade 4 — Skill 7

Round Numbers

Round 163,987 to the nearest thousand.

Step 1
Find the place to which you want to round.
↓ place to be rounded
163,987
63,987 is between 163,000 and 164,000.

Step 2
Look at the digit to its right.
↓ place to be rounded
163,987
Look at the hundreds digit. Is 9 greater or less than 5?

Step 3
Since 9 is greater than 5, the digit in the rounding place increases by 1.
So, 163,987 rounded to the nearest thousand is 164,000.
Use these rules:
• If the digit is *less than 5*, the digit in the rounding place stays the same.
• If the digit is *5 or more*, the digit in the rounding place increases by 1.

All of the digits to the right of the rounded place become zeros.

Try These

Round each number to the nearest thousand.

1. 598,457 598,000
2. 87,430,984 87,431,000
3. 4,159 4,000

Round each number to the place value of the underlined digit.

4. 24,540,871 25,000,000
5. 16,726 20,000
6. 316,554 317,000
7. 729,497 730,000

8. 758,475 760,000
9. 5,468,795 5,500,000
10. 48,596 48,600
11. 568,795 600,000

Go to the next side.

Intervention • Skills **IN29**

Practice on Your Own — Skill 7

Round 105,190,328 to the nearest million.

| **Think:** Find the place to which you want to round.
↓ place to be rounded
105,190,328 | **Next,** Look at the digit to its right.
↓ place to be rounded
105,190,328
Is 1 greater or less than 5? | Since 1 is less than 5, the digit in the rounding place stays the same.
So, 105,190,328 rounded to the nearest million is 105,000,000. |

Round to the nearest thousand.

1. 109,387 109,000
2. 473,098 473,000
3. 78,943,789 78,944,000
4. 9,821,501 9,822,000

Round to the nearest ten thousand.

5. 109,387 110,000
6. 473,098 470,000
7. 78,943,789 78,940,000
8. 9,821,501 9,820,000

Round to the nearest million.

9. 3,132,466 3,000,000
10. 67,613,429 68,000,000
11. 150,510,536 151,000,000
12. 819,453,021 819,000,000

Round each number to the place value of the underlined digit.

13. 8,675,309 8,700,000
14. 492,586 490,000
15. 2,105 2,000
16. 454,452,505 454,453,000

> **Quiz**

Round each number to the place value of the underlined digit.

17. 251,622 252,000
18. 238,296 238,000
19. 485,514 490,000
20. 224,016 224,000

21. 244,484 244,000
22. 368,812 369,000
23. 91,696,783 92,000,000
24. 141,786,442 142,000,000

Grade 4 — Skill 8

2-Digit Addition

Find 36 + 27 = ■.

Step 1 Add the ones.

Tens	Ones
3	6
+ 2	7

6 + 7 = 13 ones

Step 2 Regroup.

Tens	Ones
1	
3	6
+ 2	7
	3

Regroup 13 ones as 1 ten 3 ones.

Step 3 Add the tens.

Tens	Ones
1	
3	6
+ 2	7
6	3

1 + 3 + 2 = 6 tens

So, 36 + 27 = 63.

Try These

Find the sum.

1.
Tens	Ones
1	4
+ 4	8
5	4

2.
Tens	Ones
1	
5	9
+ 3	1
9	0

3.
Tens	Ones
1	3
+ 4	8
8	1

4.
Tens	Ones
1	6
1	7
+ 9	2

Go to the next side.

Intervention • Skills **IN35**

Practice on Your Own — Skill 8

Think:
Regroup ones when the sum of the digits is 10 or greater.

Tens	Ones
1	
5	5
+ 2	6
8	1

Find the sum.

1.
Tens	Ones
1	
1	7
+ 1	3
3	0

2.
Tens	Ones
1	
3	6
+ 2	8
6	4

3.
Tens	Ones
1	
4	5
+ 4	5
9	0

4.
Tens	Ones
1	
4	8
+ 1	7
6	5

5.
Tens	Ones
1	
4	9
+ 2	2
7	1

6.
Tens	Ones
1	
4	9
+ 2	6
7	5

7.
Tens	Ones
1	
6	6
+ 2	4
9	0

8.
Tens	Ones
1	
1	8
+ 3	5
5	3

9.
Tens	Ones
1	
5	5
+ 1	6
7	1

10.
Tens	Ones
1	
2	9
+ 3	4
6	3

11.
Tens	Ones
1	
3	7
+ 5	8
9	5

12.
Tens	Ones
1	
1	4
+ 5	7
7	1

13. 11
  + 19
  30

14. 65
  + 29
  94

15. 27
  + 33
  60

16. 36
  + 16
  52

> **Quiz**

Find the sum.

17. 25
  + 25
  50

18. 37
  + 48
  85

19. 56
  + 34
  90

20. 79
  + 19
  98

IN290 Intervention • Skills

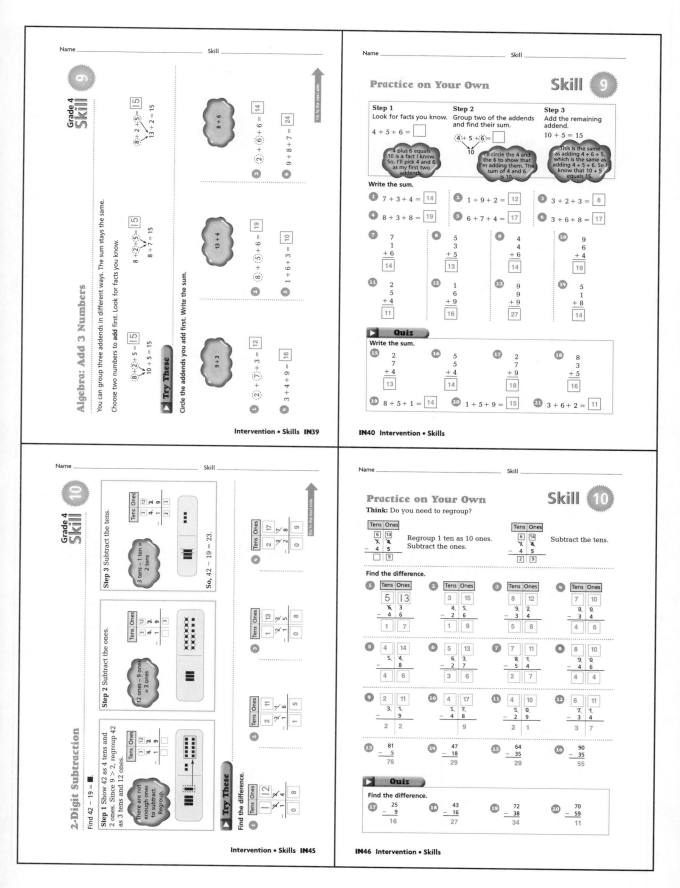

Top Left — Grade 4 Skill 9

Grade 4 Skill 9

Algebra: Add 3 Numbers

You can group three addends in different ways. The sum stays the same.

Choose two numbers to **add** first. Look for facts you know.

$(8+2)+5 = 15$
$10 + 5 = 15$

$8+(2+5)= 15$
$8 + 7 = 15$

$8+2+(5)= 15$
$13 + 2 = 15$

▶ Try These

Circle the addends you add first. Write the sum.

9 + 3
1. $(2)+(7)+3 = 12$
2. $3 + 4 + 9 = 16$

13 + 6
2. $(8)+(5)+6 = 19$
5. $1 + 6 + 3 = 10$

8 + 6
3. $(2)+(6)+6 = 14$
6. $9 + 8 + 7 = 24$

Go to the next side →

Top Right — Skill 9

Practice on Your Own — Skill 9

Step 1 Look for facts you know.
$4 + 5 + 6 =$ ☐
4 plus 6 equals 10 is a fact I know. So, I'll pick 4 and 6 as my first two addends.

Step 2 Group two of the addends and find their sum.
$(4) + 5 + (6) =$ ☐   10
I'll circle the 4 and the 6 to show that I'm adding them. The sum of 4 and 6 is 10.

Step 3 Add the remaining addend.
$10 + 5 = 15$
This is the same as adding 4 + 6 + 5, which is the same as adding 4 + 5 + 6. So I know that 10 + 5 equals 15.

Write the sum.

1. $7 + 3 + 4 = 14$
2. $1 + 9 + 2 = 12$
3. $3 + 2 + 3 = 8$
4. $8 + 3 + 8 = 19$
5. $6 + 7 + 4 = 17$
6. $3 + 6 + 8 = 17$

7. $7 + 1 + 6 = 14$
8. $5 + 3 + 5 = 13$
9. $4 + 4 + 6 = 14$
10. $9 + 6 + 4 = 19$

11. $2 + 5 + 4 = 11$
12. $1 + 6 + 9 = 16$
13. $9 + 9 + 9 = 27$
14. $5 + 1 + 8 = 14$

▶ Quiz

Write the sum.

15. $2 + 7 + 4 = 13$
16. $5 + 5 + 4 = 14$
17. $2 + 7 + 9 = 18$
18. $8 + 3 + 5 = 16$

19. $8 + 5 + 1 = 14$
20. $1 + 5 + 9 = 15$
21. $3 + 6 + 2 = 11$

Bottom Left — Grade 4 Skill 10

Grade 4 Skill 10

2-Digit Subtraction

Find $42 - 19 =$ ■

Step 1 Show 42 as 4 tens and 2 ones. Since $9 > 2$, regroup 42 as 3 tens and 12 ones.
There are not enough ones to subtract. Regroup.

Step 2 Subtract the ones. 12 ones − 9 ones = 3 ones

Step 3 Subtract the tens. 3 tens − 1 ten = 2 tens

So, $42 - 19 = 23$.

▶ Try These

Find the difference.

Go to the next side →

Bottom Right — Skill 10

Practice on Your Own — Skill 10

Think: Do you need to regroup?

Regroup 1 ten as 10 ones. Subtract the ones.   Subtract the tens.

Find the difference.

#	Tens	Ones	−	=	Tens	Ones
1	5	13	4 6		1	7
2	3	15	2 6		1	9
3	8	12	3 4		5	8
4	7	10	3 4		4	6
5		14	8		4	6
6		13	2 7		3	6
7	7	11	5 4		2	7
8	8	10	4 6		4	4
9	2	11	9		2	2
10	4	17	8			9
11	4	10	2 9		2	1
12	6	11	3 4		3	7

13. $81 - 5 = 76$
14. $47 - 18 = 29$
15. $64 - 35 = 29$
16. $90 - 35 = 55$

▶ Quiz

Find the difference.

17. $25 - 9 = 16$
18. $43 - 16 = 27$
19. $72 - 38 = 34$
20. $70 - 59 = 11$

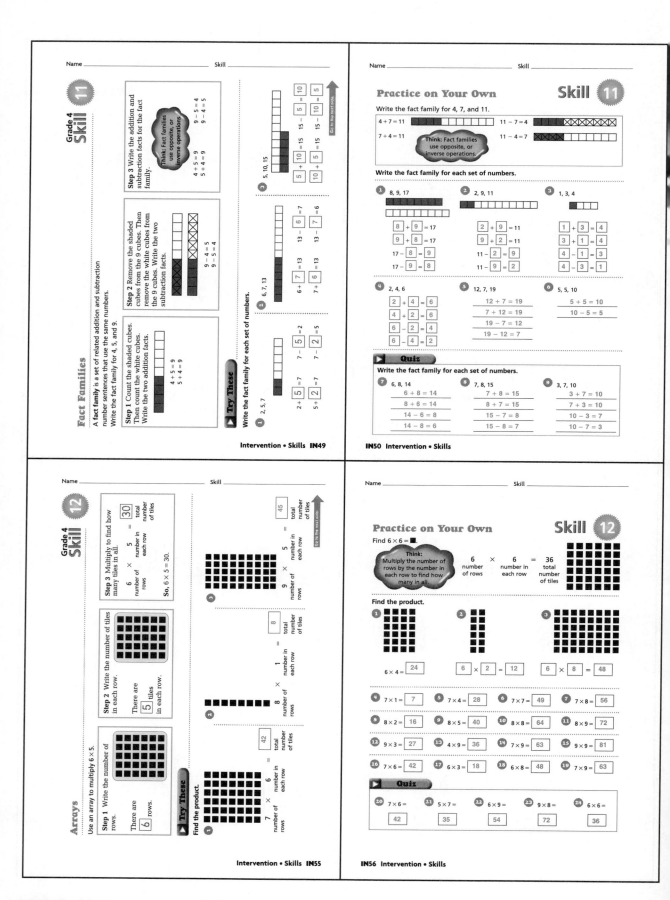

Skill 11 — Grade 4

Fact Families

A **fact family** is a set of related addition and subtraction number sentences that use the same numbers.
Write the fact family for 4, 5, and 9.

Step 1 Count the shaded cubes. Then count the white cubes. Write the two addition facts.

$$4 + 5 = 9$$
$$5 + 4 = 9$$

Step 2 Remove the shaded cubes from the 9 cubes. Then remove the white cubes from the 9 cubes. Write the two subtraction facts.

$$9 - 4 = 5$$
$$9 - 5 = 4$$

Step 3 Write the addition and subtraction facts for the fact family.

$$4 + 5 = 9$$
$$5 + 4 = 9$$
$$9 - 5 = 4$$
$$9 - 4 = 5$$

Think: Fact families use opposite, or inverse operations.

Try These

Write the fact family for each set of numbers.

1 2, 5, 7

$$2 + \boxed{5} = 7$$
$$5 + \boxed{2} = 7$$
$$7 - \boxed{5} = 2$$
$$7 - \boxed{2} = 5$$

2 6, 7, 13

$$6 + \boxed{7} = 13$$
$$7 + \boxed{6} = 13$$
$$13 - \boxed{6} = 7$$
$$13 - \boxed{7} = 6$$

3 5, 10, 15

$$5 + \boxed{10} = 15$$
$$\boxed{10} + \boxed{5} = 15$$
$$15 - \boxed{5} = 10$$
$$\boxed{10} - \boxed{5} = 5$$

Intervention • Skills **IN49**

Practice on Your Own — Skill 11

Write the fact family for 4, 7, and 11.

$$4 + 7 = 11$$
$$7 + 4 = 11$$
$$11 - 7 = 4$$
$$11 - 4 = 7$$

Think: Fact families use opposite, or inverse operations.

Write the fact family for each set of numbers.

1 8, 9, 17

$$8 + \boxed{9} = 17$$
$$9 + \boxed{8} = 17$$
$$17 - \boxed{8} = \boxed{9}$$
$$17 - \boxed{9} = \boxed{8}$$

2 2, 9, 11

$$2 + \boxed{9} = 11$$
$$\boxed{9} + \boxed{2} = 11$$
$$11 - \boxed{2} = \boxed{9}$$
$$11 - \boxed{9} = \boxed{2}$$

3 1, 3, 4

$$1 + \boxed{3} = \boxed{4}$$
$$\boxed{3} + \boxed{1} = \boxed{4}$$
$$\boxed{4} - \boxed{1} = \boxed{3}$$
$$\boxed{4} - \boxed{3} = \boxed{1}$$

4 2, 4, 6

$$\boxed{2} + \boxed{4} = \boxed{6}$$
$$\boxed{4} + \boxed{2} = \boxed{6}$$
$$\boxed{6} - \boxed{2} = \boxed{4}$$
$$\boxed{6} - \boxed{4} = \boxed{2}$$

5 12, 7, 19

$$12 + 7 = 19$$
$$7 + 12 = 19$$
$$19 - 7 = 12$$
$$19 - 12 = 7$$

6 5, 5, 10

$$5 + 5 = 10$$
$$10 - 5 = 5$$

Quiz

Write the fact family for each set of numbers.

7 6, 8, 14

$$6 + 8 = 14$$
$$8 + 6 = 14$$
$$14 - 6 = 8$$
$$14 - 8 = 6$$

8 7, 8, 15

$$7 + 8 = 15$$
$$8 + 7 = 15$$
$$15 - 7 = 8$$
$$15 - 8 = 7$$

9 3, 7, 10

$$3 + 7 = 10$$
$$7 + 3 = 10$$
$$10 - 3 = 7$$
$$10 - 7 = 3$$

IN50 Intervention • Skills

Skill 12 — Grade 4

Arrays

Use an array to multiply 6×5.

Step 1 Write the number of rows.

There are $\boxed{6}$ rows.

Step 2 Write the number of tiles in each row.

There are $\boxed{5}$ tiles in each row.

Step 3 Multiply to find how many tiles in all.

$$6 \times 5 = \boxed{30}$$
number of rows × number in each row = total number of tiles

So, $6 \times 5 = 30$.

Try These

Find the product.

1

$$7 \times 6 = \boxed{42}$$
number of rows × number in each row = total number of tiles

2

$$8 \times 1 = \boxed{8}$$
number of rows × number in each row = total number of tiles

3

$$9 \times 5 = \boxed{45}$$
number of rows × number in each row = total number of tiles

Intervention • Skills **IN55**

Practice on Your Own — Skill 12

Find $6 \times 6 = \blacksquare$.

Think: Multiply the number of rows by the number in each row to find how many in all.

$$6 \times 6 = 36$$
number of rows × number in each row = total number of tiles

Find the product.

1 $6 \times 4 = \boxed{24}$

2 $6 \times 2 = \boxed{12}$

3 $6 \times 8 = \boxed{48}$

4 $7 \times 1 = \boxed{7}$

5 $7 \times 4 = \boxed{28}$

6 $7 \times 7 = \boxed{49}$

7 $7 \times 8 = \boxed{56}$

8 $8 \times 2 = \boxed{16}$

9 $8 \times 5 = \boxed{40}$

10 $8 \times 8 = \boxed{64}$

11 $8 \times 9 = \boxed{72}$

12 $9 \times 3 = \boxed{27}$

13 $4 \times 9 = \boxed{36}$

14 $7 \times 9 = \boxed{63}$

15 $9 \times 9 = \boxed{81}$

16 $7 \times 6 = \boxed{42}$

17 $6 \times 3 = \boxed{18}$

18 $6 \times 8 = \boxed{48}$

19 $7 \times 9 = \boxed{63}$

Quiz

20 $7 \times 6 = \boxed{42}$

21 $5 \times 7 = \boxed{35}$

22 $6 \times 9 = \boxed{54}$

23 $9 \times 8 = \boxed{72}$

24 $6 \times 6 = \boxed{36}$

IN56 Intervention • Skills

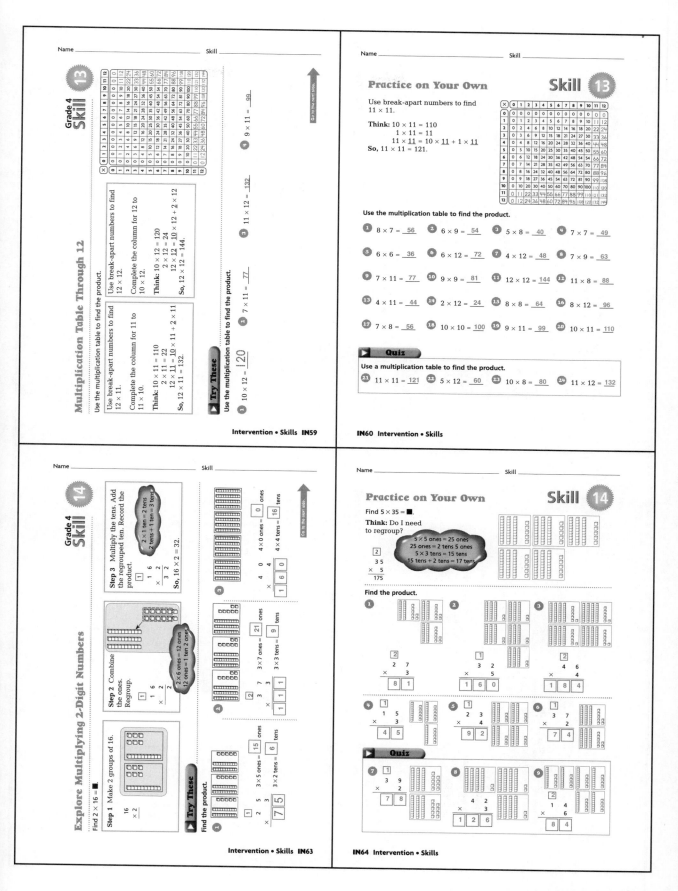

Top-left panel (Skill 13):

Grade 4
Skill 13

Multiplication Table Through 12

Use the multiplication table to find the product.

Use break-apart numbers to find
12 × 11.

Complete the column for 11 to
11 × 10.

Think: 10 × 11 = 110
2 × 11 = 22
12 × 11 = 10 × 11 + 2 × 11
So, 12 × 11 = 132.

Use break-apart numbers to find
12 × 12.

Complete the column for 12 to
10 × 12.

Think: 10 × 12 = 120
2 × 12 = 24
12 × 12 = 10 × 12 + 2 × 12
So, 12 × 12 = 144.

Try These

Use the multiplication table to find the product.

1. 10 × 12 = _120_   2. 7 × 11 = _77_   3. 11 × 12 = _132_   4. 9 × 11 = _99_

Go to the next side.

Top-right panel (Skill 13):

Practice on Your Own

Skill 13

Use break-apart numbers to find
11 × 11.

Think: 10 × 11 = 110
1 × 11 = 11
11 × 11 = 10 × 11 + 1 × 11
So, 11 × 11 = 121.

Use the multiplication table to find the product.

1. 8 × 7 = _56_   2. 6 × 9 = _54_   3. 5 × 8 = _40_   4. 7 × 7 = _49_

5. 6 × 6 = _36_   6. 6 × 12 = _72_   7. 4 × 12 = _48_   8. 7 × 9 = _63_

9. 7 × 11 = _77_   10. 9 × 9 = _81_   11. 12 × 12 = _144_   12. 11 × 8 = _88_

13. 4 × 11 = _44_   14. 2 × 12 = _24_   15. 8 × 8 = _64_   16. 8 × 12 = _96_

17. 7 × 8 = _56_   18. 10 × 10 = _100_   19. 9 × 11 = _99_   20. 10 × 11 = _110_

Quiz

Use a multiplication table to find the product.

21. 11 × 11 = _121_   22. 5 × 12 = _60_   23. 10 × 8 = _80_   24. 11 × 12 = _132_

Bottom-left panel (Skill 14):

Grade 4
Skill 14

Explore Multiplying 2-Digit Numbers

Find 2 × 16 = ■.

Step 1 Make 2 groups of 16.

16
× 2

Step 2 Combine
the ones.
Regroup.

1
1 6
× 2
2

2 × 6 ones = 12 ones
12 ones = 1 ten 2 ones

Step 3 Multiply the tens. Add
the regrouped ten. Record the
product.

1
1 6
× 2
3 2

2 × 1 ten = 2 tens
2 tens + 1 ten = 3 tens

So, 16 × 2 = 32.

Try These

Find the product.

1. 2 5   3 × 5 ones = _15_ ones
   × 3   3 × 2 tens = _6_ tens
   7 5

2. 3 7   3 × 7 ones = _21_ ones
   × 3   3 × 3 tens = _9_ tens
   1 1 1

3. 4 0   4 × 0 ones = _0_ ones
   × 4   4 × 4 tens = _16_ tens
   1 6 0

Go to the next side.

Bottom-right panel (Skill 14):

Practice on Your Own

Skill 14

Find 5 × 35 = ■.

Think: Do I need
to regroup?

5 × 5 ones = 25 ones
25 ones = 2 tens 5 ones
5 × 3 tens = 15 tens
15 tens + 2 tens = 17 tens

2
3 5
× 5
175

Find the product.

1. 2
   2 7
   × 3
   8 1

2. 1
   3 2
   × 5
   1 6 0

3. 2
   4 6
   × 4
   1 8 4

4. 1
   1 5
   × 3
   4 5

5. 1
   2 3
   × 4
   9 2

6. 1
   3 7
   × 2
   7 4

Quiz

7. 1
   3 9
   × 2
   7 8

8. 4 2
   × 3
   1 2 6

9. 2
   1 4
   × 6
   8 4

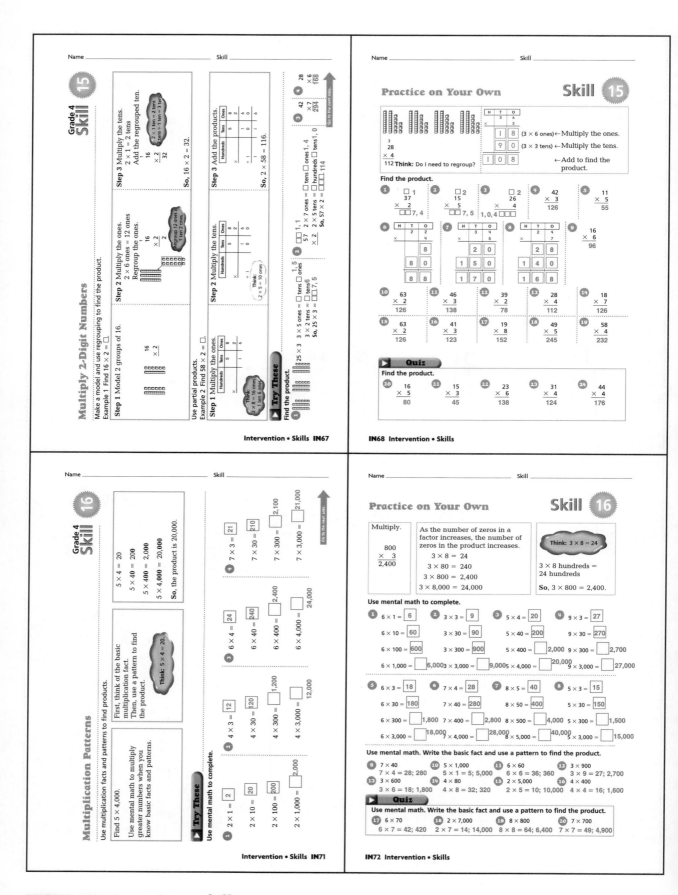

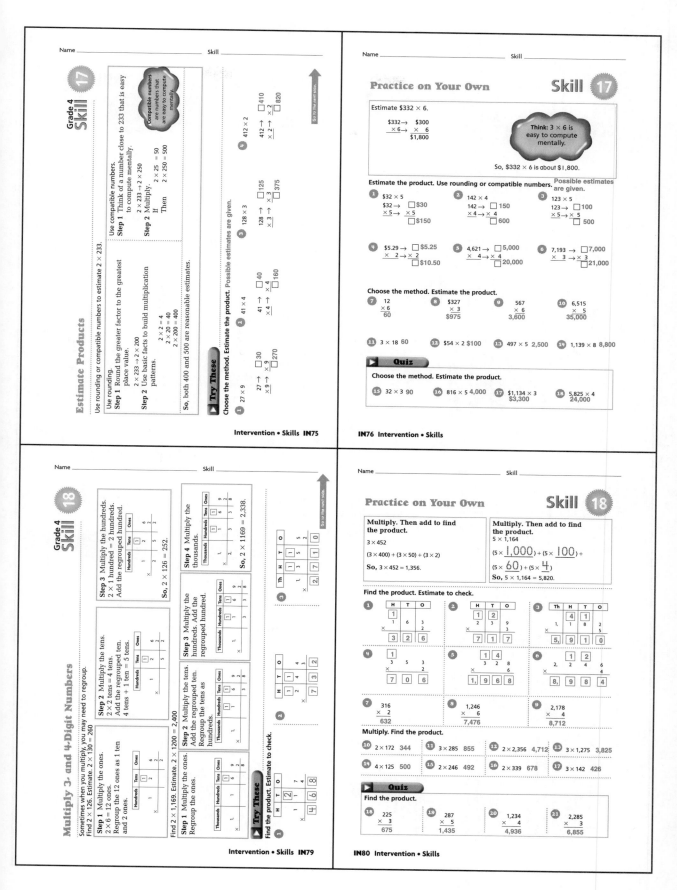

Top Left Panel (Skill 17)

Grade 4
Skill 17

Estimate Products

Use rounding or compatible numbers to estimate 2 × 233.

Use rounding.
Step 1 Round the greater factor to the greatest place value.

2 × 233 → 2 × 200

Step 2 Use basic facts to build multiplication patterns.

2 × 2 = 4
2 × 20 = 40
2 × 200 = 400

Use compatible numbers.
Step 1 Think of a number close to 233 that is easy to compute mentally.

2 × 233 → 2 × 250

Step 2 Multiply.
If   2 × 25 = 50
Then   2 × 250 = 500

> Compatible numbers are numbers that are easy to compute mentally.

So, both 400 and 500 are reasonable estimates.

Try These

Choose the method. Estimate the product. Possible estimates are given.

1 27 × 9
27 → ☐30
×9 → × 9
     ☐270

2 41 × 4
41 → ☐40
×4 → × 4
     ☐160

3 128 × 3
128 → ☐125
×3 → × 3
     ☐375

4 412 × 2
412 → ☐410
× 2 → × 2
      ☐820

Top Right Panel (Skill 17)

Practice on Your Own   **Skill 17**

Estimate $332 × 6.

$332 → $300
× 6 → × 6
      $1,800

> Think: 3 × 6 is easy to compute mentally.

So, $332 × 6 is about $1,800.

Estimate the product. Use rounding or compatible numbers. Possible estimates are given.

1 $32 × 5
$32 → ☐$30
×5 → × 5
     ☐$150

2 142 × 4
142 → ☐ 150
× 4 → × 4
      ☐ 600

3 123 × 5
123 → ☐100
×5 → × 5
     ☐ 500

4 $5.29 → ☐$5.25
× 2 → × 2
      ☐$10.50

5 4,621 → ☐5,000
× 4 → × 4
      ☐ 20,000

6 7,193 → ☐7,000
× 3 → × 3
      ☐21,000

Choose the method. Estimate the product.

7 12
× 6
60

8 $327
× 3
$975

9 567
× 6
3,600

10 6,515
× 5
35,000

11 3 × 18 60

12 $54 × 2 $100

13 497 × 5 2,500

14 1,139 × 8 8,800

Quiz

Choose the method. Estimate the product.

15 32 × 3 90

16 816 × 5 4,000

17 $1,134 × 3 $3,300

18 5,825 × 4 24,000

Bottom Left Panel (Skill 18)

Grade 4
Skill 18

Multiply 3- and 4-Digit Numbers

Sometimes when you multiply, you may need to regroup.
Find 2 × 126. Estimate. 2 × 130 = 260

Step 1 Multiply the ones.
2 × 6 = 12 ones.
Regroup the 12 ones as 1 ten and 2 ones.

Step 2 Multiply the tens.
2 × 2 tens = 4 tens.
Add the regrouped ten.
4 tens + 1 ten = 5 tens.

Step 3 Multiply the hundreds.
2 × 1 hundred = 2 hundreds.
Add the regrouped hundred.

So, 2 × 126 = 252.

Find 2 × 1,169. Estimate. 2 × 1200 = 2,400

Step 1 Multiply the ones. Regroup the ones.

Step 2 Multiply the tens. Add the regrouped ten. Regroup the tens as hundreds.

Step 3 Multiply the hundreds. Add the regrouped hundred.

Step 4 Multiply the thousands.

So, 2 × 1169 = 2,338.

Try These

Find the product. Estimate to check.

1

2

3

Bottom Right Panel (Skill 18)

Practice on Your Own   **Skill 18**

Multiply. Then add to find the product.
3 × 452
(3 × 400) + (3 × 50) + (3 × 2)
So, 3 × 452 = 1,356.

Multiply. Then add to find the product.
5 × 1,164
(5 × 1,000) + (5 × 100) + (5 × 60) + (5 × 4)
So, 5 × 1,164 = 5,820.

Find the product. Estimate to check.

1

2

3

4

5

6

7 316
× 2
632

8 1,246
× 6
7,476

9 2,178
× 4
8,712

Multiply. Find the product.

10 2 × 172 344

11 3 × 285 855

12 2 × 2,356 4,712

13 3 × 1,275 3,825

14 4 × 125 500

15 2 × 246 492

16 2 × 339 678

17 3 × 142 426

Quiz

Find the product.

18 225
× 3
675

19 287
× 5
1,435

20 1,234
× 4
4,936

21 2,285
× 3
6,855

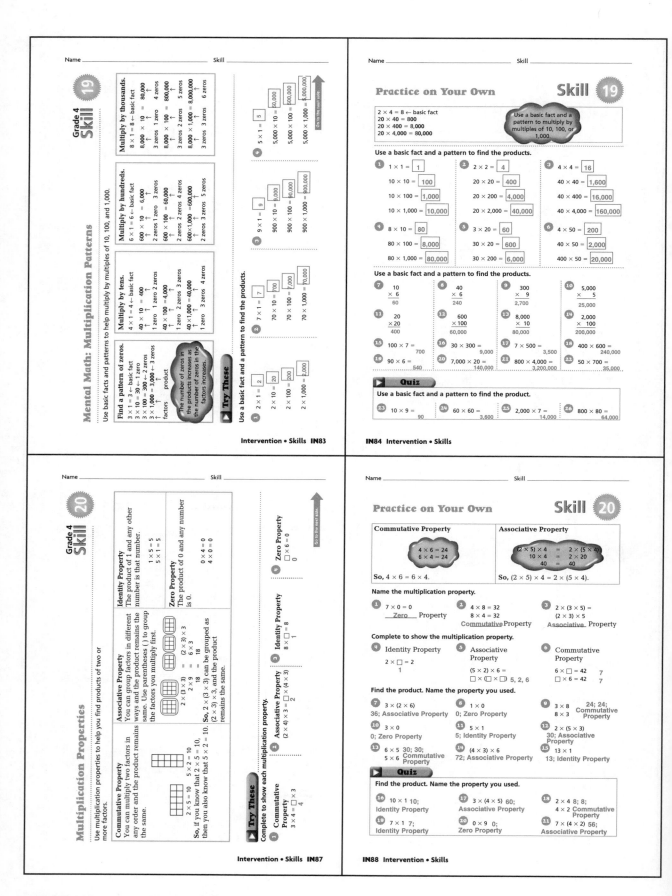

Top-left panel (Skill 19)

Grade 4
Skill 19

Mental Math: Multiplication Patterns

Use basic facts and patterns to help multiply by multiples of 10, 100, and 1,000.

Find a pattern of zeros.

$3 \times 1 = 3 \leftarrow$ basic fact
$3 \times 10 = 30 \leftarrow$ 1 zero
$3 \times 100 = 300 \leftarrow$ 2 zeros
$3 \times 1,000 = 3,000 \leftarrow$ 3 zeros
factors   product

The number of zeros in the products increases as the number of zeros in the factors increases.

Multiply by tens.
$4 \times 1 = 4 \leftarrow$ basic fact
$40 \times 10 = 400$
   1 zero 2 zeros
$40 \times 100 = 4,000$
   1 zero 3 zeros
$40 \times 1,000 = 40,000$
   1 zero 4 zeros

Multiply by hundreds.
$6 \times 1 = 6 \leftarrow$ basic fact
$600 \times 10 = 6,000$
  2 zeros 1 zero 3 zeros
$600 \times 100 = 60,000$
  2 zeros 2 zeros 4 zeros
$600 \times 1,000 = 600,000$
  2 zeros 3 zeros 5 zeros

Multiply by thousands.
$8 \times 1 = 8 \leftarrow$ basic fact
$8,000 \times 10 = 80,000$
 3 zeros 1 zero 4 zeros
$8,000 \times 100 = 800,000$
 3 zeros 2 zeros 5 zeros
$8,000 \times 1,000 = 8,000,000$
 3 zeros 3 zeros 6 zeros

Go to the next side.

▲ Try These

Use a basic fact and a pattern to find the products.

1. $2 \times 1 = 2$
$2 \times 10 = 20$
$2 \times 100 = 200$
$2 \times 1,000 = 1,000$

2. $7 \times 1 = 7$
$70 \times 10 = 700$
$70 \times 100 = 7,000$
$70 \times 1,000 = 70,000$

3. $9 \times 1 = 9$
$900 \times 10 = 9,000$
$900 \times 100 = 90,000$
$900 \times 1,000 = 900,000$

4. $5 \times 1 = 5$
$5,000 \times 10 = 50,000$
$5,000 \times 100 = 500,000$
$5,000 \times 1,000 = 5,000,000$

Intervention • Skills **IN83**

Top-right panel (Skill 19)

Practice on Your Own
Skill 19

$2 \times 4 = 8 \leftarrow$ basic fact
$20 \times 40 = 800$
$20 \times 400 = 8,000$
$20 \times 4,000 = 80,000$

Use a basic fact and a pattern to multiply by multiples of 10, 100, or 1,000.

Use a basic fact and a pattern to find the products.

1. $1 \times 1 = 1$
$10 \times 10 = 100$
$10 \times 100 = 1,000$
$10 \times 1,000 = 10,000$

2. $2 \times 2 = 4$
$20 \times 20 = 400$
$20 \times 200 = 4,000$
$20 \times 2,000 = 40,000$

3. $4 \times 4 = 16$
$40 \times 40 = 1,600$
$40 \times 400 = 16,000$
$40 \times 4,000 = 160,000$

4. $8 \times 10 = 80$
$80 \times 100 = 8,000$
$80 \times 1,000 = 80,000$

5. $3 \times 20 = 60$
$30 \times 20 = 600$
$30 \times 200 = 6,000$

6. $4 \times 50 = 200$
$40 \times 50 = 2,000$
$400 \times 50 = 20,000$

Use a basic fact and a pattern to find the products.

7. $\begin{array}{r} 10 \\ \times\ 6 \\ \hline 60 \end{array}$

8. $\begin{array}{r} 40 \\ \times\ 6 \\ \hline 240 \end{array}$

9. $\begin{array}{r} 300 \\ \times\ 9 \\ \hline 2,700 \end{array}$

10. $\begin{array}{r} 5,000 \\ \times\ 5 \\ \hline 25,000 \end{array}$

11. $\begin{array}{r} 20 \\ \times 20 \\ \hline 400 \end{array}$

12. $\begin{array}{r} 600 \\ \times 100 \\ \hline 60,000 \end{array}$

13. $\begin{array}{r} 8,000 \\ \times\ 10 \\ \hline 80,000 \end{array}$

14. $\begin{array}{r} 2,000 \\ \times\ 100 \\ \hline 200,000 \end{array}$

15. $100 \times 7 = 700$

16. $30 \times 300 = 9,000$

17. $7 \times 500 = 3,500$

18. $400 \times 600 = 240,000$

19. $90 \times 6 = 540$

20. $7,000 \times 20 = 140,000$

21. $800 \times 4,000 = 3,200,000$

22. $50 \times 700 = 35,000$

▶ Quiz

Use a basic fact and a pattern to find the product.

23. $10 \times 9 = 90$

24. $60 \times 60 = 3,600$

25. $2,000 \times 7 = 14,000$

26. $800 \times 80 = 64,000$

IN84 Intervention • Skills

Bottom-left panel (Skill 20)

Grade 4
Skill 20

Multiplication Properties

Use multiplication properties to help you find products of two or more factors.

Commutative Property
You can multiply two factors in any order and the product remains the same.

$2 \times 5 = 10 \qquad 5 \times 2 = 10$

So, if you know that $2 \times 5 = 10$, then you also know that $5 \times 2 = 10$.

Associative Property
You can group factors in different ways and the product remains the same. Use parentheses ( ) to group the factors you multiply first.

$2 \times (3 \times 3) = (2 \times 3) \times 3$
$2 \times 9 = 6 \times 3$
$18 = 18$

So, $2 \times (3 \times 3)$ can be grouped as $(2 \times 3) \times 3$, and the product remains the same.

Identity Property
The product of 1 and any other number is that number.

$1 \times 5 = 5$
$5 \times 1 = 5$

Zero Property
The product of 0 and any number is 0.

$0 \times 4 = 0$
$4 \times 0 = 0$

Go to the next side.

▲ Try These

Complete to show each multiplication property.

1. Commutative Property
$3 \times 4 = \square \times 3$
  4

2. Associative Property
$(2 \times 4) \times 3 = \square \times (4 \times 3)$
  2

3. Identity Property
$8 \times \square = 8$
  1

4. Zero Property
$\square \times 6 = 0$
  0

Intervention • Skills **IN87**

Bottom-right panel (Skill 20)

Practice on Your Own
Skill 20

Commutative Property
$4 \times 6 = 24$
$6 \times 4 = 24$
So, $4 \times 6 = 6 \times 4$.

Associative Property
$(2 \times 5) \times 4 = 2 \times (5 \times 4)$
$10 \times 4 = 2 \times 20$
$40 = 40$
So, $(2 \times 5) \times 4 = 2 \times (5 \times 4)$.

Name the multiplication property.

1. $7 \times 0 = 0$
  Zero Property

2. $4 \times 8 = 32$
$8 \times 4 = 32$
Commutative Property

3. $2 \times (3 \times 5) = (2 \times 3) \times 5$
Associative Property

Complete to show the multiplication property.

4. Identity Property
$2 \times \square = 2$
  1

5. Associative Property
$(5 \times 2) \times 6 = \square \times (\square \times \square)$ 5, 2, 6

6. Commutative Property
$6 \times \square = 42$ 7
$\square \times 6 = 42$ 7

Find the product. Name the property you used.

7. $3 \times (2 \times 6)$
36; Associative Property

8. 1×0
0; Zero Property

9. 3×8
8×3
24; 24; Commutative Property

10. 3×0
0; Zero Property

11. 5×1
5; Identity Property

12. $2 \times (5 \times 3)$
30; Associative Property

13. 6×5 5×6
30; 30; Commutative Property

14. $(4 \times 3) \times 6$
72; Associative Property

15. 13×1
13; Identity Property

▶ Quiz

Find the product. Name the property you used.

16. 10×1 10; Identity Property

17. $3 \times (4 \times 5)$ 60; Associative Property

18. 2×4 8; 8; 4×2 Commutative Property

19. 7×1 7; Identity Property

20. 0×9 0; Zero Property

21. $7 \times (4 \times 2)$ 56; Associative Property

IN88 Intervention • Skills

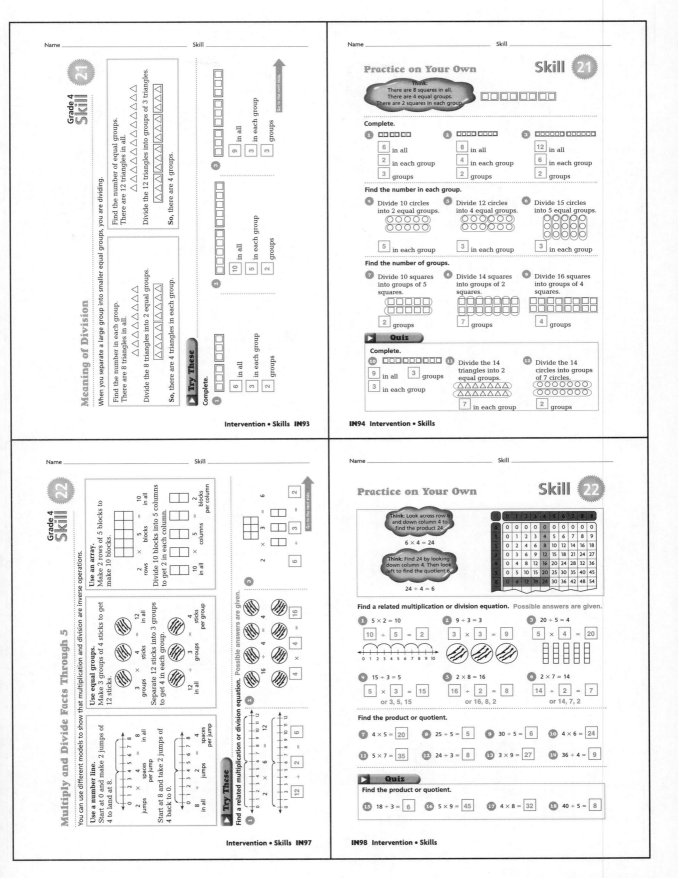

Skill 21 — Grade 4: Meaning of Division

Grade 4 Skill 21

Meaning of Division

When you separate a large group into smaller equal groups, you are dividing.

Find the number in each group.
There are 8 triangles in all.
Divide the 8 triangles into 2 equal groups.
So, there are 4 triangles in each group.

Find the number of equal groups.
There are 12 triangles in all.
Divide the 12 triangles into groups of 3 triangles.
So, there are 4 groups.

9 in all / 3 in each group / 3 groups

10 in all / 5 in each group / 2 groups

Try These

Complete.

6 in all / 3 in each group / 2 groups

Skill 21 — Practice on Your Own

Practice on Your Own   Skill 21

Think:
There are 8 squares in all.
There are 4 equal groups.
There are 2 squares in each group.

Complete.

1) 6 in all / 2 in each group / 3 groups
2) 8 in all / 4 in each group / 2 groups
3) 12 in all / 6 in each group / 2 groups

Find the number in each group.

4) Divide 10 circles into 2 equal groups. — 5 in each group
5) Divide 12 circles into 4 equal groups. — 3 in each group
6) Divide 15 circles into 5 equal groups. — 3 in each group

Find the number of groups.

7) Divide 10 squares into groups of 5 squares. — 2 groups
8) Divide 14 squares into groups of 2 squares. — 7 groups
9) Divide 16 squares into groups of 4 squares. — 4 groups

Quiz

Complete.

10) 9 in all / 3 groups / 3 in each group
11) Divide the 14 triangles into 2 equal groups. — 7 in each group
12) Divide the 14 circles into groups of 7 circles. — 2 groups

Skill 22 — Grade 4: Multiply and Divide Facts Through 5

Grade 4 Skill 22

Multiply and Divide Facts Through 5

You can use different models to show that multiplication and division are inverse operations.

Use a number line.
Start at 0 and make 2 jumps of 4 to land at 8.

2 jumps × 4 spaces per jump = 8 in all

Start at 8 and take 2 jumps of 4 back to 0.

8 in all ÷ 2 jumps = 4 spaces per jump

Use equal groups.
Make 3 groups of 4 sticks to get 12 sticks.

3 groups × 4 sticks = 12 in all

Separate 12 sticks into 3 groups to get 4 in each group.

12 in all ÷ 3 groups = 4 sticks per group

Use an array.
Make 2 rows of 5 blocks to make 10 blocks.

2 rows × 5 blocks = 10 in all

Divide 10 blocks into 5 columns to get 2 in each column.

10 in all ÷ 5 columns = 2 blocks per column

Try These

Find a related multiplication or division equation. Possible answers are given.

2 × 3 = 6   3 = 2
6

16 ÷ 4 = 4   4 × 4 = 16

2 × 6 = 12   12 ÷ 2 = 6

Skill 22 — Practice on Your Own

Practice on Your Own   Skill 22

Think: Look across row 6 and down column 4 to find the product 24.

$6 \times 4 = 24$

Think: Find 24 by looking down column 4. Then look left to find the quotient 6.

$24 \div 4 = 6$

Find a related multiplication or division equation. Possible answers are given.

1) $5 \times 2 = 10$ → $10 \div 5 = 2$
2) $9 \div 3 = 3$ → $3 \times 3 = 9$
3) $20 \div 5 = 4$ → $5 \times 4 = 20$
4) $15 \div 3 = 5$ → $5 \times 3 = 15$ — or 3, 5, 15
5) $2 \times 8 = 16$ → $16 \div 2 = 8$ — or 16, 8, 2
6) $2 \times 7 = 14$ → $14 \div 2 = 7$ — or 14, 7, 2

Find the product or quotient.

7) $4 \times 5 = 20$
8) $25 \div 5 = 5$
9) $30 \div 5 = 6$
10) $4 \times 6 = 24$
11) $5 \times 7 = 35$
12) $24 \div 3 = 8$
13) $3 \times 9 = 27$
14) $36 \div 4 = 9$

Quiz

Find the product or quotient.

15) $18 \div 3 = 6$
16) $5 \times 9 = 45$
17) $4 \times 8 = 32$
18) $40 \div 5 = 8$

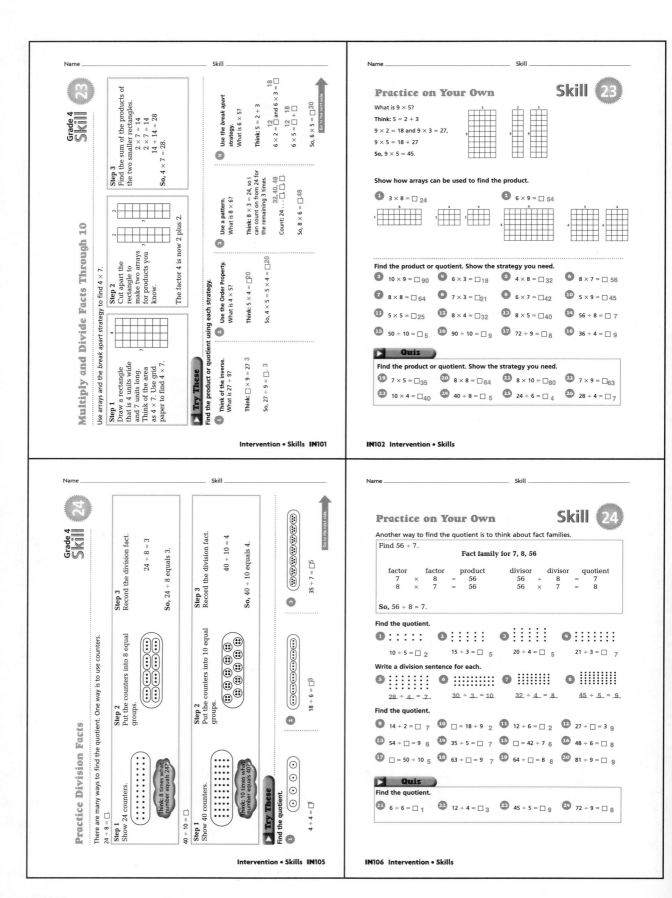

Panel 1 (top-left)

Grade 4 Skill 23

Multiply and Divide Facts Through 10

Use arrays and the *break apart* strategy to find 4×7.

Step 1
Draw a rectangle that is 4 units wide and 7 units long. Think of the area as 4×7. Use grid paper to find 4×7.

Step 2
Cut apart the rectangle to make two arrays for products you know.

The factor 4 is now 2 plus 2.

Step 3
Find the sum of the products of the two smaller rectangles.
$2 \times 7 = 14$
$2 \times 7 = 14$
$14 + 14 = 28$
So, $4 \times 7 = 28$.

▶ Try These

Find the product or quotient using each strategy.

1. Think of the inverse. What is $27 \div 9$?
Think: $\square \times 9 = 27$ 3
So, $27 \div 9 = \square$.   3

2. Use the Order Property. What is 4×5?
Think: $5 \times 4 = \square$ 20
So, $4 \times 5 = 5 \times 4 = \square$ 20

3. Use a pattern. What is 8×6?
Think: $8 \times 3 = 24$, so I can count on from 24 for the remaining 3 times.
Count: $24 \ldots \square, \square, \square$ 32, 40, 48
So, $8 \times 6 = \square$.   48

4. Use the *break apart* strategy. What is 6×5?
Think: $5 = 2 + 3$
$6 \times 2 = \square$ and $6 \times 3 = \square$ 12   18
$6 \times 5 = \square + \square$ 12   18
So, $6 \times 5 = \square$.   30

Go to the next side.

Intervention • Skills **IN101**

Panel 2 (top-right)

Practice on Your Own   Skill 23

What is 9×5?
Think: $5 = 2 + 3$
$9 \times 2 = 18$ and $9 \times 3 = 27$,
$9 \times 5 = 18 + 27$
So, $9 \times 5 = 45$.

Show how arrays can be used to find the product.

1. $3 \times 8 = \square$ 24
2. $6 \times 9 = \square$ 54

Find the product or quotient. Show the strategy you need.

3. $10 \times 9 = \square$ 90
4. $6 \times 3 = \square$ 18
5. $4 \times 8 = \square$ 32
6. $8 \times 7 = \square$ 56
7. $8 \times 8 = \square$ 64
8. $7 \times 3 = \square$ 21
9. $6 \times 7 = \square$ 42
10. $5 \times 9 = \square$ 45
11. $5 \times 5 = \square$ 25
12. $8 \times 4 = \square$ 32
13. $8 \times 5 = \square$ 40
14. $56 \div 8 = \square$ 7
15. $50 \div 10 = \square$ 5
16. $90 \div 10 = \square$ 9
17. $72 \div 9 = \square$ 8
18. $36 \div 4 = \square$ 9

▶ Quiz

Find the product or quotient. Show the strategy you need.

19. $7 \times 5 = \square$ 35
20. $8 \times 8 = \square$ 64
21. $8 \times 10 = \square$ 80
22. $7 \times 9 = \square$ 63
23. $10 \times 4 = \square$ 40
24. $40 \div 8 = \square$ 5
25. $24 \div 6 = \square$ 4
26. $28 \div 4 = \square$ 7

IN102 Intervention • Skills

Panel 3 (bottom-left)

Grade 4 Skill 24

Practice Division Facts

There are many ways to find the quotient. One way is to use counters.

$24 \div 8 = \square$

Step 1
Show 24 counters.

Think: 8 times what number equals 24?

Step 2
Put the counters into 8 equal groups.

Step 3
Record the division fact.
$24 \div 8 = 3$
So, $24 \div 8$ equals 3.

$40 \div 10 = \square$

Step 1
Show 40 counters.

Think: 10 times what number equals 40?

Step 2
Put the counters into 10 equal groups.

Step 3
Record the division fact.
$40 \div 10 = 4$
So, $40 \div 10$ equals 4.

▶ Try These

Find the quotient.

1. $4 \div 4 = \square$
2. $18 \div 6 = \square$ 3
3. $35 \div 7 = \square$ 5

Go to the next side.

Intervention • Skills **IN105**

Panel 4 (bottom-right)

Practice on Your Own   Skill 24

Another way to find the quotient is to think about fact families.

Find $56 \div 7$.

Fact family for 7, 8, 56

factor		factor		product	divisor		divisor		quotient
7	×	8	=	56	56	÷	8	=	7
8	×	7	=	56	56	×	7	=	8

So, $56 \div 8 = 7$.

Find the quotient.

1. $10 \div 5 = \square$ 2
2. $15 \div 3 = \square$ 5
3. $20 \div 4 = \square$ 5
4. $21 \div 3 = \square$ 7

Write a division sentence for each.

5. $28 \div 4 = 7$
6. $30 \div 3 = 10$
7. $32 \div 4 = 8$
8. $45 \div 5 = 9$

Find the quotient.

9. $14 \div 2 = \square$ 7
10. $\square = 18 \div 9$ 2
11. $12 \div 6 = \square$ 2
12. $27 \div 3 = \square$ 9
13. $54 \div \square = 9$ 6
14. $35 \div 5 = \square$ 7
15. $\square = 42 \div 7$ 6
16. $48 \div 6 = \square$ 8
17. $\square = 50 \div 10$ 5
18. $63 \div \square = 9$ 7
19. $64 \div \square = 8$ 8
20. $81 \div 9 = \square$ 9

▶ Quiz

Find the quotient.

21. $6 \div 6 = \square$ 1
22. $12 \div 4 = \square$ 3
23. $45 \div 5 = \square$ 9
24. $72 \div 9 = \square$ 8

IN106 Intervention • Skills

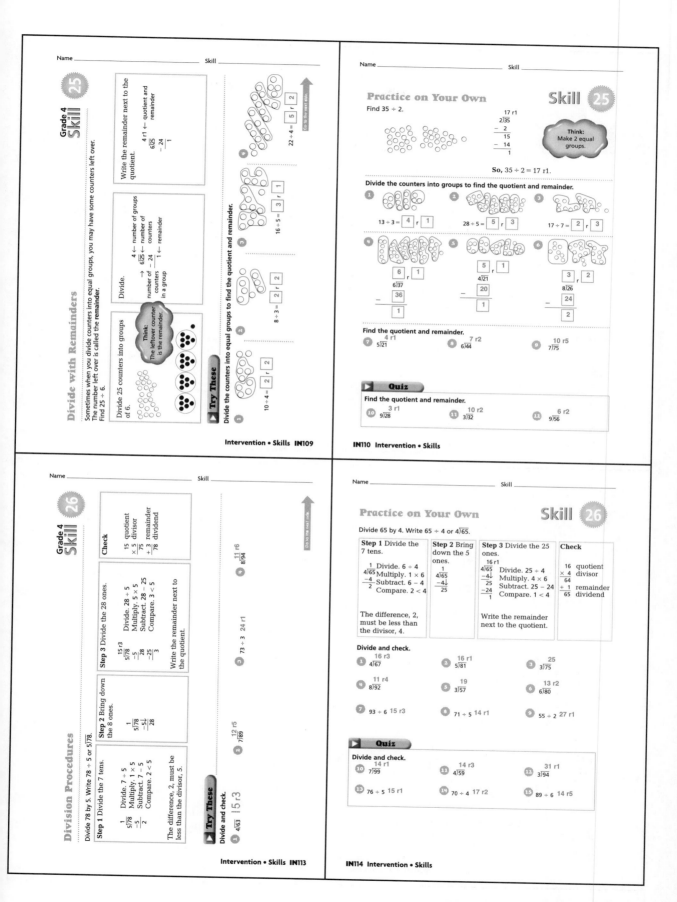

Grade 4 Skill 25

Divide with Remainders

Sometimes when you divide counters into equal groups, you may have some counters left over. The number left over is called the **remainder**.
Find 25 ÷ 6.

Divide 25 counters into groups of 6.

Think: The leftover counter is the remainder.

Divide.

number of counters in a group →
$$6\overline{)25}$$
$$-24$$
$$1$$
4 ← number of groups
number of counters
1 ← remainder

Write the remainder next to the quotient.

$$6\overline{)25} \quad 4\ r1 \leftarrow \text{quotient and remainder}$$
$$-24$$
$$1$$

$$22 \div 4 = 5\ r\ 2$$

Try These

Divide the counters into equal groups to find the quotient and remainder.

1. $10 \div 4 = \boxed{2}\ r\ \boxed{2}$

2. $8 \div 3 = \boxed{2}\ r\ \boxed{2}$

3. $16 \div 5 = \boxed{3}\ r\ \boxed{1}$

Practice on Your Own Skill 25

Find 35 ÷ 2.

$$2\overline{)35}\quad 17\ r1$$
$$-2$$
$$15$$
$$-14$$
$$1$$

Think: Make 2 equal groups.

So, 35 ÷ 2 = 17 r1.

Divide the counters into groups to find the quotient and remainder.

1. $13 \div 3 = \boxed{4}\ r\ \boxed{1}$

2. $28 \div 5 = \boxed{5}\ r\ \boxed{3}$

3. $17 \div 7 = \boxed{2}\ r\ \boxed{3}$

4. $6\overline{)37}$ $\boxed{6}\ r\ \boxed{1}$ -36 1

5. $4\overline{)21}$ $\boxed{5}\ r\ \boxed{1}$ 20 1

6. $8\overline{)26}$ $\boxed{3}\ r\ \boxed{2}$ 24 2

Find the quotient and remainder.

7. $5\overline{)21}$ **4 r1**

8. $6\overline{)44}$ **7 r2**

9. $7\overline{)75}$ **10 r5**

▶ **Quiz**

Find the quotient and remainder.

10. $9\overline{)28}$ **3 r1**

11. $3\overline{)32}$ **10 r2**

12. $9\overline{)56}$ **6 r2**

Grade 4 Skill 26

Division Procedures

Divide 78 by 5. Write 78 ÷ 5 or $5\overline{)78}$.

Step 1 Divide the 7 tens.

$$5\overline{)78}\quad 1$$
$$-5$$
$$2$$
Divide. 7 ÷ 5
Multiply. 1 × 5
Subtract. 7 − 5
Compare. 2 < 5

The difference, 2, must be less than the divisor, 5.

Step 2 Bring down the 8 ones.

$$5\overline{)78}\quad 1$$
$$-5\downarrow$$
$$28$$

Step 3 Divide the 28 ones.

$$5\overline{)78}\quad 15\ r3$$
$$-5$$
$$28$$
$$-25$$
$$3$$
Divide. 28 ÷ 5
Multiply. 5 × 5
Subtract. 28 − 25
Compare. 3 < 5

Write the remainder next to the quotient.

Check

$$15\quad \text{quotient}$$
$$\times 5\quad \text{divisor}$$
$$75$$
$$+3\quad \text{remainder}$$
$$78\quad \text{dividend}$$

Try These

Divide and check.

1. $4\overline{)63}$ **15 r3**

2. $7\overline{)89}$ **12 r5**

3. $73 \div 3$ **24 r1**

4. $8\overline{)94}$ **11 r6**

Practice on Your Own Skill 26

Divide 65 by 4. Write 65 ÷ 4 or $4\overline{)65}$.

Step 1 Divide the 7 tens.

$$4\overline{)65}\quad 1$$
$$-4$$
$$2$$
Divide. 6 ÷ 4
Multiply. 1 × 6
Subtract. 6 − 4
Compare. 2 < 4

The difference, 2, must be less than the divisor, 4.

Step 2 Bring down the 5 ones.

$$4\overline{)65}\quad 1$$
$$-4\downarrow$$
$$25$$

Step 3 Divide the 25 ones.

$$4\overline{)65}\quad 16\ r1$$
$$-4\downarrow$$
$$25$$
$$-24$$
$$1$$
Divide. 25 ÷ 4
Multiply. 4 × 6
Subtract. 25 − 24
Compare. 1 < 4

Write the remainder next to the quotient.

Check

$$16\quad \text{quotient}$$
$$\times 4\quad \text{divisor}$$
$$64$$
$$+1\quad \text{remainder}$$
$$65\quad \text{dividend}$$

Divide and check.

1. $4\overline{)67}$ **16 r3**

2. $5\overline{)81}$ **16 r1**

3. $3\overline{)75}$ **25**

4. $8\overline{)92}$ **11 r4**

5. $3\overline{)57}$ **19**

6. $6\overline{)80}$ **13 r2**

7. $93 \div 6$ **15 r3**

8. $71 \div 5$ **14 r1**

9. $55 \div 2$ **27 r1**

▶ **Quiz**

Divide and check.

10. $7\overline{)99}$ **14 r1**

11. $4\overline{)59}$ **14 r3**

12. $3\overline{)94}$ **31 r1**

13. $76 \div 5$ **15 r1**

14. $70 \div 4$ **17 r2**

15. $89 \div 6$ **14 r5**

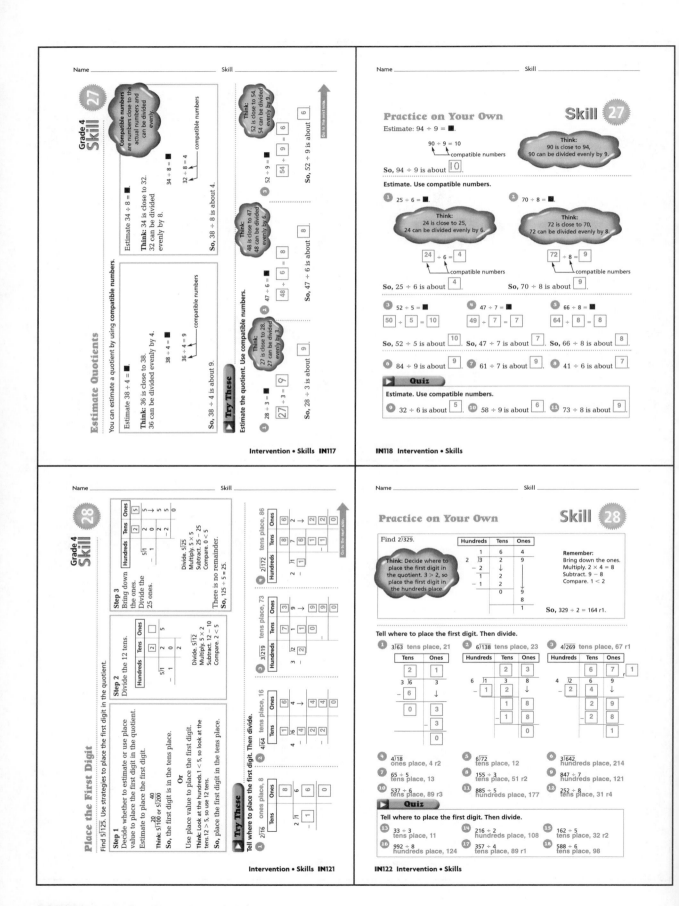

Grade 4 Skill 27

Estimate Quotients

You can estimate a quotient by using **compatible numbers**.

Compatible numbers are numbers close to the actual numbers and can be divided evenly.

Estimate $38 \div 4 = \blacksquare$.

Think: 36 is close to 38. 36 can be divided evenly by 4.

$$38 \div 4 = \blacksquare$$
$$36 \div 4 = 9$$
compatible numbers

So, $38 \div 4$ is about 9.

Estimate $34 \div 8 = \blacksquare$.

Think: 34 is close to 32. 32 can be divided evenly by 8.

$$34 \div 8 = \blacksquare$$
$$32 \div 8 = 4$$

So, $38 \div 8$ is about 4.

Try These

Estimate the quotient. Use compatible numbers.

1 $28 \div 3 = \blacksquare$

Think: 27 is close to 28. 27 can be divided evenly by 3.

$27 \div 3 = \boxed{9}$

So, $28 \div 3$ is about $\boxed{9}$.

2 $47 \div 6 = \blacksquare$

Think: 48 is close to 47. 48 can be divided evenly by 6.

$\boxed{48} \div 6 = \boxed{8}$

So, $47 \div 6$ is about $\boxed{8}$.

3 $52 \div 9 = \blacksquare$

Think: 52 is close to 54. 54 can be divided evenly by 9.

$\boxed{54} \div 9 = \boxed{6}$

So, $52 \div 9$ is about $\boxed{6}$.

Go to the next fold.

Practice on Your Own — Skill 27

Estimate: $94 \div 9 = \blacksquare$.

$$90 \div 9 = 10$$
compatible numbers

Think: 90 is close to 94, 90 can be divided evenly by 9.

So, $94 \div 9$ is about $\boxed{10}$.

Estimate. Use compatible numbers.

1 $25 \div 6 = \blacksquare$.

Think: 24 is close to 25, 24 can be divided evenly by 6.

$\boxed{24} \div 6 = \boxed{4}$
compatible numbers

So, $25 \div 6$ is about $\boxed{4}$.

2 $70 \div 8 = \blacksquare$.

Think: 72 is close to 70, 72 can be divided evenly by 8.

$\boxed{72} \div 8 = \boxed{9}$
compatible numbers

So, $70 \div 8$ is about $\boxed{9}$.

3 $52 \div 5 = \blacksquare$
$50 \div 5 = \boxed{10}$
So, $52 \div 5$ is about $\boxed{10}$.

4 $47 \div 7 = \blacksquare$
$49 \div 7 = \boxed{7}$
So, $47 \div 7$ is about $\boxed{7}$.

5 $66 \div 8 = \blacksquare$
$64 \div 8 = \boxed{8}$
So, $66 \div 8$ is about $\boxed{8}$.

6 $84 \div 9$ is about $\boxed{9}$.
7 $61 \div 7$ is about $\boxed{9}$.
8 $41 \div 6$ is about $\boxed{7}$.

Quiz

Estimate. Use compatible numbers.

9 $32 \div 6$ is about $\boxed{5}$.
10 $58 \div 9$ is about $\boxed{6}$.
11 $73 \div 8$ is about $\boxed{9}$.

Grade 4 Skill 28

Place the First Digit

Find $5\overline{)125}$. Use strategies to place the first digit in the quotient.

Step 1
Decide whether to estimate or use place value to place the first digit in the quotient.
Estimate to place the first digit.

$5\overline{)100}$ or $5\overline{)200}$ → 20, 40

So, the first digit is in the tens place.

Or

Use place value to place the first digit.
Think: Look at the hundreds. 1 < 5, so look at the tens. 12 > 5, so use 12 tens.

So, place the first digit in the tens place.

Step 2
Divide the 12 tens.

Hundreds	Tens	Ones
	2	
5)1	2	5
−1	0	
	2	

Divide. $5\overline{)12}$
Multiply. 5×2
Subtract. $12 − 10$
Compare. $2 < 5$

Step 3
Bring down the ones.
Divide the 25 ones.

Hundreds	Tens	Ones
	2	5
5)1	2	5
−1	0	
	2	5
−	2	5
		0

Divide. $5\overline{)25}$
Multiply. 5×5
Subtract. $25 − 25$
Compare. $0 < 5$
There is no remainder.
So, $125 \div 5 = 25$.

Try These

Tell where to place the first digit. Then divide.

1 $2\overline{)16}$ ones place, 8

Tens	Ones
	8
2)1	6
−1	6
	0

2 $4\overline{)64}$ tens place, 16

Tens	Ones
1	6
4)6	4
−4	↓
2	4
−2	4
	0

3 $3\overline{)219}$ tens place, 73

Hundreds	Tens	Ones
	7	3
3)2	1	9
−2	1	↓
−	1	9
		0

4 $2\overline{)172}$ tens place, 86

Hundreds	Tens	Ones
	8	6
2)1	7	2
−1	6	↓
	1	2
−1	2	
		0

Go to the next side.

Practice on Your Own — Skill 28

Find $2\overline{)329}$.

Think: Decide where to place the first digit in the quotient. 3 > 2, so place the first digit in the hundreds place.

Hundreds	Tens	Ones
1	6	4
2)3	2	9
−2	↓	
1	2	
−1	2	
	0	9
	−	8
		1

Remember:
Bring down the ones.
Multiply. $2 \times 4 = 8$
Subtract. $9 − 8$
Compare. $1 < 2$

So, $329 \div 2 = 164$ r1.

Tell where to place the first digit. Then divide.

1 $3\overline{)63}$ tens place, 21

Tens	Ones
2	1
3)6	3
−6	↓
0	3
	3
	0

2 $6\overline{)138}$ tens place, 23

Hundreds	Tens	Ones
	2	3
6)1	3	8
−1	2	↓
	1	8
	1	8
		0

3 $4\overline{)269}$ tens place, 67 r1

Hundreds	Tens	Ones
	6	7 r 1
4)2	6	9
−2	4	↓
	2	9
	2	8
		1

4 $4\overline{)18}$ ones place, 4 r2
5 $6\overline{)72}$ tens place, 12
6 $3\overline{)642}$ hundreds place, 214
7 $65 \div 5$ tens place, 13
8 $155 \div 3$ tens place, 51 r2
9 $847 \div 7$ hundreds place, 121
10 $537 \div 6$ tens place, 89 r3
11 $885 \div 5$ hundreds place, 177
12 $252 \div 8$ tens place, 31 r4

Quiz

Tell where to place the first digit. Then divide.

13 $33 \div 3$ tens place, 11
14 $216 \div 2$ hundreds place, 108
15 $162 \div 5$ tens place, 32 r2
16 $992 \div 8$ hundreds place, 124
17 $357 \div 4$ tens place, 89 r1
18 $588 \div 6$ tens place, 98

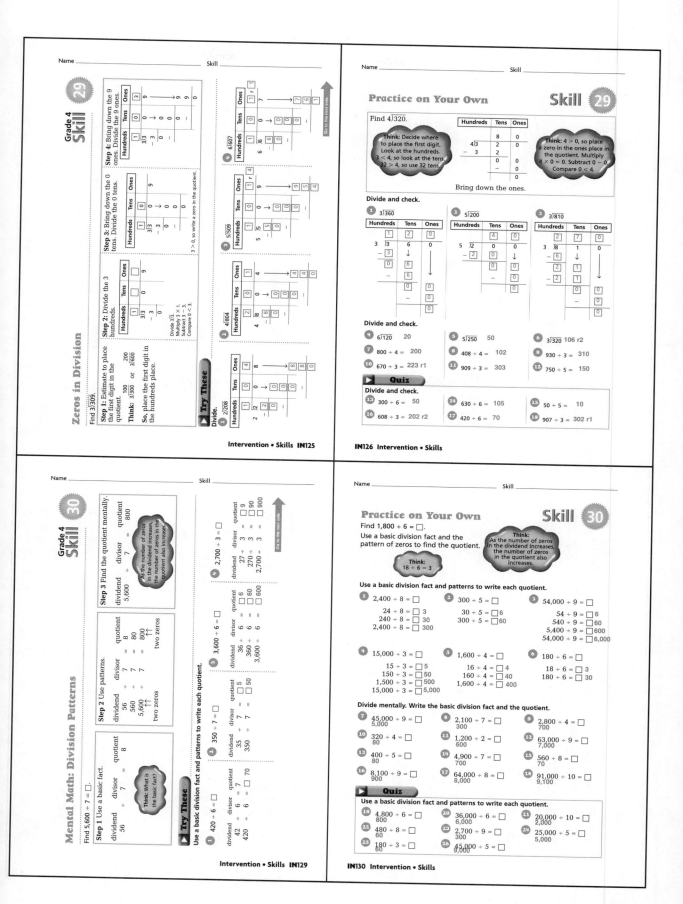

Grade 4 Skill 29

Zeros in Division

Find 3)309.

Step 1: Estimate to place the first digit in the quotient.

Think: 3)300 or 3)600
           100   200

So, place the first digit in the hundreds place.

Step 2: Divide the 3 hundreds.

Divide 3)3.
Multiply 3 × 1.
Subtract 3 − 3.
Compare 0 < 3.

Step 3: Bring down the 0 tens. Divide the 0 tens.

Step 4: Bring down the 9 ones. Divide the 9 ones.

3 > 0, so write a zero in the quotient

▶ **Try These**

Divide.

Practice on Your Own — Skill 29

Find 4)320.

	Hundreds	Tens	Ones
		8	0
4)3		2	0
− 3		2	
		0	0
			0
			0

Think: Decide where to place the first digit. Look at the hundreds. 3 < 4, so look at the tens. 32 > 4, so use 32 tens.

Think: 4 > 0, so place a zero in the ones place in the quotient. Multiply 4 × 0 = 0. Subtract 0 − 0. Compare 0 < 4.

Bring down the ones.

Divide and check.

1. 3)360
2. 5)200
3. 3)810

Divide and check.

4. 6)120   20
5. 5)250   50
6. 3)320   106 r2
7. 800 ÷ 4 =   200
8. 408 ÷ 4 =   102
9. 930 ÷ 3 =   310
10. 670 ÷ 3 =   223 r1
11. 909 ÷ 3 =   303
12. 750 ÷ 5 =   150

▶ **Quiz**

Divide and check.

13. 300 ÷ 6 =   50
14. 630 ÷ 6 =   105
15. 50 ÷ 5 =   10
16. 608 ÷ 3 =   202 r2
17. 420 ÷ 6 =   70
18. 907 ÷ 3 =   302 r1

Grade 4 Skill 30

Mental Math: Division Patterns

Find 5,600 ÷ 7 = □.

Step 1 Use a basic fact.

dividend	divisor	quotient
56	÷ 7	= 8

Think: What is the basic fact?

Step 2 Use patterns.

dividend	divisor	quotient
56	÷ 7	= 8
560	÷ 7	= 80
5,600	÷ 7	= 800

two zeros   two zeros

Step 3 Find the quotient mentally.

dividend	divisor	quotient
5,600	÷ 7	= 800

As the number of zeros in the dividend increases, the number of zeros in the quotient also increases.

▶ **Try These**

Use a basic division fact and patterns to write each quotient.

1. 420 ÷ 6 = □

dividend	divisor	quotient
42	÷ 6	= 7
420	÷ 6	= 70

2. 350 ÷ 7 = □

dividend	divisor	quotient
35	÷ 7	= 5
350	÷ 7	= 50

3. 3,600 ÷ 6 = □

dividend	divisor	quotient
36	÷ 6	= 6
360	÷ 6	= 60
3,600	÷ 6	= 600

4. 2,700 ÷ 3 = □

dividend	divisor	quotient
27	÷ 3	= 9
270	÷ 3	= 90
2,700	÷ 3	= 900

Practice on Your Own — Skill 30

Find 1,800 ÷ 6 = □.
Use a basic division fact and the pattern of zeros to find the quotient.

Think: 18 ÷ 6 = 3

Think: As the number of zeros in the dividend increases, the number of zeros in the quotient also increases.

Use a basic division fact and patterns to write each quotient.

1. 2,400 ÷ 8 = □
   24 ÷ 8 = □ 3
   240 ÷ 8 = □ 30
   2,400 ÷ 8 = □ 300

2. 300 ÷ 5 = □
   30 ÷ 5 = □ 6
   300 ÷ 5 = □ 60

3. 54,000 ÷ 9 = □
   54 ÷ 9 = □ 6
   540 ÷ 9 = □ 60
   5,400 ÷ 9 = □ 600
   54,000 ÷ 9 = □ 6,000

4. 15,000 ÷ 3 = □
   15 ÷ 3 = □ 5
   150 ÷ 3 = □ 50
   1,500 ÷ 3 = □ 500
   15,000 ÷ 3 = □ 5,000

5. 1,600 ÷ 4 = □
   16 ÷ 4 = □ 4
   160 ÷ 4 = □ 40
   1,600 ÷ 4 = □ 400

6. 180 ÷ 6 = □
   18 ÷ 6 = □ 3
   180 ÷ 6 = □ 30

Divide mentally. Write the basic division fact and the quotient.

7. 45,000 ÷ 9 = □   5,000
8. 2,100 ÷ 7 = □   300
9. 2,800 ÷ 4 = □   700
10. 320 ÷ 4 = □   80
11. 1,200 ÷ 2 = □   600
12. 63,000 ÷ 9 = □   7,000
13. 400 ÷ 5 = □   80
14. 4,900 ÷ 7 = □   700
15. 560 ÷ 8 = □   70
16. 8,100 ÷ 9 = □   900
17. 64,000 ÷ 8 = □   8,000
18. 91,000 ÷ 10 = □   9,100

▶ **Quiz**

Use a basic division fact and patterns to write each quotient.

19. 4,800 ÷ 6 = □   800
20. 36,000 ÷ 6 = □   6,000
21. 20,000 ÷ 10 = □   2,000
22. 480 ÷ 8 = □   60
23. 2,700 ÷ 9 = □   300
24. 25,000 ÷ 5 = □   5,000
25. 180 ÷ 3 = □   60
26. 45,000 ÷ 5 = □   9,000

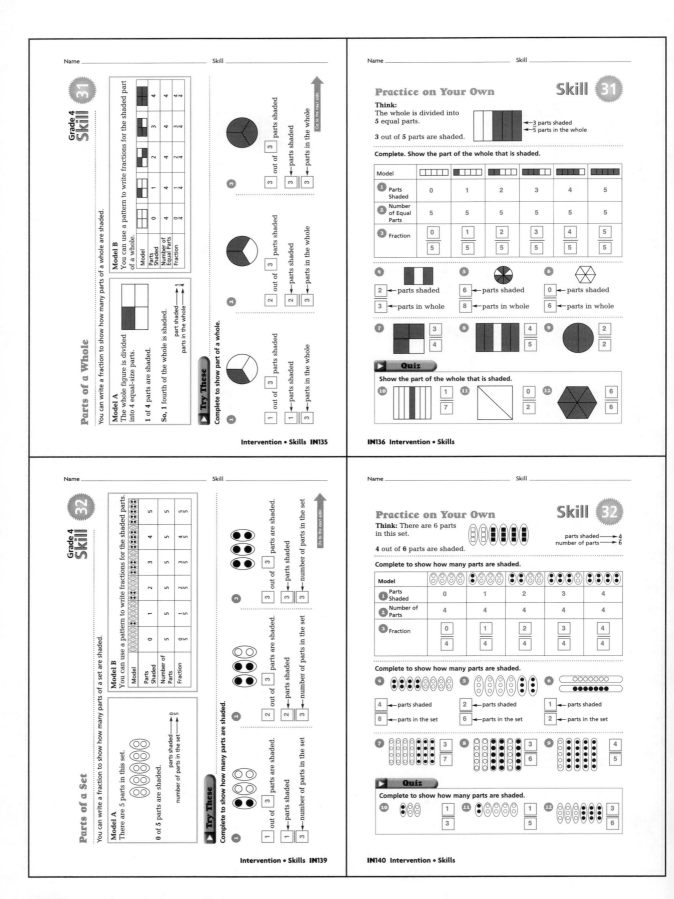

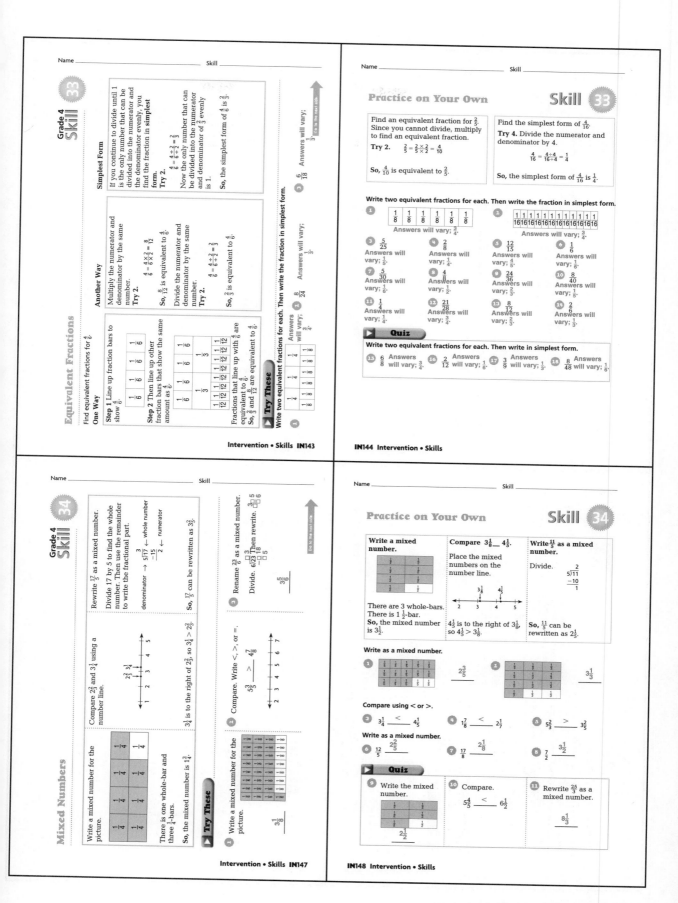

Grade 4 Skill 33

Equivalent Fractions

Find equivalent fractions for $\frac{4}{6}$.

One Way

Step 1 Line up fraction bars to show $\frac{4}{6}$.

Step 2 Then line up other fraction bars that show the same amount as $\frac{4}{6}$.

Fractions that line up with $\frac{4}{6}$ are equivalent to $\frac{4}{6}$.

So, $\frac{2}{3}$ and $\frac{8}{12}$ are equivalent to $\frac{4}{6}$.

Another Way

Multiply the numerator and denominator by the same number.
Try 2.

$$\frac{4}{6} = \frac{4 \times 2}{6 \times 2} = \frac{8}{12}$$

So, $\frac{8}{12}$ is equivalent to $\frac{4}{6}$.

Divide the numerator and denominator by the same number.
Try 2.

$$\frac{4}{6} = \frac{4 \div 2}{6 \div 2} = \frac{2}{3}$$

So, $\frac{2}{3}$ is equivalent to $\frac{4}{6}$.

Simplest Form

If you continue to divide until 1 is the only number that can be divided into the numerator and the denominator evenly, you find the fraction in **simplest form.**
Try 2.

$$\frac{4}{6} = \frac{4 \div 2}{6 \div 2} = \frac{2}{3}$$

Now the only number that can be divided into the numerator and denominator of $\frac{2}{3}$ evenly is 1.

So, the simplest form of $\frac{4}{6}$ is $\frac{2}{3}$.

Try These

Write two equivalent fractions for each. Then write the fraction in simplest form.

1. Answers will vary; $\frac{1}{3}$.
2. $\frac{8}{24}$ Answers will vary; $\frac{1}{3}$.
3. $\frac{6}{18}$ Answers will vary; $\frac{1}{3}$

Intervention • Skills **IN143**

Find an equivalent fraction for $\frac{2}{5}$. Since you cannot divide, multiply to find an equivalent fraction.

Try 2. $\frac{2}{5} = \frac{2 \times 2}{5 \times 2} = \frac{4}{10}$

So, $\frac{4}{10}$ is equivalent to $\frac{2}{5}$.

Find the simplest form of $\frac{4}{16}$.

Try 4. Divide the numerator and denominator by 4.

$\frac{4}{16} = \frac{4 \div 4}{16 \div 4} = \frac{1}{4}$

So, the simplest form of $\frac{4}{16}$ is $\frac{1}{4}$.

Write two equivalent fractions for each. Then write the fraction in simplest form.

1. Answers will vary; $\frac{3}{4}$.
2. Answers will vary; $\frac{3}{4}$.
3. $\frac{5}{25}$ Answers will vary; $\frac{1}{5}$.
4. $\frac{2}{8}$ Answers will vary; $\frac{1}{4}$.
5. $\frac{12}{15}$ Answers will vary; $\frac{4}{5}$.
6. $\frac{1}{6}$ Answers will vary; $\frac{1}{6}$.
7. $\frac{5}{30}$ Answers will vary; $\frac{1}{6}$.
8. $\frac{4}{8}$ Answers will vary; $\frac{1}{2}$.
9. $\frac{24}{36}$ Answers will vary; $\frac{2}{3}$.
10. $\frac{8}{40}$ Answers will vary; $\frac{1}{5}$.
11. $\frac{1}{4}$ Answers will vary; $\frac{1}{4}$.
12. $\frac{21}{28}$ Answers will vary; $\frac{3}{4}$.
13. $\frac{8}{12}$ Answers will vary; $\frac{2}{3}$.
14. $\frac{2}{6}$ Answers will vary; $\frac{1}{3}$.

Quiz

Write two equivalent fractions for each. Then write in simplest form.

15. $\frac{6}{8}$ Answers will vary; $\frac{3}{4}$.
16. $\frac{2}{12}$ Answers will vary; $\frac{1}{6}$.
17. $\frac{3}{9}$ Answers will vary; $\frac{1}{3}$.
18. $\frac{8}{48}$ Answers will vary; $\frac{1}{6}$.

IN144 Intervention • Skills

Grade 4 Skill 34

Mixed Numbers

Write a mixed number for the picture.

There is one whole-bar and three $\frac{1}{4}$-bars.

So, the mixed number is $1\frac{3}{4}$.

Compare $2\frac{2}{3}$ and $3\frac{1}{4}$ using a number line.

$3\frac{1}{4}$ is to the right of $2\frac{2}{3}$, so $3\frac{1}{4} > 2\frac{2}{3}$.

Rewrite $\frac{17}{5}$ as a mixed number.

Divide 17 by 5 to find the whole number. Then use the remainder to write the fractional part.

denominator $\rightarrow 5\overline{)17}$ $\leftarrow$ whole number
$\underline{-15}$
$\quad 2 \leftarrow$ numerator

So, $\frac{17}{5}$ can be rewritten as $3\frac{2}{5}$.

Try These

1. Write a mixed number for the picture.

$3\frac{1}{8}$

2. Compare. Write <, >, or =.

$5\frac{3}{5} > 4\frac{7}{8}$

3. Rename $\frac{23}{6}$ as a mixed number.

Divide. $6\overline{)23}$ Then rewrite. $\frac{23}{6} = \frac{5}{6}$
$\underline{-18}$
$\quad 5$

$3\frac{5}{6}$

Intervention • Skills **IN147**

Write a mixed number.

There are 3 whole-bars. There is $1\frac{1}{2}$-bar.
So, the mixed number is $3\frac{1}{2}$.

Compare $3\frac{1}{8}$ ___ $4\frac{1}{5}$.

Place the mixed numbers on the number line.

$4\frac{1}{5}$ is to the right of $3\frac{1}{8}$, so $4\frac{1}{5} > 3\frac{1}{8}$.

Write $\frac{11}{5}$ as a mixed number.

Divide. $5\overline{)11}$
$\underline{-10}$
$\quad 1$

So, $\frac{11}{5}$ can be rewritten as $2\frac{1}{5}$.

Write as a mixed number.

1. $2\frac{3}{5}$
2. $3\frac{1}{3}$

Compare using < or >.

3. $3\frac{1}{4} < 4\frac{4}{5}$
4. $1\frac{7}{8} < 2\frac{4}{7}$
5. $5\frac{2}{3} > 3\frac{4}{5}$

Write as a mixed number.

6. $\frac{12}{5}$ $2\frac{2}{5}$
7. $\frac{17}{8}$ $2\frac{1}{8}$
8. $\frac{7}{2}$ $3\frac{1}{2}$

Quiz

9. Write the mixed number.

$2\frac{1}{2}$

10. Compare.

$5\frac{4}{5} < 6\frac{1}{2}$

11. Rewrite $\frac{25}{3}$ as a mixed number.

$8\frac{1}{3}$

IN148 Intervention • Skills

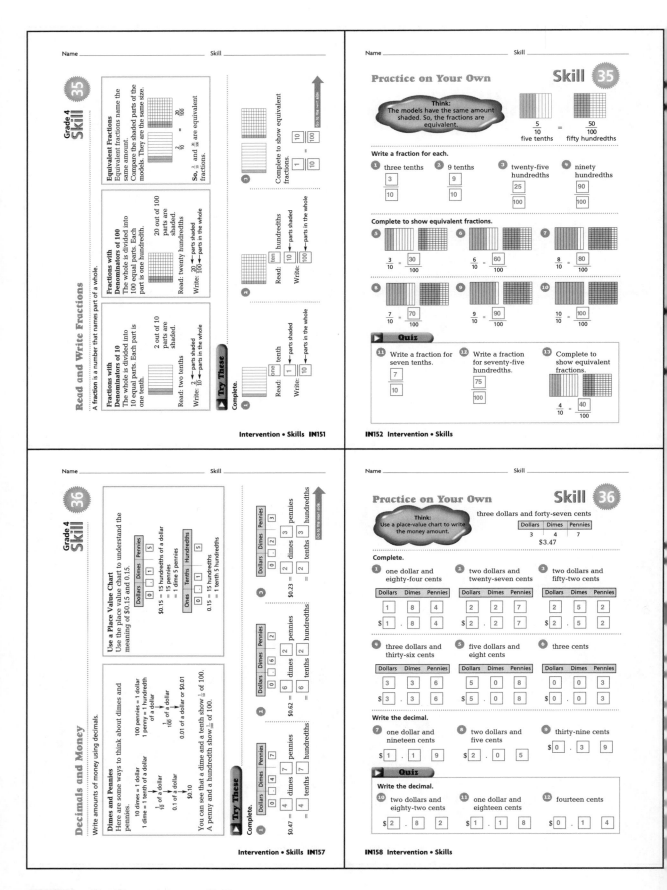

Read and Write Fractions

Grade 4 · Skill 35

A fraction is a number that names part of a whole.

Fractions with Denominators of 10
The whole is divided into 10 equal parts. Each part is one tenth.
2 out of 10 parts are shaded.
Read: two tenths.
Write: $\frac{2}{10}$ ← parts shaded ← parts in the whole

Fractions with Denominators of 100
The whole is divided into 100 equal parts. Each part is one hundredth.
20 out of 100 parts are shaded.
Read: twenty hundredths.
Write: $\frac{20}{100}$ ← parts shaded ← parts in the whole

Equivalent Fractions
Equivalent fractions name the same amount.
Compare the shaded parts of the models. They are the same size.
So, $\frac{2}{10}$ and $\frac{20}{100}$ are equivalent fractions.

▲ Try These

Complete.

1. Read: one tenth. Write: $\frac{1}{10}$ ← parts shaded ← parts in the whole
2. Read: ten hundredths. Write: $\frac{10}{100}$ ← parts shaded ← parts in the whole
3. Complete to show equivalent fractions. $\frac{\boxed{\ }}{10} = \frac{\boxed{\ }}{100}$

Practice on Your Own — Skill 35

Think: The models have the same amount shaded. So, the fractions are equivalent.

$\frac{5}{10}$ = $\frac{50}{100}$
five tenths fifty hundredths

Write a fraction for each.

1. three tenths $\frac{3}{10}$
2. 9 tenths $\frac{9}{10}$
3. twenty-five hundredths $\frac{25}{100}$
4. ninety hundredths $\frac{90}{100}$

Complete to show equivalent fractions.

5. $\frac{3}{10} = \frac{30}{100}$
6. $\frac{6}{10} = \frac{60}{100}$
7. $\frac{8}{10} = \frac{80}{100}$
8. $\frac{7}{10} = \frac{70}{100}$
9. $\frac{9}{10} = \frac{90}{100}$
10. $\frac{10}{10} = \frac{100}{100}$

▶ Quiz

11. Write a fraction for seven tenths. $\frac{7}{10}$
12. Write a fraction for seventy-five hundredths. $\frac{75}{100}$
13. Complete to show equivalent fractions. $\frac{4}{10} = \frac{40}{100}$

Decimals and Money

Grade 4 · Skill 36

Write amounts of money using decimals.

Dimes and Pennies
Here are some ways to think about dimes and pennies.
10 dimes = 1 dollar 100 pennies = 1 dollar
1 dime = 1 tenth of a dollar 1 penny = 1 hundredth of a dollar
$\frac{1}{10}$ of a dollar $\frac{1}{100}$ of a dollar
0.1 of a dollar 0.01 of a dollar or $0.01
$0.10

You can see that a dime and a tenth show $\frac{1}{10}$ of 100.
A penny and a hundredth show $\frac{1}{100}$ of 100.

Use a Place Value Chart
Use the place value chart to understand the meaning of $0.15 and 0.15.

Dollars	Dimes	Pennies
0	1	5

$0.15 = 15 hundredths of a dollar
= 15 pennies
= 1 dime 5 pennies

Ones	Tenths	Hundredths
0	1	5

0.15 = 15 hundredths
= 1 tenth 5 hundredths

▲ Try These

Complete.

1. $0.47 = | 0 | 4 | 7 | Dollars Dimes Pennies
= 4 dimes 7 pennies
= 4 tenths 7 hundredths

2. $0.62 = | 0 | 6 | 2 | Dollars Dimes Pennies
= 6 dimes 2 pennies
= 6 tenths 2 hundredths

3. $0.23 = | 0 | 2 | 3 | Dollars Dimes Pennies
= 2 dimes 3 pennies
= 2 tenths 3 hundredths

Practice on Your Own — Skill 36

Think: Use a place-value chart to write the money amount.

three dollars and forty-seven cents

Dollars	Dimes	Pennies
3	4	7

$3.47

Complete.

1. one dollar and eighty-four cents

Dollars	Dimes	Pennies
1	8	4

$1 . 8 4

2. two dollars and twenty-seven cents

Dollars	Dimes	Pennies
2	2	7

$2 . 2 7

3. two dollars and fifty-two cents

Dollars	Dimes	Pennies
2	5	2

$2 . 5 2

4. three dollars and thirty-six cents

Dollars	Dimes	Pennies
3	3	6

$3 . 3 6

5. five dollars and eight cents

Dollars	Dimes	Pennies
5	0	8

$5 . 0 8

6. three cents

Dollars	Dimes	Pennies
0	0	3

$0 . 0 3

Write the decimal.

7. one dollar and nineteen cents $1 . 1 9
8. two dollars and five cents $2 . 0 5
9. thirty-nine cents $0 . 3 9

▶ Quiz

Write the decimal.

10. two dollars and eighty-two cents $2 . 8 2
11. one dollar and eighteen cents $1 . 1 8
12. fourteen cents $0 . 1 4

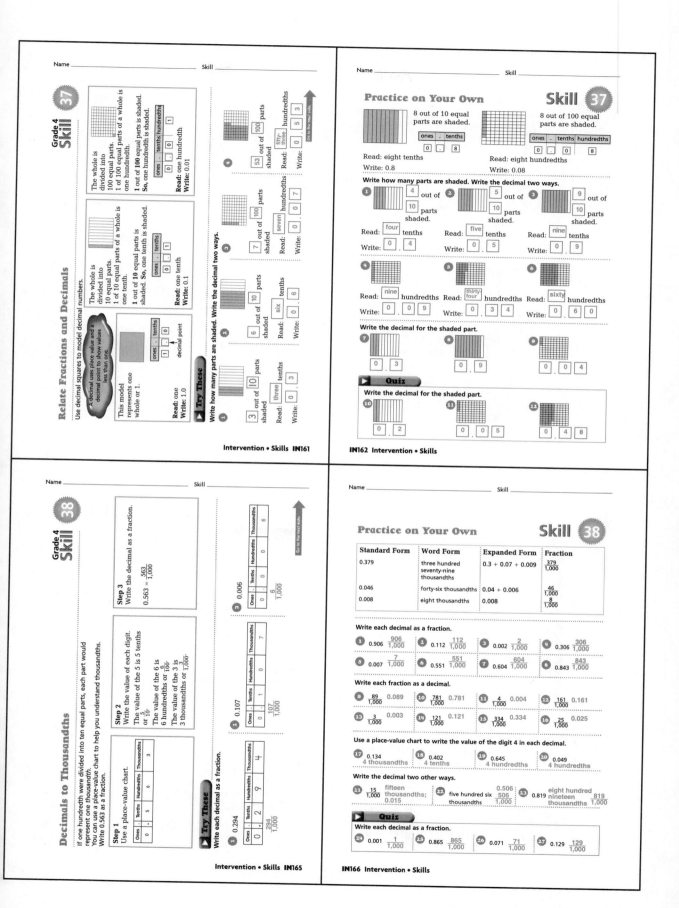

Grade 4 — Skill 37

Relate Fractions and Decimals

Use decimal squares to model decimal numbers.

A decimal uses place value and a decimal point to show values less than one.

This model represents one whole or 1.

ones	.	tenths
1	.	0

↑ decimal point

Read: one
Write: 1.0

The whole is divided into 10 equal parts.
1 of 10 equal parts of a whole is one tenth.

1 out of 10 equal parts is shaded. **So,** one tenth is shaded.

ones	.	tenths
0	.	1

Read: one tenth
Write: 0.1

The whole is divided into 100 equal parts.
1 of 100 equal parts of a whole is one hundredth.

1 out of 100 equal parts is shaded. **So,** one hundredth is shaded.

ones	.	tenths	hundredths
0	.	0	1

Read: one hundredth
Write: 0.01

Try These

Write how many parts are shaded. Write the decimal two ways.

1 3 out of 10 parts shaded
Read: three tenths
Write: 0 . 3

2 6 out of 10 parts shaded
Read: six tenths
Write: 0 . 6

3 7 out of 100 parts shaded
Read: seven hundredths
Write: 0 . 0 7

4 53 out of 100 parts shaded
Read: fifty-three hundredths
Write: 0 . 5 3

Go to the next side. ↑

Intervention • Skills IN161

Practice on Your Own — Skill 37

8 out of 10 equal parts are shaded.

ones	.	tenths
0	.	8

Read: eight tenths
Write: 0.8

8 out of 100 equal parts are shaded.

ones	.	tenths	hundredths
0	.	0	8

Read: eight hundredths
Write: 0.08

Write how many parts are shaded. Write the decimal two ways.

1 4 out of 10 parts shaded.
Read: four tenths
Write: 0 . 4

2 5 out of 10 parts shaded.
Read: five tenths
Write: 0 . 5

3 9 out of 10 parts shaded.
Read: nine tenths
Write: 0 . 9

4 Read: nine hundredths
Write: 0 . 0 9

5 Read: thirty-four hundredths
Write: 0 . 3 4

6 Read: sixty hundredths
Write: 0 . 6 0

Write the decimal for the shaded part.

7 0 . 3

8 0 . 9

9 0 . 0 4

Quiz

Write the decimal for the shaded part.

10 0 . 2

11 0 . 0 5

12 0 . 4 8

IN162 Intervention • Skills

Grade 4 — Skill 38

Decimals to Thousandths

If one hundredth were divided into ten equal parts, each part would represent one *thousandth*.
You can use a place-value chart to help you understand thousandths.
Write 0.563 as a fraction.

Step 1
Use a place-value chart.

Ones	.	Tenths	Hundredths	Thousandths
0	.	5	6	3

Step 2
Write the value of each digit.
The value of the 5 is 5 tenths or $\frac{5}{10}$.
The value of the 6 is 6 hundredths or $\frac{6}{100}$.
The value of the 3 is 3 thousandths or $\frac{3}{1,000}$.

Step 3
Write the decimal as a fraction.
$0.563 = \frac{563}{1,000}$

Try These

Write each decimal as a fraction.

1 0.294

Ones	.	Tenths	Hundredths	Thousandths
0	.	2	9	4

$\frac{294}{1,000}$

2 0.107

Ones	.	Tenths	Hundredths	Thousandths
0	.	1	0	7

$\frac{107}{1,000}$

3 0.006

Ones	.	Tenths	Hundredths	Thousandths
0	.	0	0	6

$\frac{6}{1,000}$

Go to the next side. ↑

Intervention • Skills IN165

Practice on Your Own — Skill 38

Standard Form	Word Form	Expanded Form	Fraction
0.379	three hundred seventy-nine thousandths	0.3 + 0.07 + 0.009	$\frac{379}{1,000}$
0.046	forty-six thousandths	0.04 + 0.006	$\frac{46}{1,000}$
0.008	eight thousandths	0.008	$\frac{8}{1,000}$

Write each decimal as a fraction.

1 0.906 $\frac{906}{1,000}$
2 0.112 $\frac{112}{1,000}$
3 0.002 $\frac{2}{1,000}$
4 0.306 $\frac{306}{1,000}$

5 0.007 $\frac{7}{1,000}$
6 0.551 $\frac{551}{1,000}$
7 0.604 $\frac{604}{1,000}$
8 0.843 $\frac{843}{1,000}$

Write each fraction as a decimal.

9 $\frac{89}{1,000}$ 0.089
10 $\frac{781}{1,000}$ 0.781
11 $\frac{4}{1,000}$ 0.004
12 $\frac{161}{1,000}$ 0.161

13 $\frac{3}{1,000}$ 0.003
14 $\frac{121}{1,000}$ 0.121
15 $\frac{334}{1,000}$ 0.334
16 $\frac{25}{1,000}$ 0.025

Use a place-value chart to write the value of the digit 4 in each decimal.

17 0.134 4 thousandths
18 0.402 4 tenths
19 0.645 4 hundredths
20 0.049 4 hundredths

Write the decimal two other ways.

21 $\frac{15}{1,000}$ fifteen thousandths; 0.015
22 0.506 five hundred six thousandths $\frac{506}{1,000}$
23 0.819 eight hundred nineteen thousandths $\frac{819}{1,000}$

Quiz

Write each decimal as a fraction.

24 0.001 $\frac{1}{1,000}$
25 0.865 $\frac{865}{1,000}$
26 0.071 $\frac{71}{1,000}$
27 0.129 $\frac{129}{1,000}$

IN166 Intervention • Skills

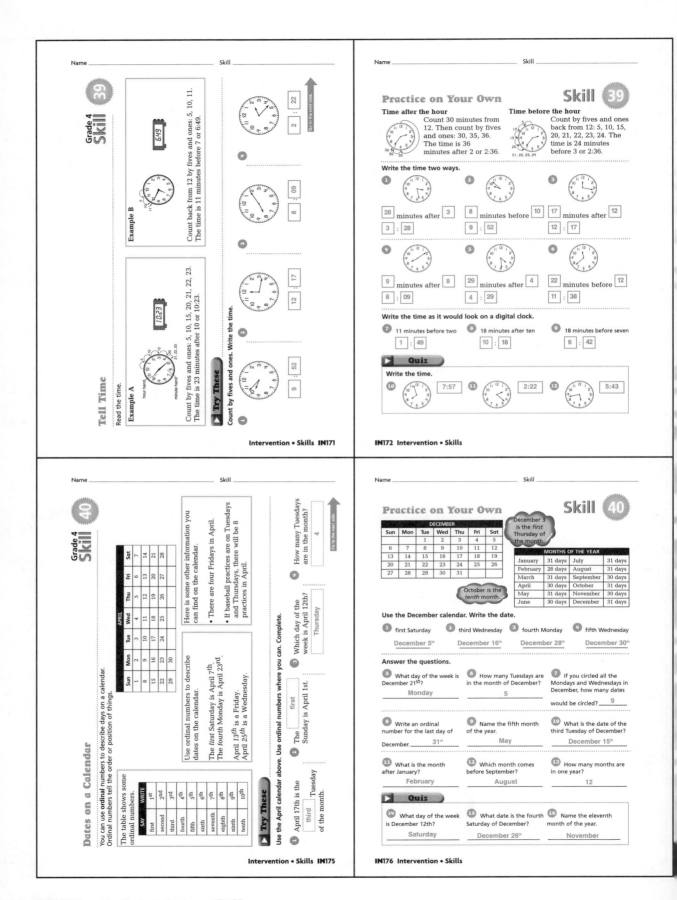

Top-left panel (Skill 39, Grade 4)

Name _____ Skill _____

Grade 4 Skill 39

Tell Time

Read the time.

Example A

hour hand / minute hand

10:23

Count by fives and ones: 5, 10, 15, 20, 21, 22, 23.
The time is 23 minutes after 10 or 10:23.

Example B

6:49

Count back from 12 by fives and ones: 5, 10, 11.
The time is 11 minutes before 7 or 6:49.

Try These

Count by fives and ones. Write the time.

1. 9 : 52

2. 12 : 17

3. 8 : 09

4. 2 : 22

Go to the next side.

Top-right panel (Skill 39)

Name _____ Skill _____

Practice on Your Own **Skill 39**

Time after the hour
Count 30 minutes from 12. Then count by fives and ones: 30, 35, 36. The time is 36 minutes after 2 or 2:36.

Time before the hour
Count by fives and ones back from 12: 5, 10, 15, 20, 21, 22, 23, 24. The time is 24 minutes before 3 or 2:36.

Write the time two ways.

1. 28 minutes after 3   3 : 28

2. 8 minutes before 10   9 : 52

3. 17 minutes after 12   12 : 17

4. 9 minutes after 8   8 : 09

5. 29 minutes after 4   4 : 29

6. 22 minutes before 12   11 : 38

Write the time as it would look on a digital clock.

7. 11 minutes before two   1 : 49

8. 18 minutes after ten   10 : 18

9. 18 minutes before seven   6 : 42

▶ **Quiz**

Write the time.

10. 7:57   11. 2:22   12. 5:43

IN172 Intervention • Skills

Bottom-left panel (Skill 40, Grade 4)

Name _____ Skill _____

Grade 4 Skill 40

Dates on a Calendar

You can use **ordinal** numbers to describe days on a calendar. Ordinal numbers tell the order or position of things.

The table shows some ordinal numbers.

SAY	WRITE
first	1st
second	2nd
third	3rd
fourth	4th
fifth	5th
sixth	6th
seventh	7th
eighth	8th
ninth	9th
tenth	10th

APRIL

Sun	Mon	Tue	Wed	Thu	Fri	Sat
1	2	3	4	5	6	7
8	9	10	11	12	13	14
15	16	17	18	19	20	21
22	23	24	25	26	27	28
29	30					

Use ordinal numbers to describe dates on the calendar.

The *first* Saturday is April 7th.
The *fourth* Monday is April 23rd.

April 13th is a Friday.
April 25th is a Wednesday.

Here is some other information you can find on the calendar.
• There are four Fridays in April.
• If baseball practices are on Tuesdays and Thursdays, there will be 8 practices in April.

Try These

Use the April calendar above. Use ordinal numbers where you can. Complete.

1. April 17th is the **third** Tuesday of the month.

2. The **first** Sunday is April 1st.

3. Which day of the week is April 12th? **Thursday**

4. How many Tuesdays are in the month? **4**

Go to the next side.

Bottom-right panel (Skill 40)

Name _____ Skill _____

Practice on Your Own **Skill 40**

December 3 is the *first* Thursday of the month.

DECEMBER

Sun	Mon	Tue	Wed	Thu	Fri	Sat
		1	2	3	4	5
6	7	8	9	10	11	12
13	14	15	16	17	18	19
20	21	22	23	24	25	26
27	28	29	30	31		

MONTHS OF THE YEAR

January	31 days	July	31 days
February	28 days	August	31 days
March	31 days	September	30 days
April	30 days	October	31 days
May	31 days	November	30 days
June	30 days	December	31 days

October is the *tenth* month.

Use the December calendar. Write the date.

1. first Saturday   December 5th

2. third Wednesday   December 16th

3. fourth Monday   December 28th

4. fifth Wednesday   December 30th

Answer the questions.

5. What day of the week is December 21st? **Monday**

6. How many Tuesdays are in the month of December? **5**

7. If you circled all the Mondays and Wednesdays in December, how many dates would be circled? **9**

8. Write an ordinal number for the last day of December. **31st**

9. Name the fifth month of the year. **May**

10. What is the date of the third Tuesday of December? **December 15th**

11. What is the month after January? **February**

12. Which month comes before September? **August**

13. How many months are in one year? **12**

▶ **Quiz**

14. What day of the week is December 12th? **Saturday**

15. What date is the fourth Saturday of December? **December 26th**

16. Name the eleventh month of the year. **November**

IN176 Intervention • Skills

Intervention • Skills IN171

Intervention • Skills IN175

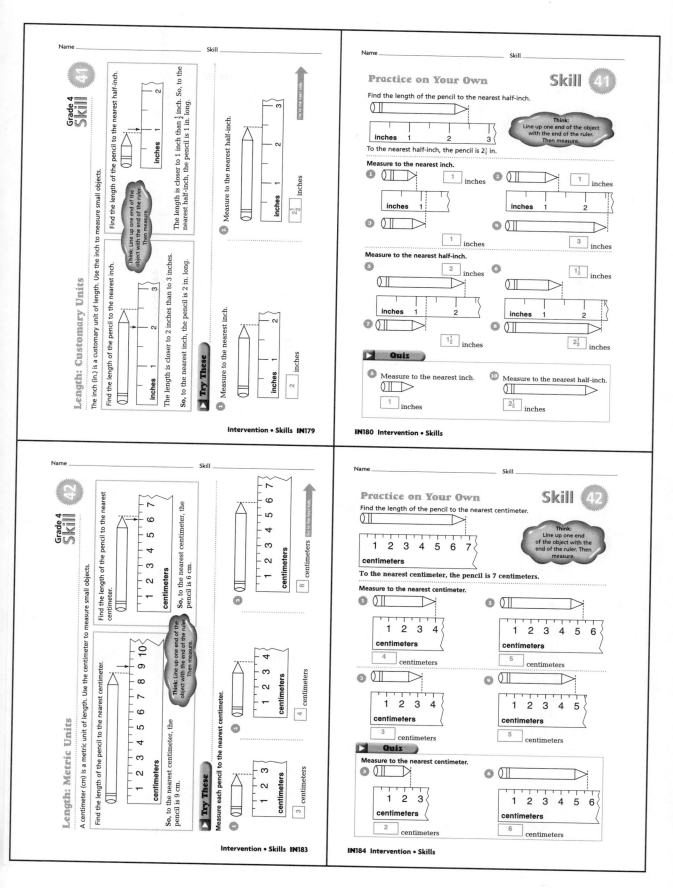

Length: Customary Units

The inch (in.) is a customary unit of length. Use the inch to measure small objects.

Find the length of the pencil to the nearest inch.

The length is closer to 2 inches than to 3 inches.

So, to the nearest inch, the pencil is 2 in. long.

Think: Line up one end of the object with the end of the ruler. Then measure.

Find the length of the pencil to the nearest half-inch.

The length is closer to 1 inch than $\frac{1}{2}$ inch. So, to the nearest half-inch, the pencil is 1 in. long.

Try These

1. Measure to the nearest inch.

2. Measure to the nearest half-inch.

Grade 4 Skill 41

Intervention • Skills IN179

Practice on Your Own — Skill 41

Find the length of the pencil to the nearest half-inch.

Think: Line up one end of the object with the end of the ruler. Then measure.

To the nearest half-inch, the pencil is $2\frac{1}{2}$ in.

Measure to the nearest inch.

1. 1 inches
2. 1 inches
3. 1 inches
4. 3 inches

Measure to the nearest half-inch.

5. 2 inches
6. $1\frac{1}{2}$ inches
7. $1\frac{1}{2}$ inches
8. $2\frac{1}{2}$ inches

Quiz

9. Measure to the nearest inch. 1 inches
10. Measure to the nearest half-inch. $2\frac{1}{2}$ inches

IN180 Intervention • Skills

Length: Metric Units

A centimeter (cm) is a metric unit of length. Use the centimeter to measure small objects.

Find the length of the pencil to the nearest centimeter.

So, to the nearest centimeter, the pencil is 9 cm.

Think: Line up one end of the object with the end of the ruler. Then measure.

Find the length of the pencil to the nearest centimeter.

So, to the nearest centimeter, the pencil is 6 cm.

Try These

Measure each pencil to the nearest centimeter.

1. 3 centimeters
2. 4 centimeters
3. 6 centimeters

Grade 4 Skill 42

Intervention • Skills IN183

Practice on Your Own — Skill 42

Find the length of the pencil to the nearest centimeter.

Think: Line up one end of the object with the end of the ruler. Then measure.

To the nearest centimeter, the pencil is 7 centimeters.

Measure to the nearest centimeter.

1. 4 centimeters
2. 5 centimeters
3. 3 centimeters
4. 5 centimeters

Quiz

Measure to the nearest centimeter.

5. 2 centimeters
6. 6 centimeters

IN184 Intervention • Skills

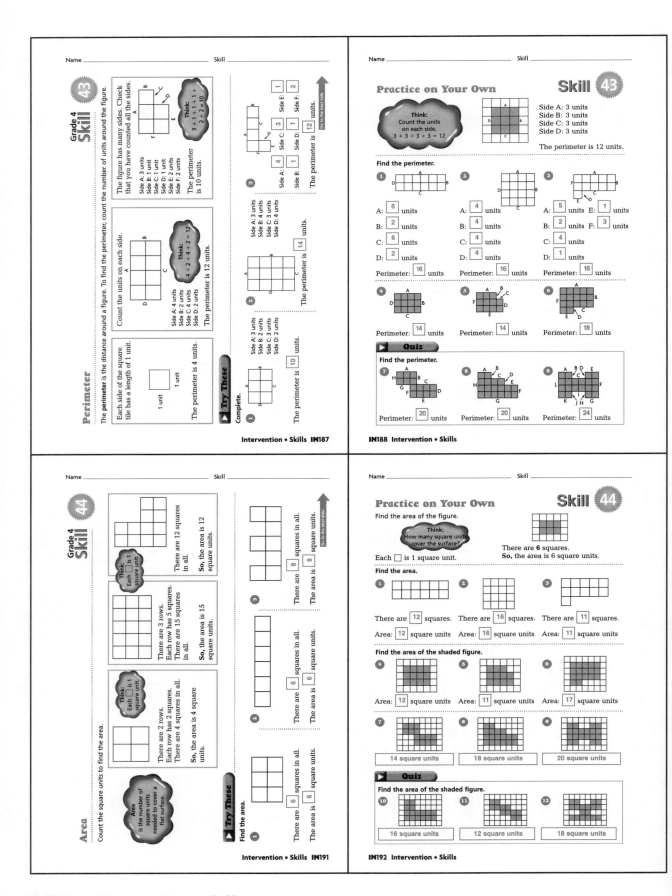

Grade 4 Skill 43

Perimeter

The **perimeter** is the distance around a figure. To find the perimeter, count the number of units around the figure.

Each side of the square tile has a length of 1 unit.

1 unit

The perimeter is 4 units.

Count the units on each side.

Side A: 4 units
Side B: 2 units
Side C: 4 units
Side D: 2 units

Think: $4 + 2 + 4 + 2 = 12$

The perimeter is 12 units.

The figure has many sides. Check that you have counted all the sides.

Side A: 3 units
Side B: 1 unit
Side C: 1 unit
Side D: 1 unit
Side E: 2 units
Side F: 2 units

Think: $3 + 1 + 1 + 1 + 2 + 2 = 10$

The perimeter is 10 units.

Try These

Complete.

1.
Side A: 3 units
Side B: 2 units
Side C: 3 units
Side D: 2 units
The perimeter is 10 units.

2.
Side A: 3 units
Side B: 4 units
Side C: 3 units
Side D: 4 units
The perimeter is 14 units.

3.
Side E: 1
Side F: 2
Side C: 3
Side D: 1
The perimeter is 12 units.

Go to the next side.

Practice on Your Own — **Skill 43**

Think: Count the units on each side. $3 + 3 + 3 + 3 = 12$

Side A: 3 units
Side B: 3 units
Side C: 3 units
Side D: 3 units

The perimeter is 12 units.

Find the perimeter.

1.
A: 6 units
B: 2 units
C: 6 units
D: 2 units
Perimeter: 16 units

2.
A: 4 units
B: 4 units
C: 4 units
D: 4 units
Perimeter: 16 units

3.
A: 5 units   E: 1 units
B: 2 units   F: 3 units
C: 4 units
D: 1 units
Perimeter: 16 units

4. Perimeter: 14 units
5. Perimeter: 14 units
6. Perimeter: 18 units

Quiz

Find the perimeter.

7. Perimeter: 20 units
8. Perimeter: 20 units
9. Perimeter: 24 units

Grade 4 Skill 44

Area

Area is the number of square units needed to cover a flat surface.

Count the square units to find the area.

Think: Each □ is 1 square unit.

There are 2 rows.
Each row has 2 squares.
There are 4 squares in all.
So, the area is 4 square units.

Think: Each □ is 1 square unit.

There are 3 rows.
Each row has 5 squares.
There are 15 squares in all.
So, the area is 15 square units.

Think: Each □ is 1 square unit.

There are 12 squares in all.
So, the area is 12 square units.

Try These

Find the area.

1.
There are 6 squares in all.
The area is 6 square units.

2.
There are 6 squares in all.
The area is 6 square units.

3.
There are 8 squares in all.
The area is 8 square units.

Go to the next side.

Practice on Your Own — **Skill 44**

Find the area of the figure.

Think: How many square units cover the surface?

Each □ is 1 square unit.

There are **6** squares.
So, the area is 6 square units.

Find the area.

1. There are 12 squares. Area: 12 square units
2. There are 16 squares. Area: 16 square units
3. There are 11 squares. Area: 11 square units

Find the area of the shaded figure.

4. Area: 12 square units
5. Area: 11 square units
6. Area: 17 square units

7. 14 square units
8. 18 square units
9. 20 square units

Quiz

Find the area of the shaded figure.

10. 16 square units
11. 12 square units
12. 18 square units

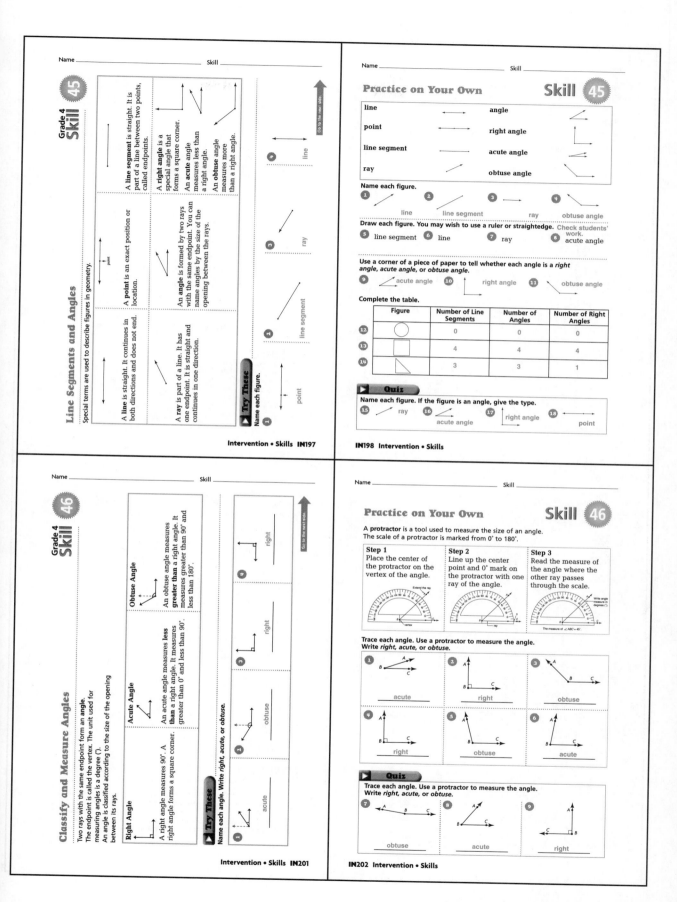

Grade 4 — Skill 45

Line Segments and Angles

Special terms are used to describe figures in geometry.

A **line** is straight. It continues in both directions and does not end.

A **point** is an exact position or location.

A **line segment** is straight. It is part of a line between two points, called endpoints.

A **ray** is part of a line. It has one endpoint. It is straight and continues in one direction.

A **right angle** is a special angle that forms a square corner.

An **angle** is formed by two rays with the same endpoint. You can name angles by the size of the opening between the rays.

An **acute angle** measures less than a right angle.

An **obtuse angle** measures more than a right angle.

▶ **Try These**

Name each figure.

1. point
2. line segment
3. ray
4. line

Go to the next side.

Intervention • Skills **IN197**

Skill 45

Practice on Your Own

line — angle
point — right angle
line segment — acute angle
ray — obtuse angle

Name each figure.

1. line
2. line segment
3. ray
4. obtuse angle

Draw each figure. You may wish to use a ruler or straightedge. Check students' work.

5. line segment
6. line
7. ray
8. acute angle

Use a corner of a piece of paper to tell whether each angle is a *right angle*, *acute angle*, or *obtuse angle*.

9. acute angle
10. right angle
11. obtuse angle

Complete the table.

Figure	Number of Line Segments	Number of Angles	Number of Right Angles
12. ○	0	0	0
13. □	4	4	4
14. △	3	3	1

▶ **Quiz**

Name each figure. If the figure is an angle, give the type.

15. ray
16. acute angle
17. right angle
18. point

IN198 Intervention • Skills

Grade 4 — Skill 46

Classify and Measure Angles

Two rays with the same endpoint form an **angle**. The endpoint is called the **vertex**. The unit used for measuring angles is a **degree (°)**. An angle is classified according to the size of the opening between its rays.

Right Angle

A right angle measures 90°. A right angle forms a square corner.

Acute Angle

An acute angle measures **less than a right angle**. It measures greater than 0° and less than 90°.

Obtuse Angle

An obtuse angle measures **greater than a right angle**. It measures greater than 90° and less than 180°.

▶ **Try These**

Name each angle. Write *right*, *acute*, or *obtuse*.

1. acute
2. obtuse
3. right
4. right

Go to the next side.

Intervention • Skills **IN201**

Skill 46

Practice on Your Own

A **protractor** is a tool used to measure the size of an angle. The scale of a protractor is marked from 0° to 180°.

Step 1
Place the center of the protractor on the vertex of the angle.

Step 2
Line up the center point and 0° mark on the protractor with one ray of the angle.

Step 3
Read the measure of the angle where the other ray passes through the scale.

Trace each angle. Use a protractor to measure the angle. Write *right*, *acute*, or *obtuse*.

1. acute
2. right
3. obtuse
4. right
5. obtuse
6. acute

▶ **Quiz**

Trace each angle. Use a protractor to measure the angle. Write *right*, *acute*, or *obtuse*.

7. obtuse
8. acute
9. right

IN202 Intervention • Skills

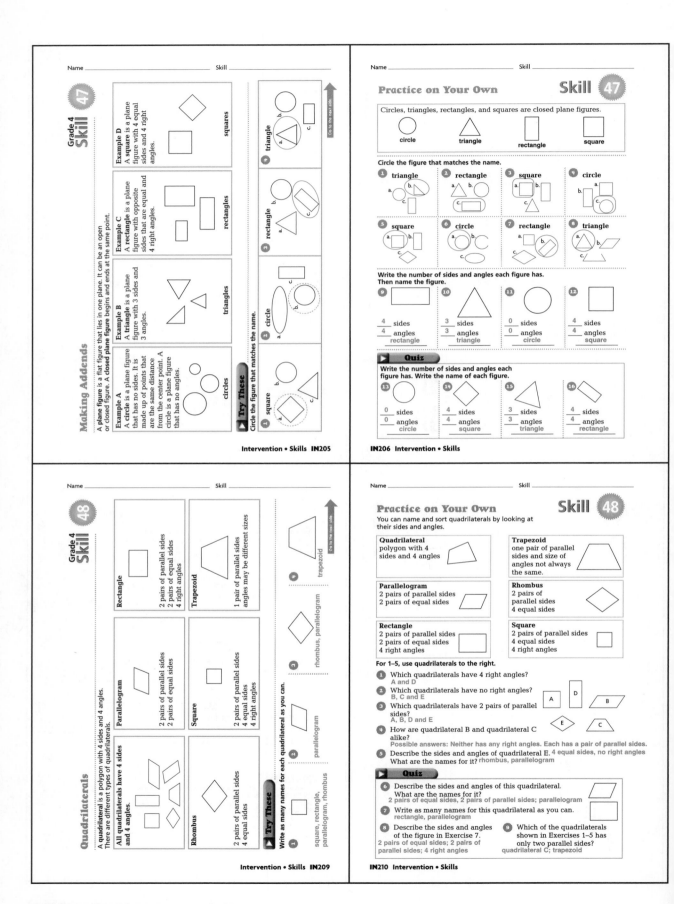

Grade 4 Skill 47

Making Addends

A plane figure is a flat figure that lies in one plane. It can be an open or closed figure. A closed plane figure begins and ends at the same point.

Example A
A circle is a plane figure that has no sides. It is made up of points that are the same distance from the center point. A circle is a plane figure that has no angles.

circles

Example B
A triangle is a plane figure with 3 sides and 3 angles.

triangles

Example C
A rectangle is a plane figure with opposite sides that are equal and 4 right angles.

rectangles

Example D
A square is a plane figure with 4 equal sides and 4 right angles.

squares

Try These
Circle the figure that matches the name.

1 square
2 circle
3 rectangle
4 triangle

Intervention • Skills IN205

Practice on Your Own — Skill 47

Circles, triangles, rectangles, and squares are closed plane figures.

circle   triangle   rectangle   square

Circle the figure that matches the name.

1 triangle
2 rectangle
3 square
4 circle
5 square
6 circle
7 rectangle
8 triangle

Write the number of sides and angles each figure has. Then name the figure.

9
 4 sides
 4 angles
 rectangle

10
 3 sides
 3 angles
 triangle

11
 0 sides
 0 angles
 circle

12
 4 sides
 4 angles
 square

Quiz

Write the number of sides and angles each figure has. Write the name of each figure.

13
 0 sides
 0 angles
 circle

14
 4 sides
 4 angles
 square

15
 3 sides
 3 angles
 triangle

16
 4 sides
 4 angles
 rectangle

IN206 Intervention • Skills

Grade 4 Skill 48

Quadrilaterals

A quadrilateral is a polygon with 4 sides and 4 angles. There are different types of quadrilaterals.

All quadrilaterals have 4 sides and 4 angles.

Parallelogram
2 pairs of parallel sides
2 pairs of equal sides

Rectangle
2 pairs of parallel sides
2 pairs of equal sides
4 right angles

Rhombus
2 pairs of parallel sides
4 equal sides

Square
2 pairs of parallel sides
4 equal sides
4 right angles

Trapezoid
1 pair of parallel sides
angles may be different sizes

Try These
Write as many names for each quadrilateral as you can.

1 square, rectangle, parallelogram, rhombus
2 parallelogram
3 rhombus, parallelogram
4 trapezoid

Intervention • Skills IN209

Practice on Your Own — Skill 48

You can name and sort quadrilaterals by looking at their sides and angles.

Quadrilateral
polygon with 4 sides and 4 angles

Trapezoid
one pair of parallel sides and size of angles not always the same.

Parallelogram
2 pairs of parallel sides
2 pairs of equal sides

Rhombus
2 pairs of parallel sides
4 equal sides

Rectangle
2 pairs of parallel sides
2 pairs of equal sides
4 right angles

Square
2 pairs of parallel sides
4 equal sides
4 right angles

For 1–5, use quadrilaterals to the right.

1 Which quadrilaterals have 4 right angles?
   A and D

2 Which quadrilaterals have no right angles?
   B, C and E

3 Which quadrilaterals have 2 pairs of parallel sides?
   A, B, D and E

4 How are quadrilateral B and quadrilateral C alike?
   Possible answers: Neither has any right angles. Each has a pair of parallel sides.

5 Describe the sides and angles of quadrilateral E. 4 equal sides, no right angles
   What are the names for it? rhombus, parallelogram

Quiz

6 Describe the sides and angles of this quadrilateral.
   What are the names for it?
   2 pairs of equal sides, 2 pairs of parallel sides; parallelogram

7 Write as many names for this quadrilateral as you can.
   rectangle, parallelogram

8 Describe the sides and angles of the figure in Exercise 7.
   2 pairs of equal sides; 2 pairs of parallel sides; 4 right angles

9 Which of the quadrilaterals shown in Exercises 1–5 has only two parallel sides?
   quadrilateral C; trapezoid

IN210 Intervention • Skills

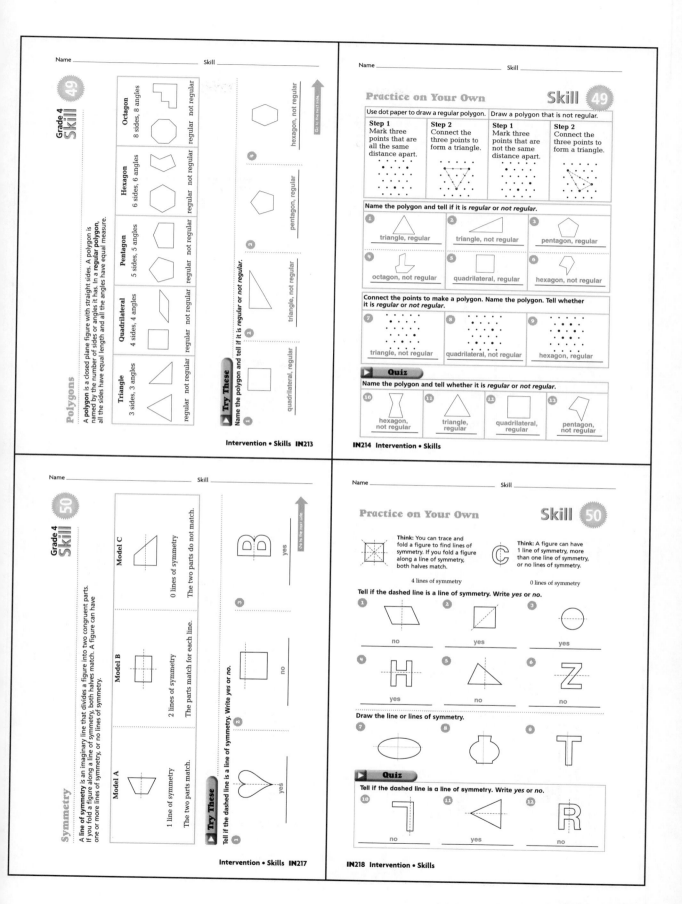

Grade 4 — Skill 49

Polygons

A **polygon** is a closed plane figure with straight sides. A polygon is named by the number of sides or angles it has. In a **regular polygon**, all the sides have equal length and all the angles have equal measure.

Triangle 3 sides, 3 angles	Quadrilateral 4 sides, 4 angles	Pentagon 5 sides, 5 angles	Hexagon 6 sides, 6 angles	Octagon 8 sides, 8 angles
regular not regular	regular not regular	regular not regular	regular not regular	regular not regular

Try These

Name the polygon and tell if it is *regular* or *not regular*.

1. quadrilateral, regular
2. triangle, not regular
3. pentagon, regular
4. hexagon, not regular

Go to the next side.

Intervention • Skills **IN213**

Practice on Your Own — Skill 49

Use dot paper to draw a regular polygon.		Draw a polygon that is not regular.	
Step 1 Mark three points that are all the same distance apart.	**Step 2** Connect the three points to form a triangle.	**Step 1** Mark three points that are not the same distance apart.	**Step 2** Connect the three points to form a triangle.

Name the polygon and tell if it is *regular* or *not regular*.

1. triangle, regular
2. triangle, not regular
3. pentagon, regular
4. octagon, not regular
5. quadrilateral, regular
6. hexagon, not regular

Connect the points to make a polygon. Name the polygon. Tell whether it is *regular* or *not regular*.

7. triangle, not regular
8. quadrilateral, not regular
9. hexagon, regular

Quiz

Name the polygon and tell whether it is *regular* or *not regular*.

10. hexagon, not regular
11. triangle, regular
12. quadrilateral, regular
13. pentagon, not regular

IN214 Intervention • Skills

Grade 4 — Skill 50

Symmetry

A **line of symmetry** is an imaginary line that divides a figure into two congruent parts. If you fold a figure along a line of symmetry, both halves match. A figure can have one or more lines of symmetry, or no lines of symmetry.

Model A	Model B	Model C
1 line of symmetry	2 lines of symmetry	0 lines of symmetry
The two parts match.	The parts match for each line.	The two parts do not match.

Try These

Tell if the dashed line is a line of symmetry. Write *yes* or *no*.

1. yes
2. no
3. yes

Go to the next side.

Intervention • Skills **IN217**

Practice on Your Own — Skill 50

Think: You can trace and fold a figure to find lines of symmetry. If you fold a figure along a line of symmetry, both halves match.

4 lines of symmetry

Think: A figure can have 1 line of symmetry, more than one line of symmetry, or no lines of symmetry.

0 lines of symmetry

Tell if the dashed line is a line of symmetry. Write *yes* or *no*.

1. no
2. yes
3. yes
4. yes
5. no
6. no

Draw the line or lines of symmetry.

7.
8.
9.

Quiz

Tell if the dashed line is a line of symmetry. Write *yes* or *no*.

10. no
11. yes
12. no

IN218 Intervention • Skills

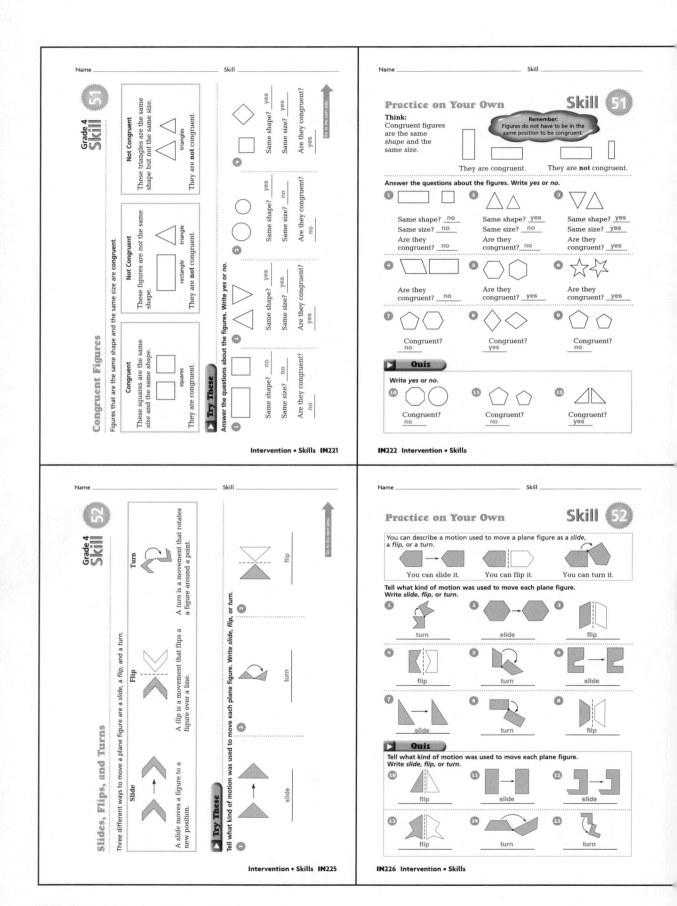

Grade 4
Skill 51

Congruent Figures

Figures that are the same shape and the same size are congruent.

Congruent	Not Congruent	Not Congruent
These squares are the same size and the same shape.	These figures are not the same shape.	These triangles are the same shape but not the same size.
squares	rectangle triangle	triangles
They are congruent.	They are **not** congruent.	They are **not** congruent.

Try These

Answer the questions about the figures. Write yes or no.

1 Same shape? no
Same size? no
Are they congruent? no

2 Same shape? yes
Same size? yes
Are they congruent? yes

3 Same shape? yes
Same size? no
Are they congruent? no

4 Same shape? yes
Same size? yes
Are they congruent? yes

Go to the next side.

Intervention • Skills **IN221**

Practice on Your Own

Skill 51

Think:
Congruent figures are the same *shape* and the same *size*.

Remember:
Figures do not have to be in the same position to be congruent.

They are congruent.   They are **not** congruent.

Answer the questions about the figures. Write yes or no.

1 Same shape? no
Same size? no
Are they congruent? no

2 Same shape? yes
Same size? no
Are they congruent? no

3 Same shape? yes
Same size? yes
Are they congruent? yes

4 Are they congruent? no

5 Are they congruent? yes

6 Are they congruent? yes

7 Congruent? no

8 Congruent? yes

9 Congruent? no

Quiz

Write yes or no.

10 Congruent? no

11 Congruent? no

12 Congruent? yes

IN222 Intervention • Skills

Grade 4
Skill 52

Slides, Flips, and Turns

Three different ways to move a plane figure are a *slide*, a *flip*, and a *turn*.

Slide
A *slide* moves a figure to a new position.

Flip
A *flip* is a movement that flips a figure over a line.

Turn
A *turn* is a movement that rotates a figure around a point.

Try These

Tell what kind of motion was used to move each plane figure. Write *slide*, *flip*, or *turn*.

1 slide

2 turn

3 flip

Go to the next side.

Intervention • Skills **IN225**

Practice on Your Own

Skill 52

You can describe a motion used to move a plane figure as a *slide*, a *flip*, or a *turn*.

You can slide it.   You can flip it.   You can turn it.

Tell what kind of motion was used to move each plane figure.
Write *slide*, *flip*, or *turn*.

1 turn

2 slide

3 flip

4 flip

5 turn

6 slide

7 slide

8 turn

9 flip

Quiz

Tell what kind of motion was used to move each plane figure.
Write *slide*, *flip*, or *turn*.

10 flip

11 slide

12 slide

13 flip

14 turn

15 turn

IN226 Intervention • Skills

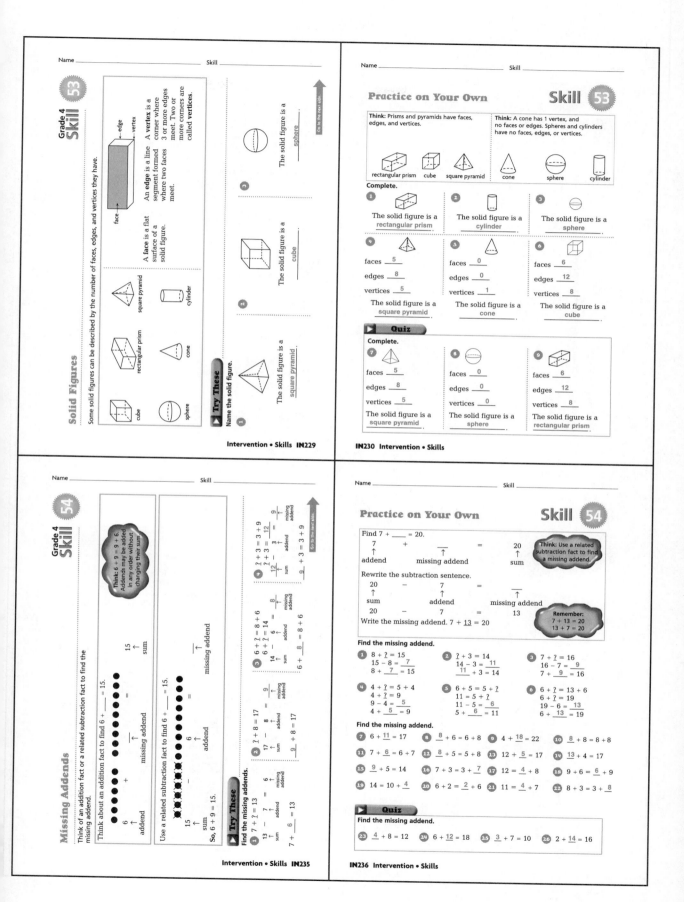

Grade 4 — Skill 53

Solid Figures

Some solid figures can be described by the number of faces, edges, and vertices they have.

A face is a flat surface of a solid figure.

An edge is a line segment formed where two faces meet.

A vertex is a corner where 3 or more edges meet. Two or more corners are called **vertices**.

cube   sphere   rectangular prism   cone   square pyramid   cylinder

The solid figure is a __sphere__.

The solid figure is a __cube__.

The solid figure is a __square pyramid__.

▶ **Try These**

Name the solid figure.

Go to the next side.

Intervention • Skills IN229

Practice on Your Own — Skill 53

Think: Prisms and pyramids have faces, edges, and vertices.

Think: A cone has 1 vertex, and no faces or edges. Spheres and cylinders have no faces, edges, or vertices.

rectangular prism   cube   square pyramid   cone   sphere   cylinder

Complete.

1. The solid figure is a __rectangular prism__

2. The solid figure is a __cylinder__

3. The solid figure is a __sphere__

4. faces __5__ edges __8__ vertices __5__ — The solid figure is a __square pyramid__

5. faces __0__ edges __0__ vertices __1__ — The solid figure is a __cone__

6. faces __6__ edges __12__ vertices __8__ — The solid figure is a __cube__

▶ **Quiz**

Complete.

7. faces __5__ edges __8__ vertices __5__ — The solid figure is a __square pyramid__

8. faces __0__ edges __0__ vertices __0__ — The solid figure is a __sphere__

9. faces __6__ edges __12__ vertices __8__ — The solid figure is a __rectangular prism__

IN230 Intervention • Skills

Grade 4 — Skill 54

Missing Addends

Think of an addition fact or a related subtraction fact to find the missing addend.

Think about an addition fact to find $6 + \underline{\quad} = 15$.

Think: $6 + 9 = 9 + 6$. Addends may be added in any order without changing their sum

$6 + \underline{\quad} = 15$

addend   missing addend   sum

Use a related subtraction fact to find $6 + \underline{\quad} = 15$.

$15 - 6 = 9$

sum   addend   missing addend

So, $6 + 9 = 15$.

▶ **Try These**

Find the missing addends.

1. $7 + \underline{?} = 13$
   $13 - 7 = \underline{6}$
   $7 + \underline{6} = 13$

2. $\underline{?} + 8 = 17$
   $17 - 8 = \underline{9}$
   $\underline{9} + 8 = 17$

3. $6 + \underline{?} = 8 + 6$
   $6 + \underline{?} = 14$
   $14 - 6 = \underline{8}$
   $6 + \underline{8} = 8 + 6$

4. $\underline{?} + 3 = 3 + 9$
   $\underline{?} + 3 = 12$
   $\underline{12} - 3 = \underline{9}$
   $\underline{9} + 3 = 3 + 9$

Go to the next side.

Intervention • Skills IN235

Practice on Your Own — Skill 54

Find $7 + \underline{\quad} = 20$.

$7 + \underline{\quad} = 20$

addend   missing addend   sum

Think: Use a related subtraction fact to find a missing addend.

Rewrite the subtraction sentence.

$20 - 7 = \underline{\quad}$

sum   addend   missing addend

$20 - 7 = 13$

Write the missing addend. $7 + \underline{13} = 20$

Remember: $7 + 13 = 20$ $13 + 7 = 20$

Find the missing addend.

1. $8 + \underline{?} = 15$
   $15 - 8 = \underline{7}$
   $8 + \underline{7} = 15$

2. $\underline{?} + 3 = 14$
   $14 - 3 = \underline{11}$
   $\underline{11} + 3 = 14$

3. $7 + \underline{?} = 16$
   $16 - 7 = \underline{9}$
   $7 + \underline{9} = 16$

4. $4 + \underline{?} = 5 + 4$
   $4 + \underline{?} = 9$
   $9 - 4 = \underline{5}$
   $4 + \underline{5} = 9$

5. $6 + 5 = 5 + \underline{?}$
   $11 = 5 + \underline{?}$
   $11 - 5 = \underline{6}$
   $5 + \underline{6} = 11$

6. $6 + \underline{?} = 13 + 6$
   $6 + \underline{?} = 19$
   $19 - 6 = \underline{13}$
   $6 + \underline{13} = 19$

Find the missing addend.

7. $6 + \underline{11} = 17$
8. $\underline{8} + 6 = 6 + 8$
9. $4 + \underline{18} = 22$
10. $\underline{8} + 8 = 8 + 8$
11. $7 + \underline{6} = 6 + 7$
12. $\underline{8} + 5 = 5 + 8$
13. $12 + \underline{5} = 17$
14. $\underline{13} + 4 = 17$
15. $\underline{9} + 5 = 14$
16. $7 + 3 = 3 + \underline{7}$
17. $12 = \underline{4} + 8$
18. $9 + 6 = \underline{6} + 9$
19. $14 = 10 + \underline{4}$
20. $6 + 2 = \underline{2} + 6$
21. $11 = \underline{4} + 7$
22. $8 + 3 = 3 + \underline{8}$

▶ **Quiz**

Find the missing addend.

23. $\underline{4} + 8 = 12$
24. $6 + \underline{12} = 18$
25. $\underline{3} + 7 = 10$
26. $2 + \underline{14} = 16$

IN236 Intervention • Skills

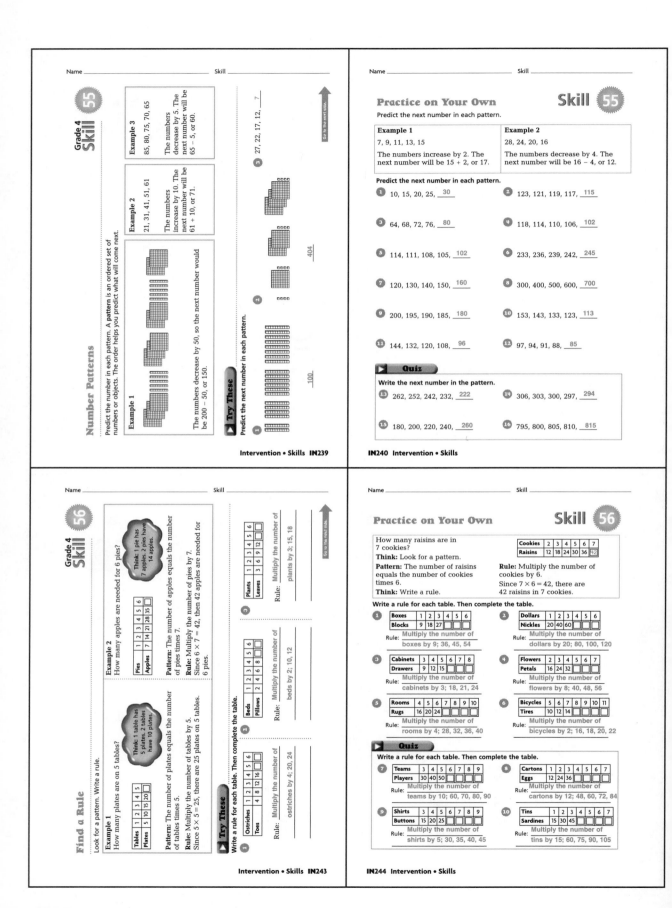

Top-Left Panel

Grade 4 Skill 55

Number Patterns

Predict the number in each pattern. A **pattern** is an ordered set of numbers or objects. The order helps you predict what will come next.

Example 1

The numbers decrease by 50, so the next number would be 200 − 50, or 150.

Example 2

21, 31, 41, 51, 61

The numbers increase by 10. The next number will be 61 + 10, or 71.

Example 3

85, 80, 75, 70, 65

The numbers decrease by 5. The next number will be 65 − 5, or 60.

▶ **Try These**

Predict the next number in each pattern.

1. _100_

2. _404_

3. 27, 22, 17, 12, __7__

Top-Right Panel

Practice on Your Own **Skill 55**

Predict the next number in each pattern.

Example 1	Example 2
7, 9, 11, 13, 15	28, 24, 20, 16
The numbers increase by 2. The next number will be 15 + 2, or 17.	The numbers decrease by 4. The next number will be 16 − 4, or 12.

Predict the next number in each pattern.

1. 10, 15, 20, 25, __30__
2. 123, 121, 119, 117, __115__
3. 64, 68, 72, 76, __80__
4. 118, 114, 110, 106, __102__
5. 114, 111, 108, 105, __102__
6. 233, 236, 239, 242, __245__
7. 120, 130, 140, 150, __160__
8. 300, 400, 500, 600, __700__
9. 200, 195, 190, 185, __180__
10. 153, 143, 133, 123, __113__
11. 144, 132, 120, 108, __96__
12. 97, 94, 91, 88, __85__

▶ **Quiz**

Write the next number in the pattern.

13. 262, 252, 242, 232, __222__
14. 306, 303, 300, 297, __294__
15. 180, 200, 220, 240, __260__
16. 795, 800, 805, 810, __815__

Bottom-Left Panel

Grade 4 Skill 56

Find a Rule

Look for a pattern. Write a rule.

Example 1
How many plates are needed for 5 tables?

Think: 1 table has 5 plates, 2 tables have 10 plates.

Tables	1	2	3	4	5
Plates	5	10	15	20	

Pattern: The number of plates equals the number of tables times 5.
Rule: Multiply the number of tables by 5.
Since 5 × 5 = 25, there are 25 plates on 5 tables.

Example 2
How many apples are needed for 6 pies?

Think: 1 pie has 7 apples, 2 pies have 14 apples.

Pies	1	2	3	4	5	6
Apples	7	14	21	28	35	

Pattern: The number of apples equals the number of pies times 7.
Rule: Multiply the number of pies by 7.
Since 6 × 7 = 42, then 42 apples are needed for 6 pies.

▶ **Try These**

Write a rule for each table. Then complete the table.

1.
Ostriches	1	2	3	4	5	6
Toes	4	8	12	16		

Rule: Multiply the number of ostriches by 4; 20, 24

2.
Beds	1	2	3	4	5	6
Pillows	2	4	6	8		

Rule: Multiply the number of beds by 2; 10, 12

3.
Plants	1	2	3	4	5	6
Leaves	3	6	9	12		

Rule: Multiply the number of plants by 3; 15, 18

Bottom-Right Panel

Practice on Your Own **Skill 56**

How many raisins are in 7 cookies?
Think: Look for a pattern.
Pattern: The number of raisins equals the number of cookies times 6.
Think: Write a rule.

Cookies	2	3	4	5	6	7
Raisins	12	18	24	30	36	42

Rule: Multiply the number of cookies by 6.
Since 7 × 6 = 42, there are 42 raisins in 7 cookies.

Write a rule for each table. Then complete the table.

1.
Boxes	1	2	3	4	5	6
Blocks	9	18	27			

Rule: Multiply the number of boxes by 9; 36, 45, 54

2.
Dollars	1	2	3	4	5	6
Nickles	20	40	60			

Rule: Multiply the number of dollars by 20; 80, 100, 120

3.
Cabinets	3	4	5	6	7
Drawers	9	12	15		

Rule: Multiply the number of cabinets by 3; 18, 21, 24

4.
Flowers	2	3	4	5	6	7
Petals	16	24	32			

Rule: Multiply the number of flowers by 8; 40, 48, 56

5.
Rooms	4	5	6	7	8	9	10
Rugs	16	20	24				

Rule: Multiply the number of rooms by 4; 28, 32, 36, 40

6.
Bicycles	5	6	7	8	9	10	11
Tires	10	12	14				

Rule: Multiply the number of bicycles by 2; 16, 18, 20, 22

▶ **Quiz**

Write a rule for each table. Then complete the table.

7.
Teams	3	4	5	6	7	8	9
Players	30	40	50				

Rule: Multiply the number of teams by 10; 60, 70, 80, 90

8.
Cartons	1	2	3	4	5	6	7
Eggs	12	24	36				

Rule: Multiply the number of cartons by 12; 48, 60, 72, 84

9.
Shirts	3	4	5	6	7	8	9
Buttons	15	20	25				

Rule: Multiply the number of shirts by 5; 30, 35, 40, 45

10.
Tins	1	2	3	4	5	6	7
Sardines	15	30	45				

Rule: Multiply the number of tins by 15; 60, 75, 90, 105

Grade 4 — Skill 57

Algebra: Missing Factors

Use a multiplication table to find missing factors.

Find $4 \times \blacksquare = 20$.

factors ———→ product

Think: 4 times what number is 20?

Step 1 Find the row for the factor, 4.
Look **across** the row. Find the product, 20.

Step 2 Look **up** the column.

Step 3 Find the missing factor. It is 5.
Complete the multiplication sentence.

$4 \times 5 = 20$
factor → row, column ← factor, product → row × column

Multiplication Table

column

×	0	1	2	3	4	5	6	7	8	9
0	0	0	0	0	0	0	0	0	0	0
1	0	1	2	3	4	5	6	7	8	9
2	0	2	4	6	8	10	12	14	16	18
3	0	3	6	9	12	15	18	21	24	27
4	0	4	8	12	16	20	24	28	32	36
5	0	5	10	15	20	25	30	35	40	45
6	0	6	12	18	24	30	36	42	48	54
7	0	7	14	21	28	35	42	49	56	63
8	0	8	16	24	32	40	48	56	64	72
9	0	9	18	27	36	45	54	63	72	81

Factors →
row →

▲ Try These

Use the multiplication table to find the missing factors.

1 $3 \times \blacksquare = 9$
Row Factor: 3   Product: 9
Missing Factor: 3
$3 \times 3 = 9$

2 $7 \times \blacksquare = 42$
Row Factor: 7   Product: 42
Missing Factor: 6
$7 \times 6 = 42$

3 $8 \times \blacksquare = 24$
Row Factor: 8   Product: 24
Missing Factor: 3
$8 \times 3 = 24$

Go to the next side.

Practice on Your Own — Skill 57

Find $\blacksquare \times 7 = 21$.

Think:
Find the column for 7.
Look **down** the column to 21.
Look **left** across the row to 3.
The missing factor is 3.

$3 \times 7 = 21$
row × column = product

×	0	1	2	3	4	5	6	7	8	9
0	0	0	0	0	0	0	0	0	0	0
1	0	1	2	3	4	5	6	7	8	9
2	0	2	4	6	8	10	12	14	16	18
3	0	3	6	9	12	15	18	21	24	27
4	0	4	8	12	16	20	24	28	32	36
5	0	5	10	15	20	25	30	35	40	45
6	0	6	12	18	24	30	36	42	48	54
7	0	7	14	21	28	35	42	49	56	63
8	0	8	16	24	32	40	48	56	64	72
9	0	9	18	27	36	45	54	63	72	81

Use the multiplication table to find the missing factors.

1 $\blacksquare \times 2 = 8$
Column Factor: 2
Product: 8
Missing Factor: 4
$4 \times 2 = 8$

2 $\blacksquare \times 5 = 30$
Column Factor: 5
Product: 30
Missing Factor: 6
$6 \times 5 = 30$

3 $\blacksquare \times 9 = 54$
Column Factor: 9
Product: 54
Missing Factor: 6
$6 \times 9 = 54$

4 $5 \times 4 = 20$

5 $6 \times 5 = 30$

6 $9 \times 4 = 36$

7 $6 \times 3 = 18$

8 $4 \times 7 = 28$

9 $8 \times 6 = 48$

▶ Quiz

Use the multiplication table to find the missing factors.

10 $9 \times 8 = 72$

11 $6 \times 2 = 12$

12 $3 \times 5 = 15$

13 $5 \times 9 = 45$

14 $8 \times 3 = 24$

15 $5 \times 7 = 35$

16 $4 \times 4 = 16$

17 $7 \times 6 = 42$

18 $8 \times 4 = 32$

19 $8 \times 8 = 64$

20 $9 \times 7 = 63$

21 $8 \times 7 = 56$

Grade 4 — Skill 58

Ordered Pairs

The horizontal and vertical lines on the map are called a grid. An ordered pair of numbers like (3,2) names a point on a grid. You can use ordered pairs to locate points on a grid.

Look at the map. Name the place at point (3,2).

1849 MINER'S MAP

○ Old oak tree
⊠ Fresh water well
■ Miner's cabin
▲ Entrance to mine
● Bear's den

Step 1 Start at point 0 on grid.

Step 2 The first number in the ordered pair tells you how many spaces to move to the right. Move 3 spaces to the right.

Step 3 The second number tells you how many spaces to move up. Move up 2 spaces.

So, the miner's cabin is located at point (3,2).

▲ Try These

Use the map above. Name the place you find at each point.

1 (1,1)
Start at point 0. Move
1 spaces to the right.
Move 1 spaces up.
The place at point (1,1)
is Old oak tree

2 (5,4)
Start at point 0. Move
5 spaces to the right.
Move 4 spaces up.
The place at point (5,4)
is Bear's den

3 (2,4)
Start at point 0. Move
2 spaces to the right.
Move 4 spaces up.
The place at point (2,4)
is Fresh water well

4 (4,5)
Start at point 0. Move
4 spaces to the right.
Move 5 spaces up.
The place at point (4,5)
is Entrance to mine

Go to the next side.

Practice on Your Own — Skill 58

Think:
The ordered pair (4,3) means move **4 spaces to the right** and then move 3 spaces up.
Remember: Start at 0.
Look at the map of the state park. Name the place at point (4,3).
The place at point (4,3) is **Campsite A.**

○ Bicycle Rack
■ Bridge
△ Lookout Tower
✕ Eagle's Nest
● Campsite A, B, & C
⊠ Nature Center
□ Water Fall
▲ Ranger's Cabin
⊗ Picnic Tables
≈ Swimming Hole
△ First Aid Station

Use the map above. Name the place you find at each point.

1 (1,1)
Start at point 0. Move
1 spaces to the right.
Move 1 spaces up.
Place: Bicycle Rack

2 (1,3)
Start at point 0. Move
1 spaces to the right.
Move 3 spaces up.
Place: Ranger's Cabin

3 (3,2)
Start at point 0. Move
3 spaces to the right.
Move 2 spaces up.
Place: Bridge

4 (2,4)
Move 2 spaces to the right.
Move 4 spaces up.
The place at point (2,4):
Water Fall

5 (4,5)
Move 4 spaces to the right.
Move 5 spaces up.
The place at point (4,5):
Eagle's Nest

6 (5,2)
Move 5 spaces to the right.
Move 2 spaces up.
The place at point (5,2):
Campsite B

▶ Quiz

Use the map above. Name the place you find at each point.

7 (4,1)
Place: Swimming Hole

8 (2,1)
Place: First Aid Station

9 (5,0)
Place: Campsite C

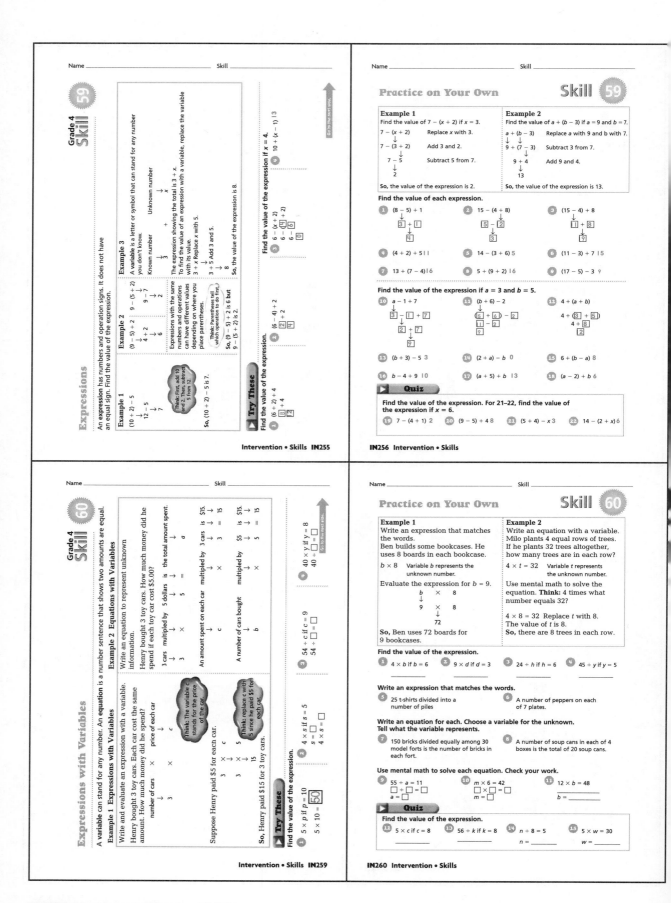

Panel: Grade 4 Skill 59 — Expressions

Expressions

An expression has numbers and operation signs. It does not have an equal sign. Find the value of the expression.

Example 1

$(10 + 2) - 5$

$12 - 5$

7

Think: First, add 10 and 2. Then, subtract 5 from 12.

So, $(10 + 2) - 5$ is 7.

Example 2

$(9 - 5) + 2$ $9 - (5 + 2)$

$4 + 2$ $9 - 7$

6 2

Expressions with the same numbers and operations can have different values depending on where you place parentheses.

Think: Parentheses tell which operation to do first.

So, $(9 - 5) + 2$ is 6 but $9 - (5 + 2)$ is 2.

Example 3

A variable is a letter or symbol that can stand for any number you don't know.

$3 + x$ Known number / Unknown number

The expression showing the total is $3 + x$.
To find the value of an expression with a variable, replace the variable with its value.

$3 + x$ Replace x with 5.

$3 + 5$ Add 3 and 5.

8

So, the value of the expression is 8.

▶ Try These

Find the value of the expression.

1. $(6 + 2) + 4$
   $8 + 4$
   $\boxed{12}$

2. $(6 - 4) + 2$
   $2 + 2$
   $\boxed{4}$

Find the value of the expression if $x = 4$.

3. $6 - (x + 2)$
   $6 - (\boxed{4} + 2)$
   $6 - \boxed{6}$
   $\boxed{0}$

4. $10 + (x - 1)$ 13

Panel: Practice on Your Own — Skill 59

Practice on Your Own — Skill 59

Example 1

Find the value of $7 - (x + 2)$ if $x = 3$.

$7 - (x + 2)$ Replace x with 3.

$7 - (3 + 2)$ Add 3 and 2.

$7 - 5$ Subtract 5 from 7.

2

So, the value of the expression is 2.

Example 2

Find the value of $a + (b - 3)$ if $a = 9$ and $b = 7$.

$a + (b - 3)$ Replace a with 9 and b with 7.

$9 + (7 - 3)$ Subtract 3 from 7.

$9 + 4$ Add 9 and 4.

13

So, the value of the expression is 13.

Find the value of each expression.

1. $(8 - 5) + 1$
   $3 + \boxed{1}$
   $\boxed{4}$

2. $15 - (4 + 8)$
   $\boxed{5} - \boxed{2}$
   $\boxed{3}$

3. $(15 - 4) + 8$
   $\boxed{1} + \boxed{8}$
   $\boxed{9}$

4. $(4 + 2) + 5$ 11

5. $14 - (3 + 6)$ 5

6. $(11 - 3) + 7$ 15

7. $13 + (7 - 4)$ 16

8. $5 + (9 + 2)$ 16

9. $(17 - 5) - 3$ 9

Find the value of the expression if $a = 3$ and $b = 5$.

10. $a - 1 + 7$
    $\boxed{3} - \boxed{1} + 7$
    $\boxed{2} + 7$
    $\boxed{9}$

11. $(b + 6) - 2$
    $(\boxed{5} + \boxed{6}) - \boxed{2}$
    $\boxed{11} - \boxed{2}$
    $\boxed{9}$

12. $4 + (a + b)$
    $4 + (\boxed{3} + \boxed{5})$
    $4 + \boxed{8}$
    $\boxed{12}$

13. $(b + 3) - 5$ 3

14. $(2 + a) - b$ 0

15. $6 + (b - a)$ 8

16. $b - 4 + 9$ 10

17. $(a + 5) + b$ 13

18. $(a - 2) + b$ 6

▶ Quiz

Find the value of the expression. For 21–22, find the value of the expression if $x = 6$.

19. $7 - (4 + 1)$ 2

20. $(9 - 5) + 4$ 8

21. $(5 + 4) - x$ 3

22. $14 - (2 + x)$ 6

Panel: Grade 4 Skill 60 — Expressions with Variables

Expressions with Variables

A variable can stand for any number. An equation is a number sentence that shows two amounts are equal.

Example 1 Expressions with Variables

Write and evaluate an expression with a variable.
Henry bought 3 toy cars. Each car cost the same amount. How much money did he spend?

number of cars × price of each car

$3 × c$

Think: The variable c stands for the price of the car.

Suppose Henry paid $5 for each car.

$3 × c$
$3 × 5$
15

Think: replace c with 5 since he paid $5 for each car.

So, Henry paid $15 for 3 toy cars.

Example 2 Equations with Variables

Write an equation to represent unknown information.
Henry bought 3 toy cars. How much money did he spend if each toy car cost $5.00?

3 cars multiplied by 5 dollars is the total amount spent.

3 × 5 = a

An amount spent on each car multiplied by 3 cars is $15.

c × 3 = 15

A number of cars bought multiplied by $5 is $15.

b × 5 = 15

▶ Try These

Find the value of the expression.

1. $5 × p$ if $p = 10$
   $5 × 10 = \boxed{50}$

2. $4 × s$ if $s = 5$
   $s = \boxed{5}$
   $4 × s = \boxed{}$

3. $54 + c$ if $c = 9$
   $54 + \boxed{} = \boxed{}$

4. $40 × y$ if $y = 8$
   $40 + \boxed{} = \boxed{}$

Panel: Practice on Your Own — Skill 60

Practice on Your Own — Skill 60

Example 1

Write an expression that matches the words.
Ben builds some bookcases. He uses 8 boards in each bookcase.

$b × 8$ Variable b represents the unknown number.

Evaluate the expression for $b = 9$.

$b × 8$
$9 × 8$
72

So, Ben uses 72 boards for 9 bookcases.

Example 2

Write an equation with a variable.
Milo plants 4 equal rows of trees. If he plants 32 trees altogether, how many trees are in each row?

$4 × t = 32$ Variable t represents the unknown number.

Use mental math to solve the equation. **Think:** 4 times what number equals 32?

$4 × 8 = 32$ Replace t with 8. The value of t is 8.
So, there are 8 trees in each row.

Find the value of the expression.

1. $4 × b$ if $b = 6$

2. $9 × d$ if $d = 3$

3. $24 ÷ h$ if $h = 6$

4. $45 ÷ y$ if $y = 5$

Write an expression that matches the words.

5. 25 t-shirts divided into a number of piles

6. A number of peppers on each of 7 plates.

Write an equation for each. Choose a variable for the unknown. Tell what the variable represents.

7. 150 bricks divided equally among 30 model forts is the number of bricks in each fort.

8. A number of soup cans in each of 4 boxes is the total of 20 soup cans.

Use mental math to solve each equation. Check your work.

9. $55 ÷ a = 11$
   $\boxed{} ÷ \boxed{} = \boxed{}$
   $a = \boxed{}$

10. $m × 6 = 42$
    $\boxed{} × \boxed{} = \boxed{}$
    $m = \boxed{}$

11. $12 × b = 48$
    $b = $ _____

▶ Quiz

Find the value of the expression.

12. $5 × c$ if $c = 8$

13. $56 ÷ k$ if $k = 8$

14. $n ÷ 8 = 5$
    $n = $ _____

15. $5 × w = 30$
    $w = $ _____

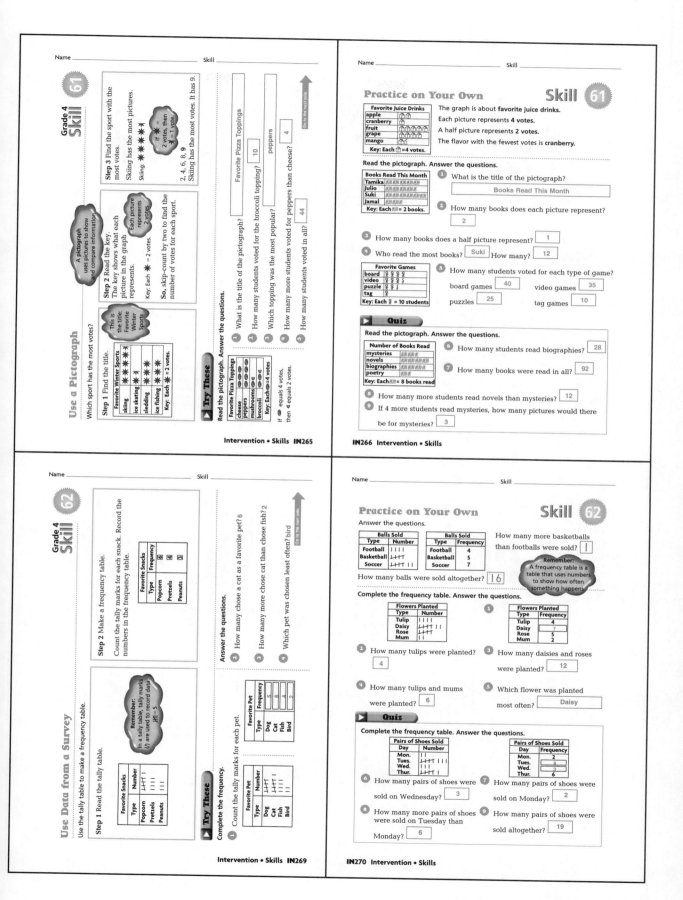

Top Left Quadrant

Grade 4
Skill 61

Use a Pictograph

Which sport has the most votes?

A pictograph uses pictures to show and compare information.

Step 1 Find the title.

This is the title: Favorite Winter Sports

Favorite Winter Sports	
skiing	✶✶✶✶
ice skating	✶✶
sledding	✶✶✶
ice fishing	✶
Key: Each ✶ = 2 votes.	

Step 2 Read the key.
The key shows what each picture in the graph represents.

Each picture represents 2 votes.

Key: Each ✶ = 2 votes.

Step 3 Find the sport with the most votes.
Skiing has the most pictures.

Skiing: ✶ ✶ ✶ ✶
2, 4, 6, 8, 9
Skiing has the most votes. It has 9.

If ✶ = 2 votes, then
✶ = 1 vote.

So, skip-count by two to find the number of votes for each sport.

▶ **Try These**

Read the pictograph. Answer the questions.

Favorite Pizza Toppings	
cheese	◔◔◔◔
peppers	◔◔◔◔◔
mushrooms	◔◔◔
broccoli	◔◔
Key: Each ◔=4 votes	

If ◔ equals 4 votes,
then ◖ equals 2 votes.

① What is the title of the pictograph? **Favorite Pizza Toppings**

② How many students voted for the broccoli topping? **10**

③ Which topping was the most popular? **peppers**

④ How many more students voted for peppers than cheese? **4**

⑤ How many students voted in all? **44**

Go to the next side.

Intervention • Skills **IN265**

Top Right Quadrant

Practice on Your Own
Skill 61

Favorite Juice Drinks	
apple	🥤🥤
cranberry	🥤
fruit	🥤🥤🥤🥤
grape	🥤🥤🥤
mango	🥤🥤
Key: Each 🥤 = 4 votes.	

The graph is about **favorite juice drinks.**
Each picture represents **4 votes.**
A half picture represents **2 votes.**
The flavor with the fewest votes is **cranberry.**

Read the pictograph. Answer the questions.

Books Read This Month	
Tamika	📕📕📕📕
Julio	📕📕📕
Suki	📕📕📕📕📕📕
Jamal	📕📕
Key: Each 📕 = 2 books.	

① What is the title of the pictograph? **Books Read This Month**

② How many books does each picture represent? **2**

③ How many books does a half picture represent? **1**

④ Who read the most books? **Suki** How many? **12**

Favorite Games	
board	♀♀♀♀
video	♀♀♀
puzzle	♀♀
tag	♀
Key: Each ♀ = 10 students	

⑤ How many students voted for each type of game?
board games **40**   video games **35**
puzzles **25**   tag games **10**

▶ **Quiz**

Read the pictograph. Answer the questions.

Number of Books Read	
mysteries	📖📖📖
novels	📖📖📖📖
biographies	📖📖📖📖
poetry	📖
Key: Each 📖 = 8 books read	

⑥ How many students read biographies? **28**

⑦ How many books were read in all? **92**

⑧ How many more students read novels than mysteries? **12**

⑨ If 4 more students read mysteries, how many pictures would there be for mysteries? **3**

IN266 Intervention • Skills

Bottom Left Quadrant

Grade 4
Skill 62

Use Data from a Survey

Use the tally table to make a frequency table.

Step 1 Read the tally table.

Favorite Snacks	
Type	Number
Popcorn	ⅢⅠⅠ
Pretzels	ⅠⅠⅠⅠ
Peanuts	ⅠⅠⅠ

Remember:
In a tally table, tally marks (∣) are used to record data. Ⅲ = 5

Step 2 Make a frequency table.
Count the tally marks for each snack. Record the numbers in the frequency table.

Favorite Snacks	
Type	Frequency
Popcorn	8
Pretzels	4
Peanuts	3

▶ **Try These**

Complete the frequency.

① Count the tally marks for each pet.

Favorite Pet	
Type	Number
Dog	ⅢⅠⅠ
Cat	Ⅲ
Fish	ⅠⅠⅠⅠ
Bird	ⅠⅠ

Favorite Pet	
Type	Frequency
Dog	5
Cat	5
Fish	4
Bird	2

Answer the questions.

② How many chose a cat as a favorite pet? **6**

③ How many more chose cat than chose fish? **2**

④ Which pet was chosen least often? **bird**

Go to the next side.

Intervention • Skills **IN269**

Bottom Right Quadrant

Practice on Your Own
Skill 62

Answer the questions.

Balls Sold	
Type	Number
Football	ⅠⅠⅠⅠ
Basketball	Ⅲ
Soccer	ⅢⅠⅠ

Balls Sold	
Type	Frequency
Football	4
Basketball	5
Soccer	7

How many more basketballs than footballs were sold? **1**

Remember:
A frequency table is a table that uses numbers to show how often something happens.

How many balls were sold altogether? **16**

Complete the frequency table. Answer the questions.

Flowers Planted	
Type	Number
Tulip	ⅠⅠⅠⅠ
Daisy	ⅢⅠⅠ
Rose	Ⅲ
Mum	ⅠⅠ

①
Flowers Planted	
Type	Frequency
Tulip	4
Daisy	7
Rose	5
Mum	2

② How many tulips were planted? **4**

③ How many daisies and roses were planted? **12**

④ How many tulips and mums were planted? **6**

⑤ Which flower was planted most often? **Daisy**

▶ **Quiz**

Complete the frequency table. Answer the questions.

Pairs of Shoes Sold	
Day	Number
Mon.	ⅠⅠ
Tues.	ⅢⅠⅠⅠ
Wed.	ⅢⅠⅠⅠ
Thur.	ⅢⅠ

Pairs of Shoes Sold	
Day	Frequency
Mon.	2
Tues.	8
Wed.	3
Thur.	6

⑥ How many pairs of shoes were sold on Wednesday? **3**

⑦ How many pairs of shoes were sold on Monday? **2**

⑧ How many more pairs of shoes were sold on Tuesday than Monday? **6**

⑨ How many pairs of shoes were sold altogether? **19**

IN270 Intervention • Skills

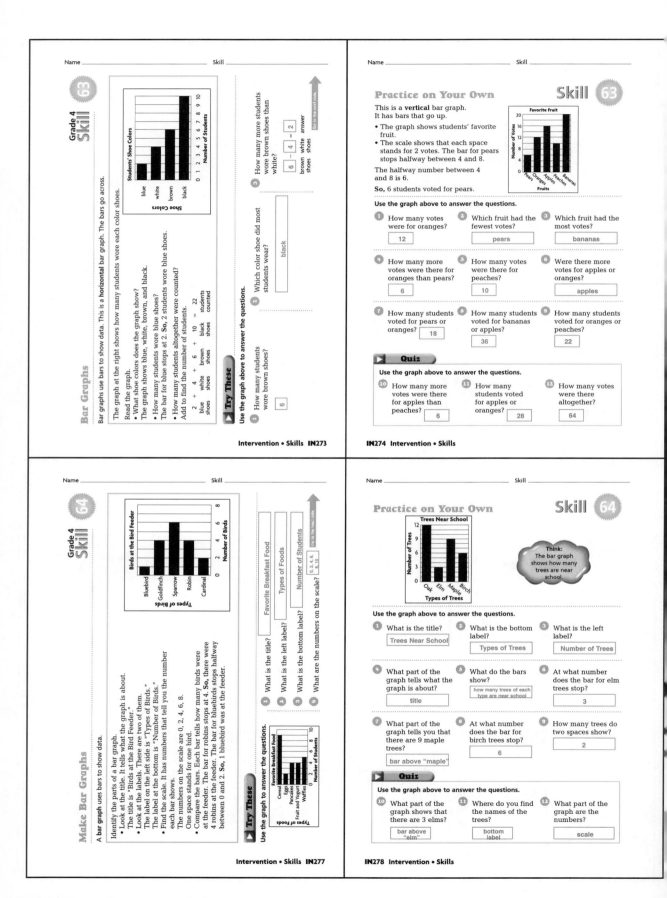

Top-left panel (Skill 63)

Grade 4 Skill 63

Bar Graphs

Bar graphs use bars to show data. This is a **horizontal** bar graph. The bars go across.

The graph at the right shows how many students wore each color shoes.

Students' Shoe Colors

Read the graph.
- What shoe colors does the graph show?
  The graph shows blue, white, brown, and black.
- How many students wore blue shoes?
  The bar for blue stops at 2. **So,** 2 students wore blue shoes.
- How many students altogether were counted?
  Add to find the number of students.

$$2 + 4 + 6 + 10 = 22$$
blue / white / brown / black / students
shoes / shoes / shoes / shoes / counted

▲ **Try These**

Use the graph above to answer the questions.

1. How many students wore brown shoes?
   6

2. Which color shoe did most students wear?
   black

3. How many more students wore brown shoes than white?
   $6 - 4 = 2$
   brown / white / answer
   shoes / shoes

Intervention • Skills **IN273**

Top-right panel (Skill 63)

Practice on Your Own **Skill 63**

This is a **vertical** bar graph.
It has bars that go up.
- The graph shows students' favorite fruit.
- The scale shows that each space stands for 2 votes. The bar for pears stops halfway between 4 and 8.

The halfway number between 4 and 8 is 6.

So, 6 students voted for pears.

Favorite Fruit

Use the graph above to answer the questions.

1. How many votes were for oranges? 12
2. Which fruit had the fewest votes? pears
3. Which fruit had the most votes? bananas
4. How many more votes were there for oranges than pears? 6
5. How many votes were there for peaches? 10
6. Were there more votes for apples or oranges? apples
7. How many students voted for pears or oranges? 18
8. How many students voted for bananas or apples? 36
9. How many students voted for oranges or peaches? 22

▶ **Quiz**

Use the graph above to answer the questions.

10. How many more votes were there for apples than peaches? 6
11. How many students voted for apples or oranges? 28
12. How many votes were there altogether? 64

IN274 Intervention • Skills

Bottom-left panel (Skill 64)

Grade 4 Skill 64

Make Bar Graphs

A **bar graph** uses bars to show data.

Identify the parts of a bar graph.
- Look at the title. It tells what the graph is about.
  The title is "Birds at the Bird Feeder."
- Look at the labels. There are two of them.
  The label on the left side is "Types of Birds."
  The label at the bottom is "Number of Birds."
- Find the scale. It has numbers that tell you the number each bar shows.
  The numbers on the scale are 0, 2, 4, 6, 8.
  One space stands for one bird.
- Compare the bars. Each bar tells how many birds were at the feeder. The bar for robins stops at 4. **So,** there were 4 robins at the feeder. The bar for bluebirds stops halfway between 0 and 2. **So,** 1 bluebird was at the feeder.

Birds at the Bird Feeder

▲ **Try These**

Use the graph to answer the questions.

Favorite Breakfast Food

1. What is the title?
   Favorite Breakfast Food
2. What is the left label?
   Types of Foods
3. What is the bottom label?
   Number of Students
4. What are the numbers on the scale?
   0, 2, 4, 6, 8, 10

Intervention • Skills **IN277**

Bottom-right panel (Skill 64)

Practice on Your Own **Skill 64**

Trees Near School

Think:
The bar graph shows how many trees are near school.

Use the graph above to answer the questions.

1. What is the title?
   Trees Near School
2. What is the bottom label?
   Types of Trees
3. What is the left label?
   Number of Trees
4. What part of the graph tells what the graph is about?
   title
5. What do the bars show?
   how many trees of each type are near school
6. At what number does the bar for elm trees stop?
   3
7. What part of the graph tells you that there are 9 maple trees?
   bar above "maple"
8. At what number does the bar for birch trees stop?
   6
9. How many trees do two spaces show?
   2

▶ **Quiz**

Use the graph above to answer the questions.

10. What part of the graph shows that there are 3 elms?
    bar above "elm"
11. Where do you find the names of the trees?
    bottom label
12. What part of the graph are the numbers?
    scale

IN278 Intervention • Skills

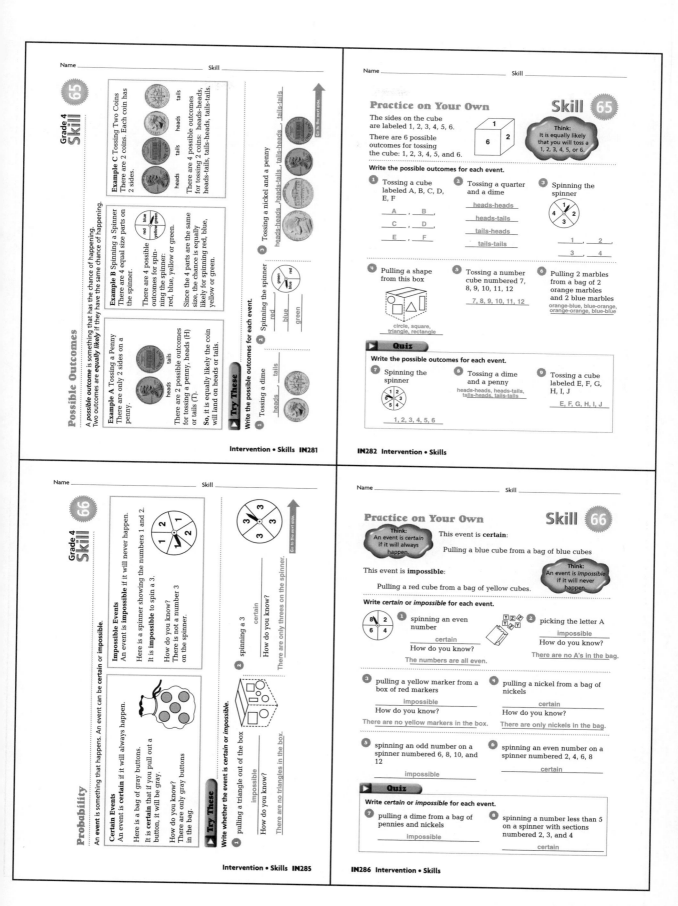

Panel 1 (top-left) — Skill 65

Name _____ Skill _____

Grade 4
Skill 65

Possible Outcomes

A *possible outcome* is something that has the chance of happening.
Two outcomes are **equally likely** if they have the same chance of happening.

Example A Tossing a Penny
There are only 2 sides on a penny.

heads   tails

There are 2 possible outcomes for tossing a penny, heads (H) or tails (T).

So, it is equally likely the coin will land on heads or tails.

Example B Spinning a Spinner
There are 4 equal size parts on the spinner.

There are 4 possible outcomes for spinning the spinner: red, blue, yellow or green.

Since the 4 parts are the same size, the chance is equally likely for spinning red, blue, yellow or green.

Example C Tossing Two Coins
There are 2 coins. Each coin has 2 sides.

heads   tails
heads   tails

There are 4 possible outcomes for tossing 2 coins: heads-heads, heads-tails, tails-heads, tails-tails.

▲ Try These

Write the possible outcomes for each event.

1. Tossing a dime
   heads , tails

2. Spinning the spinner
   red
   blue
   green

3. Tossing a nickel and a penny
   heads-heads, heads-tails, tails-heads, tails-tails

Go to the next side. →

Intervention • Skills **IN281**

Panel 2 (top-right) — Skill 65

Name _____ Skill _____

Practice on Your Own

Skill 65

The sides on the cube are labeled 1, 2, 3, 4, 5, 6.

There are 6 possible outcomes for tossing the cube: 1, 2, 3, 4, 5, and 6.

Think: It is equally likely that you will toss a 1, 2, 3, 4, 5, or 6.

Write the possible outcomes for each event.

1. Tossing a cube labeled A, B, C, D, E, F
   A , B
   C , D
   E , F

2. Tossing a quarter and a dime
   heads-heads
   heads-tails
   tails-heads
   tails-tails

3. Spinning the spinner
   1 , 2
   3 , 4

4. Pulling a shape from this box
   circle, square, triangle, rectangle

5. Tossing a number cube numbered 7, 8, 9, 10, 11, 12
   7, 8, 9, 10, 11, 12

6. Pulling 2 marbles from a bag of 2 orange marbles and 2 blue marbles
   orange-blue, blue-orange, orange-orange, blue-blue

▶ Quiz

Write the possible outcomes for each event.

7. Spinning the spinner
   1, 2, 3, 4, 5, 6

8. Tossing a dime and a penny
   heads-heads, heads-tails, tails-heads, tails-tails

9. Tossing a cube labeled E, F, G, H, I, J
   E, F, G, H, I, J

IN282 Intervention • Skills

Panel 3 (bottom-left) — Skill 66

Name _____ Skill _____

Grade 4
Skill 66

Probability

An **event** is something that happens. An event can be **certain** or **impossible**.

Certain Events
An event is **certain** if it will always happen.

Here is a bag of gray buttons.

It is **certain** that if you pull out a button, it will be gray.

How do you know?
There are only gray buttons in the bag.

Impossible Events
An event is **impossible** if it will never happen.

Here is a spinner showing the numbers 1 and 2.

It is **impossible** to spin a 3.

How do you know?
There is not a number 3 on the spinner.

▲ Try These

Write whether the event is **certain** or **impossible**.

1. pulling a triangle out of the box
   impossible
   How do you know?
   There are no triangles in the box.

2. spinning a 3
   certain
   How do you know?
   There are only threes on the spinner.

Go to the next side. →

Intervention • Skills **IN285**

Panel 4 (bottom-right) — Skill 66

Name _____ Skill _____

Practice on Your Own

Skill 66

Think: An event is *certain* if it will always happen.

This event is **certain**:
   Pulling a blue cube from a bag of blue cubes.

This event is **impossible**:
   Pulling a red cube from a bag of yellow cubes.

Think: An event is *impossible* if it will never happen.

Write **certain** or **impossible** for each event.

1. spinning an even number
   certain
   How do you know?
   The numbers are all even.

2. picking the letter A
   impossible
   How do you know?
   There are no A's in the bag.

3. pulling a yellow marker from a box of red markers
   impossible
   How do you know?
   There are no yellow markers in the box.

4. pulling a nickel from a bag of nickels
   certain
   How do you know?
   There are only nickels in the bag.

5. spinning an odd number on a spinner numbered 6, 8, 10, and 12
   impossible

6. spinning an even number on a spinner numbered 2, 4, 6, 8
   certain

▶ Quiz

Write **certain** or **impossible** for each event.

7. pulling a dime from a bag of pennies and nickels
   impossible

8. spinning a number less than 5 on a spinner with sections numbered 2, 3, and 4
   certain

IN286 Intervention • Skills

Check What You Know

Enrichment

Name _____

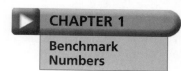

How Many?

• Place 10 counters in a plastic bag and set aside.
• Place several handfuls of counters in another plastic bag, without counting them.

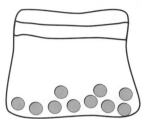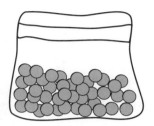

1. Use the bag with 10 counters to estimate how many counters are in the second bag. Record your estimate in the row of the table for Round 1.

ROUND	ESTIMATE	ACTUAL NUMBER	DIFFERENCE
1			
2			
3			
4			
5			

2. Remove the counters from the second bag and count them. Write the actual number in the table. Find the difference between the actual number and the estimate and write this number in the table. If the difference is less than 6, given yourself a point.

3. Do 4 more rounds the same way and total your score. Play again until you get a total score of 4 or 5.

Name _____

Crack the Code

Study the code.

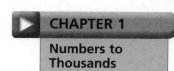

Code	Symbol Value
⬣	1,000
▲	100
■	10
●	1

Example

Code: ⬣▲▲■■■■●●●

Standard form: 1,243

Word form: one thousand, two hundred forty-three

Crack the code and complete the table.

CODE	STANDARD FORM	WORD FORM
⬣⬣▲■■■●●●●●●		
⬣■■■■●●●●		
		three thousand, two hundred seven
		one thousand, four hundred twenty-five
	2,603	
	3,018	

Name _____

Off to School

All the elementary schools in Center City sold books at a Book
Festival. The table shows how many books each grade sold. Use
the table to answer each question.

GRADE	BOOKS SOLD
Kindergarten	583
Grade 1	594
Grade 2	1,031
Grade 3	982
Grade 4	1,221
Grade 5	980
Grade 6	752

1. Which grade sold more books, Grade 1 or Grade 6?

_____

2. Which grade sold the most books?

_____

3. Which grade sold more books, Grade 2 or Grade 5?

_____

4. Which grade sold the fewest books?

_____

5. Which grade sold fewer books, Grade 4 or Grade 5?

_____

6. Which grades sold more than 800 books?

_____

7. Which grades sold fewer books than Grade 5?

_____

8. Which grades sold between 600 and 1,000 books?

_____

9. List the grades in order from the one with the least books to the one with the most.

_____

_____

_____

10. Round the number of books that the Grade 2 collected to the nearest hundred.

_____

Off to School

11. Round the number of books that the Grade 6 sold to the nearest hundred.

_____

12. Round the number of books that the Grade 1 collected to the nearest ten.

_____

13. Rounded to the nearest ten, which grade sold 1,030 books?

_____

14. Rounded to the nearest 10, which grade sold 1,220 books?

_____

15 Round the number of books that the Kindergarten sold to the nearest ten.

_____

16. Round the number of books that the Grade 3 sold to the nearest ten.

_____

17. Which two grades sold the same number of books when rounded to the nearest hundred and to the nearest ten?

_____

18. Which two grades sold the same number of books when rounded to the nearest hundred, but not to the nearest ten?

_____

19. Round the number of books that Grade 4 sold to the nearest hundred.

_____

20. Round the number of books that Grade 6 sold to the nearest hundred.

_____

21. List the grades in order from the one with the most books to the one with the least.

_____

_____

22. Which grade sold fewer books, Kindergarten or Grade 1?

_____

Name _____

Play Ball!

The Eagles baseball team wants to order new baseballs and gloves. Each baseball costs $4 and each glove costs $18. The team only has $90 to spend on balls and gloves. The table organizes the information.

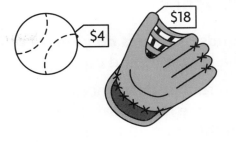

BASEBALLS					
Number	1	2	3	4	5
Cost	$4	$8	$12	$16	$20

GLOVES					
Number	1	2	3	4	5
Cost	$18	$36	$54	$72	$90

1. If the team buys 3 baseballs, how many gloves can it buy?

_____

2. If the team buys 3 gloves, how many baseballs can it buy?

_____

3. Suppose the team manager spent $88. What did she buy?

_____

4. Suppose the team manager spent $36 on gloves and $20 on baseballs. What can she buy with the money left?

_____

5. How much more do 4 gloves and 3 baseballs cost than 3 gloves and 6 baseballs?

_____

6. How much more do 3 gloves and 2 baseballs cost than 2 gloves and 5 baseballs?

_____

7. The team manager bought 1 glove and 2 baseballs on Monday, 1 glove and no baseballs on Tuesday, and 1 glove and 4 baseballs on Wednesday. How much did she spend in all?

_____

Name _____

Giraffe Story

What kinds of stories do giraffes tell?
Solve the puzzle to find out.

Find each sum or difference.
Then write the letter that is next
to the problem on all the lines
above the answer.

1. $\begin{array}{r} 350 \\ + 260 \end{array}$ **G**	2. $\begin{array}{r} 934 \\ + 382 \end{array}$ **F**	3. $\begin{array}{r} 347 \\ - 129 \end{array}$ **I**
4. $\begin{array}{r} 579 \\ + 268 \end{array}$ **R**	5. $\begin{array}{r} 625 \\ - 347 \end{array}$ **S**	6. $\begin{array}{r} 862 \\ - 561 \end{array}$ **E**
7. $\begin{array}{r} 736 \\ + 485 \end{array}$ **A**	8. $\begin{array}{r} 419 \\ + 893 \end{array}$ **T**	9. $\begin{array}{r} 800 \\ - 248 \end{array}$ **L**

_____ _____ _____ _____ _____ _____ _____ _____
610   218   847   1,221   1,316   1,316   301   278

_____ _____ _____ _____
1,312   301   552   552

_____ _____ _____ _____   _____ _____ _____ _____ _____
1,312   1,221   552   552   1,312   1,221   552   301   278

IN328 Check What You Know Enrichment

Name _____

What's Missing?

Find the starting number.

Example

$?$ ⟶ | Add 7. | ⟶ 12

Solution Since $5 + 7 = 12$, the missing number is 5.

1. $?$ ⟶ | Add 4. | ⟶ 9

_____

2. $?$ ⟶ | Add 6. | ⟶ 16

_____

3. $?$ ⟶ | Add 7. | ⟶ 15

_____

4. $?$ ⟶ | Add 9. | ⟶ 14

_____

5. $?$ ⟶ | Add 3. | ⟶ 9

_____

6. $?$ ⟶ | Add 7. | ⟶ 14

_____

Find the missing number in each fact family.

7. $6 + 8 = $ ☐

$14 - 6 = $ ☐

8. $12 + 5 = $ ☐

$17 - 5 = $ ☐

9. $11 + 8 = $ ☐

$19 - 8 = $ ☐

10. $9 + 6 = $ ☐

$15 - 6 = $ ☐

11. $4 + 9 = $ ☐

$13 - 4 = $ ☐

12. $8 + 4 = $ ☐

$12 - 8 = $ ☐

Name _____

Party Time

You are planning a party. Four people can sit around one table and six people can sit around two tables put together.
The diagrams show how this can be done.

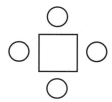 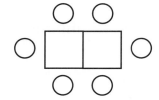

Solve.

1. How many people can be seated around 3 tables? Complete the diagram.

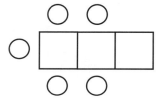

_____

2. How many people can be seated around 4 tables? Complete the diagram.

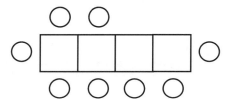

_____

3. Complete the table.

NUMBER OF TABLES	NUMBER OF PEOPLE
1	4
2	6
3	
4	

4. Use the table to find a pattern. How many people can be seated around 5 tables?

_____

5. How many people can be seated around 7 tables?

_____

6. How many people can be seated around 10 tables?

_____

7. How many tables do you need to seat 18 people?

_____

8. How many tables do you need to seat 24 people?

_____

Tick Tock

Write the time under each clock. Find the next time in the pattern.

1.

_____   _____   _____   _____

2.

_____   _____   _____   _____

3.

_____   _____   _____   _____

Write the time. Find the next time in the pattern.

4. 15 minutes   six o'clock   quarter   half past 6
before 6   after 6

_____   _____   _____   _____

5. 24 minutes   34 minutes   16 minutes   6 minutes
after ten   after ten   before   before
                                        eleven   eleven

_____   _____   _____   _____

Check What You Know Enrichment IN331

A Month of Fun Days

JULY						
Sunday	Monday	Tuesday	Wednesday	Thursday	Friday	Saturday
		1	2	3	4	5
6	7	8	9	10	11	12
13	14	15	16	17	18	19
20	21	22	23	24	25	26
27	28	29	30	31		

Use the calendar.

1. What day of the week is July 22?

   _____

2. What day of the week is the Fourth of July?

   _____

3. What date is the second Wednesday in July?

   _____

4. What date is the third Monday in July?

   _____

5. If you circled all the dates for Fridays and Saturdays in July, how many dates would be circled?

   _____

6. If swimming lessons are on Mondays and Thursdays, how many swimming lessons will there be in July?

   _____

7. What is the pattern in the dates for Thursdays in July: 3, 10, 17, 24, 31?

   _____

8. You go to camp for 6 days, starting July 12. What date do you come home?

   _____

Name _____

I'll Buy It!

Your school sells supplies during lunch time.
The prices of several things are shown in the pictograph.

Use the pictograph to answer the questions.

SCHOOL COUNTER PRICES	
Pencil	○ ○ ○
Pen	○ ○ ○ ○ ◖
Eraser	○ ◖
Note Pad	○ ○ ○ ○ ○ ○ ○

Key: Each ○ = 10¢.

1. How much does a note pad cost?

   _____

2. How much does a pen cost?

   _____

3. If a pencil was 5 cents more, how much would it cost?

   _____

4. If an eraser was 5 cents more, how much would it cost?

   _____

5. How much does it cost to buy a pencil and an eraser?

   _____

6. How much does it cost to buy a pen and a pencil?

   _____

7. How much more does a pen cost than a pencil?

   _____

8. How much more does a note pad cost than a pen?

   _____

9. If a pencil is 10 cents more, how many symbols would there be for the pencil?

   _____

10. If a pen is 5 cents more, how many symbols would there be for the pen?

    _____

My Favorite Color

1. Ask 30 fourth-grade students to name their favorite color. Record their answers as tallies in the tally chart.

FAVORITE COLORS TALLY CHART	
Color	**Number of Students**
Red	
Blue	
Orange	
Other	

2. Use the tally chart to complete the frequency table.

FAVORITE COLORS FREQUENCY TABLE	
Color	**Number of Students**
Red	
Blue	
Orange	
Other	

3. How many students chose red or blue?

_____

4. How many students chose blue or orange?

_____

5. How many more students said red than orange (or orange than red)?

_____

6. How many more students said blue than red (or red than blue)?

_____

7. How many students named a favorite color?

_____

8. If 3 more students named blue, how many tally marks would be shown for that color?

_____

Name _____

What's the Weight?

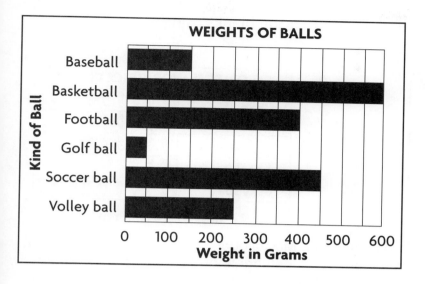

WEIGHTS OF BALLS

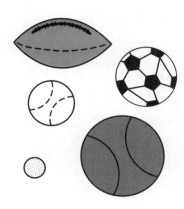

1. What is the title of the graph?

_____

2. What is the label at the left side of the graph?

_____

3. The weights of the balls are given in what units?

_____

4. Which is the heaviest ball?

_____

5. Which ball is the lightest?

_____

6. How much does a volleyball weigh?

_____

7. Which ball weighs 400 grams?

_____

8. How much does a basketball and a baseball weigh together?

_____

Name _____

Pictographs in Class

Read each of the pictographs below. Then fill in the blanks using the information in the graph.

1.

FAVORITE SPORT OF GRADE 6	
basketball	👤 👤 👤 👤
baseball	👤 👤 👤
football	👤 👤 👤 👤 👤 👤
soccer	👤 👤 👤
swimming	👤 👤 👤 👤

Key 👤 = 5 students.

Sixth grade students were asked to choose their _____. The same number of students chose _____ and _____. The most popular sport was _____. The number of students who chose basketball was ____. ____ students chose swimming.

2.

FAVORITE FLAVOR OF ICE CREAM	
chocolate	🍦 🍦 🍦 🍦 🍦 🍦
vanilla	🍦 🍦 🍦 🍦 🍦
strawberry	🍦 🍦 🍦 🍦 🍦 🍦 🍦
chocolate chip	🍦 🍦 🍦
rocky road	🍦 🍦 🍦 🍦 🍦 🍦 🍦 🍦 🍦

Key 🍦 = 2 children.

Mr. McCullough's class surveyed a total of ____ students on their favorite ice cream flavors. They found that the most popular flavor is _____, which ____ students chose. The least favorite flavor is _____. Twice as many students chose _____ as chose _____.

3.

SPELLING TEST SCORES	
Lisa	☆ ☆ ☆ ☆ ☆ ☆ ☆ ☆
Jon	☆ ☆ ☆ ☆ ☆ ☆ ☆ ☆ ☆
Felicia	☆ ☆ ☆ ☆ ☆ ☆ ☆
Raul	☆ ☆ ☆ ☆ ☆ ☆ ☆ ☆
Mica	☆ ☆ ☆ ☆ ☆ ☆
Renee	☆ ☆ ☆ ☆ ☆ ☆ ☆
Allie	☆ ☆ ☆ ☆ ☆ ☆ ☆ ☆ ☆ ☆
Jay	☆ ☆ ☆ ☆ ☆
Tenesha	☆ ☆ ☆ ☆ ☆ ☆
Quentin	☆ ☆ ☆ ☆ ☆ ☆ ☆

Key ☆ = 10 points.

Students in Mr. Freeman's class made a graph of their _____ scores. There were ____ students who got a 90 or above on the test. ____ students scored a 70 or less. The most frequent score was ____. Mica got the same score as ____.

4.

TIME SPENT DOING HOMEWORK	
Maria	⧖ ⧖ ⧖
Philip	⧖ ⧖ ⧖ ⧖ ⧖
Stacy	⧖ ⧖
Ted	⧖ ⧖
Anh	⧖ ⧖ ⧖

Key ⧖ = 10 minutes.

In Mrs. Green's class, ____ students were asked how much time they spent doing their homework. _____ and _____ spent the same amount of time working, The time spent by _____ was 3 times as great as the time spent by _____. _____ worked 10 minutes less than Maria.

Silly Symbols

Ancient people used the letters of their alphabet to make both words and numbers. Imagine using our letters for numbers. Let each letter represent the number under it in the table.

A	B	C	D	E	F	G	H	I	R	S	T	U	V	W	X	Y	Z
1	2	3	4	5	6	7	8	9	10	20	30	40	50	60	70	80	90

So TE = 35   and   D × F = SD
                              4 × 6 = 24

Solve each problem. Write your answers as numbers and letters.

1.

B × E = _____

2 × 5 = _____

2.

C × G = _____

3 × 7 = _____

3.

B × H = _____

2 × 8 = _____

4.

SH ÷ G = _____

28 ÷ 7 = _____

5.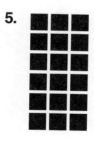

RH ÷ F = _____

18 ÷ ____ = _____

6.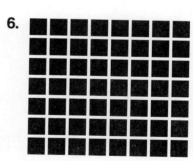

VF ÷ H = _____

56 ÷ ____ = _____

7. F × B = _____

____ × ____ = ____

8. C × E = _____

____ × ____ = ____

9. I × I = _____

____ × ____ = ____

Name _____

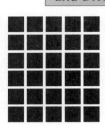
10.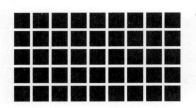

$E \times I =$ _____

_____ $\times$ _____ = _____

11.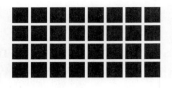

$D \times H =$ _____

_____ $\times$ _____ = _____

12.

$F \times E =$ _____

_____ $\times$ _____ = _____

13.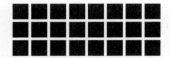

$SD \div C =$ _____

_____ $\div$ _____ = _____

14.

$RB \div D =$ _____

_____ $\div$ _____ = _____

15.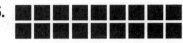

$RH \div B =$ _____

_____ $\div$ _____ = _____

16. $D \times R =$ _____

_____ $\times$ _____ = _____

17. $H \times F =$ _____

_____ $\times$ _____ = _____

18. $H \times I =$ _____

_____ $\times$ _____ = _____

19. $UB \div F =$ _____

_____ $\div$ _____ = _____

20. $TE \div E =$ _____

_____ $\div$ _____ = _____

21. $TF \div D =$ _____

_____ $\div$ _____ = _____

22. $C \times I =$ _____

_____ $\times$ _____ = _____

23. $E \times D =$ _____

_____ $\times$ _____ = _____

24. $B \times G =$ _____

_____ $\times$ _____ = _____

25. $V \div E =$ _____

_____ $\div$ _____ = _____

26. $TF \div F =$ _____

_____ $\div$ _____ = _____

27. $WC \div I =$ _____

_____ $\div$ _____ = _____

Name _____

Number Clues

Choose the number that fits all the clues.

1.

Number Clues
• When you multiply it by 3, the product is 15.
• When you multiply it by 6, the product is 30.

The number is _____.

2.

Number Clues
• When you multiply it by 2, the product is 8.
• When you multiply it by 8, the product is 32.

The number is _____.

3.

Number Clues
• When you multiply it by 4, the product is 36.
• When you multiply it by 7, the product is 63.

The number is _____.

4.

Number Clues
• When you multiply it by 7, the product is 21.
• It is the quotient of 21 divided by 7.

The number is _____.

5.

Number Clues
• When you multiply it by 4, the product is 24.
• It is the quotient of 24 divided by 4.

The number is _____.

6.

Number Clues
• When you multiply it by 6, the product is 48.
• When 48 is divided by it, the quotient is 6.

The number is _____.

7.

Number Clues
• It is the product of 5 and 7.
• When you divide it by 5 the quotient is 7.

The number is _____.

Name _____

Little Rascal

Tina did her homework correctly, but her little brother erased some of the digits. Replace the digits he erased to complete the patterns.

1. $3 \times 6 = 1\ \underline{\ \ }$

$3 \times 6\ \underline{\ \ } = 1\ \underline{\ \ }\ \underline{\ \ }$

$3 \times 6\ \underline{\ \ }\ 0 = 1,\ \underline{\ \ }\ 0\ 0$

2. $\underline{\ \ } \times 2 = 1\ 6$

$\underline{\ \ } \times 2\ 0 = 1\ 6\ \underline{\ \ }$

$\underline{\ \ } \times 2\ 0\ 0 = 1,\ 6\ \underline{\ \ }\ \underline{\ \ }$

3. $4 \times \underline{\ \ } = 2\ 8$

$4 \times \underline{\ \ }\ \underline{\ \ } = 2\ 8\ 0$

$4 \times \underline{\ \ }\ 0\ 0 = 2,\ 8\ \underline{\ \ }\ \underline{\ \ }$

4. $\underline{\ \ } \times 5 = 3\ 0$

$\underline{\ \ } \times 5\ 0 = 3\ \underline{\ \ }\ \underline{\ \ }$

$\underline{\ \ } \times 5\ 0\ 0 = 3,\ \underline{\ \ }\ \underline{\ \ }\ \underline{\ \ }$

5. $2 \times \underline{\ \ } = 1\ 8$

$2 \times \underline{\ \ }\ \underline{\ \ } = 1\ 8\ \underline{\ \ }$

$\underline{\ \ } \times \underline{\ \ }\ 0\ 0 = 1,\ \underline{\ \ }\ \underline{\ \ }\ \underline{\ \ }$

6. $\underline{\ \ } \times 7 = 3\ 5$

$\underline{\ \ } \times \underline{\ \ }\ \underline{\ \ } = 3\ \underline{\ \ }\ 0$

$5 \times \underline{\ \ }\ \underline{\ \ }\ 0 = 3,\ 5\ \underline{\ \ }\ \underline{\ \ }$

7. $\underline{\ \ } \times 5 = \underline{\ \ }\ \underline{\ \ }$

$\underline{\ \ } \times 5\ 0 = 4\ 0\ 0$

$\underline{\ \ } \times \underline{\ \ }\ 0\ 0 = 4,\ 0\ \underline{\ \ }\ \underline{\ \ }$

8. $9 \times \underline{\ \ } = \underline{\ \ }\ \underline{\ \ }$

$9 \times \underline{\ \ }\ 0 = 3\ 6\ \underline{\ \ }$

$9 \times \underline{\ \ }\ 0\ 0 = \underline{\ \ },\ \underline{\ \ }\ 0\ 0$

9. $7 \times \underline{\ \ } = 5\ 6$

$7 \times \underline{\ \ }\ 0 = \underline{\ \ }\ \underline{\ \ }\ 0$

$7 \times \underline{\ \ }\ \underline{\ \ }\ 0 = \underline{\ \ },\ \underline{\ \ }\ \underline{\ \ }\ \underline{\ \ }$

10. $\underline{\ \ } \times \underline{\ \ } = 2\ 7$

$\underline{\ \ } \times 9\ 0 = 2\ \underline{\ \ }\ \underline{\ \ }$

$\underline{\ \ } \times \underline{\ \ }\ 0\ 0 = \underline{\ \ },\ 7\ \underline{\ \ }\ \underline{\ \ }$

11. $\underline{\ \ } \times 7 = \underline{\ \ }\ \underline{\ \ }$

$\underline{\ \ } \times 7\ 0 = 4\ 2\ \underline{\ \ }$

$\underline{\ \ } \times 7\ 0\ 0 = 4,\ 2\ \underline{\ \ }\ \underline{\ \ }$

12. $9 \times \underline{\ \ } = \underline{\ \ }\ \underline{\ \ }$

$9 \times \underline{\ \ }\ 0 = \underline{\ \ }\ \underline{\ \ }\ \underline{\ \ }$

$9 \times \underline{\ \ }\ \underline{\ \ }\ \underline{\ \ } = \underline{\ \ },\ \underline{\ \ }\ 0\ 0$

Name _____

Model Matching

Find the model that matches each problem. Write the letter
of the model next to the problem. Then use the model to find
the product.

1.
$$\begin{array}{r} 14 \\ \times\ 2 \\ \hline \end{array}$$
Model _____

2.
$$\begin{array}{r} 16 \\ \times\ 3 \\ \hline \end{array}$$
Model _____

3.
$$\begin{array}{r} 23 \\ \times\ 4 \\ \hline \end{array}$$
Model _____

4.
$$\begin{array}{r} 26 \\ \times\ 3 \\ \hline \end{array}$$
Model _____

5.
$$\begin{array}{r} 17 \\ \times\ 4 \\ \hline \end{array}$$
Model _____

6.
$$\begin{array}{r} 15 \\ \times\ 3 \\ \hline \end{array}$$
Model _____

A.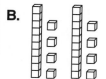

B.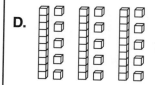

C.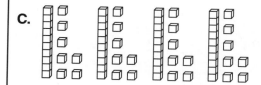

D.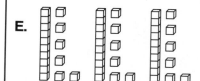

E.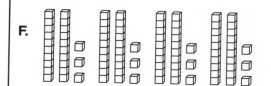

F.

Facts Search

Find three numbers across or down that can make a
multiplication fact. Circle the numbers. Write the operation
and equal sign. There are 16 facts and one is shown. A number
may be used more than once.

8	(5 × 5 = 25)			8	15	9
	7	8	6	12	3	2
5	5	1	0	4	8	3
	2	6	12	22	8	5
15	9	7	2	32	3	0
	24	3	9	27	1	10
10	45	4	7	28	3	4
	9	7	18	8	8	2
1	5	9	6	4	3	12
	9	15	17	24	9	0
7	3	36	3	5	3	15
	81	64	20	8	3	24
30	6	2	18	14	35	45
	6	1	6	7	7	49

Name _____

Shortcut

Use the patterns to find the products. List the ones with the same product.

1. A 6×10

_____

D 60×10

_____

G 600×10

_____

B 6×100

_____

E 60×100

_____

H 600×100

_____

C $6 \times 1,000$

_____

F $60 \times 1,000$

_____

Same as B: _____

Same as C: _____

Same as F: _____

---

2. A 10×3

_____

D 100×3

_____

G $1,000 \times 3$

_____

B 10×30

_____

E 100×30

_____

H $1,000 \times 30$

_____

C 10×300

_____

F 100×300

_____

Same as B: _____

Same as C: _____

Same as F: _____

---

3. A 7×10

_____

D $7 \times 1,000$

_____

G $70 \times 1,000$

_____

B 7×100

_____

E 70×100

_____

H 700×100

_____

C 70×10

_____

F 700×10

_____

Same as B: _____

Same as D: _____

Same as G: _____

Food Fuel

You get calories from food. You then burn calories when you walk, run, or even sleep. A man burns about 65 calories an hour sleeping and a woman burns about 55.

Use the information in the paragraph and in the table. You may use base-ten blocks to solve.

FOOD CALORIES PER SERVING	
Food	Calories
Cheddar cheese	95
Bologna	57
Hard-cooked egg	75
Grapes	35
Corn tortilla	65
Carrots	30

1. About how many calories does a man burn by sleeping 3 hours?

_____

2. About how many calories does a woman burn by sleeping 4 hours?

_____

3. How many calories are in 5 servings of carrots?

_____

4. How many calories are in 2 servings of bologna?

_____

5. How many calories are in 4 servings of corn tortillas?

_____

6. How many calories are in 5 servings of grapes?

_____

7. How many calories are in 4 servings of cheddar cheese?

_____

8. How many calories are in 3 servings of carrots?

_____

Paper Products

- Write the numbers 0–9 on slips of paper.
- Place them in a small bowl.
- Draw a number from the bowl and write it in one box of the first game. Replace the paper in the bowl. Continue drawing until all the boxes are filled, trying to make the largest product possible.
- When a row is filled, estimate each product and guess which one is the greatest product.
- Then find each product. You win if your guess was correct.

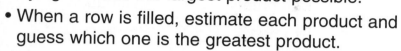

Game 1

× ☐   × ☐   × ☐   × ☐

Estimate: _____   Estimate: _____   Estimate: _____   Estimate: _____

Product: _____   Product: _____   Product: _____   Product: _____

Greatest Product Guess: _____   Actual: _____

Game 2

× ☐   × ☐   × ☐   × ☐

Estimate: _____   Estimate: _____   Estimate: _____   Estimate: _____

Product: _____   Product: _____   Product: _____   Product: _____

Greatest Product Guess: _____   Actual: _____

Name _____

Game 3

☐ ☐
× ☐
‾‾‾‾‾‾‾

☐ ☐
× ☐
‾‾‾‾‾‾‾

☐ ☐
× ☐
‾‾‾‾‾‾‾

☐ ☐
× ☐
‾‾‾‾‾‾‾

Estimate: _____   Estimate: _____   Estimate: _____   Estimate: _____

Product: _____   Product: _____   Product: _____   Product: _____

Greatest Product Guess: _____   Actual: _____

Game 4

☐ ☐
× ☐
‾‾‾‾‾‾‾

☐ ☐
× ☐
‾‾‾‾‾‾‾

☐ ☐
× ☐
‾‾‾‾‾‾‾

☐ ☐
× ☐
‾‾‾‾‾‾‾

Estimate: _____   Estimate: _____   Estimate: _____   Estimate: _____

Product: _____   Product: _____   Product: _____   Product: _____

Greatest Product Guess: _____   Actual: _____

Game 5

☐ ☐
× ☐
‾‾‾‾‾‾‾

☐ ☐
× ☐
‾‾‾‾‾‾‾

☐ ☐
× ☐
‾‾‾‾‾‾‾

☐ ☐
× ☐
‾‾‾‾‾‾‾

Estimate: _____   Estimate: _____   Estimate: _____   Estimate: _____

Product: _____   Product: _____   Product: _____   Product: _____

Greatest Product Guess: _____   Actual: _____

IN346 Check What You Know Enrichment

Name _____

Picture That

Use the facts in the picture to solve each problem.

1.

Marty spent $8 for drinks. How much did each drink cost?

_____

2.

How many bags can you fill with 4 treats in each?

_____

3.

15 feet

3 feet

How many of the shorter pieces can you cut from the longer piece?

_____

4.

18 ounces   6 ounces

How many glasses can you fill from the pitcher?

_____

5.

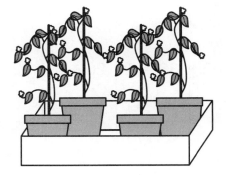

How many boxes do you need to buy to hold 20 plants?

_____

6.

Shirt: $5

receipt
----
total $30

How many T-shirts were bought?

_____

The Bear Facts

Why don't bears wear shoes?
Solve the puzzle to find out.

Find each quotient. Write the quotient on the line below the problem. Use the chart to match the quotient with a letter. Then write the letter on the line below the quotient.

A	F	B	E	H	R	P	T	Y
1	2	3	4	5	6	7	8	9

$32 \div 4$ | $40 \div 8$ | $24 \div 6$ | $18 \div 2$

____ | ____ | ____ | ____

____ ____ ____ ____

$21 \div 3$ | $48 \div 8$ | $16 \div 4$ | $18 \div 9$ | $32 \div 8$ | $42 \div 7$

____ | ____ | ____ | ____ | ____ | ____

____ ____ ____ ____ ____ ____

$27 \div 9$ | $28 \div 7$ | $12 \div 12$ | $54 \div 9$ | $16 \div 8$ | $36 \div 9$ | $20 \div 5$ | $72 \div 9$

____ | ____ | ____ | ____ | ____ | ____ | ____ | ____

____ ____ ____ ____   ____ ____ ____ ____

IN348 Check What You Know Enrichment

Name _____

Starry Quotients

Do the following for each exercise:
• Write a division expression for the model.
• Rewrite the expression, using compatible numbers.
• Use the compatible numbers to estimate the quotient.
• Use the model to find the quotient and remainder.
• Compare the quotient to the estimate. Answer the question.
  Write *yes* or *no*.

1.

Division expression: _____ ÷ _____

Compatible number expression:

_____ ÷ _____

Estimate: _____

Quotient and remainder: _____ r_____

Is the quotient close to the estimate?

_____

2.

Division expression: _____ ÷ _____

Compatible number expression:

_____ ÷ _____

Estimate: _____

Quotient and remainder: _____ r_____

Is the quotient close to the estimate?

_____

3.

Division expression: _____ ÷ _____

Compatible number expression:

_____ ÷ _____

Estimate: _____

Quotient and remainder: _____ r_____

Is the quotient close to the estimate?

_____

4.

Division expression: _____ ÷ _____

Compatible number expression:

_____ ÷ _____

Estimate: _____

Quotient and remainder: _____ r_____

Is the quotient close to the estimate?

_____

Check What You Know Enrichment IN349

Name _____

5.

Division expression: _____ ÷ _____

Compatible number expression:

_____ ÷ _____

Estimate: _____

Quotient and remainder: _____ r_____

Is the quotient close to the estimate?

_____

6.

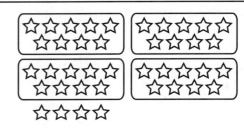

Division expression: _____ ÷ _____

Compatible number expression:

_____ ÷ _____

Estimate: _____

Quotient and remainder: _____ r_____

Is the quotient close to the estimate?

_____

7.

Division expression: _____ ÷ _____

Compatible number expression:

_____ ÷ _____

Estimate: _____

Quotient and remainder: _____ r_____

Is the quotient close to the estimate?

_____

8.

Division expression: _____ ÷ _____

Compatible number expression:

_____ ÷ _____

Estimate: _____

Quotient and remainder: _____ r_____

Is the quotient close to the estimate?

_____

9.

Division expression: _____ ÷ _____

Compatible number expression:

_____ ÷ _____

Estimate: _____

Quotient and remainder: _____ r_____

Is the quotient close to the estimate?

_____

A Riddle of Zeros

What did the 0 say to the 4?

Find each quotient using mental math. Then look in the code box to find the letter that matches the answer. Write the matching letter in the circle next to the answer. BEWARE! Not all of the answers will be used.

1. $16 \div 2$ = _____ ○

2. $240 \div 4$ = _____

3. $800 \div 2$ = _____ ○

4. $72 \div 8$ = _____ ○

5. $1,600 \div 8$ = _____

6. $640 \div 8$ = _____ ○

7. $2,800 \div 4$ = _____

8. $900 \div 3$ = _____ ○

9. $350 \div 5$ = _____ ○

10. $160 \div 8$ = _____ ○

11. $4,200 \div 7$ = _____ ○

12. $150 \div 3$ = _____ ○

13. $8,100 \div 9$ = _____

14. $720 \div 8$ = _____ ○

15. $48 \div 8$ = _____ ○

16. $4,500 \div 9$ = _____ ○

17. $320 \div 8$ = _____ ○

18. $900 \div 9$ = _____ ○

19. $270 \div 9$ = _____ ○

20. $5,600 \div 7$ = _____

Code				
6 = U	20 = U	50 = D	90 = N	400 = A
8 = I	30 = R	70 = O	100 = E	500 = M
9 = M	40 = B	80 = A	300 = R	600 = N

Name _____

Number, Please!

Solve each riddle. Shade the corresponding number in the picture.

1. My divisor is 6.
   I am greater than 2 × 6.
   I am less than 20.
   My remainder is 4.
   What dividend am I?

   _____

2. My divisor is 4.
   I am greater than 30.
   I am less than 9 × 4.
   My remainder is 1.
   What dividend am I?

   _____

3. My divisor is 9.
   I am greater than 50.
   I am less than 6 × 9.
   My remainder is 6.
   What dividend am I?

   _____

4. My divisor is 8.
   I am greater than 10.
   I am less than 8 × 2.
   My remainder is 7.
   What dividend am I?

   _____

5. My divisor is 7.
   I am greater than 4 × 7.
   I am less than 5 × 7.
   My remainder is 2.
   What dividend am I?

   _____

6. My divisor is 5.
   I am greater than 8 × 5.
   I am less than 9 × 5.
   My remainder is 4.
   What dividend am I?

   _____

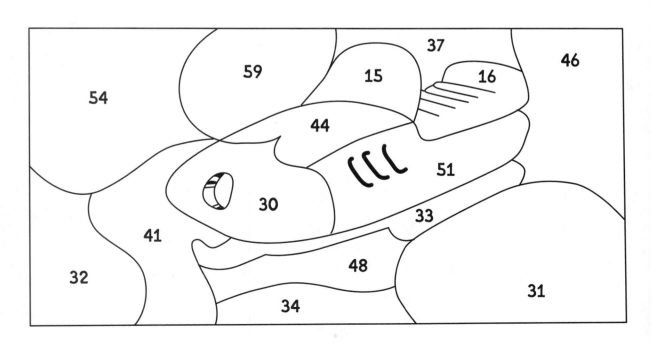

IN352 Check What You Know Enrichment

Name _____

Sporty Products

Solve.

1. A baseball team has 9 players. How many players are there on 4 baseball teams?

   _____

2. A park has 6 baseball fields. Each field has 4 bases. How many bases are in the park?

   _____

3. A Little League baseball team played 7 innings. They scored the same number of runs each inning and 21 runs in all. How many runs did the team score in one inning?

   _____

4. A basketball game has 4 quarters. The Cubs scored 7 points each quarter. How many points did the team score in all?

   _____

5. A baseball field has 4 bases. The park manager has 20 bases. How many baseball fields can she make?

   _____

6. The Cubs basketball team has 2 totally different starting lineups. They have 10 players in all. How many players are in a starting lineup?

   _____

7. Two teams scored a total of 18 points in the first half of a basketball game. At the end of the half, they were tied. How many points did each team score?

   _____

8. A gym has 5 bags of basketballs with the same number of balls in each. It has 25 basketballs in all. How many are in each bag?

   _____

A Sad Bird

What kind of bird is sad? Solve the puzzle to find out. Shade the squares and then write the letter formed in the blank below.

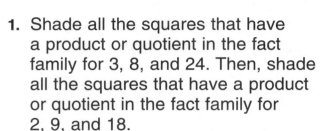

1. Shade all the squares that have a product or quotient in the fact family for 3, 8, and 24. Then, shade all the squares that have a product or quotient in the fact family for 2, 9, and 18.

4 × 6	3 × 8	2 × 9	24 ÷ 4	3 × 6
3 × 4	8 × 3	6 × 3	3 × 8	5 × 3
16 ÷ 2	24 ÷ 3	18 ÷ 2	14 ÷ 2	3 × 9
2 × 8	24 ÷ 8	18 ÷ 6	18 ÷ 9	6 × 4
5 × 7	2 × 9	9 × 2	21 ÷ 7	18 ÷ 3

2. Shade all the squares that have a product or quotient in the fact family for 4, 7, and 28. Then, shade all the squares that have a product or quotient in the fact family for 5, 6, and 30.

4 × 7	5 × 8	18 ÷ 9	24 ÷ 4	3 × 6
6 × 5	8 × 3	6 × 4	3 × 9	5 × 3
28 ÷ 7	25 ÷ 5	14 ÷ 2	15 ÷ 3	3 × 9
5 × 6	24 ÷ 8	48 ÷ 6	18 ÷ 3	6 × 4
7 × 4	30 ÷ 6	30 ÷ 5	28 ÷ 4	36 ÷ 4

3. Shade all the squares that have a product or quotient in the fact family for 3, 7, and 21. Then, shade all the squares that have a product or quotient in the fact family for 4, 9, and 36.

5 × 6	4 × 9	18 ÷ 2	36 ÷ 4	3 × 4
3 × 8	7 × 3	6 × 3	3 × 7	5 × 5
16 ÷ 2	21 ÷ 3	18 ÷ 2	21 ÷ 7	3 × 9
2 × 9	36 ÷ 4	18 ÷ 6	36 ÷ 9	6 × 7
5 × 7	3 × 7	9 × 4	21 ÷ 7	18 ÷ 3

4. Shade all the squares that have a product or quotient in the fact family for 6, 8, and 48. Then, shade all the squares that have a product or quotient in the fact family for 5, 9, and 45.

3 × 8	6 × 8	5 × 9	48 ÷ 6	24 ÷ 4
36 ÷ 6	9 × 5	8 × 3	6 × 4	3 × 9
9 × 6	48 ÷ 8	45 ÷ 5	14 ÷ 2	15 ÷ 3
24 ÷ 6	8 × 6	24 ÷ 8	42 ÷ 6	18 ÷ 3
5 × 8	5 × 9	48 ÷ 6	45 ÷ 9	28 ÷ 4

A _____ _____ _____ _____ bird is sad.
     1   2   3   4

Name _____

Find the Figures

Look carefully at the picture below. Use a blue crayon and circle the right angles. Circle the acute angles in red. Circle the obtuse angles in green. Circle the line segments in yellow. Circle the rays in purple.

Name _____

Straw Angles

Use straws to make each angle. Then compare your straw angle to a corner of your desk. Tell if each angle is a *right* angle, *greater than* a right angle, or *less than* a right angle.

1.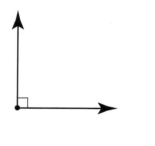

_____

2.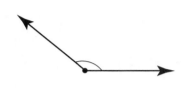

_____

3.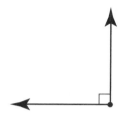

_____

4.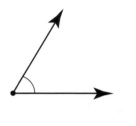

_____

5.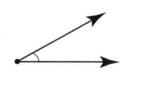

_____

6.

_____

7.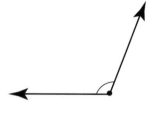

_____

8.

_____

9.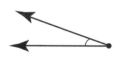

_____

10.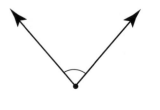

_____

11.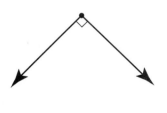

_____

12.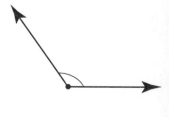

_____

Name _____

What's the Angle?

Find the angle in the design that matches the number below.
Tell if each angle is *acute*, *right*, or *obtuse*.

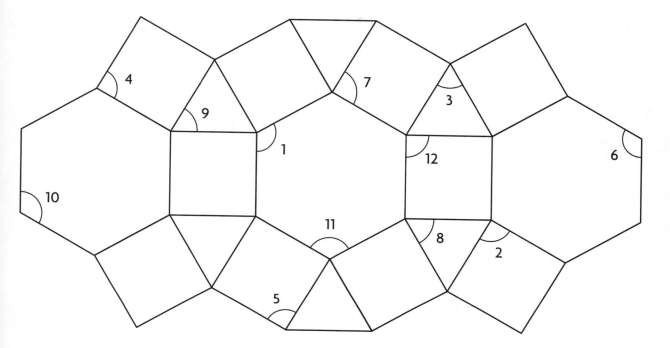

1. _____   2. _____   3. _____

4. _____   5. _____   6. _____

7. _____   8. _____   9. _____

10. _____   11. _____   12. _____

Plane Figure Puzzle

Read the clues. Color the figures.
Then write the name of each figure.

1. If a plane figure has 4 right angles and 2 pairs of equal sides, color it blue.

2. If a plane figure has 2 right angles and 5 sides, color it red.

3. If a plane figure has no right angles and 3 equal sides, color it green.

4. If a plane figure has no right angles and no sides that are equal, color it yellow.

5. If a plane figure has 4 right angles and 4 sides that are equal, color it brown.

6. If a plane figure has 2 equal sides and 3 angles less than right angles, color it pink.

7. If a plane figure has no equal sides and no angles, color it orange.

8. If a plane figure has one right angle, color it purple.

9. If a plane figure has 4 equal sides and no right angles, color it gray.

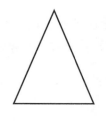

_____   _____

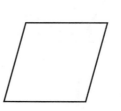
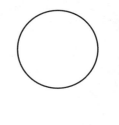

_____   _____

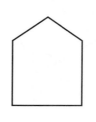
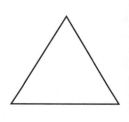

_____   _____

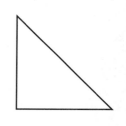

_____   _____

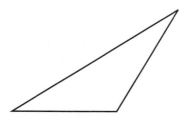

_____   _____

Name _____

Cut It Out!

Trace the following figures onto thin paper and cut them out.
Copy the letters onto your cut-out figures.

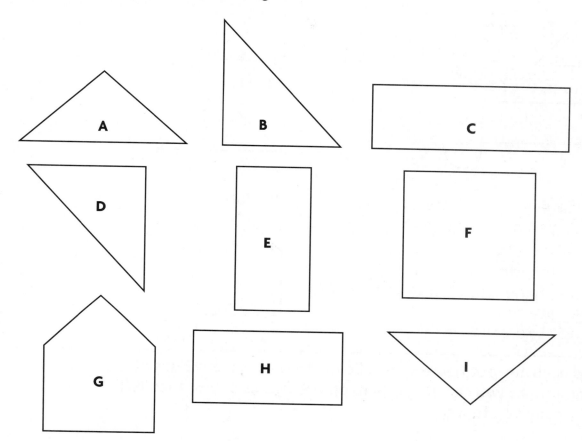

Are the figures the same size and shape? Put your cut-out figures
together to find out. Write *yes* or *no*.

1. A and D

_____

2. B and D

_____

3. A and B

_____

4. A and I

_____

5. B and I

_____

6. C and E

_____

7. C and H

_____

8. C and F

_____

9. E and H

_____

Name _____

Use your cut-out figures to draw the slide, flip or turn.

10. slide

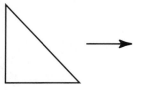

11. flip

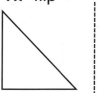

12. turn

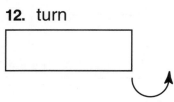

13. flip

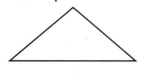

14. slide

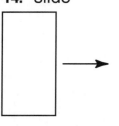

15. turn

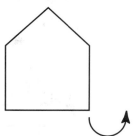

Fold each cut-out figure shown below to find as many lines of
symmetry as you can. Draw them on the figures below, then tell
how many you found.

16.

There is _____ line
of symmetry.

17.

There are _____
lines of symmetry.

18.

There are _____
lines of symmetry.

19.

There are _____
lines of symmetry.

20.

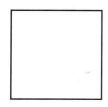

There are _____
lines of symmetry.

21.

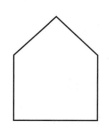

There is _____ line
of symmetry.

Place to Place

Use the number line to name the number each place represents.

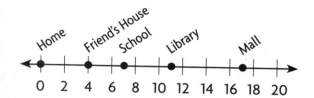

Example: Home is 0.

1. Friend's House _____

2. Library _____

3. School _____

4. Mall _____

Use the number line to compare. Write $<$, $>$, or $=$.

5. Home to   Home to
   Sten   Ada

   35 ◯ 20

6. Home to   Home to
   McElroy   Colby

   85 ◯ 60

7. Home to   Home to
   Ada   Colby

   20 ◯ 60

8. Home to   Home to
   Sten   Payne

   35 ◯ 42

Use the number line to add and subtract.

9. How much farther is it from Home to School than from Home to your Aunt's House?

   $7 - 2 =$ _____

10. How far is it from Home to your Friend's House and from there to School?

    $4 + 3 =$ _____

11. How much farther is it from Home to the Store than from Home to School?

    $10 - 7 =$ _____

Name _____

Being Happy

Solve the puzzle to find something happy.

Connect each set of points in the order they are listed.

1. (0, 5)
(2, 7)
(5, 7)
(7, 5)
(7, 3)
(5, 1)
(2, 1)
(0, 3)
(0, 5)

2. (2, 5)
(2, 6)
(3, 6)
(3, 5)
(2, 5)

3. (5, 6)
(4, 6)
(4, 5)
(5, 5)
(5, 6)

4. (1, 3)
(2, 2)
(5, 2)
(6, 3)

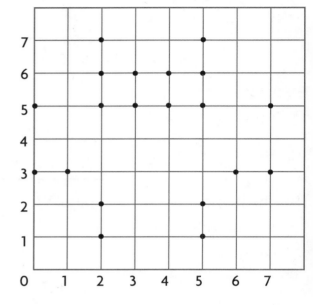

5. Make your own puzzle using the grid on the right.
List the coordinates below.

_____

_____

_____

_____

_____

_____

_____

_____

_____

Name _____

They're All Equal

1. Divide the whole into equal parts to show fourths,
   four different ways.

2. Shade each whole above to show $\frac{3}{4}$.

_____

3. Divide the whole into equal parts to show thirds,
   two different ways.

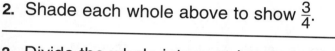

4. Shade each whole above to show $\frac{2}{3}$.

_____

5. Divide the whole into equal parts to show sixths,
   four different ways.

6. Shade each whole above to show $\frac{1}{6}$.

_____

7. Divide the whole into equal parts to show halves,
   four different ways.

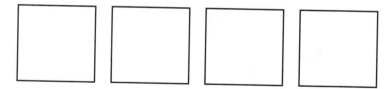

8. Shade each whole above to show $\frac{1}{2}$.

Name _____

How Many Parts?

Materials: Pattern blocks, yarn

Take 10 pattern blocks. Use the blocks and write a fraction for each.

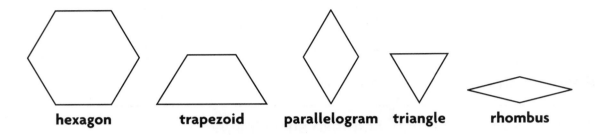

| hexagon | trapezoid | parallelogram | triangle | rhombus |

1. What fraction of the blocks are △ ?

   _____

2. What fraction of the blocks are ◇ ?

   _____

3. What fraction of the blocks are ⏢ ?

   _____

4. What fraction of the blocks are ▢ ?

   _____

Use yarn to make 5 groups with 2 blocks in each group.

5. What fraction of the blocks is in 3 groups?

   _____

6. What fraction of the blocks is in 5 groups?

   _____

7. How many blocks are in $\frac{2}{5}$?

   _____

8. How many blocks are in $\frac{4}{5}$?

   _____

IN364 **Check What You Know Enrichment**

How Many?

Complete to show the fraction of the clock face that is shaded.
Then use <, >, or = to compare the shaded areas.

1.
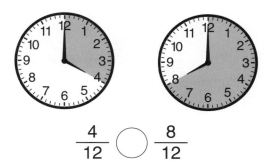

$$\frac{4}{12} \bigcirc \frac{8}{12}$$

2.
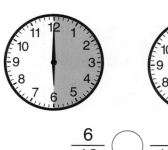

$$\frac{6}{12} \bigcirc \frac{}{12}$$

3.
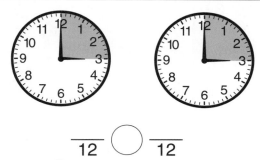

$$\frac{}{12} \bigcirc \frac{}{12}$$

4.
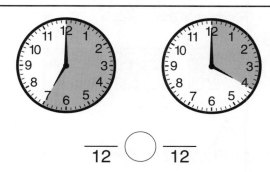

$$\frac{}{12} \bigcirc \frac{}{12}$$

5.

$$\frac{}{12} \bigcirc \frac{}{12}$$

6.
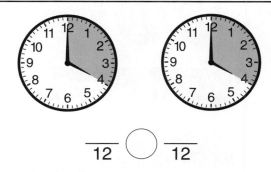

$$\frac{}{12} \bigcirc \frac{}{12}$$

7.
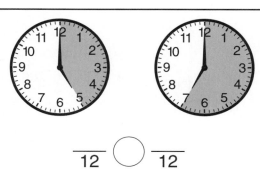

$$\frac{}{12} \bigcirc \frac{}{12}$$

8.
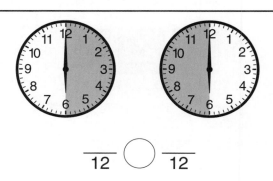

$$\frac{}{12} \bigcirc \frac{}{12}$$

Name _____

All Mixed Up!

Match the model to a mixed number and the mixed number
to a fraction. Draw lines to each.

1. 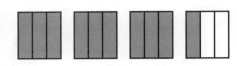 $2\frac{3}{4}$ $\frac{8}{3}$

2.  $1\frac{5}{6}$ $\frac{7}{2}$

3. 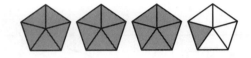 $3\frac{1}{3}$ $\frac{11}{6}$

4. 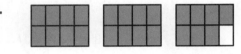 $3\frac{3}{8}$ $\frac{16}{5}$

5.  $2\frac{1}{4}$ $\frac{11}{4}$

6.  $2\frac{7}{8}$ $\frac{9}{4}$

7.  $3\frac{1}{5}$ $\frac{23}{8}$

8.  $2\frac{2}{3}$ $\frac{10}{3}$

9.  $2\frac{1}{2}$ $\frac{27}{8}$

10. 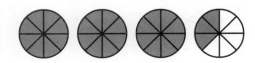 $3\frac{1}{2}$ $\frac{5}{2}$

IN366 Check What You Know Enrichment

Name _____

What Are the Chances?

Use paper clips and pencils to make two spinners.

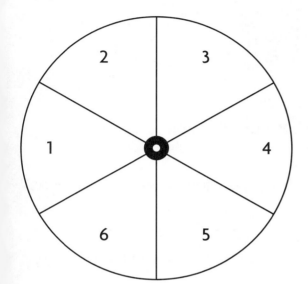 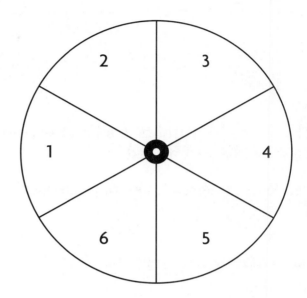

1. Spin both pointers once. What is the sum of the numbers?
   What are all of the possible sums?

   _____

2. Spin both pointers 25 times. Complete this table. Make
   a tally mark to record the sum of the two numbers you get.

Sum	2	3										
Tally												

3. Which sum did you get most often?

   _____

4. Which sums did you not get at all or did you get least
   often?

   _____

Name _____

Legs and Laundry

There are _____ shirts in all on the clothesline. Write a fraction
to show the part named.

1. What fraction have long sleeves?

_____

2. What fraction have short sleeves?

_____

3. What fraction have numbers?

_____

4. What fraction have stripes?

_____

5. What fraction have numbers or
stripes?

_____

6. What fraction have both
numbers and short sleeves?

_____

There are _____ animals in all. Write a fraction to show the part
named.

7. What fraction have exactly 4 legs?

_____

8. What fraction has exactly 2 legs?

_____

9. What fraction have 4 or more legs?

_____

10. What fraction have fur?

_____

Name _____

Map Maker

You can use a ruler to measure distances on a map.

To measure the distance between two points on Karen's map, place one end of your ruler on the point next to the first place. Then find the mark on your ruler that is closest to the point that you are measuring to.

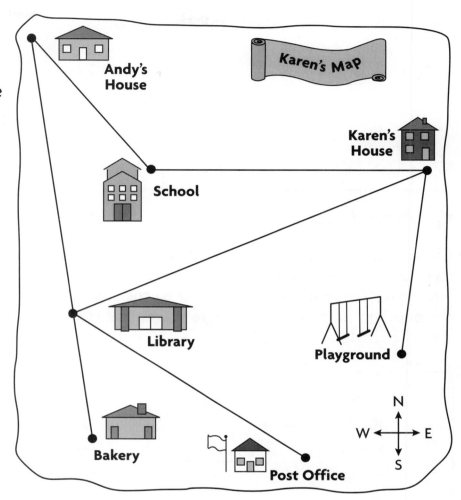

Karen's Map

Andy's House

Karen's House

School

Library

Playground

Bakery

Post Office

N
W ← → E
S

Use your ruler to measure the distance to the nearest half inch.

1. from Karen's house to library

2. from library to post office

_____

_____

3. from Andy's house to bakery

4. from Andy's house to school

_____

_____

5. from Karen's house to playground

6. from bakery to library

_____

_____

Name _____

Lost Digits

Be a math detective and find the missing digits.

1.

```
    3 ☐
  ×   8
  ☐  8  8
```

2.

```
  5,  2   8   0
      ×      ☐
  2  1,  ☐  ☐  0
```

3.

```
      1   2
      ×      ☐
  ☐  0  ☐
```

Quotient Map

Choose an empty triangle below that has two arrows pointing to it. Look at the numbers in the boxes pointing to the triangle you chose. Divide the larger number by the smaller number. Put the quotient in the empty triangle you chose. Fill in all the empty triangles.

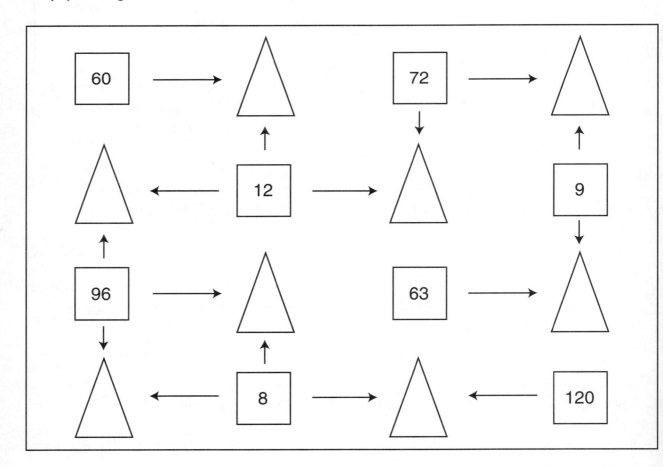

A Turtle Crawl

A turtle crawls from point A to point H.

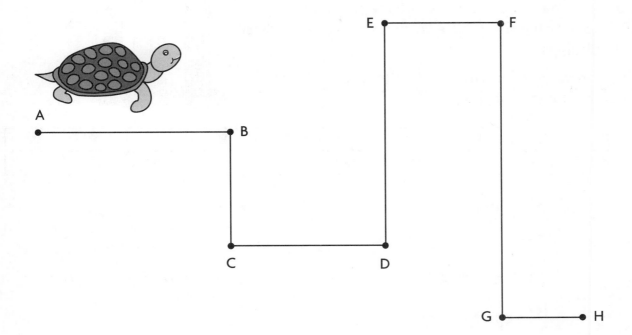

Use your centimeter ruler to find each distance.

1. A to B

_____

2. B to C

_____

3. C to D

_____

4. D to E

_____

5. F to G

_____

6. G to H

_____

7. B to F

_____

8. D to G

_____

Name _____

Going Up, and Up, and Up. . .

The two tallest buildings in the world are in Kuala Lumpur, Malaysia. They actually are two towers that are the same height. Each is 1,483 feet tall and has 88 floors. Solve the puzzle to find the name of these tall buildings.

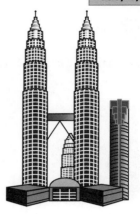

Find the value of n. Then write the letter of that value to the left of the problem.

A	E	I	N	O	P	R	S	T	W
70	100	380	40	38	7,000	1,000	400	10	4

_____ 1. $7 \times 1,000 = n$

  $n =$ _____

_____ 2. $15 \times n = 1,500$

  $n =$ _____

_____ 3. $30 \times n = 300$

  $n =$ _____

_____ 4. $n \times 8 = 8,000$

  $n =$ _____

_____ 5. $100 \times n = 3,800$

  $n =$ _____

_____ 6. $n \times 10 = 400$

  $n =$ _____

_____ 7. $100 \times n = 7,000$

  $n =$ _____

_____ 8. $10 \times n = 4,000$

  $n =$ _____

_____ 9. $590 \times n = 5,900$

  $n =$ _____

_____ 10. $n \times 1,000 = 38,000$

  $n =$ _____

_____ 11. $n \times 1,000 = 4,000$

  $n =$ _____

_____ 12. $7 \times n = 700$

  $n =$ _____

_____ 13. $48 \times n = 48,000$

  $n =$ _____

_____ 14. $100 \times n = 40,000$

  $n =$ _____

Name _____

Pieces and Parts

Write a decimal to show what part of each grid is
shaded and what part is not shaded.

1.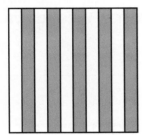

Shaded: _____

Not shaded: _____

2.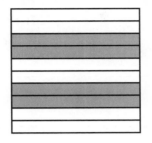

Shaded: _____

Not shaded: _____

3.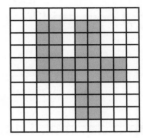

Shaded: _____

Not shaded: _____

4.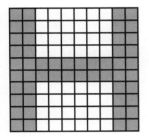

Shaded: _____

Not shaded: _____

5.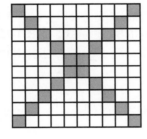

Shaded: _____

Not shaded: _____

6.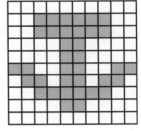

Shaded: _____

Not shaded: _____

Draw and shade a design for each grid. Then write a
decimal to show what part of the grid is shaded
and what part is not shaded.

7.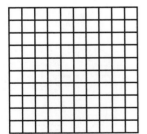

Shaded: _____

Not shaded: _____

8.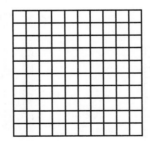

Shaded: _____

Not shaded: _____

9.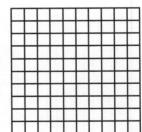

Shaded: _____

Not shaded: _____

Check What You Know Enrichment IN373

Riddle Me This

Answer the riddles.

1. I am a coin. I equal 0.1 of a dollar. What coin am I?

    _____

2. I am a decimal. I am four dollars and thirty-five cents. What decimal am I?

    _____

3. I am a decimal. I am two dollars and seventy-five cents. What decimal am I?

    _____

4. I am a coin. I equal 0.01 of a dollar. What coin am I?

    _____

5. I am a decimal. I have two tenths. What decimal am I?

    _____

6. I am a decimal. I have seven tenths. What decimal am I?

    _____

7. I am a decimal. I have sixty-four hundredths. What decimal am I?

    _____

8. I am a decimal. I have twenty-three hundredths. What decimal am I?

    _____

9. I am a fraction. My denominator is 100. I equal $\frac{4}{10}$. What fraction am I?

    _____

10. I am a fraction. My denominator is 100. I equal $\frac{9}{10}$. What fraction am I?

     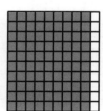

    _____

Name _____

Methuselah

The oldest living tree is named Methuselah. Methuselah lives in California and is estimated to be about 4,700 years old. That's a lot of birthdays! What kind of tree is Methuselah? Solve the puzzle to find out. Write the letter of each answer above the exercise number below.

Round each to the nearest hundred.

1. 687 _____

2. 425 _____

3. 252 _____

4. 245 _____

5. 479 _____

Round each to the nearest ten.

6. 321 _____

7. 148 _____

8. 575 _____

9. 416 _____

10. 412 _____

11. 235 _____

B	580
C	420
E	700
I	410
L	500
N	150
O	200
P	240
R	300
S	400
T	320

___ ___ ___ ___ ___ ___ ___   ___ ___ ___ ___   ___ ___ ___ ___
 8   3 10   2   6   5   1   9   4   7   1   11 10   7   1

Name _____

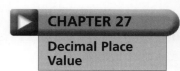
A Place for a Pattern

In each box, find the value of the digit 1. If the digit represents tenths, color the box red. If the digit represents hundredths, color the box blue. If the digit represents thousandths, color the box yellow. Look for a pattern when you complete the coloring.

0.157	0.13	0.017	0.149	0.102
0.143	0.316	0.301	0.214	0.18
0.91	0.551	0.413	0.291	0.818
0.001	0.512	0.071	0.013	0.481
0.619	0.081	0.183	0.781	0.51
0.221	0.124	0.109	0.14	0.471

Name _____

Perimeter Puzzles

Count to find the perimeter of each figure. Then order the
perimeters from least to greatest, and use the letters of each
problem to solve the riddle.

1. **H**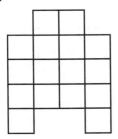

2. **E**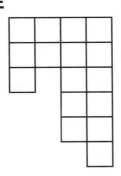

3. **L**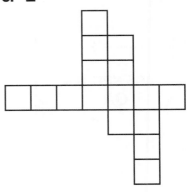

4. **R**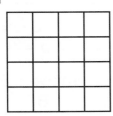

5. **P**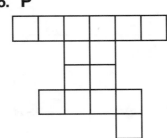

6. **N**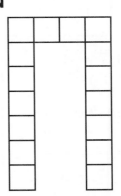

7. **A**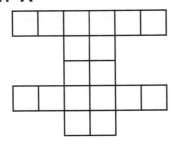

8. **E**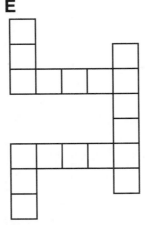

9. **A**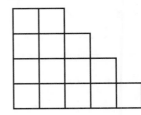

How do rabbits travel?

In a ___ ___ ___ ___ ___ ___ ___ ___ ___
    16   18   20   22   26   28   30   34   38

Name _____

Overall Expressions

Find the value of each expression. If the answer is incorrect, cross out the box. Then write the remaining letters on the lines below to solve the riddle.

$3 + 4 + a$ if $a = 2$ answer: 9 CA	$b + 3 + 1$ if $b = 6$ answer: 12 MA	$5 + c + 7$ if $c = 5$ answer: 32 TH	$d + 3 + 8$ if $d = 9$ answer: 20 BB
$5 + 8 + e$ if $e = 7$ answer: 21 IS	$f + 1 + 2$ if $f = 8$ answer: 11 AG	$5 + 4 + g$ if $g = 1$ answer: 9 MY	$8 + 1 + h + 3$ if $h = 2$ answer: 13 BE
$j + 7 + 3 + 1$ if $j = 4$ answer: 14 ST	$k + 6 + 3$ if $k = 9$ answer: 19 SU	$8 + m + 6$ if $m = 9$ answer: 23 EP	$7 + 4 + n$ if $n = 8$ answer: 19 AT
$p + 7 + 5 + 3$ if $p = 9$ answer: 25 BJ	$q + 8 + 4 + 4$ if $q = 8$ answer: 22 EC	$r + 9 + 9$ if $r = 2$ answer: 20 CH	$7 + s + 4 + 9$ if $s = 2$ answer: 23 TO

What did the farmer use to fix his overalls?

A __ __ __ __ __ __ __   __ __ __ __ __

Mystery Multiplication

Find the value of each expression. Then use your answers to fill in the mystery numbers in the table. The sum of the numbers in each row equals the numbers at the right. The sum of the numbers in each column equals the numbers at the bottom. The sum of the diagonals equals the numbers shown at the corners.

1. $5 \times n$, if $n = 6$ _____

2. $9 \times z$, if $z = 5$ _____

3. $9 \times t$, if $t = 2$ _____

4. $4 \times m$, if $m = 7$ _____

5. $2 \times w$, if $w = 7$ _____

6. $7 \times v$, if $v = 6$ _____

7. $4 \times e$, if $e = 1$ _____

8. $2 \times s$, if $s = 11$ _____

9. $7 \times h$, if $h = 5$ _____

10. $4 \times p$, if $p = 3$ _____

					152
5	37	47			164
11			34		134
41	0	41	26		130
29		29	45	35	152
	35			19	104
104	121	133	163	163	145

Name _____

Polyominos

A polyomino has more than one square. Count to find the area
of each polyomino.

1.

Area = _____ squares

2.

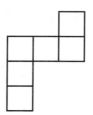

Area = _____ squares

3.

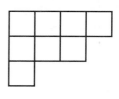

Area = _____ squares

4.

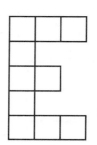

Area = _____ squares

5.

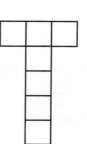

Area = _____ squares

6.

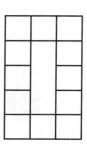

Area = _____ squares

7.

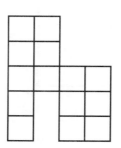

Area = _____ squares

8.

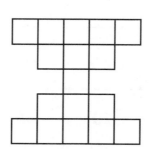

Area = _____ squares

9.

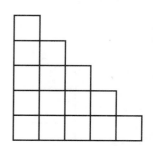

Area = _____ squares

Name _____

It's Solid

Match each solid figure with its name in Column 1 and with two facts about it from Column 2. Write the letters under each picture.

1.

_____

2.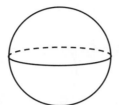

_____

3.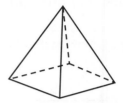

_____

4.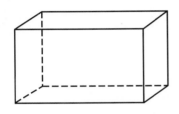

_____

5.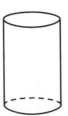

_____

6.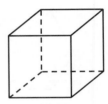

_____

Column 1

a. square pyramid

b. cylinder

c. rectangular prism

d. sphere

e. cube

f. cone

Column 2

g. 6 flat surfaces

h. 5 flat surfaces

i. 2 flat surfaces

j. 1 flat surface

k. 0 flat surfaces

l. 8 corners

m. 5 corners

n. 0 corners

Name _____

The Missing Half

Each figure below was once a square, rectangle, triangle, circle, pentagon, octagon, or hexagon. Each has been cut in half with one of the halves removed. Complete the plane figure.
Write its name on the line.

1.

_____

2.

_____

3.

_____

4.

_____

5.

_____

6.

_____

Missing Factors

Fill in the missing factors to complete the tables.

7.

×	_1_	_____	_____
2 × _4_	8	16	24
3 × _____	15	30	45
2 × _____	12	24	36

8.

×	_2_	_____	_____
_9_ × 2	36	72	90
_____ × 7	14	28	35
_____ × 5	20	40	50

9.

×	_____	_____	_____
2 × _____	24	32	12
3 × _____	36	48	18
9 × _____	54	72	27

10.

×	_____	_____	_____
9 × _____	90	72	54
2 × _____	50	40	30
8 × _____	80	64	48

Name _____

How Many?

- Place 10 counters in a plastic bag and set aside.
- Place several handfuls of counters in another plastic bag, without counting them.

1. Use the bag with 10 counters to estimate how many counters are in the second bag. Record your estimate in the row of the table for Round 1. Answers will vary.

ROUND	ESTIMATE	ACTUAL NUMBER	DIFFERENCE
1			
2			
3			
4			
5			

2. Remove the counters from the second bag and count them. Write the actual number in the table. Find the difference between the actual number and the estimate and write this number in the table. If the difference is less than 6, given yourself a point.

3. Do 4 more rounds the same way and total your score. Play again until you get a total score of 4 or 5.

Name _____

Crack the Code

Study the code.

Code	Symbol Value
⬣	1,000
▲	100
■	10
●	1

Example

Code: ⬣▲▲■■■■■●●●

Standard form: 1,243

Word form: one thousand, two hundred forty-three

Crack the code and complete the table.

CODE	STANDARD FORM	WORD FORM
⬣⬣▲■■■●●●●●●	2,136	two thousand, one hundred thirty-six
⬣■■■■●●●●●	1,045	one thousand, forty-five
⬣⬣⬣▲▲●●●●●●●	3,207	three thousand, two hundred seven
⬣▲▲▲▲■■●●●●●	1,425	one thousand, four hundred twenty-five
⬣⬣▲▲▲▲▲▲●●●	2,603	two thousand, six hundred three
⬣⬣⬣■●●●●●●●●	3,018	three thousand, eighteen

Name _____

Off to School

All the elementary schools in Center City sold books at a Book Festival. The table shows how many books each grade sold. Use the table to answer each question.

GRADE	BOOKS SOLD
Kindergarten	583
Grade 1	594
Grade 2	1,031
Grade 3	982
Grade 4	1,221
Grade 5	980
Grade 6	752

1. Which grade sold more books, Grade 1 or Grade 6?
   Grade 6

2. Which grade sold the most books?
   Grade 4

3. Which grade sold more books, Grade 2 or Grade 5?
   Grade 2

4. Which grade sold the fewest books?
   Kindergarten

5. Which grade sold fewer books, Grade 4 or Grade 5?
   Grade 5

6. Which grades sold more than 800 books?
   Grades 2, 3, 4, and 5

7. Which grades sold fewer books than Grade 5?
   Kindergarten, Grade 1, Grade 6

8. Which grades sold between 600 and 1,000 books?
   Grades 3, 5, 6

9. List the grades in order from the one with the least books to the one with the most.
   Kindergarten, Grade 1, Grade 6,
   Grade 5, Grade 3, Grade 2,
   Grade 4

10. Round the number of books that the Grade 2 collected to the nearest hundred.
    1,000

Name _____

Off to School

11. Round the number of books that the Grade 6 sold to the nearest hundred.
    800

12. Round the number of books that the Grade 1 collected to the nearest ten.
    590

13. Rounded to the nearest ten, which grade sold 1,030 books?
    Grade 2

14. Rounded to the nearest 10, which grade sold 1,220 books?
    Grade 4

15. Round the number of books that the Kindergarten sold to the nearest ten.
    580

16. Round the number of books that the Grade 3 sold to the nearest ten.
    980

17. Which two grades sold the same number of books when rounded to the nearest hundred and to the nearest ten?
    Grade 3 and Grade 5

18. Which two grades sold the same number of books when rounded to the nearest hundred, but not to the nearest ten?
    Kindergarten and Grade 1

19. Round the number of books that Grade 4 sold to the nearest hundred.
    1,200

20. Round the number of books that Grade 6 sold to the nearest hundred.
    800

21. List the grades in order from the one with the most books to the one with the least.
    Grade 4, Grade 2, Grade 3, Grade 5,
    Grade 6, Grade 1, and Kindergarten

22. Which grade sold fewer books, Kindergarten or Grade 1?
    Kindergarten

Worksheet 1 (top-left)

Play Ball!

The Eagles baseball team wants to order new baseballs and gloves. Each baseball costs $4 and each glove costs $18. The team only has $90 to spend on balls and gloves. The table organizes the information.

BASEBALLS					
Number	1	2	3	4	5
Cost	$4	$8	$12	$16	$20

GLOVES					
Number	1	2	3	4	5
Cost	$18	$36	$54	$72	$90

1. If the team buys 3 baseballs, how many gloves can it buy?

___4 gloves___

2. If the team buys 3 gloves, how many baseballs can it buy?

___9 baseballs___

3. Suppose the team manager spent $88. What did she buy?

___4 gloves and 4 baseballs___

4. Suppose the team manager spent $36 on gloves and $20 on baseballs. What can she buy with the money left?

___1 glove and 4 baseballs___

5. How much more do 4 gloves and 3 baseballs cost than 3 gloves and 6 baseballs?

___$6___

6. How much more do 3 gloves and 2 baseballs cost than 2 gloves and 5 baseballs?

___$6___

7. The team manager bought 1 glove and 2 baseballs on Monday, 1 glove and no baseballs on Tuesday, and 1 glove and 4 baseballs on Wednesday. How much did she spend in all?

___$78___

Check What You Know Enrichment **IN327**

Worksheet 2 (top-right)

Giraffe Story

What kinds of stories do giraffes tell?
Solve the puzzle to find out.

Find each sum or difference. Then write the letter that is next to the problem on all the lines above the answer.

1. $350 + 260$ **G** = 610	2. $934 + 382$ **F** = 1,316	3. $347 - 129$ **I** = 218
4. $579 + 268$ **R** = 847	5. $625 - 347$ **S** = 278	6. $862 - 561$ **E** = 301
7. $736 + 485$ **A** = 1,221	8. $419 + 893$ **T** = 1,312	9. $800 - 248$ **L** = 552

G	I	R	A	F	F	E	S
610	218	847	1,221	1,316	1,316	301	278

T	E	L	L
1,312	301	552	552

T	A	L	L	T	A	L	E	S
1,312	1,221	552	552	1,312	1,221	552	301	278

IN328 Check What You Know Enrichment

Worksheet 3 (bottom-left)

What's Missing?

Find the starting number.

Example

[?] ⟶ [Add 7.] ⟶ 12

Solution Since 5 + 7 = 12, the missing number is 5.

1. [?] ⟶ [Add 4.] ⟶ 9
___5___

2. [?] ⟶ [Add 6.] ⟶ 16
___10___

3. [?] ⟶ [Add 7.] ⟶ 15
___8___

4. [?] ⟶ [Add 9.] ⟶ 14
___5___

5. [?] ⟶ [Add 3.] ⟶ 9
___6___

6. [?] ⟶ [Add 7.] ⟶ 14
___7___

Find the missing number in each fact family.

7. $6 + 8 = \boxed{14}$
$14 - 6 = \boxed{8}$

8. $12 + 5 = \boxed{17}$
$17 - 5 = \boxed{12}$

9. $11 + 8 = \boxed{19}$
$19 - 8 = \boxed{11}$

10. $9 + 6 = \boxed{15}$
$15 - 6 = \boxed{9}$

11. $4 + 9 = \boxed{13}$
$13 - 4 = \boxed{9}$

12. $8 + 4 = \boxed{12}$
$12 - 8 = \boxed{4}$

Check What You Know Enrichment **IN329**

Worksheet 4 (bottom-right)

Party Time

You are planning a party. Four people can sit around one table and six people can sit around two tables put together. The diagrams show how this can be done.

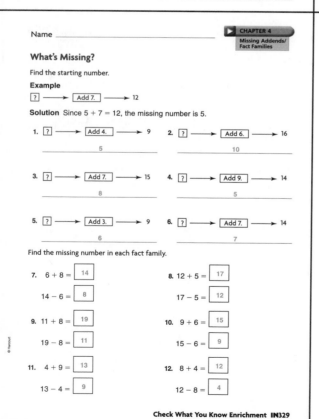

Solve.

1. How many people can be seated around 3 tables? Complete the diagram.

___8 people___

2. How many people can be seated around 4 tables? Complete the diagram.

___10 people___

3. Complete the table.

NUMBER OF TABLES	NUMBER OF PEOPLE
1	4
2	6
3	8
4	10

4. Use the table to find a pattern. How many people can be seated around 5 tables?

___12 people___

5. How many people can be seated around 7 tables?

___16 people___

6. How many people can be seated around 10 tables?

___22 people___

7. How many tables do you need to seat 18 people?

___8 tables___

8. How many tables do you need to seat 24 people?

___11 tables___

IN330 Check What You Know Enrichment

Tick Tock

Write the time under each clock. Find the next time in the pattern.

1.

3:30   4:00   4:30   5:00   5:30

2.

11:15   11:45   12:15   12:45   1:15

3.

2:08   2:13   2:18   2:23   2:28

Write the time. Find the next time in the pattern.

4.

15 minutes before 6	six o'clock	quarter after 6	half past 6	
5:45	6:00	6:15	6:30	6:45

5.

24 minutes after ten	34 minutes after ten	16 minutes before eleven	6 minutes before eleven	
10:24	10:34	10:44	10:54	11:04

Check What You Know Enrichment IN331

A Month of Fun Days

JULY						
Sunday	Monday	Tuesday	Wednesday	Thursday	Friday	Saturday
		1	2	3	4	5
6	7	8	9	10	11	12
13	14	15	16	17	18	19
20	21	22	23	24	25	26
27	28	29	30	31		

Use the calendar.

1. What day of the week is July 22?

Tuesday

2. What day of the week is the Fourth of July?

Friday

3. What date is the second Wednesday in July?

July 9

4. What date is the third Monday in July?

July 21

5. If you circled all the dates for Fridays and Saturdays in July, how many dates would be circled?

8

6. If swimming lessons are on Mondays and Thursdays, how many swimming lessons will there be in July?

9

7. What is the pattern in the dates for Thursdays in July: 3, 10, 17, 24, 31?

Add 7

8. You go to camp for 6 days, starting July 12. What date do you come home?

July 18

IN332 Check What You Know Enrichment

I'll Buy It!

Your school sells supplies during lunch time.
The prices of several things are shown in the pictograph.
Use the pictograph to answer the questions.

SCHOOL COUNTER PRICES	
Pencil	○ ○ ○
Pen	○ ○ ○ ○ ◖
Eraser	○ ◖
Note Pad	○ ○ ○ ○ ○ ○ ○

Key: Each ○ = 10¢.

1. How much does a note pad cost?

70¢

2. How much does a pen cost?

45¢

3. If a pencil was 5 cents more, how much would it cost?

35¢

4. If an eraser was 5 cents more, how much would it cost?

20¢

5. How much does it cost to buy a pencil and an eraser?

45¢

6. How much does it cost to buy a pen and a pencil?

75¢

7. How much more does a pen cost than a pencil?

15¢

8. How much more does a note pad cost than a pen?

25¢

9. If a pencil is 10 cents more, how many symbols would there be for the pencil?

4 symbols

10. If a pen is 5 cents more, how many symbols would there be for the pen?

5 symbols

Check What You Know Enrichment IN333

My Favorite Color

1. Ask 30 fourth-grade students to name their favorite color. Record their answers as tallies in the tally chart.

FAVORITE COLORS TALLY CHART	
Color	Number of Students
Red	
Blue	
Orange	
Other	

2. Use the tally chart to complete the frequency table.

FAVORITE COLORS FREQUENCY TABLE	
Color	Number of Students
Red	
Blue	
Orange	
Other	

Check students' answers based on their data.

3. How many students chose red or blue?

4. How many students chose blue or orange?

5. How many more students said red than orange (or orange than red)?

6. How many more students said blue than red (or red than blue)?

7. How many students named a favorite color?

8. If 3 more students named blue, how many tally marks would be shown for that color?

IN334 Check What You Know Enrichment

What's the Weight?

WEIGHTS OF BALLS

Kind of Ball: Baseball, Basketball, Football, Golf ball, Soccer ball, Volley ball

Weight in Grams: 0 100 200 300 400 500 600

1. What is the title of the graph?

_____ Weights of Balls _____

2. What is the label at the left side of the graph?

_____ Kind of Ball _____

3. The weights of the balls are given in what units?

_____ grams _____

4. Which is the heaviest ball?

_____ basketball _____

5. Which ball is the lightest?

_____ golf ball _____

6. How much does a volleyball weigh?

_____ 250 grams _____

7. Which ball weighs 400 grams?

_____ football _____

8. How much does a basketball and a baseball weigh together?

_____ 750 grams _____

Check What You Know Enrichment IN335

Pictographs in Class

Read each of the pictographs below. Then fill in the blanks using the information in the graph.

2. 60; rocky road; 18; chocolate chip; chocolate; chocolate chip

1.

FAVORITE SPORT OF GRADE 6	
basketball	👤👤👤👤👤
baseball	👤👤👤👤👤
football	👤👤👤👤
soccer	👤👤👤👤👤
swimming	👤👤👤👤

Key 👤 = 5 students.

Sixth grade students were asked to choose their _____. The same number of students chose _____ and _____. The most popular sport was _____. The number of students who chose basketball was ____. ____ students chose swimming.

favorite sport; baseball; soccer; football; 25; 20

2.

FAVORITE FLAVOR OF ICE CREAM	
chocolate	🍦🍦🍦🍦
vanilla	🍦🍦🍦
strawberry	🍦🍦🍦🍦🍦
chocolate chip	🍦🍦🍦
rocky road	🍦🍦🍦🍦🍦🍦🍦

Key 🍦 = 2 children.

Mr. McCullough's class surveyed a total of ____ students on their favorite ice cream flavors. They found that the most popular flavor is _____, which ____ students chose. The least favorite flavor is _____. Twice as many students chose _____ as chose _____.

See above.

3.

SPELLING TEST SCORES	
Lisa	☆☆☆☆☆☆
Jon	☆☆☆☆☆☆☆
Felicia	☆☆☆☆☆
Raul	☆☆☆☆☆☆
Mica	☆☆☆☆☆
Renee	☆☆☆☆☆☆
Allie	☆☆☆☆☆☆☆
Jay	☆☆☆☆☆
Tenesha	☆☆☆☆☆☆☆☆
Quentin	☆☆☆☆☆

Key ☆ = 10 points.

Students in Mr. Freeman's class made a graph of their _____ scores. There were ____ students who got a 90 or above on the test. ____ students scored a 70 or less. The most frequent score was ____. Mica got the same score as ____.

spelling test; 4; 3; 80; Tenesha

4.

TIME SPENT DOING HOMEWORK	
Maria	⏳⏳⏳⏳
Philip	⏳⏳⏳⏳⏳
Stacy	⏳⏳
Ted	⏳⏳⏳
Anh	⏳⏳⏳⏳

Key ⏳ = 10 minutes.

In Mrs. Green's class, ____ students were asked how much time they spent doing their homework. _____ and _____ spent the same amount of time working. The time spent by _____ was 3 times as great as the time spent by _____. _____ worked 10 minutes less than Maria.

5; Maria and Anh; Philip; Stacy; Ted

IN336 Check What You Know Enrichment

Silly Symbols

Ancient people used the letters of their alphabet to make both words and numbers. Imagine using our letters for numbers. Let each letter represent the number under it in the table.

A	B	C	D	E	F	G	H	I	R	S	T	U	V	W	X	Y	Z
1	2	3	4	5	6	7	8	9	10	20	30	40	50	60	70	80	90

So TE = 35 and D × F = SD
              4 × 6 = 24

Solve each problem. Write your answers as numbers and letters.

1. B × E = R
2 × 5 = 10

2. C × G = SA
3 × 7 = 21

3. B × H = RF
2 × 8 = 16

4. SH ÷ G = D
28 ÷ 7 = 4

5. RH ÷ F = C
18 ÷ 6 = 3

6. VF ÷ H = G
56 ÷ 8 = 7

7. F × B = RB
6 × 2 = 12

8. C × E = RE
3 × 5 = 15

9. I × I = YA
9 × 9 = 81

Check What You Know Enrichment IN337

---

10. E × I = UE
5 × 9 = 45

11.

12. F × E = T
6 × 5 = 30

D × H = TB
4 × 8 = 32

13. SD ÷ C = H
24 ÷ 3 = 8

14. RB ÷ D = C
12 ÷ 4 = 3

15. RH ÷ B = I
18 ÷ 2 = 9

16. D × R = U
4 × 10 = 40

17. H × F = UH
8 × 6 = 48

18. H × I = XB
8 × 9 = 72

19. UB ÷ F = G
42 ÷ 6 = 7

20. TE ÷ E = G
35 ÷ 5 = 7

21. TF ÷ D = I
36 ÷ 4 = 9

22. C × I = SG
3 × 9 = 27

23. E × D = S
5 × 4 = 20

24. B × G = RD
2 × 7 = 14

25. V × E = R
50 ÷ 5 = 10

26. TF ÷ F = F
36 ÷ 6 = 6

27. WC ÷ I = G
63 ÷ 9 = 7

IN338 Check What You Know Enrichment

Number Clues

Choose the number that fits all the clues.

1.
Number Clues
- When you multiply it by 3, the product is 15.
- When you multiply it by 6, the product is 30.

The number is __5__.

2.
Number Clues
- When you multiply it by 2, the product is 8.
- When you multiply it by 8, the product is 32.

The number is __4__.

3.
Number Clues
- When you multiply it by 4, the product is 36.
- When you multiply it by 7, the product is 63.

The number is __9__.

4.
Number Clues
- When you multiply it by 7, the product is 21.
- It is the quotient of 21 divided by 7.

The number is __3__.

5.
Number Clues
- When you multiply it by 4, the product is 24.
- It is the quotient of 24 divided by 4.

The number is __6__.

6.
Number Clues
- When you multiply it by 6, the product is 48.
- When 48 is divided by it, the quotient is 6.

The number is __8__.

7.
Number Clues
- It is the product of 5 and 7.
- When you divide it by 5 the quotient is 7.

The number is __35__.

Check What You Know Enrichment **IN339**

Little Rascal

Tina did her homework correctly, but her little brother erased some of the digits. Replace the digits he erased to complete the patterns.

1. $3 \times 6 = 1\,\underline{8}$
   $3 \times 6\,\underline{0} = 1\,\underline{8}\,\underline{0}$
   $3 \times 6\,\underline{0}\,0 = 1,\underline{8}\,00$

2. $\underline{8} \times 2 = 16$
   $\underline{8} \times 20 = 16\,\underline{0}$
   $\underline{8} \times 200 = 1,6\,\underline{0}\,\underline{0}$

3. $4 \times \underline{7} = 28$
   $4 \times \underline{7}\,\underline{0} = 280$
   $4 \times \underline{7}\,00 = 2,8\,\underline{0}\,\underline{0}$

4. $\underline{6} \times 5 = 30$
   $\underline{6} \times 50 = 3\,\underline{0}\,\underline{0}$
   $\underline{6} \times 500 = 3,\underline{0}\,\underline{0}\,\underline{0}$

5. $2 \times \underline{9} = 18$
   $2 \times \underline{9}\,\underline{0} = 18\,\underline{0}$
   $\underline{2} \times \underline{9}\,00 = 1,\underline{8}\,\underline{0}\,0$

6. $\underline{5} \times 7 = 35$
   $\underline{5} \times \underline{7}\,\underline{0} = 3\,\underline{5}\,0$
   $5 \times \underline{7}\,\underline{0}\,0 = 3,5\,\underline{0}\,\underline{0}$

7. $\underline{8} \times 5 = \underline{4}\,\underline{0}$
   $\underline{8} \times 50 = 400$
   $\underline{8} \times \underline{5}\,00 = 4,0\,\underline{0}\,\underline{0}$

8. $9 \times \underline{4} = \underline{3}\,\underline{6}$
   $9 \times \underline{4}\,\underline{0} = 36\,\underline{0}$
   $9 \times \underline{4}\,00 = \underline{3},\underline{6}\,00$

9. $7 \times \underline{8} = 56$
   $7 \times \underline{8}\,\underline{0} = \underline{5}\,\underline{6}\,0$
   $7 \times \underline{8}\,\underline{0}\,0 = \underline{5},\underline{6}\,\underline{0}\,\underline{0}$

10. $\underline{3} \times \underline{9} = 27$
    $\underline{3} \times 90 = 2\,\underline{7}\,\underline{0}$
    $\underline{3} \times \underline{9}\,00 = \underline{2},7\,\underline{0}\,\underline{0}$

11. $\underline{6} \times 7 = \underline{4}\,\underline{2}$
    $\underline{6} \times 70 = 42\,\underline{0}$
    $\underline{6} \times 700 = 4,2\,\underline{0}\,\underline{0}$

12. $9 \times \underline{5} = \underline{4}\,\underline{5}$
    $9 \times \underline{5}\,0 = \underline{4}\,\underline{5}\,\underline{0}$
    $9 \times \underline{5}\,\underline{0}\,\underline{0} = \underline{4},\underline{5}\,00$

IN340 Check What You Know Enrichment

Model Matching

Find the model that matches each problem. Write the letter of the model next to the problem. Then use the model to find the product.

1. $\begin{array}{r} 14 \\ \times\ 2 \\ \hline 28 \end{array}$ Model __B__

2. $\begin{array}{r} 16 \\ \times\ 3 \\ \hline 48 \end{array}$ Model __E__

3. $\begin{array}{r} 23 \\ \times\ 4 \\ \hline 92 \end{array}$ Model __F__

4. $\begin{array}{r} 26 \\ \times\ 3 \\ \hline 78 \end{array}$ Model __A__

5. $\begin{array}{r} 17 \\ \times\ 4 \\ \hline 68 \end{array}$ Model __C__

6. $\begin{array}{r} 15 \\ \times\ 3 \\ \hline 45 \end{array}$ Model __D__

Check What You Know Enrichment **IN341**

Facts Search

Find three numbers across or down that can make a multiplication fact. Circle the numbers. Write the operation and equal sign. There are 16 facts and one is shown. A number may be used more than once.

8	5 × 5 = 25		8	15	9
7	8	6	12 × 3		2
5	5	1	0	4	8 × 3
	2 × 6 = 12		22 =	8	5
15	9	7	2	32 ×	3 = 0
24 =	3 × 9 = 27		1		10
10	45	4 × 7 = 28	= 3		4
	9	7 × 18	8	8	2
1 ×	5	9	6	4 × 3 = 12	
9	15 = 17 ×	24	9	0	
7 =	3	36	3	5 × 3 = 15	
81	64	20 =	8 × 3 = 24		
30	6	2	18	14	35	45
6 × 1 = 6		7 × 7 = 49			

IN342 Check What You Know Enrichment

Intervention • Skills IN387

Shortcut

Use the patterns to find the products. List the ones with the same product.

1. A 6×10
_____60_____

D 60×10
_____600_____

G 600×10
_____6,000_____

B 6×100
_____600_____

E 60×100
_____6,000_____

H 600×100
_____60,000_____

C $6 \times 1,000$
_____6,000_____

F $60 \times 1,000$
_____60,000_____

Same as B: ___D___   Same as C: ___E, G___   Same as F: ___H___

2. A 10×3
_____30_____

D 100×3
_____300_____

G $1,000 \times 3$
_____3,000_____

B 10×30
_____300_____

E 100×30
_____3,000_____

H $1,000 \times 30$
_____30,000_____

C 10×300
_____3,000_____

F 100×300
_____30,000_____

Same as B: ___D___   Same as C: ___E, G___   Same as F: ___H___

3. A 7×10
_____70_____

D $7 \times 1,000$
_____7,000_____

G $70 \times 1,000$
_____70,000_____

B 7×100
_____700_____

E 70×100
_____7,000_____

H 700×100
_____70,000_____

C 70×10
_____700_____

F 700×10
_____7,000_____

Same as B: ___C___   Same as D: ___E, F___   Same as G: ___H___

Food Fuel

You get calories from food. You then burn calories when you walk, run, or even sleep. A man burns about 65 calories an hour sleeping and a woman burns about 55.

Use the information in the paragraph and in the table. You may use base-ten blocks to solve.

FOOD CALORIES PER SERVING	
Food	**Calories**
Cheddar cheese	95
Bologna	57
Hard-cooked egg	75
Grapes	35
Corn tortilla	65
Carrots	30

1. About how many calories does a man burn by sleeping 3 hours?
_____195 calories_____

2. About how many calories does a woman burn by sleeping 4 hours?
_____220 calories_____

3. How many calories are in 5 servings of carrots?
_____150 calories_____

4. How many calories are in 2 servings of bologna?
_____114 calories_____

5. How many calories are in 4 servings of corn tortillas?
_____260 calories_____

6. How many calories are in 5 servings of grapes?
_____175 calories_____

7. How many calories are in 4 servings of cheddar cheese?
_____380 calories_____

8. How many calories are in 3 servings of carrots?
_____90 calories_____

Paper Products

- Write the numbers 0–9 on slips of paper.
- Place them in a small bowl.
- Draw a number from the bowl and write it in one box of the first game. Replace the paper in the bowl. Continue drawing until all the boxes are filled, trying to make the largest product possible.
- When a row is filled, estimate each product and guess which one is the greatest product.
- Then find each product. You win if your guess was correct.

Check students' estimates and products.

Game 1

$\times$ ☐☐ $\times$ ☐☐ $\times$ ☐☐ $\times$ ☐☐

Estimate: _____   Estimate: _____   Estimate: _____   Estimate: _____
Product: _____   Product: _____   Product: _____   Product: _____

Greatest Product Guess: _____   Actual: _____

Game 2

$\times$ ☐☐ $\times$ ☐☐ $\times$ ☐☐ $\times$ ☐☐

Estimate: _____   Estimate: _____   Estimate: _____   Estimate: _____
Product: _____   Product: _____   Product: _____   Product: _____

Greatest Product Guess: _____   Actual: _____

Game 3

$\times$ ☐☐ $\times$ ☐☐ $\times$ ☐☐ $\times$ ☐☐

Estimate: _____   Estimate: _____   Estimate: _____   Estimate: _____
Product: _____   Product: _____   Product: _____   Product: _____

Greatest Product Guess: _____   Actual: _____

Game 4

$\times$ ☐☐ $\times$ ☐☐ $\times$ ☐☐ $\times$ ☐☐

Estimate: _____   Estimate: _____   Estimate: _____   Estimate: _____
Product: _____   Product: _____   Product: _____   Product: _____

Greatest Product Guess: _____   Actual: _____

Game 5

$\times$ ☐☐ $\times$ ☐☐ $\times$ ☐☐ $\times$ ☐☐

Estimate: _____   Estimate: _____   Estimate: _____   Estimate: _____
Product: _____   Product: _____   Product: _____   Product: _____

Greatest Product Guess: _____   Actual: _____

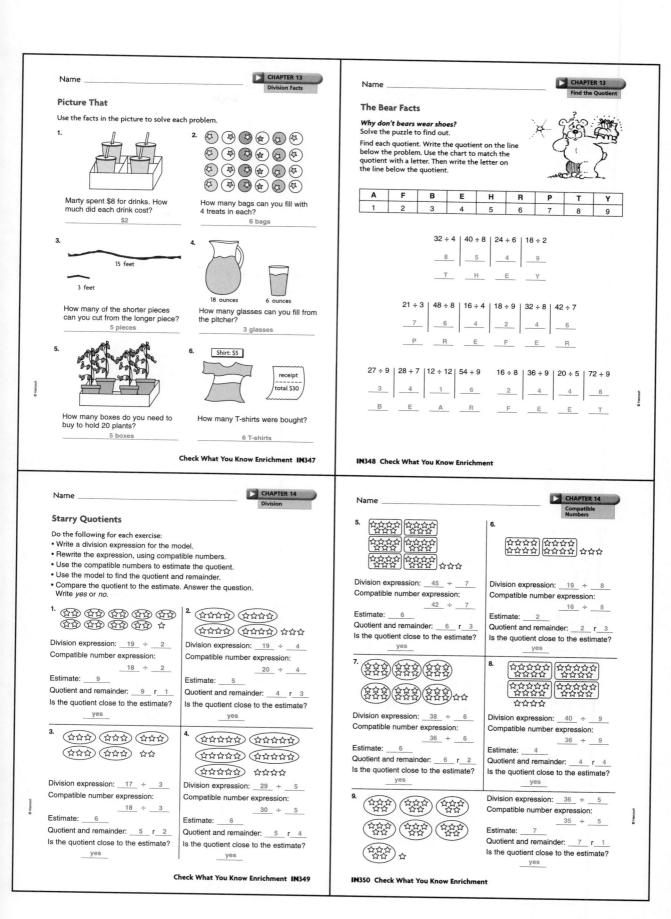

Picture That

Name _____

Use the facts in the picture to solve each problem.

1. Marty spent $8 for drinks. How much did each drink cost?
_____$2_____

2. How many bags can you fill with 4 treats in each?
_____6 bags_____

3. 15 feet / 3 feet
How many of the shorter pieces can you cut from the longer piece?
_____5 pieces_____

4. 18 ounces / 6 ounces
How many glasses can you fill from the pitcher?
_____3 glasses_____

5. How many boxes do you need to buy to hold 20 plants?
_____5 boxes_____

6. Shirt: $5 / receipt total $30
How many T-shirts were bought?
_____6 T-shirts_____

Check What You Know Enrichment **IN347**

The Bear Facts

Name _____

Why don't bears wear shoes?
Solve the puzzle to find out.

Find each quotient. Write the quotient on the line below the problem. Use the chart to match the quotient with a letter. Then write the letter on the line below the quotient.

A	F	B	E	H	R	P	T	Y
1	2	3	4	5	6	7	8	9

32 ÷ 4	40 ÷ 8	24 ÷ 6	18 ÷ 2
8	5	4	9
T	H	E	Y

21 ÷ 3	48 ÷ 8	16 ÷ 4	18 ÷ 9	32 ÷ 8	42 ÷ 7
7	6	4	2	4	6
P	R	E	F	E	R

27 ÷ 9	28 ÷ 7	12 ÷ 12	54 ÷ 9	16 ÷ 8	36 ÷ 9	20 ÷ 5	72 ÷ 9
3	4	1	6	2	4	4	8
B	E	A	R	F	E	E	T

IN348 Check What You Know Enrichment

Starry Quotients

Name _____

Do the following for each exercise:
• Write a division expression for the model.
• Rewrite the expression, using compatible numbers.
• Use the compatible numbers to estimate the quotient.
• Use the model to find the quotient and remainder.
• Compare the quotient to the estimate. Answer the question.
  Write *yes* or *no*.

1. Division expression: __19__ ÷ __2__
Compatible number expression: __18__ ÷ __2__
Estimate: __9__
Quotient and remainder: __9__ r __1__
Is the quotient close to the estimate? __yes__

2. Division expression: __19__ ÷ __4__
Compatible number expression: __20__ ÷ __4__
Estimate: __5__
Quotient and remainder: __4__ r __3__
Is the quotient close to the estimate? __yes__

3. Division expression: __17__ ÷ __3__
Compatible number expression: __18__ ÷ __3__
Estimate: __6__
Quotient and remainder: __5__ r __2__
Is the quotient close to the estimate? __yes__

4. Division expression: __29__ ÷ __5__
Compatible number expression: __30__ ÷ __5__
Estimate: __6__
Quotient and remainder: __5__ r __4__
Is the quotient close to the estimate? __yes__

Check What You Know Enrichment **IN349**

Name _____

5. Division expression: __45__ ÷ __7__
Compatible number expression: __42__ ÷ __7__
Estimate: __6__
Quotient and remainder: __6__ r __3__
Is the quotient close to the estimate? __yes__

6. Division expression: __19__ ÷ __8__
Compatible number expression: __16__ ÷ __8__
Estimate: __2__
Quotient and remainder: __2__ r __3__
Is the quotient close to the estimate? __yes__

7. Division expression: __38__ ÷ __6__
Compatible number expression: __36__ ÷ __6__
Estimate: __6__
Quotient and remainder: __6__ r __2__
Is the quotient close to the estimate? __yes__

8. Division expression: __40__ ÷ __9__
Compatible number expression: __36__ ÷ __9__
Estimate: __4__
Quotient and remainder: __4__ r __4__
Is the quotient close to the estimate? __yes__

9. Division expression: __36__ ÷ __5__
Compatible number expression: __35__ ÷ __5__
Estimate: __7__
Quotient and remainder: __7__ r __1__
Is the quotient close to the estimate? __yes__

IN350 Check What You Know Enrichment

A Riddle of Zeros

What did the 0 say to the 4?

Find each quotient using mental math. Then look in the code box to find the letter that matches the answer. Write the matching letter in the circle next to the answer. BEWARE! Not all of the answers will be used.

1. $16 \div 2$ = ___8___ ①
2. $240 \div 4$ = ___60___
3. $800 \div 2$ = ___400___ Ⓐ
4. $72 \div 8$ = ___9___ Ⓜ
5. $1,600 \div 8$ = ___200___
6. $640 \div 8$ = ___80___ Ⓐ
7. $2,800 \div 4$ = ___700___
8. $900 \div 3$ = ___300___ Ⓡ
9. $350 \div 5$ = ___70___ Ⓞ
10. $160 \div 8$ = ___20___ Ⓤ
11. $4,200 \div 7$ = ___600___ Ⓝ
12. $150 \div 3$ = ___50___ Ⓓ

13. $8,100 \div 9$ = ___900___
14. $720 \div 8$ = ___90___ Ⓝ
15. $48 \div 8$ = ___6___ Ⓤ
16. $4,500 \div 9$ = ___500___ Ⓜ
17. $320 \div 8$ = ___40___ Ⓑ
18. $900 \div 9$ = ___100___ Ⓔ
19. $270 \div 9$ = ___30___ Ⓡ
20. $5,600 \div 7$ = ___800___

Code				
6 = U	20 = U	50 = D	90 = N	400 = A
8 = I	30 = R	70 = O	100 = E	500 = M
9 = M	40 = B	80 = A	300 = R	600 = N

Check What You Know Enrichment **IN351**

Number, Please!

Solve each riddle. Shade the corresponding number in the picture.

1. My divisor is 6.
   I am greater than 2×6.
   I am less than 20.
   My remainder is 4.
   What dividend am I?
   ___16___

2. My divisor is 4.
   I am greater than 30.
   I am less than 9×4.
   My remainder is 1.
   What dividend am I?
   ___33___

3. My divisor is 9.
   I am greater than 50.
   I am less than 6×9.
   My remainder is 6.
   What dividend am I?
   ___51___

4. My divisor is 8.
   I am greater than 10.
   I am less than 8×2.
   My remainder is 7.
   What dividend am I?
   ___15___

5. My divisor is 7.
   I am greater than 4×7.
   I am less than 5×7.
   My remainder is 2.
   What dividend am I?
   ___30___

6. My divisor is 5.
   I am greater than 8×5.
   I am less than 9×5.
   My remainder is 4.
   What dividend am I?
   ___44___

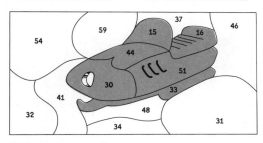

IN352 Check What You Know Enrichment

Sporty Products

Solve.

1. A baseball team has 9 players. How many players are there on 4 baseball teams?
   ___36 players___

2. A park has 6 baseball fields. Each field has 4 bases. How many bases are in the park?
   ___24 bases___

3. A Little League baseball team played 7 innings. They scored the same number of runs each inning and 21 runs in all. How many runs did the team score in one inning?
   ___3 runs___

4. A basketball game has 4 quarters. The Cubs scored 7 points each quarter. How many points did the team score in all?
   ___28 points___

5. A baseball field has 4 bases. The park manager has 20 bases. How many baseball fields can she make?
   ___5 fields___

6. The Cubs basketball team has 2 totally different starting lineups. They have 10 players in all. How many players are in a starting lineup?
   ___5 players___

7. Two teams scored a total of 18 points in the first half of a basketball game. At the end of the half, they were tied. How many points did each team score?
   ___9 points___

8. A gym has 5 bags of basketballs with the same number of balls in each. It has 25 basketballs in all. How many are in each bag?
   ___5 balls___

Check What You Know Enrichment **IN353**

A Sad Bird

What kind of bird is sad? Solve the puzzle to find out. Shade the squares and then write the letter formed in the blank below.

1. Shade all the squares that have a product or quotient in the fact family for 3, 8, and 24. Then, shade all the squares that have a product or quotient in the fact family for 2, 9, and 18.

4 × 6	3 × 8	2 × 9	24 ÷ 4	3 × 6
3 × 4	8 × 3	6 × 3	3 × 8	5 × 3
16 ÷ 2	24 ÷ 3	18 ÷ 2	14 ÷ 2	3 × 9
2 × 8	24 ÷ 8	18 ÷ 6	18 ÷ 9	6 × 4
5 × 7	2 × 9	9 × 2	21 ÷ 7	18 ÷ 3

2. Shade all the squares that have a product or quotient in the fact family for 4, 7, and 28. Then, shade all the squares that have a product or quotient in the fact family for 5, 6, and 30.

4 × 7	5 × 8	18 ÷ 9	24 ÷ 4	3 × 6
6 × 5	8 × 3	6 × 4	3 × 9	5 × 3
28 ÷ 7	25 ÷ 5	14 ÷ 2	15 ÷ 3	3 × 9
5 × 6	24 ÷ 8	48 ÷ 6	18 ÷ 3	6 × 4
7 × 4	30 ÷ 6	30 ÷ 5	28 ÷ 4	36 ÷ 4

3. Shade all the squares that have a product or quotient in the fact family for 3, 7, and 21. Then, shade all the squares that have a product or quotient in the fact family for 4, 9, and 36.

5 × 6	4 × 9	18 ÷ 2	36 ÷ 4	3 × 4
3 × 8	7 × 3	6 × 3	3 × 7	5 × 5
16 ÷ 2	21 ÷ 7	18 ÷ 2	21 ÷ 7	3 × 9
2 × 9	36 ÷ 4	18 ÷ 6	36 ÷ 9	6 × 7
5 × 7	3 × 7	9 × 4	21 ÷ 7	18 ÷ 3

4. Shade all the squares that have a product or quotient in the fact family for 6, 8, and 48. Then, shade all the squares that have a product or quotient in the fact family for 5, 9, and 45.

3 × 8	6 × 8	5 × 9	48 ÷ 6	24 ÷ 4
36 ÷ 6	9 × 5	8 × 3	6 × 4	3 × 9
9 × 6	48 ÷ 8	45 ÷ 5	14 ÷ 2	15 ÷ 3
24 ÷ 6	8 × 6	24 ÷ 8	42 ÷ 6	18 ÷ 3
5 × 8	5 × 9	48 ÷ 6	45 ÷ 9	28 ÷ 4

A _B_ _L_ _U_ _E_ bird is sad.
   1   2   3   4

IN354 Check What You Know Enrichment

IN390 Intervention • Skills

Find the Figures

Look carefully at the picture below. Use a blue crayon and circle the right angles. Circle the acute angles in red. Circle the obtuse angles in green. Circle the line segments in yellow. Circle the rays in purple.

Check students' work. Possible answers: right angles— the inside of the picture frame, the legs of the table where they join the top, the top of the pendulum area of the clock; acute angles—some of the spindles of the banister, the pendulum arm, the table corners, the picture frame along the outer edges; obtuse angles—on the lower corners of the table, the clock hands, the inner edges of the picture frame, and some of the spindles of the banister; line segments—in the banister spindles, the frame around the banister, the frame around the picture and on the table top; rays—the two hands on the clock

Check What You Know Enrichment **IN355**

Straw Angles

Use straws to make each angle. Then compare your straw angle to a corner of your desk. Tell if each angle is a *right* angle, *greater than* a right angle, or *less than* a right angle.

1. 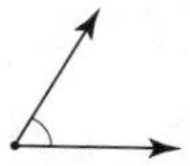 less than
2.  greater than
3. 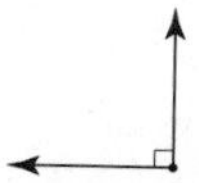 right
4. 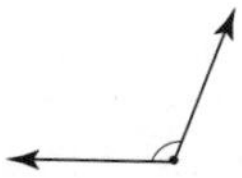 greater than
5. 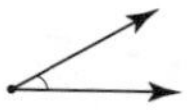 less than
6.  greater than
7. 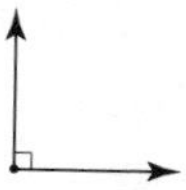 right
8.  greater than
9. 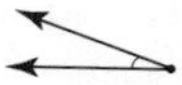 less than
10.  less than
11.  right
12. 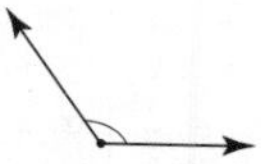 greater than

IN356 Check What You Know Enrichment

What's the Angle?

Find the angle in the design that matches the number below. Tell if each angle is *acute, right,* or *obtuse.*

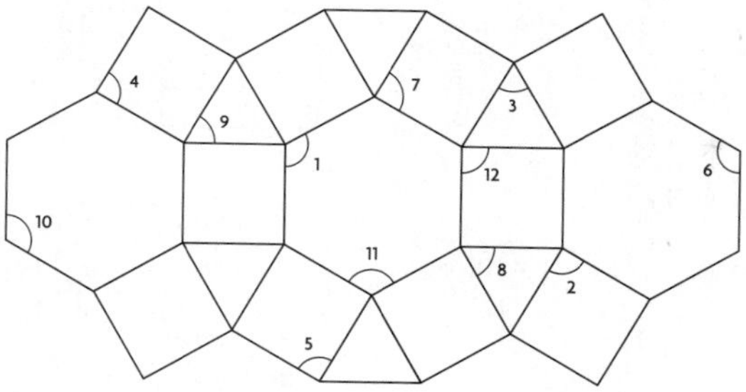

1. obtuse
2. right
3. acute
4. right
5. right
6. obtuse
7. right
8. acute
9. acute
10. obtuse
11. obtuse
12. right

Check What You Know Enrichment **IN357**

Plane Figure Puzzle

Read the clues. Color the figures. Then write the name of each figure.

1. If a plane figure has 4 right angles and 2 pairs of equal sides, color it blue.

2. If a plane figure has 2 right angles and 5 sides, color it red.

3. If a plane figure has no right angles and 3 equal sides, color it green.

4. If a plane figure has no right angles and no sides that are equal, color it yellow.

5. If a plane figure has 4 right angles and 4 sides that are equal, color it brown.

6. If a plane figure has 2 equal sides and 3 angles less than right angles, color it pink.

7. If a plane figure has no equal sides and no angles, color it orange.

8. If a plane figure has one right angle, color it purple.

9. If a plane figure has 4 equal sides and no right angles, color it gray.

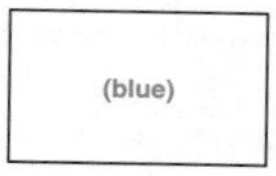

(blue) rectangle

(pink) isosceles triangle

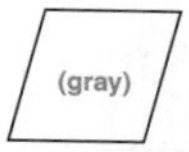

(gray) rhombus

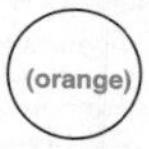

(orange) circle

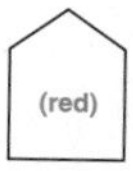

(red) pentagon

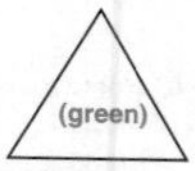

(green) equilateral triangle

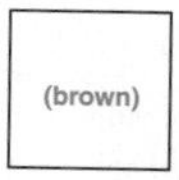

(brown) square

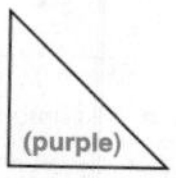

(purple) right triangle

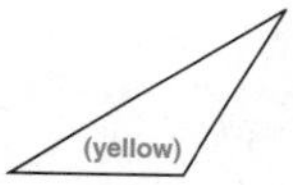

(yellow) scalene triangle

(blue) rectangle

IN358 Check What You Know Enrichment

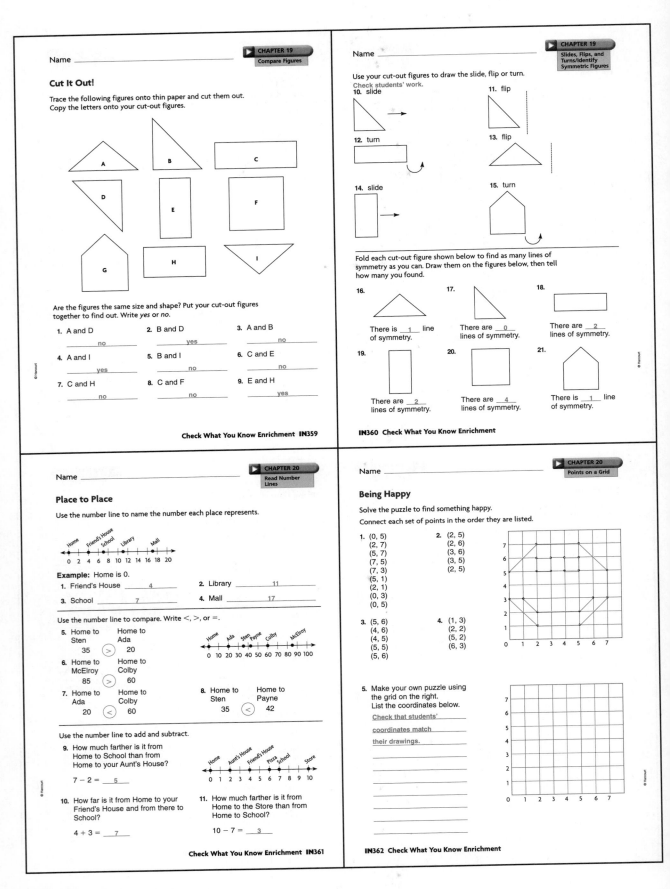

Name _____

Cut It Out!

Trace the following figures onto thin paper and cut them out.
Copy the letters onto your cut-out figures.

A   B   C

D   E   F

G   H   I

Are the figures the same size and shape? Put your cut-out figures
together to find out. Write **yes** or **no**.

1. A and D   2. B and D   3. A and B
   _____no_____   _____yes_____   _____no_____

4. A and I   5. B and I   6. C and E
   _____yes_____   _____no_____   _____no_____

7. C and H   8. C and F   9. E and H
   _____no_____   _____no_____   _____yes_____

Check What You Know Enrichment IN359

Name _____

Use your cut-out figures to draw the slide, flip or turn.
Check students' work.

10. slide   11. flip

12. turn   13. flip

14. slide   15. turn

Fold each cut-out figure shown below to find as many lines of
symmetry as you can. Draw them on the figures below, then tell
how many you found.

16.   17.   18.

There is __1__ line   There are __0__   There are __2__
of symmetry.   lines of symmetry. lines of symmetry.

19.   20.   21.

There are __2__   There are __4__   There is __1__ line
lines of symmetry.   lines of symmetry. of symmetry.

IN360 Check What You Know Enrichment

Name _____

Place to Place

Use the number line to name the number each place represents.

Home Friend's House School Library Mall
0 2 4 6 8 10 12 14 16 18 20

Example: Home is 0.

1. Friend's House _____4_____   2. Library _____11_____

3. School _____7_____   4. Mall _____17_____

Use the number line to compare. Write <, >, or =.

5. Home to   Home to   Home Ada Sten Payne Colby McElroy
   Sten   Ada
   35   >   20   0 10 20 30 40 50 60 70 80 90 100

6. Home to   Home to
   McElroy   Colby
   85   >   60

7. Home to   Home to   8. Home to   Home to
   Ada   Colby   Sten   Payne
   20   <   60   35   <   42

Use the number line to add and subtract.

9. How much farther is it
   Home to School than from   Home Aunt's House Friend's House Pizza School Store
   Home to your Aunt's House?
                                 0 1 2 3 4 5 6 7 8 9 10
   7 − 2 = __5__

10. How far is it from Home to your   11. How much farther is it from
    Friend's House and from there to   Home to the Store than from
    School?   Home to School?
    4 + 3 = __7__   10 − 7 = __3__

Check What You Know Enrichment IN361

Name _____

Being Happy

Solve the puzzle to find something happy.
Connect each set of points in the order they are listed.

1. (0, 5)   2. (2, 5)
   (2, 7)   (2, 6)
   (5, 7)   (3, 6)
   (7, 5)   (3, 5)
   (7, 3)   (2, 5)
   (5, 1)
   (2, 1)
   (0, 3)
   (0, 5)

3. (5, 6)   4. (1, 3)
   (4, 6)   (2, 2)
   (4, 5)   (5, 2)
   (5, 5)   (6, 3)
   (5, 6)

5. Make your own puzzle using
   the grid on the right.
   List the coordinates below.
   Check that students'
   coordinates match
   their drawings.
   _____
   _____
   _____
   _____
   _____

IN362 Check What You Know Enrichment

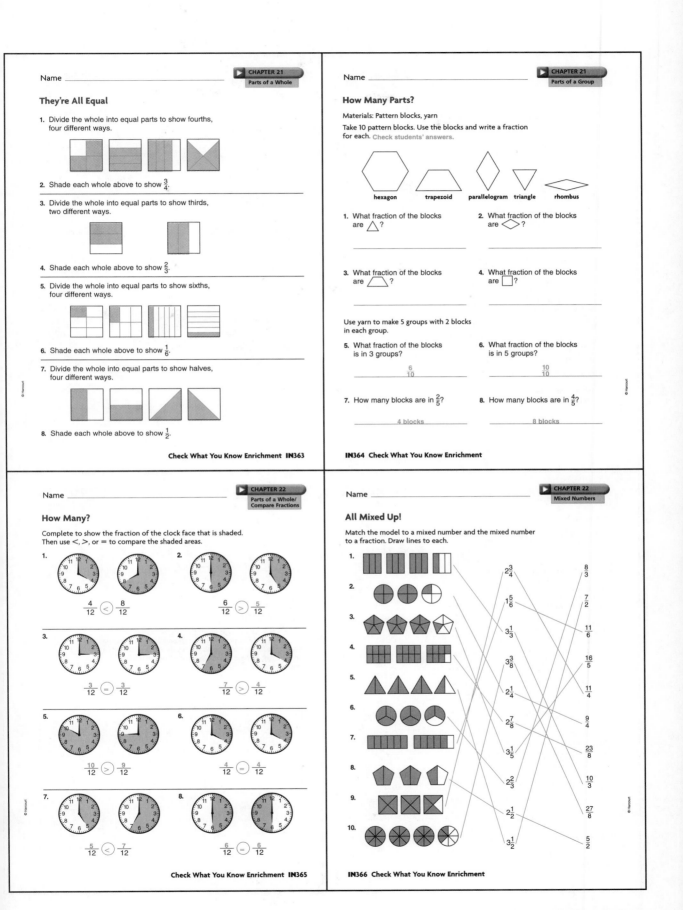

Name _____

They're All Equal

1. Divide the whole into equal parts to show fourths, four different ways.

2. Shade each whole above to show $\frac{3}{4}$.

3. Divide the whole into equal parts to show thirds, two different ways.

4. Shade each whole above to show $\frac{2}{3}$.

5. Divide the whole into equal parts to show sixths, four different ways.

6. Shade each whole above to show $\frac{1}{6}$.

7. Divide the whole into equal parts to show halves, four different ways.

8. Shade each whole above to show $\frac{1}{2}$.

Check What You Know Enrichment **IN363**

Name _____

How Many Parts?

Materials: Pattern blocks, yarn

Take 10 pattern blocks. Use the blocks and write a fraction for each. Check students' answers.

hexagon   trapezoid   parallelogram   triangle   rhombus

1. What fraction of the blocks are △ ?

_____

2. What fraction of the blocks are ◇ ?

_____

3. What fraction of the blocks are ⬡ ?

_____

4. What fraction of the blocks are ☐ ?

_____

Use yarn to make 5 groups with 2 blocks in each group.

5. What fraction of the blocks is in 3 groups?

$\frac{6}{10}$

6. What fraction of the blocks is in 5 groups?

$\frac{10}{10}$

7. How many blocks are in $\frac{2}{5}$?

4 blocks

8. How many blocks are in $\frac{4}{5}$?

8 blocks

IN364 Check What You Know Enrichment

Name _____

How Many?

Complete to show the fraction of the clock face that is shaded. Then use <, >, or = to compare the shaded areas.

1. $\frac{4}{12}$ < $\frac{8}{12}$

2. $\frac{6}{12}$ > $\frac{5}{12}$

3. $\frac{3}{12}$ = $\frac{3}{12}$

4. $\frac{7}{12}$ > $\frac{4}{12}$

5. $\frac{10}{12}$ > $\frac{9}{12}$

6. $\frac{4}{12}$ = $\frac{4}{12}$

7. $\frac{5}{12}$ < $\frac{7}{12}$

8. $\frac{6}{12}$ = $\frac{6}{12}$

Check What You Know Enrichment **IN365**

Name _____

All Mixed Up!

Match the model to a mixed number and the mixed number to a fraction. Draw lines to each.

1.
2.
3.
4.
5.
6.
7.
8.
9.
10.

$2\frac{3}{4}$ $\frac{8}{3}$

$1\frac{5}{6}$ $\frac{7}{2}$

$3\frac{1}{3}$ $\frac{11}{6}$

$3\frac{3}{8}$ $\frac{16}{5}$

$2\frac{1}{4}$ $\frac{11}{4}$

$2\frac{7}{8}$ $\frac{9}{4}$

$3\frac{1}{5}$ $\frac{23}{8}$

$2\frac{2}{3}$ $\frac{10}{3}$

$2\frac{1}{2}$ $\frac{27}{8}$

$3\frac{1}{2}$ $\frac{5}{2}$

IN366 Check What You Know Enrichment

What Are the Chances?

Use paper clips and pencils to make two spinners.

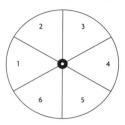 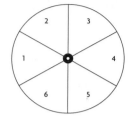

1. Spin both pointers once. What is the sum of the numbers? What are all of the possible sums?

   Answers will vary; 2, 3, 4, 5, 6, 7, 8, 9, 10, 11, 12

2. Spin both pointers 25 times. Complete this table. Make a tally mark to record the sum of the two numbers you get.

   Check students' work.

Sum	2	3								
Tally										

3. Which sum did you get most often?

   _____ Answers will vary. _____

4. Which sums did you not get at all or did you get least often?

   _____ Answers will vary. _____

Legs and Laundry

There are ___7___ shirts in all on the clothesline. Write a fraction to show the part named.

1. What fraction have long sleeves?
   $\frac{2}{7}$

2. What fraction have short sleeves?
   $\frac{5}{7}$

3. What fraction have numbers?
   $\frac{3}{7}$

4. What fraction have stripes?
   $\frac{1}{7}$

5. What fraction have numbers or stripes?
   $\frac{4}{7}$

6. What fraction have both numbers and short sleeves?
   $\frac{2}{7}$

There are ___8___ animals in all. Write a fraction to show the part named.

7. What fraction have exactly 4 legs?
   $\frac{4}{8}$, or $\frac{1}{2}$

8. What fraction has exactly 2 legs?
   $\frac{1}{8}$

9. What fraction have 4 or more legs?
   $\frac{6}{8}$, or $\frac{3}{4}$

10. What fraction have fur?
   $\frac{3}{8}$

Map Maker

You can use a ruler to measure distances on a map.

To measure the distance between two points on Karen's map, place one end of your ruler on the point next to the first place. Then find the mark on your ruler that is closest to the point that you are measuring to.

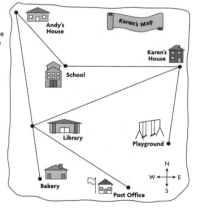

Use your ruler to measure the distance to the nearest half inch.

1. from Karen's house to library
   _____ 4 inches _____

2. from library to post office
   _____ 3 inches _____

3. from Andy's house to bakery
   _____ $4\frac{1}{2}$ inches _____

4. from Andy's house to school
   _____ 2 inches _____

5. from Karen's house to playground
   _____ 2 inches _____

6. from bakery to library
   _____ $1\frac{1}{2}$ inches _____

Lost Digits

Be a math detective and find the missing digits.

1.
$$\begin{array}{r} 3\;\boxed{6} \\ \times\;\;8 \\ \hline \boxed{2}\;8\;8 \end{array}$$

2.
$$\begin{array}{r} 5,2\,8\,0 \\ \times\;\;\;\;\boxed{4} \\ \hline 2\,1,\boxed{1}\,\boxed{2}\,0 \end{array}$$

3.
$$\begin{array}{r} 1\;\boxed{2} \\ \times\;\boxed{9} \\ \hline \boxed{1}\,0\,\boxed{8} \end{array}$$

Quotient Map

Choose an empty triangle below that has two arrows pointing to it. Look at the numbers in the boxes pointing to the triangle you chose. Divide the larger number by the smaller number. Put the quotient in the empty triangle you chose. Fill in all the empty triangles.

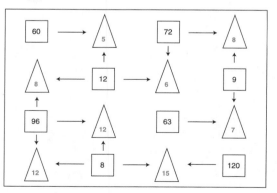

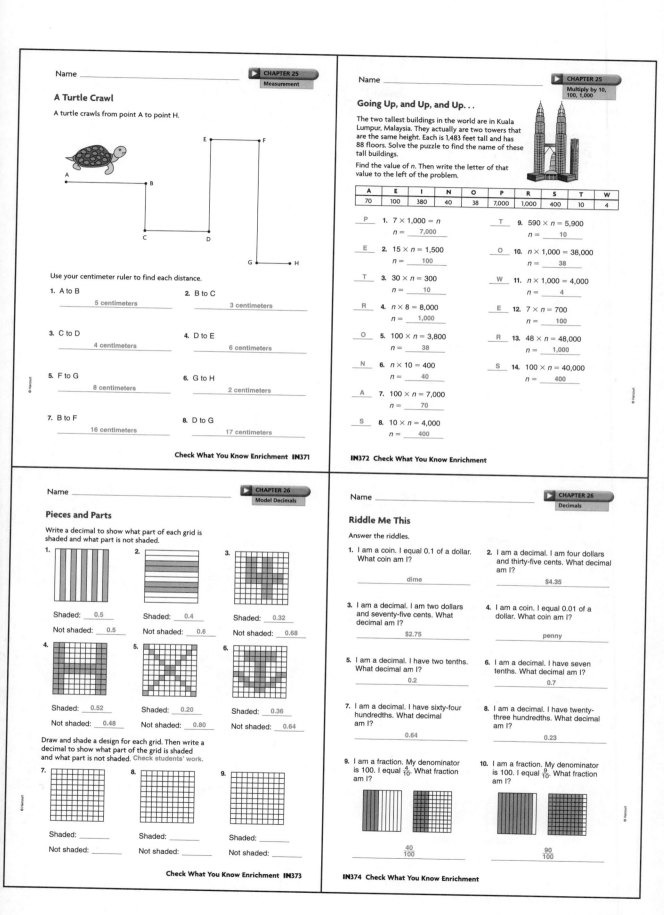

A Turtle Crawl

A turtle crawls from point A to point H.

Use your centimeter ruler to find each distance.

1. A to B
   5 centimeters

2. B to C
   3 centimeters

3. C to D
   4 centimeters

4. D to E
   6 centimeters

5. F to G
   8 centimeters

6. G to H
   2 centimeters

7. B to F
   16 centimeters

8. D to G
   17 centimeters

Check What You Know Enrichment **IN371**

Going Up, and Up, and Up. . .

The two tallest buildings in the world are in Kuala Lumpur, Malaysia. They actually are two towers that are the same height. Each is 1,483 feet tall and has 88 floors. Solve the puzzle to find the name of these tall buildings.

Find the value of n. Then write the letter of that value to the left of the problem.

A	E	I	N	O	P	R	S	T	W
70	100	380	40	38	7,000	1,000	400	10	4

P 1. $7 \times 1,000 = n$
   $n =$ 7,000

E 2. $15 \times n = 1,500$
   $n =$ 100

T 3. $30 \times n = 300$
   $n =$ 10

R 4. $n \times 8 = 8,000$
   $n =$ 1,000

O 5. $100 \times n = 3,800$
   $n =$ 38

N 6. $n \times 10 = 400$
   $n =$ 40

A 7. $100 \times n = 7,000$
   $n =$ 70

S 8. $10 \times n = 4,000$
   $n =$ 400

T 9. $590 \times n = 5,900$
   $n =$ 10

O 10. $n \times 1,000 = 38,000$
   $n =$ 38

W 11. $n \times 1,000 = 4,000$
   $n =$ 4

E 12. $7 \times n = 700$
   $n =$ 100

R 13. $48 \times n = 48,000$
   $n =$ 1,000

S 14. $100 \times n = 40,000$
   $n =$ 400

IN372 Check What You Know Enrichment

Pieces and Parts

Write a decimal to show what part of each grid is shaded and what part is not shaded.

1. Shaded: 0.5
   Not shaded: 0.5

2. Shaded: 0.4
   Not shaded: 0.6

3. Shaded: 0.32
   Not shaded: 0.68

4. Shaded: 0.52
   Not shaded: 0.48

5. Shaded: 0.20
   Not shaded: 0.80

6. Shaded: 0.36
   Not shaded: 0.64

Draw and shade a design for each grid. Then write a decimal to show what part of the grid is shaded and what part is not shaded. Check students' work.

7. Shaded: _____
   Not shaded: _____

8. Shaded: _____
   Not shaded: _____

9. Shaded: _____
   Not shaded: _____

Check What You Know Enrichment **IN373**

Riddle Me This

Answer the riddles.

1. I am a coin. I equal 0.1 of a dollar. What coin am I?
   dime

2. I am a decimal. I am four dollars and thirty-five cents. What decimal am I?
   $4.35

3. I am a decimal. I am two dollars and seventy-five cents. What decimal am I?
   $2.75

4. I am a coin. I equal 0.01 of a dollar. What coin am I?
   penny

5. I am a decimal. I have two tenths. What decimal am I?
   0.2

6. I am a decimal. I have seven tenths. What decimal am I?
   0.7

7. I am a decimal. I have sixty-four hundredths. What decimal am I?
   0.64

8. I am a decimal. I have twenty-three hundredths. What decimal am I?
   0.23

9. I am a fraction. My denominator is 100. I equal $\frac{4}{10}$. What fraction am I?
   $\frac{40}{100}$

10. I am a fraction. My denominator is 100. I equal $\frac{9}{10}$. What fraction am I?
    $\frac{90}{100}$

IN374 Check What You Know Enrichment

Name _____

Methuselah

The oldest living tree is named Methuselah. Methuselah lives in California and is estimated to be about 4,700 years old. That's a lot of birthdays! What kind of tree is Methuselah? Solve the puzzle to find out. Write the letter of each answer above the exercise number below.

Round each to the nearest hundred.

1. 687 _____ 700
2. 425 _____ 400
3. 252 _____ 300
4. 245 _____ 200
5. 479 _____ 500

Round each to the nearest ten.

6. 321 _____ 320
7. 148 _____ 150
8. 575 _____ 580
9. 416 _____ 420
10. 412 _____ 410
11. 235 _____ 240

B	580
C	420
E	700
I	410
L	500
N	150
O	200
P	240
R	300
S	400
T	320

B R I S T L E   C O N E   P I N E
8 3 10 2 6 5 1   9 4 7 1   11 10 7 1

Name _____

A Place for a Pattern

In each box, find the value of the digit 1. If the digit represents tenths, color the box red. If the digit represents hundredths, color the box blue. If the digit represents thousandths, color the box yellow. Look for a pattern when you complete the coloring.

0.157	0.13	0.017	0.149	0.102
red	red	blue	red	red
0.143	0.316	0.301	0.214	0.18
red	blue	yellow	blue	red
0.91	0.551	0.413	0.291	0.818
blue	yellow	blue	yellow	blue
0.001	0.512	0.071	0.013	0.481
yellow	blue	yellow	blue	yellow
0.619	0.081	0.183	0.781	0.51
blue	yellow	red	yellow	blue
0.221	0.124	0.109	0.14	0.471
yellow	red	red	red	yellow

Name _____

Perimeter Puzzles

Count to find the perimeter of each figure. Then order the perimeters from least to greatest, and use the letters of each problem to solve the riddle.

1. H

16

2. E

22

3. L

28

4. R
20

5. P
26

6. N
34

7. A

30

8. E
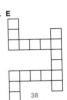
38

9. A

18

How do rabbits travel?

In a H A R E   P L A N E
     16 18 20 22 26 28 30 34 38

Name _____

Overall Expressions

Find the value of each expression. If the answer is incorrect, cross out the box. Then write the remaining letters on the lines below to solve the riddle.

$3 + 4 + a$ if $a = 2$ correct answer: 9 CA	$b + 3 + 1$ if $b = 6$ incorrect answer: 12 MA	$5 + c + 7$ if $c = 5$ incorrect answer: 32 TH	$d + 3 + 8$ if $d = 9$ correct answer: 20 BB
$5 + 8 + e$ if $e = 7$ incorrect answer: 21 IS	$f + 1 + 2$ if $f = 8$ correct answer: 11 AG	$5 + 4 + g$ if $g = 1$ incorrect answer: 9 MY	$8 + 1 + h + 3$ if $h = 2$ incorrect answer: 13 BE
$j + 7 + 3 + 1$ if $j = 4$ incorrect answer: 14 ST	$k + 6 + 3$ if $k = 9$ incorrect answer: 19 SU	$8 + m + 6$ if $m = 9$ correct answer: 23 EP	$7 + 4 + n$ if $n = 8$ correct answer: 19 AT
$p + 7 + 5 + 5$ if $p = 9$ incorrect answer: 25 BJ	$q + 8 + 4 + 4$ if $q = 5$ incorrect answer: 22 EC	$r + 9 + 9$ if $r = 2$ correct answer: 20 CH	$7 + s + 4 + 9$ if $s = 2$ incorrect answer: 23 TO

What did the farmer use to fix his overalls?

A C A B B A G E P A T C H
CABBAGE PATCH

Mystery Multiplication

Find the value of each expression. Then use your answers to fill in the mystery numbers in the table. The sum of the numbers in each row equals the numbers at the right. The sum of the numbers in each column equals the numbers at the bottom. The sum of the diagonals equals the numbers shown at the corners.

1. $5 \times n$, if $n = 6$ 30
2. $9 \times z$, if $z = 5$ 45
3. $9 \times t$, if $t = 2$ 18
4. $4 \times m$, if $m = 7$ 28
5. $2 \times w$, if $w = 7$ 14
6. $7 \times v$, if $v = 6$ 42
7. $4 \times e$, if $e = 1$ 4
8. $2 \times s$, if $s = 11$ 22
9. $7 \times h$, if $h = 5$ 35
10. $4 \times p$, if $p = 3$ 12

					152
5	37	47	30	45	164
11	35	12	34	42	134
41	0	41	26	22	130
29	14	29	45	35	152
18	35	4	28	19	104
104	121	133	163	163	145

Polyominos

A polyomino has more than one square. Count to find the area of each polyomino.

1. Area = 6 squares
2. Area = 6 squares
3. Area = 8 squares
4. Area = 10 squares
5. Area = 7 squares
6. Area = 12 squares
7. Area = 14 squares
8. Area = 17 squares
9. Area = 15 squares

It's Solid

Match each solid figure with its name in Column 1 and with two facts about it from Column 2. Write the letters under each picture.

1. f, j, n
2. d, k, n
3. a, h, m
4. c, g, l
5. b, i, n
6. e, g, l

Column 1
a. square pyramid
b. cylinder
c. rectangular prism
d. sphere
e. cube
f. cone

Column 2
g. 6 flat surfaces
h. 5 flat surfaces
i. 2 flat surfaces
j. 1 flat surface
k. 0 flat surfaces
l. 8 corners
m. 5 corners
n. 0 corners

The Missing Half

Each figure below was once a square, rectangle, triangle, circle, pentagon, octagon, or hexagon. Each has been cut in half with one of the halves removed. Complete the plane figure. Write its name on the line.

1. rectangle
2. circle
3. pentagon
4. hexagon
5. triangle
6. octagon

Missing Factors

Fill in the missing factors to complete the tables.

7.

×	1	2	3
2 × 4	8	16	24
3 × 5	15	30	45
2 × 6	12	24	36

8.

×	2	4	5
9 × 2	36	72	90
1 × 7	14	28	35
2 × 5	20	40	50

9.

×	6	8	3
2 × 2	24	32	12
3 × 2	36	48	18
9 × 1	54	72	27

10.

×	5	4	3
9 × 2	90	72	54
2 × 5	50	40	30
8 × 2	80	64	48